Order of
First Families of North Carolina
Ancestor Biographies
Vol. 1

Order of First Families of North Carolina Ancestor Biographies Vol. 1

"The First Two Hundred"

compiled by

John Anderson Brayton
Memphis, Tennessee

Copies may be obtained from the author:
1900 Central Avenue
Memphis, TN 38104

Published for the author by Otter Bay Books
Baltimore, Maryland

Library of Congress Control Number 2010942209
ISBN 978-0-8063-5531-3

Made in the United States of America

Table of Contents

documents, "[__]" means the text was illegible, and "[--]" means that there was a gap in the text. Jan, Feb, Mar, Apr, Aug, Sept, Oct, Nov, Dec, are my own abbreviations for the various months.

I would like to thank the Board of the **Order of First Families of North Carolina** for their consistent support of and enthusiasm for this project; Jo Betts Barrett Baxley for her uncanny ability to proofread against the greatest odds—*i.e.*, repetition, and this writer's *soi-disant* flowers of rhetoric; and the late Dr. William Marion Mann for having had the idea to form this organization in the first place.

John Anderson Brayton
March 2011
Memphis, Tennessee

Short Biographies of Ancestors, both Primary and Supplemental With Children and their Spouses of the First Generation

The requirement for an ancestor's eligibility in the roster of the **Order of First Families of North Carolina** is that he or she show residence in the provincial colony on or before 12 July 1729. Marriage to a resident before that date will usually suffice for the requirement, but not always. The resident need not have died in the colony of North Carolina—he or she can have lived there for some duration, and then removed elsewhere.

For the sake of brevity, minimal references will be given, without footnotes. For example, Perquimans Co., NC, vital records have normally been taken from two sources: Weynette Parks Haun's *Perquimans County, North Carolina, Births, Marriages, Deaths, & Flesh Marks, 1659-1820*, and William Wade Hinshaw, ed., *Encyclopedia of American Quaker Genealogy*, vol. 1 *North Carolina*. Other Monthly Meetings transcribed and abstracted by Hinshaw have likewise been investigated: Vol. 2, *Records and Minutes of Four of the Oldest Monthly Meetings... Philadelphia Yearly Meeting of Friends*; and Vol. 6, *Virginia*. The Quaker records will be distinguished from Mrs. Haun's publication as they appear in Hinshaw, with the month given as a number, and periods between the remaining elements of the date. Luckily we have two registers of vital records which have been employed in this work: [1] Weynette Parks Haun, *Old Albemarle County North Carolina Pasquotank Precinct (County) Births, Marriages, Deaths, Brands and Flesh Marks, & County Claims 1691-1833*, for Pasquotank County, cited as Pasquotank Register; and [2] Weynette Parks Haun, *Perquimans County North Carolina, Births, Marriages, Deaths, & Flesh Marks, 1659-1820*, for Perquimans.

The North Carolina Secretary of State collections are referenced either as loose wills, or as recorded copies found in the S.S. Record Books, or volumes. Unrecorded wills found in the various county repositories are also referenced as "loose wills."

Virginia records fall mostly into the categories of court records and various treatments taken from Fred Dorman's *Adventurers of Purse and Person*, 4th edition. Where biographies are found in William S. Powell's excellent *Dictionary of North Carolina Biography*, 6 vols., they are so noted. Some family genealogies have proved worthy of citation, but this writer depends more faithfully upon original source documents. William Perry Johnston's *Journal of North Carolina Genealogy* contains some excellent articles on early families, and those have been examined.

Children of the first generation have been added with their respective marriages, based on the research of individual members and of this writer. The lists will probably not be complete, and any additions will be welcome. The "+" plus sign indicates that a descent through that particular child has been approved and established. The blank sign "[__]" does not necessarily mean that there is no information about that person—only that this compiler has not yet had access to it, or that his own research has not resolved the problem. Persons who have researched these families far longer than this writer has will doubtless be able to fill in many of the gaps herein.

This publication is naturally a work in progress, and corrections and additions are welcome. Of course it is to be understood that the length of the sketches below is in no way a function of the ancestor's supposed "prominence" either in the history of North Carolina or in the minds of his or her descendants.

A word about style. Normally genealogists arrange the order of dates as day, month, and year, except for the Quaker records. I have, however, used the Quaker method of month, day, and year in numbers, as reported by Hinshaw, without any attempt to "modernize," especially since the Quaker new year began in March. I do not know whether they made the same adjustment in their calendar that the rest of the English-speaking kingdom made in 1750.

Spouses of ancestors and their children, and their spouses are all listed in bold-face. Spouses who happen to be descendants of other OFFNC ancestors will appear with a generational exponent to the right of their first name, identifying their distance from that ancestor.

This writer has attempted to verify and discover as much as possible about the origins and ancestry of each ancestor as possible, especially those whose lineage has never appeared in publication. For instance, the ancestry of Edward^{1} Cannon (even though he no longer qualifies as an ancestor) and his wife Sarah^{1} Dawley has been explored back into Norfolk Co., VA; the parents of the OFFNC ancestors and their wives are appended a generational exponent "A", and *their* parents, "B," and so on. When it becomes necessary to discuss the siblings of an OFFNC ancestor, those siblings are given an exponent of "1" as well. Generational exponents enclosed in brackets, such as Richard$^{[4]}$ Pace, always refer to genealogy established previously in *Adventurers of Purse and Person*, 4th ed. Those exponents with parentheses, such as "Henry$^{(2)}$ White," are used to discuss complicated descents from families pertinent to the OFFNC.

The reference "Mitchell" is Thornton W. Mitchell, *North Carolina Wills: A Testator Index, 1665-1900, Corrected and Revised Edition*. "Bradley" refers to Dr. Stephen E. Bradley's abstracts of *Early Records of North Carolina* series.

Reference works to avoid, if possible: [1] Mrs. Watson Winslow's *History of Perquimans County*; not only did she indulge in frequent genealogical whimsy, she did not understand the subtleties of alphabetical order nor even the not-so-subtleties of simple arithmetic. [2] Mrs. Marilu Smallwood's *Some Colonial and Revolutionary Families of North Carolina*; some of her research is, alas, giddy; [3] **Anything** by Worth S. Ray, except, possibly, his *Index to Hathaway*.

The following mark [✠] indicates that descent through that ancestor has been temporarily closed. The facts listed in the sketch of that ancestor are all perfectly valid (especially that ancestor's eligibility), but mistakes in the lineage of members formerly using that ancestor have been detected.

OFFNC ESTABLISHED ANCESTORS AND THEIR CHILDREN

1. Albert$^{(1)}$ Albertson, Sr., born *ca.* 1640, died testate "at his own house," 28 Feb 1701, Perquimans, his will recorded 4 Apr 1702, Perquimans Co., NC, NC Secretary of State loose wills. He married $^{24}/_{25}$ Dec 1668, Perquimans Co., NC, **Mary Gosbey**, who died testate between 8 Dec 1720 and 10 Jan $172^{0}/_{1}$, Perquimans, NC Secretary of State loose wills, recorded in NC Secretary of State vol. 875, p. 315. According to Caroline B. Whitley's *North Carolina Headrights, A List of Names, 1663-1744*, p. 147, Albert Albertson, planter registered rights for 290 acres of land in Perquimans precinct, 2 May 1694: Albert Alberson, Mary his wife, Albert and Esau his sons, Susannah, and Hannah his daughters.

Mary (Gosbey) Albertson has not yet been connected with the other Gosbeys of the Albemarle, but she may have been related to an older Hannah [__] Gosbey who on 1 Mar $169^{3}/_{4}$ patented 300 acres of land for her son John and 200 acres for daughter Sarah, according to NC Land Patent Book 1, p. 5, both tracts being on the east side of Sutton's Creek in Perquimans.

The various web entries for the Albertson and Gosbey families have provided some of the most entertaining and delightful fiction ever encountered by this writer. He is *almost* speechless. Yet, there is no proof that Albertson was born in Sweden, or in any other Scandinavian country.

The Children of Albert Albertson and Mary Gosbey, born Perquimans:

[1] a. **Albert^{2} Albertson**, Jr., born 15 July 1669, married **Elizabeth** [__].
[2] b. **Susann^{2} Albertson**, born 19 Feb 1670.
[3] c. **Esaue^{2} Albertson**, born 19 Aug 1672, married 7 Jan $170^{0}/_{1}$, Perquimans, **Sarah^{2} Sexton**.
[4] d. **Hannah^{2} Albertson**, born 11 Dec 1675, married 7 June 1693, Perquimans, **Joseph^{2} Nicholson**.
[5] e. **Peter^{2} Albertson**, born 30 June 1677, married 17 Aug 1701, Perquimans, **Ann Jones**.
[6]+ f. **Nathaniel^{2} Albertson**, born *ca.* 1680, his will was proved Jan $175^{2}/_{3}$, Perquimans, NC Secretary of State loose wills; married **Abigail^{3} Nicholson**.

2. Nathaniel$^{(2)}$ Albertson, the son of **Albert$^{(1)}$ Albertson** and Mary Gosbey who were married in Perquimans on 25 Dec 1668, was born by 1680, Perquimans Co., NC, and his will was proved Jan $175^{2}/_{3}$, Perquimans, NC Secretary of State loose wills. Listed as the son of Albert^{A} Albertson, Nathaniel married 12 July 1705, Perquimans (also registered at Perquimans Monthly Meeting), **Abigail^{3} Nicholson**, born 24 Sept 1689, Perquimans Co., NC, the daughter of **Samuel^{2}**

Nicholson (Christopher[1]) and **Elizabeth**[2] **Charles** (William[1]), who were married there 16 Dec 1688.

All the children listed below except for Sarah (Albertson) Davis were named in Nathaniel Albertson's will. Sarah's marriage was found in William Wade Hinshaw's "Addenda to Perquimans Monthly Meeting Minutes," in his *Encyclopedia of American Quaker Genealogy*, vol. 1 *North Carolina.* She was described therein as the daughter of Nathaniel Albertson. Daughter Elizabeth's marriage was found there as well.

The Children of Nathaniel Albertson and Abigail Nicholson:

[1] a. **Joshua**[2] **Albertson**, died testate between 5 Aug an d Oct 1753, Perquimans Co., NC, Secretary of State loose wills; married **Mary** [__].

[2] b. **William**[2] **Albertson**, died testate between 31.5.1784 and 10 Sept 1784, Perquimans Co., NC, Will Book C, p. 278; married **Sarah** [__].

[3] c. **Sarah**[2] **Albertson**, married 8.3.1723, Perquimans Monthly Meeting, Lower Meeting House, **Richard Davis** "of Virginia."

[4] d. **Hannah**[2] **Albertson**.

[5]+ e. **Elizabeth**[2] **Albertson**, married 9.11.1725, Perquimans Monthly Meeting, Lower Meeting House, **Samuel**[2] **Newby**.

[6] f. **Aaron**[2] **Albertson**, died testate between 15 Oct 1769 and Apr 1782, Perquimans Co., NC, Will Book C, p. 245; married 10.7.1729, Perquimans Monthly Meeting, **Ann Gilbert**.

[7] g. **Lydda**[2] **Albertson**, married 1.14.1744, Perquimans Monthly Meeting, Old Neck Meeting House, **Thomas Trueblood**, son of Amos of Pasquotank.

3. Simon Alderson, Sr., died testate after 9 Jan 171$^2/_3$, Bath Co., NC, his will recorded in NC Secretary of State vol. 875, p. 80. The fact that he styled himself as Simon, Sr., indicates the presence of someone of the same name in his family who was of age—in this case, his son Simon, Jr. The name Alderson existed in Virginia in seventeenth century Essex, Lancaster, Surry, and Westmoreland counties, but no connection with the North Carolina colonist has yet been made. According to Caroline B. Whitley's *North Carolina Headrights, A List of Names, 1663-1744*, p. 80, Simon Alderson, on 14 Apr 1702, received 350 acres for the following importation rights: Simon Allderson, Ellenor Allderson, Simond, Jr., Mary Hittson, Eliz. Allderson, Sarah Allderson, and Thomas Platt. Although he named wife **Elizabeth** [__] in his will, this list of headrights proves that his first wife was **Eleanor** [__], and that she was the mother of Simond[2], Jr., Elizabeth[2] and Sarah[2]. We cannot, therefore, assign daughter Jane to either Eleanor or Elizabeth with any certainty.

Simon Alderson named his last three children in his will, but the existence of daughter Sarah, who must have died young, is deduced from his importation list, cited above.

The Children of Simon Alderson and Eleanor [__]:

[1] a. **Sarah[2] Alderson,** *died young.*

[2] b. **Simon[2] Alderson**, Jr., born by 1690, died testate before his original will was proved Dec 1740, Beaufort Co., NC, his will recorded in NC Land Grant Book 4, no. 131, and filed among NC Secretary of State loose wills; married **Elizabeth** [__].

[3]+ c. **Elizabeth[2] Alderson**, married **Joell[1] Martin**, who died testate between 24 Oct 1715 and 3 July 1716, Bath Co., NC, his will not only filed among NC Secretary of State loose wills, but also recorded both in NC Secretary of State vol. 875, p. 131, and in Beaufort Co., NC, Deed Book 1, p. 269, as Joel "Marten."

The Child of Simon Alderson and [__]:

[4] d. **Jane[2] Alderson**, married [__] **Averidge**.

4. John Alston, the son of Solomon[A] Alston and his wife Mary [__], was baptized 16 Apr 1677, Wethersfield, Essex, according to an extremely welcome article by David L. Kent, "English Origins of the Alston Family of the Carolinas," in *The South Carolina Magazine of Ancestral Research*, vol. 34, no. 2 [Spring 2006], pp. 63-68. Alston died testate between 20 Jan 1755 and 2 Dec 1758, Chowan Co., NC, his will was filed among NC Secretary of State loose wills. He married **Mary** [__], named in his will, and who was not *née* Clark. His first appearance in the North Carolina records was 17 Apr 1703, Perquimans Co., NC, as a witness to a letter of attorney from Henry Baker of Virginia to Samuel Swann. This can be found in *The Colonial Records of North Carolina*, 2nd ser., vol. 4, *North Carolina Higher-Court Records, 1702-1708*, pp. 58-60. There is a good biographical sketch of John Alston in William S. Powell's *Dictionary of North Carolina Biography*, vol. 1, *A-C*, p. 27; it is infinitely more reliable than the egregious Dr. Joseph Groves' *The Alstons and Allstons of North and South Carolina*. Further information on this family can be found in *Order of First Families of North Carolina, Ancestor Registry*, no. 1.

The Children of John Alston and Mary [__], all born Chowan Precinct, NC:

[1]+ a. **Joseph John[2] Alston**, born *ca.* 1703, died testate between 5 Jan 1780

and Aug 1781, Halifax Co., NC, Will Book 3, p. 10; married first, **Elizabeth** (possibly "Chancy"); second, 1750, Norfolk Co., VA, **Euphan Wilson**, daughter of Willis Wilson of Norfolk. Co., VA, who died testate between 28 Apr 1758 and Sept 1760, Norfolk Co., VA, Will Book 1, 1755-1772, p. 50a. Euphan's children, according to the will of her father, were Willis[3], Henry[3], and Mary[3] Alston.

[2]+ b. **Solomon[2] Alston**, born *ca.* 1705, died testate between 4 Sept 1780 and Jan 1785, Warren Co., NC, Will Book 4, p. 70; married *ca.* 1728, **Ann Hinton**, daughter of John and Mary (Hardy) Hinton.

[3]+ c. **William[2] Alston**, died intestate before 21 Feb 1744, Edgecombe Co., NC; he married, as her first husband, **Hannah Kimbrough**.

[4] d. **Phillip[2] Alston**, died testate between 11 Nov 1783 and July 1784, Warren Co., NC, Will Book 4, p. 35; he married after 1743, **Winifred[2] Whitmel**.

[5] e. **James[2] Alston**, died testate between 28 Feb and May 1761, Orange Co., NC, Will Book A, p. 13; married after 1741, **Christian Lillington**, daughter of George Lillington and wife Hannah [__] of Craven Co., NC.

[6] f. **Mary[2] Alston**, married first, **Henry Guston**; second, *ca.* 18 Feb 1743, Chowan Co., NC, prenuptial agreement, **William Seward**; there were no children by either marriage.

[7]+ g. **Elizabeth[2] Alston**, born *ca.* 1710, died after 30 May 1792, Halifax Co., NC; she married first, *ca.* 1729, Chowan Co., NC, **Samuel[3] Williams**, son of **William[2] Williams**, who died testate between Oct 1753 and Feb $175^3/_4$, Edcgecombe Co., NC, Secretary of State loose wills second, *ca.* 29 July 1765, Halifax Co., NC, Deed Book 9, p. 313 (prenuptial settlement), **Richard Burt**.

[8]+ h. **Sarah[2] Alston**, born *ca.* 1712, married *ca.* 1735, Bertie Co., NC, **Thomas Kearney**, who died testate after 16 Aug 1764, Halifax Co., NC, Will Book 1, p. 146.

[9] i. **Charity[2] Alston**, died testate between 24 Mar and May court 1764, Northampton Co., NC, Will Book 1, p. 94; she married first, **Robert Hilliard**, who died testate between 13 Apr 1743 and May 1751, Edgecombe Co., NC, Secretary of State loose wills; second, as his second wife, *ca.* 3 Apr 1754, Edgecombe Co., NC, prenuptial agreement, **John Dawson**, who died testate between Nov 1750 and Feb 1762, Northampton Co., NC, Will Book 1, p. 69.

[10] j. **Martha[2] Alston**, died before 20 Jan 1755, married 29 Jan 1752, Chowan Co., NC (marriage bond, Leml. Wilson "of Virginia," bondsmen: Jos. Blount, James Trotter; wit: Arthur Allen, Lemll. Cartwright), **Lemuel Wilson**. No issue. Estate records in Edenton Court indicate that when Lemuel Wilson died before 27 May 1766 in

Beaufort Co., NC; his executrix was Winifred [__], a second wife. See Dr. Stephen E. Bradley, Jr., *Edenton District North Carolina Loose Estates Papers, 1756-1806*, vol. 3, *Norcom-Young*, item #423-424. Obviously his will has been lost, but his wife Winifred died testate *ca*. Mar 1783, Beaufort Co., NC, Will Book F, p. 122 (585), as Winifred *Willson*. There were children by Lemuel's second marriage.

5. John Archbell, cordwainer, was born about 1679 and died intestate between 16 Sept 1720—his last recorded purchase of land (from Walter Jones) in Beaufort Co., NC, Deed Book 1, p. 321—and 24 Jan 1739, at which time his widow **Frances** of Duck Creek, Beaufort Co., NC, transferred her dower to their son Nathan[2] Archbell, in Beaufort Co., NC, Deed Book 2, p. 322. Archbell's first recorded appearance was in Northumberland Co., VA, as a headright for George Eskridge, registered 18 Oct 1704, according to Northumberland Co., VA, Order Book, No. 5, p. 322. John Archbell married by 18 Mar $171^{3}/_{4}$, Northumberland Co., VA, **Frances [__] Clifford**, the widow of Robert Clifford of Northumberland, according to Northumberland Order Book 6 (1713-1719), p. 24. She died sometime after the Jan 1739 settlement of her dower, Beaufort Co., NC. John Archbell, identified as a resident of Bath on 18 Jan $171^{6}/_{7}$, purchased 83 acres of land from Thomas Morris, according to Beaufort Co., NC, Deed Book 1, p. 204.

For reasons which are not yet clear, Edward Doe, in his will dated 19 Aug 1751, and recorded in Beaufort Co., NC, Old Wills, p. 41, made a bequest to Mary[3] Archbell, the daughter of his "well beloved Nathan & Francis Archabald."

The Child of John Achbell and Frances [__] Clifford:

[1]+ a. **Nathan[2] Archbell**, born 1714-19, died testate after 10 Feb 1790, Beaufort Co., NC, Old Wills, p. 243; married **Frances** [__].

6. William Bailey was born by 1610 and died *ca*. 1676, possibly in Newport, Rhode Island, although it has not been clearly established that he ever returned there from the Albemarle. His first mention in the Rhode Island records is on 14 June 1655, wherein he purchased land in Newport of Gabriel Hicks. By 5 Mar 1656, he was called William Bailey, "Sr.," at which time he and Gabriel Hicks sold land in Newport to Joshua Coggeshall of Portsmouth. Although John Osborne Austin has chronicled the Rhode Island activities of William Bailey in *The Genealogical Dictionary of Rhode Island*, p. 9, there are many mistakes and omissions in Austin's account. Austin gives Bailey the following children: John, Joseph, *Edward*, *Hugh*, and *Stephen* [italics mine], omitting any references to possible daughters. However, it is apparent that William Bailey and his wife Grace made a journey to the Albemarle and resided there for an undetermined length of time. According to two accounts in Caroline B. Whitley's *North Carolina Headrights, A List of Names, 1663-1744*, p. 85, on 12 Apr 1694, John Stepney proved 11 transportation rights: John Stepney, Marcy Stepney, [--], Grace Baley, John Baley, Wm. Bayley, junior, Saml. Bayley, Experience [--], Jane Bayley, Sarah Bayley, and Mercy Bayley; on p. 182, *ca.* 1695, [William Bailey's stepson] John Stepney received 300 acres of land for importation of the following persons, John Stepny, Mercy (Bailey) Stepny, Wm. Baily, Grace Baly, Jno. Baily, and Wm. Baly, Jr. Although these importation rights were nearly always recorded long after the arrival of the petitioner and his or her headrights in the Albemarle, we may say that William Bailey lived in Perquimans precinct from around 1660 to 1676.

William Bailey married *ca.* 1634, **Grace** [__], who married second, after her husband's death (by 1676), Thomas Lawton of Portsmouth, Rhode Island. Theirs was not a happy marriage due to Thomas' frequent absences from Portsmouth; moreover, Grace continually importuned the town council for support. In his will, dated 6 June 1674, proved 1681, Portsmouth, Thomas Lawton declared that "although Grace *have* not behaved herself towards me as a wife ought to do towards a husband," he left her, nevertheless, the property with which she had come into her second marriage, according to Austin, p. 123. Her offending behavior was not described. Grace [__] Bailey was not the daughter of Hugh Parsons and the widow Elizabeth [__] England as Austin incorrectly posited, having misinterpreted the language of Hugh Parsons' bequest to his one Bailey grandson. Probably, Grace's son William[2] Bailey, Jr., after having returned to Rhode Island, married a daughter of the Parsons and had an only son Hugh[3] Bailey, named after his maternal grandfather, and left a bequest in that grandfather's will. William Perry Johnson, writing on the Baileys in *The Journal of North Carolina Genealogy*, vol. 13, no. 1 [Spring 1967], pp. 1835-40, was the first to correct these mistakes in Austin.

The identity of John[2] Bailey's wife was obtained from Jane Fletcher Fiske, *Rhode Island General Court of Trials, 1671-1704*, p. 107, "Newport Court Book A," in which, on 6 Sept 1681, the indictment of John Baily of Portsmouth for fornication with the widow Sutton Browne was "quashed." They were in fact already married.

The Children of William Bailey and Grace [__]:

[1] a. **William[2] Bailey**, Jr., born *ca.* 1635, married [__] **Parsons**.

[2]+ b. **Abigail[2] Bailey**, born *ca.* 1643, married first, 14 [--] *ca.* 1659, in Rhode Island, registered in Perquimans, **William[1] Charles**; she married second, 21 [--], Perquimans, **John Lacy**, the testator of 1.10.1682; third, 6 May 1683, Perquimans, **Francis Toms**.

[3] c. **Mercy[2] Bailey**, married [--], *ca.* 1679, Perquimans Register, **John Stepney**, the son of John and Bennett [__] Stepney.

[4] d. **Samuel[2] Bailey**, possibly married **Elizabeth Rogers**, daughter of Thomas and Sarah Rogers of Rhode Island.

[5] e. **Experience[2] Bailey**.

[6] f. **Jane[2] Bailey**.

[7] g. **Sarah[2] Bailey**.

[8] h. **John[2] Bailey**, born 1653, died 13 Jan 1736, buried Middletown, Newport Co., RI, will dated 8 May 1733, proved 2 Feb 1736; married *ca.* Mar 1680, Newport, RI, **Sutton [__] Browne**, born 1655, died 18 Feb 1730, Middletown, according to Austin, p. 123.

7. Henry Baker II of "Buckland," the son of Henry[A] Baker I and wife Mary [__] of Nansemond and Isle of Wight counties, VA, was born by 1680, Isle of Wight Co., VA, and died testate between 9 Jan 1737 and 1 May 1738, Chowan Co., NC. His will was recorded in NC Land Grant Book 4, no. 81. Henry II was named in his father's will, dated 10 June 1707 and proved 28 July 1712, Isle of Wight Co., VA, Will & Deed Book 2, p. 539. His father's widow Mary left a will naming all her children, dated 5 Mar 1732 and proved 23 Sept 1723, Isle of Wight Co., VA, Will Book 4, p. 22. Henry Baker II married first, [__], alleged fancifully to be Angelica Bray. He married second, as her first husband, **Ruth[3] Chancey**, named in his will, the daughter of Sarah Keile and Hon. **Edmund[2] Chancey** of Pasquotank Co., NC, who in turn named his daughter and all but two of Ruth and Henry's children in his own will dated 15 Mar 1753, NC Secretary of State loose wills. According to NC Secretary of State C.C.R. 179, Miscellaneous Estates, 1669-1759, the file for Henry Baker, 1739-1745, there is found the record of a lawsuit between Edward Bunton and James Castellaw versus Wm. Gunn and wife Ruth of Chowan, the said Ruth being the widow of the said Henry Baker, revealing a second marriage for her. William Gunn was listed as a resident of Brunswick Co., VA, in a deed dated 15 Mar 1738, Bertie Co., NC, Deed Book E, p. 462, a purchase of 400 acres on the north side of the Roanoak River from Thomas Wilson and his wife Mary. Ruth and William Gunn appeared only once together in the records of Bertie, in a deed dated 24 Feb 1740, Bertie Co., NC, Deed Book F, p. 287, in which they sold four Negro slaves, Tom, Benbow, Dina, and her child—a mulatto boy named Daniel, now in the possession of George Gould—to Benjamin Hill.

The Nansemond land Henry Baker inherited from his parents was cut off into that part of Chowan which would eventually become Hertford Co., NC. Baker had established a ferry in Chowan by Mar 1724, at which time he appointed Edward Moseley as his attorney to sue Col. William Maule for operating a ferry at the same place on the Chowan River, a location previously confirmed by the Chowan court as Baker's own, according to the *Colonial Records of North Carolina*, 2nd ser., vol. 6, *North Carolina Higher-Court Minutes, 1724-1730*, p. 29. There is an excellent treatment of this generation of the family in David B. Gammon's *Eastern North Carolina Families*, vol. 1, pp. 11-34. Unfortunately, an examination of the parish registers of Buckland, Kent, long thought to be the seat of this family, revealed no particular presence of the name Baker. There are, however, other parishes of that name in Berkshire, Buckingham, Gloucester, Hertford, Somerset, Surrey, and Devon.

Henry II named the following children in his will: Henry², John², Blake², Mary², Sarah², David², Ruth², and Zadock². He also named his brothers Lawrence and James, the latter of whom left Henry III a bequest in his will dated 14 Sept 1754 and recorded 2 Dec 1756, Isle of Wight Co., VA, Will Book 6, p. 250.

The Child of Henry Baker II and [__]:

[1]+ a. **Henry² Baker III**, died in Hertford Co., NC; said to have married **Catherine Booth** of Southampton Co., VA.

The Children of Henry Baker II and Ruth Chancey, named in the will of their grandfather Chancey:

[2]+ b. **Mary² Baker**, born *ca.* 1723, Chowan; married, as his first wife, 5 July 1742, **Tscharner³ de Graffenreid** (Christopher²⁻¹), born 28 Nov 1722, Williamsburg,VA, died testate between 8 Feb and 10 Apr 1794, Lunenburg Co., VA, Will Book 4, p. 57.

[3] c. **David² Baker**, *died before 1753.*

[4] d. **Sarah² Baker**, born *ca.* 1728, according to Chowan Co., NC, Court Minutes, 1730-1745, p. 131, dated Sept 1742, at which time she was adjudged to be 14 years of age and therefore capable of choosing a guardian. She first chose Thomas Luten, then Zachariah Chancey.

[5] e. **Ruth² Baker**, born 1734, died 4 Dec 1817, aged 83 years, Warren Co., NC, according to the Raleigh *Register*, and described as the mother of "Mrs. Blake Baker, Esq.;" married first, **Christopher Billups**, died testate between 18 Jan 1782 and 9 July 1789, Lunenburg Co., VA, Will Book 4, p. 62; second, [**Thomas**?] **Scott**.

[6] f. **Zadock² Baker**, married [__] **Wynn**.

[7] g. **John² Baker**, died intestate 1773, Hertford (his estate papers filed in Chowan); married first, 5 Sept 1754, Chowan Co., NC (marriage bond), **Elizabeth Wilson**; second, **Mary Anne** [__].

[8] h. **Blake² Baker**, died testate between 176[--] and 1769, Halifax Co., NC, Will Book 1, p. 250, made a bequest to his sister **Ruth² Billups**; married **Mary (Kinchen) McKinnie**, the widow of **Richard² McKinnie**, who died intestate before 17 May 1775, Halifax Co.,

NC, Inventories of Estates, 1773-1779, p. 16.

8. Thomas Barecock/Barcock died testate between 1 Jan 1721 and 17 Jan $172^{1}/_{2}$, Pasquotank Co., NC, Secretary of State loose wills. He married first, [__]^{2} **Jennings**, the daughter of **William**^{1} **Jennings** and Margaret [__]. He married second, **Margaret** [__]. According to Caroline B. Whitley, *North Carolina Headrights, A List of Names, 1663-1744*, p. 168, on 29 Oct 1695, Thomas Barecock registered his importation rights for 200 acres: himself, his wife Margaret, and a servant named William. Thomas Barecock was called the son-in-law of William Jennings, and William Jennings, in his 1687 will, named his godson William Barcock, the son of Thomas. This suggests that William^{2} was his grandson by an unnamed daughter who died before Thomas registered his importation rights (which named his second wife Margaret), and that second wife Margaret [__] was the mother of the rest of his children. The name Barcock or Barecock eventually devolved into the somewhat more euphonic "Barco."

Although referred to but not named in the will of her husband, Elizabeth^{2} Upton is identified as widow and executrix of John Upton on 17 Oct 1717, Pasquotank Co., NC, Deed Book A, p. 165. Jane Browne, the wife of William^{2} Barecock was the daughter of John Browne, the testator of Pasquotank and his wife Margaret [__] Browne, who married second, [__] Peggs. John Browne died testate between 15 Feb $169^{8}/_{9}$ and 17 Oct 1699, his will filed among the NC Secretary of State loose wills. He named wife Margaret, sons Daniel and Peter, and daughters Margaret and "Jeane."

There is a long sketch on Thomas Barecock in Jesse Forbes Pugh's *Three Hundred Years Along the Pasquotank*, pp. 26-27. My only disagreement with Mr. Pugh's treatment of the family revolves around the maternity of the children. I can only guarantee that son William^{2} was the son of **William Jennings**' unnamed daughter. From Pasquotank deeds, it appears that the name Forbes had variants besides Forbus—Forbush was another.

The Children of Thomas Barecock and [__] Jennings:

[1] a. **William**^{2} **Barecock**, born before 1687, died testate between 5 Mar $173^{0}/_{1}$ and July 1731, Pasquotank Co., NC, Secretary of State loose wills; married **Jane Browne**.

The Children of Thomas Barecock and Margaret [__]:

[2] b. **Elizabeth**^{2} **Barecock**, married **John Upton**, who died testate between 30 June 1715 and 15 Sept 1720, Pasquotank Co., NC, NC Secretary of State loose wills, also recorded in NC Secretary of State vol. 875, p. 234 and vol. 875, p. 326.

[3] c. **Sarah**^{2} **Barecock**, married **John Sanderlin**, who died intestate by 13

Oct 1747, Pasquotank Co., NC, according to Pasquotank Court Minutes, 1737-1755, p. 88; eldest son Robert[3] administered the estate, which was divided among the widow, and the Sanderrlin orphans: Robert[3], John[3], Joseph[3], Prissilla[3], Mary[3] Sanderlin, and possibly Joseph Sanderlin Collingsworth.

[4] d. **Priscilla[2] Barecock**, married [__] **Gregory**.

[5]+ e. **Margaret[2] Barecock**, married **Richard[1] Gregory**, who died testate between 17 May 1719 and 15 Sept 1720, Pasquotank Co., NC, will recorded in Secretary of State vol. 875, p. 235.

[6] f. **Martha[2] Barecock**, married **John Forbes/Forbus**, who died testate between 24 Nov 1747 and July 1750, Pasquotank Co., NC, Secretary of State loose wills; he named wife Martha executrix.

[7] g. **Rebecca[2] Barecock**, married **James Forbes/Forbus**; they witnessed the $173^0/_1$ will of William[2] Barecock.

9. Edward[(1)] Barnes, the son of James[A] Barnes, the testator of 2 Mar $17^{19}/_{20}$, Isle of Wight Co., VA, The Great Book, p. 55, and his wife Sarah [__], was born say 1691, Isle of Wight, and died testate between 15 Dec 1760 and Mar 1762, Edgecombe Co., NC, Will Book A, p. 91. He married **Sarah Pope**, the daughter of John[A] Pope of Isle of Wight and Southampton counties, VA, who named her in his will proved 14 July 1751, Southampton Co., VA, Will Book 1, p. 46. In Oct 1726 Edward Barnes was granted 550 acres of land in Bertie Co., NC, and sold that tract, on the west side of the Chowan River adjoining Richard Holland, to Godfrey Lee on 11 May 1728, according to Bertie Co., NC, Deed Book B, p. 400. Sarah died after the probate of Edward's will.

The Children of Edward Barnes and Sarah Pope**:**

[1] a. **Nathan[2] Barnes**, died testate before Apr 1777, Edgecombe Co., NC, Will Book A, p. 247; married [__].

[2] b. **William[2] Barnes**.

[3]+ c. **Jacob[2] Barnes**, born *ca.* 1726, died testate Jan 1764, Edgecombe Co., NC, Will Book A, p. 128; married **Juland** [__].

[4] d. **Abraham[2] Barnes**.

[5] e. **Mourning[2] Barnes**, married **John[3] Fiveash**, the son of [__] Fiveash and **Phillis[2] Fort**.

[6] f. **Charity[2] Barnes**, married [__] **Sims**.

[7]+ g. **Mary[2] Barnes**, married **Robert[2] Sims**, Sr., will dated 1791, Wayne Co., NC, Will Book A, p. 91.

[8] h. **Elizabeth[2] Barnes**, married **Jesse Leigh**.

[9] i. **Patience[2] Barnes**.

[10]+ j. **Joseph[2] Barnes**, born *ca.* 1715, died testate before his father,

between 7 Apr and Aug 1751, Northampton Co., NC, NC Secretary of State loose wills; married **Elizabeth** [__].

[11] k. [**Daughter**][2] **Barnes**, married [__] **Wiggins**.

[12] l. **Sarah**[2] **Barnes**, married **Benjamin Amason**.

10. Jacob[(2)] **Barnes**, the son of **Edward**[(1)] **Barnes** and Sarah Pope, was born *ca.* 1726, Bertie Co., NC, and died testate 1764, Edgecombe Co., NC. In cases concerning the qualification of ancestors such as such as Jacob Barnes and his brother Joseph Barnes, it has been necessary to prove that each was born before or during the time their father lived in colonial North Carolina, especially since Edward had a narrow window of opportunity to qualify as an OFFNC ancestor. Jacob died testate Jan 1764, his will dated 16 Jan, Edgecombe d Co., NC, Will Book A, p. 128. He named wife **Juland** [__] in his will. Sons Archelaus[2] and Jacob[2] were divised equal halves of land on Contentnea Creek. The land he bequeathed to son James[2] he acquired from John Wiggins in Edgecombe Co., NC, Deed Book OO, p. 108, dated 2 May 1760, 200 acres on the south bank of White Oak Swamp, near his own land, some of which he had acquired on 17 June 1758, Edgecombe Co., NC, Deed Book 6, p. 315, from James Speir: 300 acres on north side of White Oak Swamp.

Jacob Barnes appeared first in the records of Northampton Co., NC, as a witness to various deeds, the first being with his brother Joseph in a sale of land from William Gay of Edgecombe to Joseph Whitley, dated 19 Oct 1748, Northampton Co., NC, Deed Book 1, p. 355. If we may assume that Jacob was more or less of age in 1748, then that would give him a birth date of around 1726, the year his father appeared in the records of Bertie.

The Children of Jacob Barnes and Juland [__]:

[1]+ a. **Jesse**[2] **Barnes**, died testate between 11 Dec 1804 and 1811, Wayne Co., NC, Will Book B, p. 414; he married 2 Feb 1761, Edgecombe Co., NC (marriage bond), **Orpha**[3] **Fort**, the daughter of **George**[2] **Fort**, the testator of 1761.

[2] b. **James**[2] **Barnes**.

[3] c. **Brissulla**[2]**/Prescilla Barnes**, married **John**[4] **Williams** (John[3], Anthony[2], **Lewis**[1]), the son of John Williams and Prudence Jones, who died testate between 16 June and July 1790, Duplin Co., NC Will Book A, p. 503.

[4] d. **Jerusha**[2] **Barnes**.

[5] e. **Joseph**[2] **Barnes**.

[6] f. **Jacob**[2] **Barnes**, died intestate Aug 1764, Edgecombe, as revealed in Estates Records for his father; married **Mourning** [__]

[7] g. **Archelaus**[2] **Barnes**, died testate Feb 1807, his will dated 4 Feb,

Edgecombe Co., NC, Will Book D, p. 264; married **Peggy** [__], who died testate between 2 Mar and Aug 1816, Edgecombe Co., NC, Will Book E, p. 143.

[8] h. **Patty² Barnes**.

[9] i. **Abraham² Barnes**.

11. Joseph⁽²⁾ Barnes was the son of **Edward⁽¹⁾ Barnes** and Sarah Pope. In cases concerning the qualification of ancestors such as Jacob Barnes and his brother Joseph Barnes, it has been necessary to prove that each was born before or during the time their father lived in colonial North Carolina, especially since Edward had a narrow window of opportunity to qualify as an OFFNC ancestor. With Joseph Barnes, this is not a problem if we can assume that he was at least 21 years old (and therefore born before 1720) when he first purchased land in Northampton Co., NC. On 28 July 1741, according to Northampton Co., NC, Deed Book 1, p. 12, Joseph Barnes purchased land from James Colding and Foruzan Morris, 140 acres adjoining James Maney and other lands of the grantee, on Miry Marsh Branch, the tract being part of a patent of 464 acres granted John Daveson 1 Apr 1723. Joseph Barnes died testate between Apr 1751 and Aug 1751, Northampton Co., NC, while his father Edward was still alive. Joseph's will was probated in the NC Secretary of State collection. He married **Elizabeth** [__], mentioned, although not by name, in the 1760 will of her father-in-law, indicating that she was still alive.

The Children of Joseph and Elizabeth [__] Barnes:

[1] a. **Jacob² Barnes**, born say 1741, died testate between 25 Jan 1780 and Oct 1781, Nash Co., NC, Will Book 1, p. 21; inherited 100A from his father and was mentioned in the will of his grandfather Edward Barnes; he married **Elizabeth (Skinner) Ricks** of Nash Co., NC, the sister of Samuel Skinner and the widow of **Isaac⁽³⁾ Ricks**; Elizabeth returned to Edgecombe and died testate there between 6 June 1789 and May 1794, Edgecombe Co., NC, Will Book C, p. 175, naming her brother Samuel Skinner and his son Theophilus.

[2] b. **Michael/Mycah² Barnes**, born say 1743, inherited 140A from his father, plus a tract on the Chowan River from his grandfather.

[3]+ c. **Demsey² Barnes**, born say 1745, died testate between Mar 25 and Aug 1807, Edgecombe Co., NC, Will Book D, p. 283; married by 1764, **Sarah** [__].

[4] d. **Jethro² Barnes**, born say 1747, died 1 Sept 1812, intestate, Edgecombe Co., NC; children from estate division: Jesse³ Barnes, Jethro³ Barnes, William³ Barnes, Michael³ Barnes, Enos³ Barnes, Elizabeth³ wife of John Marchman, Sarah³, wife of John Parish.

[5] e. **James[2] Barnes**, born say 1749, died between 12 Mar and May 1805, Edgecombe Co., NC, Will Book D, p. 223; he married **Julan** [__]; children: Wiley[3], William[3], Reddick[3], Bryan[3], John[3], James[3], Mary[3] Bridgers, Sarah[3] Barnes, Elizabeth[3] Barnes, Susanna[3] Barnes.

12. John Bass was born *ca.* 1673 and died testate between 18 Jan and Feb 1732, Bertie Co., NC, his will filed among the NC Secretary of State loose wills. He married first, 8 Jan 1696, Perquimans Co., NC, **Love Harris**, both of whom were therein identified as residents of Nansemond Co., VA. She predeceased her husband, given that he named second wife **Mary** [__] in his will. John Bass received a patent for 460 acres on the north side of Morattock River in Bertie, on 14 Apr 1727, according to NC Patent Book 3, p. 227. Bass genealogy has been complicated by the appearance of fictional Bible records for the early generations, and by a persistent belief in descent from the very clearly childless Nathaniel Bass of London and Bristol Parish, VA, who died before 30 Aug 1654, and whose estate was settled onto his three surviving sisters in England in 1658, and **not onto any sentient being in Virginia**! See the late Daphne Gentry's excellent article "Nathaniel Basse," in the *Dictionary of Virginia Biography*, vol. 1, *Aaroe-Blanchfield*, pp. 382-83. The name John Bass does not exist in the colonial Henrico Co., VA, records.

Mary [__] Bass married second, by 21 Nov 1748, [__] Staples, according to Northampton Co., NC, Deed Book 1, p. 356. In this deed, she sold 1/3 of her dower under the will of John Bass, Sr., to her stepson John Bass, Jr., or 1/3 of the interest in the plantation on which she then lived.

It is possible that Elizabeth (Bass) Taylor was married previously to [__] Johnston before the deed from her brother listed below. Of course, this has not been proved.

The Children of John Bass and Love Harris:

[1]+ a. **Edward[2] Bass**, born *ca.* 1698, died *ca.* 1779, Dobbs Co., NC; married [__].

[2] b. **John[2] Bass**, born *ca.* 1700, sold 200 acres of land to brother William[2] Bass, bequeathed by his father's will, 30 Dec 1742, Northampton Co., NC, Deed Book 1, p. 56; died testate between 14 June and Sept 1777, Northampton Co., NC, Will Book 1, p. 292; married **Elizabeth** [__], who signed with him on a deed dated 4 Mar 1748, Northampton Co., NC, Deed Book 1, p. 343, but died before signing of his will.

[3] c. **William[2] Bass**.

[4] d. **Jeudath/Judith[2] Bass**, married **William Canady**, who was named in the deed from John[2] Bass to Willliam[2] Bass quoted above; William Cannady and wife Judith of Edgecombe sold 100 acres on

Uraha Swamp adjoining James Hutcherson and the swamp to John Dawson, dated 7 Apr 1744, Northampton Co., NC, Deed book 1, p. 175.

[5] e. **Sarah^2 Bass**, married **Lewis Anderson**; Lewis Anderson, his wife Sarah, and Shadrack Anderson, all of Granville Co., NC, sold to Jetha^3 Bass (the son of John^2 Bass, Jr.,) 100 acres on north side of Uraha Swamp which Sarah had inherited under the will of her father John^1 Bass, 10 Nov 1755, Northampton Co., NC, Deed Book 2, p. 233. Lewis is almost certainly the testator who signed his will 20 Jan 1783, proved May 1785, Granville Co., NC, Will Book 1, p. 439, naming among others eldest son Shadrack^3, son Lewis^3, and numerous grandchildren.

[6] f. **[Daughter]^2 Bass**, married [__] **Johnston.**

[7] g. **Lovey^2 Bass**, as "Lovewell" Bass on 7 May 1761, along with her "heirs of Northampton Co.," sold 100 acres on the north side of Uraha Swamp to Jethro^3 Bass, Northampton Co., NC, Deed Book 3, p. 121. This was her bequest under the will of her father.

[8] h. **Mary^2 Bass.**

[9] i. **Aaron^2 Bass.**

[10] j. **Patience^2 Bass.**

[11] k. **Moses^2 Bass.**

[12] l. **Elizabeth^2 Bass**, married **Edward Taylor**, according to a deed from her brother John Bass, who for filial love borne to his sister Elizabeth, "now wife of Edward Taylor of Northampton," gave to her son John^3 Taylor, 100 acres on south side of Hunting Quarter Swamp, Northampton Co., NC, Deed Book 1, p. 321, dated 6 Nov 1747.

13. William Bateman was born say 1660, probably in Norfolk Co., VA, and died testate between 30 Mar 1703 and 25 Apr 1704, Currituck Co., NC, NC Secretary of State loose wills. The name of his wife does not appear in the probate records, although she was referred to in his will. In 1717, an "Eals," almost certainly "Alice" Beatman was listed as delinquent on taxation for 100 acres in "Coratuk," according to William Doub Bennett's *Currituck County, North Carolina Eighteenth Century Tax & Militia Records*, p. 37. In 1718, both "Eals" and Isabel "Beatman" were taxed each on 100 acres of land as "Virginia people," p. 43, tracts which were bequeathed to them under the terms of their father's will.

The Norfolk connection is important in establishing the marriage of Isabell^2 Bateman and **George Powers**. According to Norfolk Co., VA, Deed Book 11, p. 45, dated 19 Jan 173$^1/_2$, George and Isabel Powers sold land formerly belonging to Joseph Bateman containing 37 acres, part of a larger patent of 148 acres at the Cypress Swamp adjoining Isles Cooper and John Penney, the latter of whom was the grantee. Isabell (Bateman) Powers is the only child of William Bateman to survive of whom there is any trace whatsoever in the records, and it is very tempting to assume that all the other siblings died, leaving her the sole heir of her brother. This is perhaps an oversimplification. There is no known connection between this family and the Jonathan Bateman family of Perquimans.

The Children of William Bateman and [__]:

[1] a. **Mary[2] Bateman.**

[2]+ b. **Isabell[2] Bateman**, died testate between 23 Nov and 20 Dec 1757, NC Secretary of State loose wills, and recorded in NC Secretary of State vol. 880, p. 233; married by 1720, **George[1] Powers**, who died testate between 27 Mar 1754 and June 1755, Currituck, his will filed among NC Secretary of State loose wills.

[3] c. **Ellise/Alice[2] Bateman.**

[4] d. **Joseph[2] Bateman**, *died childless*, by $173^{1}/_{2}$, Norfolk Co., VA.

[5] e. **William[2] Bateman.**

[6] f. **Elizabeth[2] Bateman.**

[7] g. **Samuel[2] Bateman.**

14. Abraham Baum appeared on the 1715 tax list for Currituck Co., NC, according to William Doub Bennett's *Currituck County, North Carolina, Eighteenth Century Tax & Militia Records*, p. 9, as Abraham "Bome." Baum died testate between 18 Sept 1729 and 7 Apr 1730, Currituck Co., NC. His will, which does not exist among the Currituck or NC Secretary of State records, was located by R. S. Spencer, whose research was included in Elizabeth Baum Hanbury's *Currituck Legacy, The Baum Family of North Carolina.* Mr. Spencer found the will (which this writer inspected) of Abraham Baum among the Hayes Collection of the Southern Historical Collection, housed at Wilson Library, University of North Carolina, Chapel Hill, NC, Microfilm Reel 2, 1694-1770, folder for 1729. Abraham married **Appolonia** [__], who married second, Joseph Winship of Currituck, who died testate between 2 Apr 1733 and 6 Jan 1746, his will filed among NC Secretary of State loose wills. There were no children by her second marriage. The lost will of Abraham Baum is also referred to in Currituck Co., NC, Deed Book 2, p. 389, dated 26 Mar 1771, in which John[2] Baum of Pasquotank deeded Currituck land on the North River to Abraham Litchfield which Abraham Baum had left in his last will and testament to his son Peter[2], obviously the childless brother of the grantor.

The Children of Abraham Baum and Appolonia [__]:

[1] a. **Peter^2 Baum**, will dated 28 Nov 1770, Currituck Co., NC.
[2]+ b. **Maurice^2 Baum**, will proved 14 July 1784, Currituck Co., NC, Will Book 1, p. 187; married **Martha** [__]. Maurice Baum's daughter Rhoda^3 married Hezekiah^3 Spruill (Joseph^2, **Godfrey^1**).
[3] c. **John^2 Baum**, married [__].
[4] d. **Adam^2 Baum**, will dated 26 Dec 1769, proved June 1770, Currituck Co., NC, Will Book 1, p. 52; married **Frances** [__].
[5] e. **Elizabeth^2 Baum**.
[6] f. **Mary^2 Baum**.
[7] g. **Sarah^2 Baum**.

15. William Bennett, almost certainly the son of William^A Bennett, Sr., and Sarah^A Walker, was born between 1680 and 1690, Isle of Wight Co., VA, and died testate 17 July 1758 and Feb 1765, Northampton Co., NC, Will Book 1, p. 112. He married **Grace** [__], whom he named in his will. William Bennett was granted 400 acres in Chowan Co., NC, 9 Mar 1717, according to North Carolina Land Patent Book 3, p. 41. A sketch of this family can be found in *Order of First Families of North Carolina, Ancestor Registry*, no. 1. More information on the descendants of the Bennetts and Hills can be found in John Bennett Boddie's *Seventeenth Century Isle of Wight*. The speculation existed that Grace [__] Bennet was *née* Van Schuyler, as proposed in *Boddie and Allied Families*, but there is no foundation for this theory whatsoever.

The Children of William Bennett and Grace [__], first two born Isle of Wight Co., VA; third born Chowan Co., NC; and fourth born Bertie Co., NC:
[1]+ a. **Mary^2 Bennett**, born *ca.* 1713, married *ca.* 1730, **William Boddie**, who died intestate *ca.* 1757, Northampton Co., NC.
[2]+ b. **Anne^2 Bennett**, born *ca.* 1715, married *ca.* 1732, **Robert$^{[4]}$ Ruffin**, who died testate between 28 Mar and Aug 1767, Northampton Co., NC, Will Book 1, p. 153.
[3] c. **William^2 Bennett**, Jr., born *ca.* 1717, died 17 Nov 1757, St. George's Parish, South Carolina; married, as her first husband, 20 Mar 1747, Northampton Co., NC, **Mary Kearney**, who married second, 4 Oct 1759, St. George's Parish, South Carolina, James Cary who died intestate *ca.* Dec 1782; she died testate between 6 Nov 1801 and 26 June 1801 [*sic*], Surry Co., VA, Will Book 1, p, 720.
[4]+ d. **Grace^2 Bennett**, born 26 Apr 1721, died testate between 27 Aug and Nov 1772, St. John's Parish, Bute Co., NC, Will Book 1, p. 247; she married Mar 1739, **Green$^{(4)}$ Hill** (Richard^3, Sion^2, Robert^1), who was born 20 Nov 1714, Surry Co., VA, and died testate between 14 Aug 1766 and Mar 1769, Northampton Co., NC, Will Book 1, p. 172.

16. Ann Bigg, the daughter of John^{A} Bigg and Johanna [__] of Norfolk Co., VA, was born *ca.* 1644 and died *ca.* 1712, Chowan Co., NC. She married first, **Richard Batchelor**, son of William^{A} Bachelor, a Quaker said to be from Buckinghamshire (where the name occurs), whose will was dated 12 Mar $168^{0}/_{1}$ and proved 17 Oct 1682, Norfolk Co., VA, Will Book 4, p. 128. In the will of her father John^{A} Bigg, dated 4 Sept 1694, proved 15 Mar $169^{6}/_{7}$, Norfolk Will Book 6, p. 77, Ann was called "Ann Faux." Ann married second, after 1682, as his first wife, **James Fewox**, who died testate between 5 May $171^{0}/_{1}$ and 9 Jan $171^{1}/_{2}$, Chowan Co., NC, his will filed among NC Secretary of State loose wills. She was named therein, but not as his executrix—a task he assigned in his will to Mary Lawson, the widow of Nathaniel Lawson. On 30 July 1700, James Fewox proved his right to 250 acres of land by the importation of James Fewox and An his wife, Robt. Fewox, Eady Batchellor, and Edward Batchellor, according to Caroline B. Whitley's *North Carolina Headrights, A List of Names, 1663-1744*, p. 31. The early generations in Lyle Keith Williams' *The Batchelor Family* are somewhat reliable, except for the fact that the author identifies John Bigg's wife as a Norsworthy, and attributes a second marriage to Ann (Bigg) Batchelor with Charles Shaw.

James Fewox married second, according to Dr. Stephen E. Bradley, Jr.'s, *Early Records of North Carolina*, vol. 9, *Colonial Court Records—Estate Papers, 1665-1775, A-Gibson*, item #196, Mary [__] Lawson, who married third, Col. Thomas Pollock. James Fewox described Mary in his will as the widow of Nathaniel Lawson and named her children John and Mary, Jr. In a document dated 14 July 1712, Mary Lawson was listed therein as Fewox's widow, although Ann was named in his will as his wife. Ann must have died between signing and probate; and the fact that Mary Lawson was named executrix suggests that Ann was not well and that James knew she might not live to execute properly. On 20 Apr 1714, according to Chowan Co., NC, Deed Book B#1, p. 34, Mary Lawson styled herself as "Mary Lawson the widow of Col. Thomas Pollock, deceased," which should come as a great surprise to everyone, since this marriage has gone unnoticed. Mary mortgaged in this record land whereon William Hardy lived, which she had purchased of Robert Fewox—an indication that this is indeed our same Mary Lawson. On 24 Mar 1717, Chowan Co., NC, Deed Book B#1, p. 541, Robert Fewox of Albemarle sold to John Hassell a plantation inherited from his father James Fewox (by James' will) which he could possess after the decease of Mary Lawson. This indicated that Mary [__] Lawson-Fewox-Pollock was deceased, as she disappeared from the records after this point.

Proof for the marriage of Edith^{2} Batchelor to William Hardy is found in Chowan Co., NC, Deed Book B#1, p. 80, dated 9 Apr 1715, in which she, Edy Hardy, relinquished to her loving [half] brother Edward^{2} Fewox her right of dower in a sale of land on Riders Creek on Scopernong River from her husband William Hardy to John Hassell. Although Edy[2] Hardy's son Lam[3] Hardy received a bequest under the will of James Fewox, Edy[2] was clearly named in the will of her father Richard Batchelor of Norfolk. According to Chowan Co., NC, Deed Book B#1, pp. 3-5, dated 19 Apr 1715, Robert[2] Fewox and wife Martha acknowledged deed of sale to William Hardy. Willliam Hardy's last appearence in Bertie is in Deed Book G, p. 335, dated 2 Jan $175^0/_1$, in which Edward Rasor sold him 300 acres of land in Middle Swamp of Salmon Creek. Later on in May, son Lamb Hardy sold Gov. Gabriel Johnston a tract of 270 acres on Salmon Creek which his father William Hardy had conveyed as a deed of gift, according to Bertie Co., NC, Deed Book G, p. 357, dated 1 May 1751. Those are William's last two traces, and we may assume that he died between Jan and May 1751.

There seems to be much indecision over the pronounciation of the surname "Fewox." Phonetically the spelling "Faux" in John Biggs' will may actually be the closest, accounting for the disappearance of the (semi) intervocalic "w" in place-names such as "Greenwich" and "Dulwich."

The Children of Richard Batchelor and Ann Bigg:

[1] a. **John[2] Batchelor**, born *ca.* 1665.

[2]+ b. **Joseph[2] Batchelor**, born *ca.* 1668, died testate by 21 Feb $173^4/_5$, Norfolk Co., VA, Will Book 12, p. 79; married **Mary** [__].

[3] c. **Edward[2] Batchelor**, born *ca.* 1671.

[4] d. **Richard[2] Batchelor**, born *ca.* 1674.

[5] e. **Alice[2] Batchelor**.

[6]+ f. **Edith[2] Batchelor**, married **William[2] Hardy** of Scuppernong, died intestate between 2 Jan $175^0/_1$ and 1 May 1751, Bertie Co., NC, according to Deed Book G, p. 335 and p. 357.

The Children of James Fewox and Ann (Bigg) Batchelor:

[7] g. **Robert[2] Fewox**, of Scuppernong, married **Martha** [__], according to Chowan Co., NC, Deed Book B#1, p. 85, as early as 8 Sept 1714, at which time she signed with him in a sale of land to William Hardy.

[8] h. **Edward[2] Fewox**, did he marry **Bridget** [__], who exhibited his [now non-existant] will in Chowan Court, Apr 1736, Chowan Co., NC, Court Minutes, 1735-1738, p. 35, with Aron Blanchard as a surety?

17. Benjamin Blanchard made a will on 5 June 1719 while still a resident of Nansemond Co., VA, but the will was proved in North Carolina among the Secretary of State loose wills. Previously on 16 Aug 1716, he was taxed on 646 acres of land in Chowan, according to Albemarle County [NC] Papers, 1678-1737, vols. 1-3, p. 271. He married **Catharine** [__], named in his will, who died sometime after 1721, Chowan Precinct, at which time she was taxed on 435 acres of land, according to the same Albemarle record mentioned above, p. 342. The land on which Benjamin Blanchard lived on in Nansemond was cut off into North Carolina. Benjamin's first appearance in the North Carolina records was as a patentee, on 16 Oct 1701, whereon he received 455 acres in Chowan precinct upon Warick Swamp, according to NC Land Patent Book 1, p. 113. He had a brother Ephraim[1] Blanchard who died testate between 22 July 1745 and Apr 1749, Chowan Co., NC, Secretary of State loose wills, who named his wife Isabell [__] and whose son Aron[2] was a witness to Benjamin's will. Brother Ephraim's children were the following: Aron, Micajah, Ephraim, and [Daughter] married to [__] Griffin. Benjamin made a deed of gift to his "loving" brother Ephraim in Chowan Co., NC, Deed Book B#1, p. 304, dated 31 July 1716. The theory that they were originally from the Boston, MA, area cannot be substantiated with records.

Information concerning the "testamentary dispositions" of Benjamin's children who died intestate in Chowan (with notice of their own offspring as well) can be found in Jonathan B. Butcher, "Probate Records in Chowan County, N.C., Bound Miscellaneous Papers, 1694-1799," *The North Carolina Genealogical Society Journal*, vol. 7, no. 1 [February 1981], p. 21.

The Children of Benjamin Blanchard and Catherine [__]:

[1] a. **Robert[2] Blanchard**, according to the Chowan Co., NC, Court Minutes, 1730-1745, p. 44, Robert[2] Blanchard was dead by 17 Jan 1733 leaving widow **Mary** [__], who administered his estate. His orphan son Amos[3] made the choice of James Hinton as guardian on 15 Apr 1742, Chowan Co., NC, Court Minutes, 1730-1745, p. 103; according to the probate records compiled by Jonathan Butcher referenced above, Mary [__] married second, James Hinton, vol. 3, p. 14, Apr 1742. Blanchard left [as children] "two males and one female, the female now being married."

[2] b. **Absalom[2] Blanchard**, died intestate before 1758, Chowan Co., NC; married **Mary** [__], who must have married, second, Joseph Wimberley.

[3] c. **Benjamin[2] Blanchard**, will dated 3 Apr 1762, Chowan Co., NC, Will Book A, p. 212; married **Sarah[(2)] Hinton**, who died testate (at great age) between 8 Mar and May 1782, Gates Co., NC, Will Book 1, p. 25; besides naming her brother William Hinton as an executor, we have the following proof of her ancestry: in Chowan Co., NC, Miscellaneous Papers, 1685-1744, Book I, p. 111, concerning the division of the estate of William[1] Hinton [brother of **John[1] Hinton**], deceased (widow Elizabeth), dated 21 Apr 1737, daughter Sarah Hinton was identified as "Sarah Hinton now Blanchard."

[4]+ d. **Catherine**[2] **Blanchard**, married by 1716, Chowan Co., NC, **William**[1] **Weston**, who died testate after 12 Nov 1747, Bertie Precinct, NC Secretary of State loose wills.

18. Capt. **James Blount**, a leader in Culpepper's rebellion, was born by 1640 and died testate between 10 Mar and 17 July 1686, Chowan precinct, Albemarle Co., NC. The will of James Blount was recorded in NC Secretary of State vol. 874.2, p. 120. He married first, [__], the mother of his children, who died between 27 Sept 1670, when she appeared as a [nameless] witness in court, and 13 June 1683, at which time Blount's second marriage had taken place—Blount obtained administration on Robert Riscoe's estate. Blount married second, **Anna** (**Willix**) **Riscoe**, the daughter of Belshassar Willix of Exeter, New Hampshire, and the widow of Robert Riscoe of the Albemarle. Anna married third, the egregious Seth Sothel, and fourth, John Lear. There is an excellent biographical sketch of Capt. James Blount in William S. Powell's *Dictionary of North Carolina Biography*, vol. 1, *A-C*, p. 179.

Daughter Elizabeth[2] (Blount) Hawkins was located in an undated Colonial Estates record for James[3] Blount (Thomas[2]) of Bath Co., NC. In Dr. Stephen E. Bradley, Jr., *Early Records of North Carolina*, vol. 9, *Colonial Court Records—Estates Papers, 1665-1775, A-Gibson*, pp. 23-24, item 44: John Slocom and wife Mary, the administratrix of James[3] Blunt, gentleman, decd., witnessed on the back of the paper by John Hawkins and Elizabeth Hawkins. These were mother and son.

Much information, although some of it (intrinsically) confusing, has been provided by Caroline B. Whitley in *North Carolina Headrights, A List of Names, 1663-1744*. On p. 38 of that work is the following notice: "Capt. Blounts' own proper rights in one warrant, Thos. Blounts all in one warrant. These rights of Thomas Blount to be put into one warrant for his brother James, that is, James, his wife, and son; 1674." This establishes the fact that James Blount, Jr., was married by 1674. On p. 103, dated 1694, James Blount, Jr., claimed three rights: James Blount [himself], John Blount [his son], and Elizabeth Blount [his wife]. Following is the notice that James kept 50 acres for himself, and assigned the other 150 acres to his brother Mr. Thomas Blount. This information seems somewhat less opaque when the warrant on p. 105 is read: "Tho. Blount. 500 acres, for transportation of 10 persons, 29 Mar 1680: James Blount, Ursula Rodgers, James Blount, Jr., Eliz. his wife, Jno. Blount, Jno. Currier, Edw. Roe, his [--], Nightingale and two Children not baptized." This establishes at least that James Blount, Jr., married Elizabeth [__], although the persons in that warrant with different surnames do not appear to be related to the Blount family.

The Children of James Blount and [__]:

[1] a. **Eliabeth^2 Blount**, married [__] **Hawkins**.

[2] b. **Ann^2 Blount**, married [__] **Slocum**.

[3]+ c. Capt. **Thomas^2 Blount**, born *ca.* 1665, died testate between 3 Sept 1701 and 30 Oct 1701, NC Secretary of State loose wills, and recorded in Secretary of State vol. 874.2, p. 7; married first [__]; second, 13 [--] *ca.* $168^5/_6$ [only the day of the month survived mutilation in the register, but the other marriages were performed around 1685], Perquimans Co., NC, **Mary (Perry) Scott**, who died testate between 26 Sept 1716 and 31 Oct 1717, Chowan, NC Secretary of State loose wills; she was the daughter of Jeremiah Perry, the 1694 testator of Chowan, and widow of Joshua Scott of Albemarle, who died testate after 8 Jan $168^5/_6$, NC Secretary of State loose wills; she married third, by 18 Aug 1715, her first mention as his wife, Chowan Co., NC, Deed Book B#1, p. 207, John Bayley of Chowan, who died testate before July 1716, NC Secretary of State loose wills; this union is also confirmed by a deed from her fourth husband, Capt. Thomas Lee of Chowan, dated 9 Jan $171^6/_7$, who described her as his wife and the relict of John Bailey on 9 Jan $171^6/_7$, Chowan Co., NC, Deed Book B#1, p. 412; she married fourth, Capt. Thomas Lee, who barely predeceased her and died testate between 17 Mar $171^6/_7$ and 6 July 1719, Chowan, NC Secretary of State loose wills.

[4]+ d. **John^2 Blount**, born 16 Sept 1669, died testate 17 Mar $172^5/_6$, Chowan Co., NC, Secretary of State loose wills; married 11 June 1695, Perquimans, **Elizabeth Davis** "of Henrico, daughter of John and Mary [Burton] Davis;" she died testate between 8 Feb 1732 and 12 Mar $173^2/_3$, Chowan, NC Secretary of State loose wills.

[5] e. **James^2 Blount**, Jr., died testate between 12 Feb 1716 and 27 Mar 1717, Chowan Co., NC, Secretary of State loose wills; he named wife **Elizabeth** [__] in his will, whom he married by 1674, and who was named in the importation rights of his brother Thomas^2. In his will, James^2 named daughters Anne^3 Blount, Elizabeth^3 Yelverton, Mary^3 and Sarah^3 Blount, sons John^3 and James^3, and grandchildren James^4 and John^4 Yelverton, and Sarah^4 Philips. On 23 Aug 1718, John^3 Blount sold to John's brother-in-law Edward Wingate land bequeathed to Ann^3 (Blount) now Wingate by the will of their father James^2 Blount.

19. John$^{(3)}$ Blount, the son of **James$^{(2)}$ Blount**, Jr., and Elizabeth [__], was born well before 1680, Chowan precinct, NC, and died intestate after 3 July 1721, Chowan Co., NC, at which time he made a deed of gift of 640 acres on the north side of Moratuck River, joining James Blount and Thomas Busby, to his son James[2] Blount, according to Chowan Co., NC, Deed Book F#1, p. 154. On that same day, James[2] and his wife Katherine [__] sold that land to Francis Parker of Nansemond Co., VA, according to Chowan Co., NC, Deed Book F#1, p. 155. The descendants of this John Blount removed to Pitt Co., NC. The name of John Blount's wife has not appeared in the records.

On 15 July 1721, James[2] and Katherine sold 600 acres on the southwest Chowan River adjoining Maule's Haven to William Maule, according to Bertie Co., NC, Deed Book A, p. 1. The next year on 12 Feb 1722, according to the same volume, p. 56, they sold to William Hinton of the Upper parish of Nansemond Co., VA, 640 acres betweeen Moratuck and Cashay on the Villager Pond, part of a 640-acre patent dated 30 Mar 1721. On 3 Feb 1724, James[2] and wife Katherine sold to George Stevens 160 acres on Sandy Run, which had been granted to Owen McDaniel on 1 Mar 1719, Bertie Co., NC, Deed Book A, p. 400. According to Bertie Co., NC, Deed Book A, p. 422, dated 30 July 1716, James[2] had received a patent dated 19 Jan $171^{5}/_{6}$ in Chowan, which he and his wife sold to Samuel Woodard—200A on the south side of the Chowan River adjoining William Maul's corner tree. This deed had been registered in Chowan but was reconfirmed in Bertie. Their last transaction together in Bertie occurred on 28 Aug 1733, Deed Book D, p. 69, in which they sold 200 acres adjoining the Cashy Swamp to their "well beloved friend" Thomas Watson.

The Children of John Blount and [__]:

[1]+ a. **James[2] Blount**, born *ca.* 1690, died after 2 Sept 1764, Pitt Co., NC; married by 30 July 1716, Chowan Co., NC, **Katherine** [__].

20. Capt. **Thomas Blount**, the son of Capt. **James Blount** and his first wife [__], was born *ca.* 1665, died testate between 3 Sept 1701 and 30 Oct 1701, NC Secretary of State loose wills, and recorded in Secretary of State vol. 874.2, p. 7; married first [__]; second, 13 [--] *ca.* $168^{5}/_{6}$ [only the day of the month survived mutilation in the register, but the other marriages were performed around 1685], Perquimans Co., NC, **Mary (Perry) Scott**, who died testate between 26 Sept 1716 and 31 Oct 1717, Chowan, NC Secretary of State loose wills. She has been identified as the daughter of Jeremiah and Jane [__] Perry, the former of whom died testate between 18 Oct 1694 and Oct 1695, Chowan, NC Secretary of State loose wills. His will was also recorded in NC Secretary of State vol. 874.2, p. 65. Jeremiah named Christian[2] Blount the daughter of Thomas[1] Blount.

Most of the children of Thomas Blount's second marriage found it either necessary or desireable to identify themselves as such in the records. Thomas[2], Jr., of Bath Co., NC, on 24 Jan $171^{6}/_{7}$, Gent., described himself as the eldest son of Capt. Thomas Blount of Albemarle, deceased, by Mary his wife, late wife of

Joshua Scott of Perquimans and of Thomas Lee of Chowan. The abstract of this record, cited from Margaret M. Hofmann's *Chowan Precinct, North Carolina, 1696 to 1723, Genealogical Abstracts of Deed Books*, p. 117, Chowan Co., NC, Deed Book B#1, p. 407, identifies Mary's former husband as "Joseph;" however, according to *North Carolina Higher-Court Records, 1697-1701*, p. 372, she was listed as the widow of *Joshua* Scott.

Joshua Scott of Perquiman died testate after 8 Jan $168^5/_6$, NC Secretary of State loose wills, naming grandchildren. After Thomas Blount's death, Ann (Perry) Scott-Blount married third, by 18 Aug 1715, Chowan, her earliest mention as his wife, Chowan Co., NC, Deed Book B#1, p. 207, John Bayley, who died testate before July 1716, NC Secretary of State loose wills. This union is also confirmed by a deed from her fourth husband, Capt. Thomas Lee of Chowan, dated 9 Jan $171^6/_7$, who described her as his wife and the relict of John Bailey on 9 Jan $171^6/_7$, Chowan Co., NC, Deed Book B#1, p. 412. She married fourth, Capt. Thomas Lee, who barely predeceased her and died testate between 17 Mar $171^6/_7$ and 6 July 1719, Chowan, NC Secretary of State loose wills.

The Children of Thomas Blount and [__]:

[1] a. **James[2] Blount**, removed to Bath Co., NC, by 18 Nov 1706, according to Chowan Co., NC, Deed Book W#1, p. 81, in which he gave back five Negro slaves to Mary Blount (specifically omitting to call her his mother), which he had received under the will of his father Thomas; he married first **Katherine Tyler**, the daughter of Nicholas Tyler; he married second, her sister **Mary Tyler**, who married second, almost certainly as his second wife, John Slocum, who died testate between 20 Mar and 19 Sept 1722, Craven precinct, NC Secretary of State loose wills. John was the son or grandson of Anthony Slockum, the testator of 26 Nov 1688, NC Secretary of State loose wills, who named Slocum grandchildren in his will. An interesting lawsuit is included in *North Carolina Higher-Court Records, 1697-1701*, pp. 468-69, dated *ca.* 1700-1702, in which Attorney General Richard Plater declared the second marriage of James Blount of Bath Co., NC, to Mary Tyler, daughter of Nicholas, unlawful, particularly in view of the fact that James had first married her sister Katherine Tyler. However, it was decided that a verdict was not within the jurisdiction of that court, which may partially explain why such marriages were not considered incestuous in North Carolina, but were so in Virginia until the 1940s. Both Tyler sisters were included in the list of Nicholas Tyler's headrights in Caroline B. Whitley's *North Carolina Headrights, A List of Names, 1663-1744*, p. 43. Both fathers of the couple, Capt. Thomas Blount and Nicholas Tyler were taken into custody, each for having been "very

great promoter and Abettor of the aforesaid unlawfull Mariage." The date of Capt. Blount's death further narrows the date of the document to 1700-1701.

[2] b. **Sarah^{2} Blount**, married [__] **Peirce**.

The Children of Thomas Blount and Mary (Perry) Scott:

[3] c. **Thomas^{2} Blount**, born *ca.* 1688, removed to Bath Co., NC, by $171^{6}/_{7}$, according to the deed listed above, died intestate by 19 Feb 1734, the signing of Churchill^{2} Reading's will; he married **Ann^{2} Reading**, the daughter of **Lyonell^{1} Reading** and Mary.

[4] d. **Christian^{2} Blount**, born *ca.* 1690, married **William Ludford**, who died testate between 2 Oct 1732 and 2 Apr 1733, Pasquotank Co., NC, Secretary of State loose wills.

[5] e. **Mary^{2} Blount**.

[6] f. **Billah^{2} Blount**, married **Kellem Tyler**, son of Nicholas Tyler and wife Katharine (and brother to James Blount's two wives), who registered their importation rights on 5 July 1697, according to Caroline B. Whitley's *North Carolina Headrights, A List of Names, 1663-1744*, p. 43. She was a legatee under the will of James Pollock, dated 23 Feb 1700, Chowan Co., NC, Secretary of State loose wills.

[7] g. **Ann^{2} Blount**, married [__] **Wilson**.

[8] h. **John^{2} Blount**.

[9] i. **Zilpha^{2} Blount**, married by 30 Oct 1722, **John Edwards**, mariner, according to Chowan Co., NC, Deed Book C#1, p. 309, in which he described his wife as the recipient of a bequest in the last will and testament of her mother Mary, "in pursuance of the will of her father, Thomas Blount."

[10]+ j. **Benjamin^{2} Blount**, died testate between 1 Feb 1739 and June 1740, Tyrrell Co., NC, Secretary of State loose wills married **Elizabeth^{2} Everitt**, born *ca.* 1703, who married second, *ca.* 1741, William Ray.

[11] k. **Jacob^{2} Blount** escaped mention in both parents' wills, and is identified in a deed of gift from his brother Benjamin^{2} on 18 Jan 1718, Chowan Co., NC, Deed Book B#1, p. 17, a gift of land which Benjamin's mother had bequeathed him—640 acres known as Rich Neck on Kendrick's Creek—and which he gave to brother Jacob in pursuance of their father's will; married **Elizabeth** [__], according to Chowan Co., NC, Deed Book B#1, p. 537, dated 30 Jan 1718, in which he sold the tract recently "assigned" him by his brother Benjamin^{2}.

21. John Bond, the son of John Bond, Sr., the 15 Feb 1687 testator of Isle of Wight Co., VA, Will & Deed Book 2, p. 274, and his wife [__], *née* Bell [John Bond, Sr., named his wife's brother John Bell], was born say 1685, Isle of Wight Co., VA, and died testate between 8 July and Sept 1749, Beaufort Co., NC. His will was filed among the NC Secretary of State loose wills. According to *The Colonial Records of North Carolina*, 2nd ser., vol. 7, *Records of the Executive Council, 1664-1734*, p. 171, John Bond, on 2 May 1727, was re-elected as a Commissioner of the Peace for Beaufort and Hyde precincts. The name of his wife is unknown, but a possible clue to her identity may be Bond's bequest of a Negro slave named Jack to his cousin Martha Spring.

Lydia (Wallis) Bond was named as a daughter of Mary [__] and William Wallis of Beaufort, the latter of whom who died testate between 29 Dec 1748 and 13 Mar 1749, NC Secretary of State loose wills.

The Children of John Bond and [__]:

[1] a. **William^2 Bond**.
[2]+ b. **John^2 Bond**, born *ca.* 1722, Beaufort, died intestate 1750, Beaufort, his inventory filed Sept Court 1750; married **Lydia Wallis**.
[3] c. **James^2 Bond**.
[4] d. **Robert^2 Bond**.
[5] e. **Richard^2 Bond**.
[6] f. **Marey^2 Bond**.
[7] g. **Sarah^2 Bond**.
[8] h. **Anna^2 Bond**.

22. Richard Bond was born *ca.* 1670 and died testate at 5:00 PM, 23 Jan 172$^7/_8$, Nansemond Co., VA, according to probate information found in his will dated 15 Jan 172$^7/_8$, filed among Chowan Co., NC, loose wills. He married first, [__], whose name does not appear in the records. He married second, **Sarah** (perhaps *née* Sumner, according to a descendant), not named in his will but who presented it for probate to the court of Chowan. Sarah married second, James Coston of Chowan, which information can be found in Chowan Co., NC, Miscellaneous Papers, 1685-1744, p. 110, dated Apr 1737, on which date Richard's son Henry^2 petitioned the court to receive his legacy from his new step-father, James Coston of Maherrin Neck. Richard^1 Bond was in Nansemond by 1704, at which time he was listed with 90 acres of land in Annie Laurie Wright Smith's *Quit Rents of Virginia, 1704*, p. 10. Another shorter version of Richard Bond's Chowan will was filed among NC Secretary of State loose wills.

Information concerning the "testamentary dispositions" of Richard Bond's children (with notice of their own offspring as well) who died intestate in

Chowan can be found in Jonathan B. Butcher, "Probate Records in Chowan County, N.C., Bound Miscellaneous Papers, 1694-1799," *The North Carolina Genealogical Society Journal*, vol. 7, no. 1 [February 1981], pp. 21-22. For the Vail connection, see the "Drummond" chapter, pp. 187-89, in *Order of First Families of North Carolina, Ancestor Registry*, no. 1. Guy Hill of Gates, who died testate between 6 Mar and Aug 1787, Gates Co., NC, Will Book 1, p. 67, named his brother-in-law Richard Bond and one Moses Hill as sole executors of his last will and testament. There is insufficient information to determine how the two were related.

The Children of Richard Bond and [__]:

[1]+ a. **Richard^2 Bond**, born *ca.* 1700-05, Chowan, died testate between 12 Feb 1793 and Nov 1795, Gates Co., NC, Will Book 1, p. 134; married [__].

[2] b. **Henry^2 Bond**, died intestate before 20 June 1786, Chowan Co., NC; married, as her first husband, **Elizabeth^3 Vail**, born *ca.* 1750, Chowan, daughter of **John^2 Vail** and Elizabeth Swann; Elizabeth (Vail) Bond married second, [__] Pambrun/Pembrune.

[3] c. **William^2 Bond.**

[4] d. **Lewis^2 Bond**, died intestate before Jan 1762, Chowan Co., NC; married [__].

[5] e. **Hance^2 Bond**, died intestate by16 Apr 1752, Chowan Co., NC; married **Sarah** [__], according to Chowan Co., NC, Court Minutes, 1746-1748, p. 185, dated Jan 1748, in which she prayed administration on her husband's estate.

[6] f. **Mary^2 Bond.**

✠ **23.** Capt. **Thomas Bonner** was born say 1650 and died testate between 6 Mar and 24 Nov 1685, Albemarle Co., NC. He married **Mary** [__], named in his will, filed among the NC Secretary of State loose wills. A Henry and a William Bonner were witnesses to Capt. Thomas' will, but no relationship between the three was indicated, even though one might reasonably assume that son Thomas^2 was the heir and that Henry and William, putative younger sons, were otherwise provided for. His wife Mary was pregnant when Capt. Thomas died, and Thomas made provisions for that child. What happen to that child, whether male or female, has not been revealed by the records.

There is no actual proof of any connection between this Thomas of 1685 and any of the other Thomas Bonners in the Albemarle. Nor is there any actual indication of just how old Thomas^2 the son of Thomas of Albemarle was in 1685 when his father died. We have, unfortunately, no accompanying records for the older Thomas, no indications of where his property lay, nor any indications about the survival of his widow and the posthumously born child (if any).

It has been incorrectly assumed by many Bonner descendants (and by this writer as well) that the Thomas Bonner who appeared in the Chowan records as a resident of Nansemond Co., VA, with "now" wife Elizabeth, was the intermediate generation between the Captain of the Albemarle and the Sherrif of Beaufort Co., NC. It can be demonstrated by land records that this younger Thomas[A] and Elizabeth remained in what would become Bertie and that Thomas[A] died there testate, between 11 Nov 1755 and Apr $175^{6}/_{7}$ [*sic*], NC Secretary of State loose wills. However, Thomas[B] Bonner, Jr., the son of this elder Thomas[A], the testator of 1755, remained in Bertie long enough to sell his bequest from his father some ten years later, making it impossible for him to be Sheriff Thomas of Beaufort, according to a deed dated 26 Jan 1757, Bertie Co., NC, Deed Book H, p. 383. Shortly thereafter, on 1 June 1757, Bertie Co., NC, Deed Book I, p. 23, this tract of 100 acres on the west side of Cashy Road, sold above to Christopher Hollomon, was in the possession of James Byram, who sold it to Amos Hinton, describing the original possessor as Thomas Bonner, *Sr.* If there were more specific records of William and Henry Bonner, who may have resided in Nansemond, there might be more hope of filling out the pedigree.

Thomas[A] Bonner had a brother John[A] Bonner of Chowan, who barely predeceased him, dying unmarried and testate between 11 Nov 1753 and Jan 1754, Chowan Co., NC, Secretary of State loose wills. The testator also named Howcutt nephews and nieces, indicating that [__][A] Bonner, a sister had married into that family.

Thomas[A] Bonner and wife Elizabeth [__] appeared briefly in the deeds of Chowan beginning on 18 Oct 1714 as residents of Nansemond Co., VA, in the following instruments: [1] sale of land to Samuel Pattchat [Patchet] of Chowan, 50 acres on the west side of Matchacomack Creek called "Thomas Bonner's tract," according to Chowan Co., NC, Deed Book B#1, p. 57; [2] power of attorney to Capt. Henry Bonner of Chowan to acknowledge the sale of the above cited 50 acres, Chowan Co., NC, Deed Book B#1, p. 59. Then in 1721, as residents of Chowan they sold land on Potacasie Creek (which Bonner had purchased of **Thomas**[1] **Brown**) to **Leonard**[1] and Mullford **Langston**, according to Chowan Co., NC, Deed Book F#1, pp. 176-78. The deed referred to was a sale of 180 acres, Chowan Co., NC, Deed Book B#1, p. 458, dated 9 July 1717.

The records have not provided us with enough information to identify Captain Bonner's son Thomas with any accuracy. It seems unlikely, finally, that he survived.

24. Sheriff **Thomas Bonner** of Beaufort Co., NC, cooper, died testate between 1 Nov 1764 and June 1765, Beaufort Co., NC. His will was recorded in Beaufort

Co., NC, Will Book A, p. 285. He married by 1730, **Abigail** [__], who died after 16 Mar 1779, the date on which her son Henry[2] referred to her as still living on her own property in Beaufort Co., NC. Thomas Bonner witnessed a deed of sale from John Jordan to Margaret Foreman in October of 1716, according to Beaufort Co., NC, Deed Book 1, p. 199. He purchased 188 acres of land from William Sidley of Bath on 2 Oct 1716, according to the same record.

Although the Christian name Henry runs suggestively through the entire Bonner family, our Thomas Bonner could not be the son of Henry Bonner of Chowan (as this writer once mistakenly thought), since that Thomas Bonner was still a resident of Chowan as late as 18 Apr 1746, at which time John Bonner, for love and good will to his brother, gave him [Thomas] 130 acres of land, Chowan Co., NC, Deed Book E-1, p. 123. Moreover, Henry Bonner of Chowan, in his will dated 21 Sept 1738, NC Secretary of State loose wills, clearly described his son Thomas as a minor.

The principal reason which excludes Sheriff Bonner from being the young son of Captain Bonner is the age of the Sheriff. It is very unlikely that he was born well before 1685 given that he did not die until the 1760s.

The Children of Thomas Bonner and Abigail [__]:

[1]+ a. **Henry[2] Bonner**, will dated 16 Mar 1779, Beaufort Co., NC, Old Will Book, p. 145; married **Elizabeth[3] Snoad**, daughter of **John Snoad** and **Ann[2] Martin** (Joel[1]).

[2]+ b. **James[2] Bonner**, born *ca.* 1719, Bath Co., NC, married first, **Anne[3] Snoad**, sister of William Snoad who died testate between 15 Mar 1746 and 8 Apr 1747, Beaufort Co., NC, Secretary of State loose wills, daughter of **John Snoad** and **Ann[2] Martin** (**Joel[1]**); he married second, **Mary[2] Maule**, daughter of Dr. **Patrick[1] Maule**.

[3] c. **Elizabeth[2] Bonner**.

[4] d. **Sarah[2] Bonner**, married **Hardy[2] Bryan** (**Edward[1]**), who died testate between 28 Feb and May 1760, Craven Co., NC, Secretary of State loose wills.

[5] e. **Abigail[2] Bonner**, married **Simon Jones**.

[6] f. **Mary[2] Bonner**, married **John Harvey**.

[7]+ g. **Anne[2] Bonner**, married **Edward[2] Salter**, who died by 28 July 1768, Pitt Co., NC, Deed Book C, p. 19, in which his son Edward[3] sold land formerly belonging to his father, deceased.

[8] h. **Thomas[2] Bonner**.

25. Joseph Boon, almost certainly the son of testator Nicholas[A] Boon and wife Mary [__] of Chowan [see below], was born by 1690, possibly in Isle of Wight Co., VA, and died testate after the signing of his will on 19 Feb 1728, Chowan

Co., NC, filed among NC Secretary of State loose wills. The name of his wife does not appear in the records of Chowan, although she was mentioned but not named in Joseph's will. She appeared [see below] with her husband in a Bertie deed dated 27 Jan $172^7/_8$ as **Elizabeth** [__]. In his will, Joseph named sister Martha Bayley, a clue, perhaps, to his or his wife's origins.

Joseph's father Nicholas^A died testate in Chowan, but his will bears neither date of signing nor date of probate, NC Secretary of State loose wills. A Nicholas Boon, almost certainly Joseph's father, appeared in a suit instituted by William Ruffin dated 8 Feb 1667, in Isle of Wight Co., VA, Will & Deed Book 1, p. 107. Other than that, there are few "footprints" left by the family. Joseph Boon does not appear at all therein. If the Nicholas of Isle of Wight were of age in 1667, then the language of his will, which gave his sons their "liberty" at 16, suggests that he died in the late 1600s. This is an "educated" guess based on the idea that son Joseph was of age as late as 1719 when he received his first patent. From his father, Joseph received the lower portion of an undivided 300-acre tract on the Little Swamp.

Joseph^1 willed a plantation to his son James^2 which he had patented in his son James's name on 7 Nov 1723—210 acres in Bertie precinct in Maherrin Woods, adjoining Joseph Boon and Hope Meadow, found in NC Land Patent Book 3, p. 175. Joseph^1 willed 100 acres on Ochonechey Neck at Roanoak to son Joseph^2 Boon, Jr. He willed 180 acres on the south side of the Maherrin River to son Thomas^2 Boon, which was part of a 680-acre patent registered to Joseph^1 on 1 Mar $17^{19}/_{20}$, according to NC Land Patent Book 8, p. 178—except that in the original record the amout was for 480 acres, on the south side of the Maherring River, adjoining the northwest side of Kerbys Creek. In Bertie Co., NC, Deed Book B, p. 426, the amount is "remembered" as 400 acres, 200 acres of which were sold by Joseph and his wife **Elizabeth** of Chowan to Richard Bayley on 27 Jan $172^7/_8$: "200 acres at Kirbey's Creek and Spring Branch on the south side of the Meherrin River, part of a patent of 400 acres dated 1 Mar 1719." On the same day in NC Land Patent Book 8, p. 193, Joseph Boon patented 495 acres of land in Chowan on the south side of Meherrin River, adjoining Richard Milton, [__] Sherwood, Jon. Courtney, the Little Swamp, William Boon, and the Cream Pond Swamp. Richard *Bailey* sold this same tract on 6 Feb 1739, in Bertie Co., NC, Deed Book F, p. 61. Joseph^1 willed son Ralph^2 Boon 380 acres whereon the testator then lived. According to Bertie Co., NC, Deed Book B, p. 57, on 9 Nov 1725, Joseph^1 purchased 40 more acres on the south side of Maherrin River, adjoining William Boon, which was part of a 500-acre patent, dated 1 Apr 1723.

Three different Boons had wives named Alice.

The Children of Joseph Boon and Elizabeth [__]:

[1] a. **James^2 Boon** removed to Craven Co., NC, by 1 Jan 1739, according

to Bertie Co., NC, Deed Book F, p. 60, wherein he sold 100 acres on the south side of the Maherrin River adjoining Arthur Williams on the north side of Kirby's Creek at the Spring Branch, to John Taylor, Sr., which had been part of a patent granted Joseph^{1} Boon on 1 Mar 1719.

[2] b. **Joseph^{2} Boon.**
[3]+ c. **Thomas^{2} Boon**, born 1713, will dated 14 Mar 1796, proved Mar 1800, Northampton Co., NC, Will Book 2, p. 193; married **Alice** [__].
[4] d. **Ralph^{2} Boon.**
[5] e. **Mary^{2} Boon.**
[6] f. **Elizabeth^{2} Boon.**

26. Thomas Boswell, Sr., was born by 1677 and was dead by 14 July 1737, Perquimans, according to Perquimans Co., NC, Deed Book D, no. 2, in which his son James^{2} of Pasquotank described his father as deceased. Thomas married, as her second husband, after Oct 1698, Perquimans Co., NC, **Ann^{3} (Waller) Massagny**, born *ca.* 1681, Perquimans Co, NC, the widow of Benjamin Massagny and the daughter of **Thomas Waller** and **Elizabeth^{2} Durant**.

The Child of Benjamin Massagny and Ann Waller, born Perquimans:
[1] a. **Sarah^{2} Massagny**, born 4 Feb 1696.

The Children of Thomas Boswell, Sr., and Ann (Waller) Massagny, born Perquimans:
[2] b. **Elizabeth^{2} Boswell**, born 27 Apr 1702.
[3]+ c. **William^{2} Boswell**, born 25 Dec 1703, died testate between 1.12. $173^{4}/_{5}$ and 17 Feb $173^{4}[/_{5}]$, Perquimans Co., NC, Secretary of State loose wills; married **Margaret Nicholson**.
[4]+ d. **James^{2} Boswell**, born 9 Jan $171^{2}/_{3}$, died by 1766, Perquimans Co., NC; married [__].
[5] e. **Joshua^{2} Boswell**, born 5 Dec 1715, died testate Apr 1762, Perquimans Co., NC, Will book C, p. 25; married **Mary** [__].

27. John Branch, whose ancestry is unknown, was born by 1695 and died intestate by 1759, Halifax Co., NC. He married **Ann Brown**, the daughter of Martha^{A} [__] and William^{A} Brown, the latter of whom died testate between 15 Dec 1718 and 21 July 1719, Chowan Co., NC, and whose will was recorded in NC Secretary of State vol. 875, p. 152. William^{A} Brown was the brother of **Thomas^{1} Brown** of Chowan, and the other son of John^{B} Brown and Mary^{B}

Boddie of Isle of Wight Co., VA. Under the terms of her father's will, Ann Brown, unmarried at the signing of the document, inherited 150 acres of land "Lying upon y[e] head of her brother John." The reader will see [below] that this land was referred to in Halifax Co., NC, Deed Book 8. It has been assumed that John Branch was a resident of colonial NC at the time of this marriage. A good treatment of the family of John Branch can be found in "Branch of Halifax County, North Carolina," in John Bennett Boddie, *Historical Southern Families*, vol. 9, pp. 262-65.

According to Chowan Co., NC, Deed Book F#1, p. 38, dated [--] July 1718, Martha[A] [__] Brown married second, shortly after the death of her husband, William Murphery of Chowan, and conveyed land given to Martha by her first husband, 640 acres at the Cypress Gut—the plantation which Arthur Davis lived on—to Barnaby McKinney. This makes the possibility that she was Martha Gray, the daughter of testator Richard Gray of Isle of Wight Co., VA, extremely unlikely. Richard Gray, in his will dated 11 Nov 1724, recorded 27 Mar 1727, Isle of Wight Co., VA, Will Book 3, p. 22, made a bequest to daughter Martha *Brown*, not Murphery. Surely he would have known that his daughter had already been remarried for some 6 years.

The records of John[1] Branch, "Sr.," are disappointingly sparse. His first activity in the land transfers is referred to in a complicated deed, dated 12 Nov 1763, involving the Stewart and Millikin families, in which Thomas Stewart and his wife, the former Ann Millikin, sold land to James Young, including a tract of 160 acres purchased from John Branch and wife Ann on 8 Aug 1730, adjoining John Brown, "up the Cypress Swamp Gut on the south side of the Morratock River," Halifax Co., NC, Deed Book 8, p. 354, land which Ann had been bequeathed in the will of her father. The 1730 transaction cannot be located. John[1] Branch's first notice in the Edgecombe deeds occurred on 19 Feb 1747/8, Edgecombe Co., NC, Deed Book 3, p. 187, in a transfer of 100 acres on the Beech Swamp, being ½ of a tract which he had "taken up," to his son John[2] Branch, Jr. This implies that he had received some type of grant for 200 acres, but this cannot be located. His next appearance can be found in a sale with his son, John[2], both of Edgecombe, of 100 acres on the north side of Beach Swamp, as per patent to John, Sr. (which patent cannot be located), found in Edgecombe Co., NC, Deed Book 2, p. 201, dated 18 Jan 1755. These two sales thus disposed of John Branch's so-called patent of 200 acres. This deed is referred to later in Halifax Co., NC, Deed Book 7, p. 67, dated 13 Sept 1759, in which Henry Pope sold to John Branch (not distinguished by either "Jr." or "Sr.") this same tract—now of 91 acres. We may assume that John Branch was deceased by 1759. Any further designation of "Sr." and "Jr." would now refer to John[2] and his son John[3].

John[2] Branch, Jr., appeared with his wife Ann in the Edgecombe deeds first on 6 Oct 1748, wherein he sold 100 acres on the south side of Beech Swamp to William Campbell, Edgecombe Co., NC, Deed Book 3, p. 353, clearly the land sold to him by his father, as noted above. On 29 Aug 1785, Halifax Co., NC, Deed Book 15, p. 525, John² Branch and wife Rebecca sold to Joel Dilliard 150 acres adjoining the Reedy Branch, Richard Barrott, and the Beaverdam Swamp. **Rebecca⁴ Branch** was left a bequest in the will of her father **John³ Bradford**, who died testate between 13 Apr and Nov 1787, Halifax Co., NC, Will Book 3, p. 140. Rebecca was the product of the first of John Bradford's marriages: to Patience Reed, said by John Bennett Boddie in *Southside Virginia Families*, vol. 1, "Barker-Bradford-Taylor of Flowerdieu Hundred," pp. 75-84, to be the daughter of a Henry Read. **John³ Bradford** was the son of John Bradford and **Rebecca² Pace**, the daughter, in turn of **Richard¹ Pace**.

William² Branch is listed as a son of John¹ Branch due principally to his presence as a witness to and as neighboring land-owner in the various transactions of John¹ Branch, Sr., and John² Branch, Jr. In Halifax Co., NC, Deed Book 8, p. 62, dated 22 Jan 1762, William² Branch still owned land next to that of (deceased) John¹ Branch, Sr., indicated in a sale from John² Branch and his wife Ann to Richard Landstill, for 151 acres on the Beach Swamp. Obviously the land of John, Sr., recently deceased, was still in intestate probate and had not yet been fully distributed to the heirs.

The Children of John Branch and Ann Brown:

[1] a. **William² Branch**, Sr., born 1719, died testate between 24 Oct 1793 and Feb 1794, Halifax Co., NC, Will Book 3, p. 218; married **Elizabeth** [__], named in his will.

[2]+ b. **John² Branch**, Sr., born before 1727, died testate between 21 Nov 1805 and May 1806, Halifax Co., NC, Will Book 3, p. 453; married first, by 1748, Edgecombe, Co., NC, **Ann** [__]; second, by 1786, Halifax, Co., NC, **Rebecca⁴ Bradford**, born 25 Dec 1752; third, **Elizabeth Norwood**, born 1770, the daughter of John Norwood, who died testate between 13 Nov and Dec 1802, Franklin Co., NC, Will Book D, and his second wife widow Leah (Lenoir) Whitaker, who died testate between 18 Dec 1819 and Dec 1831, Franklin Co., NC, Will Book J, p. 176.

28. William Bridgers, the son of Joseph^A Bridgers and Elizabeth^A Norsworthy, was born say 1670, Isle of Wight Co., VA, and died testate between 2 Nov 1729 and May 1730, Bertie Co., NC, his will was filed among the NC Secretary of State loose wills. Bridgers married [__] **Godwin**, the daughter of William^A Godwin and Elizabeth^A Wright of Isle of Wight Co., VA. Her father William Godwin named her as "[--] Bridger" in his mutilated will dated 21 Nov 1710, Isle of Wight Co., VA, Great Book, p. 52. William Bridgers was a resident of Chowan Co., NC, by 16 July 1718, according to Chowan Co., NC, Deed Book

B#1, p. 372, at which time he purchased 150 acres of land on the north side of Meherrin River adjoining the Dividing Run. A sketch of this family can be found in *Order of First Families of North Carolina, Ancestor Registry*, no. 1.

On 23 Feb 172$^{4}/_{5}$, William[1] Bridgers made a deed of gift to his sons Joseph[2] and Samuel[2] Bridgers of land which he had purchased of James Gee on the north side of Meherrin: 200 acres on the easternmost side to son Joseph[2], and the remainder to son Samuel[2]. If Samuel should die without issue, then his portion to revert to son Benjamin[2].

The Children of William Bridgers and [__] Godwin:

[1] a. **William[2] Bridgers**, predeceased his father, dying testate between 11 Mar and Nov 1729, NC Secretary of State loose wills; married, as her first husband, **Sarah[2] Dew**, died testate between 7 Dec 1753 and Feb 1754, Northampton Co., NC, Secretary of State loose wills; she married second, **William[2] Cotton**.

[2] b. **Joseph[2] Bridgers**, married **Mary** [__], according to Edgecombe Co., NC, Deed Book 3, p.142, dated 5 Aug 1747.

[3]+ c. **Samuel[2] Bridgers**, born *ca.* 1696, married *ca.* 1729, Bertie Co., NC, **Mary Johnson**. In Northampton Co., NC, Deed Book 2, p. 302, Mary [__] Johnson made a deed of gift to granddaughter Mary Johnson[3] Bridgers, on15 June 1756.

[4] d. **Benjamin[2] Bridgers**, married after 1729, Bertie Co., NC, **Sarah[2] (Bryant) Drake,** the widow of **John[1] Drake**.

[5] e. **Mary[2] Bridgers**.

[6] f. **Elizabeth[2] Bridgers**.

29. Henry Bright was born say 1660, possibly in Norfolk Co., VA, and died testate between 23 May and July Court 1749, Currituck Co., NC, his will filed among the NC Secretary of State loose wills. His first appearance in the Norfolk records was on 4 Nov 1685 wherein he purchased 210 acres on the north side of Deep Creek from Isaac Seabourne of Elizabeth River in Lower Norfolk, recorded in Norfolk Co., VA, Deed Book 4 [16 Aug 1675-6 Oct 1686], p. 210a. The name of his wife, which does not appear in the North Carolina records, was located in Norfolk Co.,VA, Deed Book 7 [5 Sept 1703-15 May 1706], p. 45, wherein on 24 Dec 1703 he and wife **Elizabeth** [__] sold the same tract acquired from Seabourne to Thomas Tucker. Henry Bright was listed on the 1714 tax list for Currituck Co., NC, as found in William Doub Bennett's *Currituck County, North Carolina, Eighteenth Century Tax & Militia Records*, p. 7.

The main question in Bright genealogy is whether this Henry was the son of the John Bright who died testate in Beaufort. The1715 tax lists of Currituck provide a son for Henry not named in Henry[1]'s will: Richard[2], distinguished from Richard, Sr., and Richard, Jr., consistently as "Richard son of Henry," according to William Doub Bennett, *Currituck County North Carolina Eighteenth Century Tax and Militia Records*, p. 8. This younger Richard^2 predeceased his father.

The Children of Henry Bright and Elizabeth [__]:

[1] a. **Richard^2 Bright**, died testate between 12 Dec 1734 and 6 Nov 1735, Currituck Co., NC, Secretatry of State loose wills, also recorded in NC Secretary of State vol. 876, p. 425; he married **Elizabeth** [__].

[2]+ b. **John^2 Bright**, died testate between 29 July 1777 and 16 Dec 1780, Currituck Co., NC, Will Book 1, p. 162; married **Isabel^2 Powers**.

[3] c. **Maryann^2 Bright**.

[4] d. **Lucy^2 Bright**.

[5] e. **Caleb^2 Bright**.

[6] f. **Silas^2 Bright**, died testate between 28 Nov 1795 and 23 Apr 1796, Currituck Co., NC, Will Book 2, p. 74; he married **Frances** [__], who married second, Simon Wilson.

[7] g. **Henry^2 Bright**, Jr., died testate between 15 Nov 1765 and July 1766, Currituck Co., NC, Will Book 1, p. 32; he married **Ann** [__].

[8] h. **Cortney^2 Bright**.

30. John Bright died testate 9 Jan 1720, the day on which his will was signed and proved, Hyde precinct, Bath Co., NC. He married **Elizabeth** [__], named in his will recorded in Beaufort Co., NC, Old Will Book, pp. 1-2. A John Bright with wife Elizabeth of the "Southern Branch of Elizabeth River in the County of Lower / Norfolk planter," sold part of the plantation which John lived on, called Little Ridge, to John's brother Richard Bright on 16 Feb 1690, according to Norfolk Co., VA, Deed Book 5, part 1 [2 Dec 1686-19 Nov 1695], p. 147.

On 16 Mar 170$^1/_2$, John and Elizabeth Bright gave their power of attorney to Capt. Lemuel Wilson to sell the plantation they lived on to James Wilson, according to Norfolk Co., VA, Deed Book 6 [1695-1703], p. 233. This suggests that they were either already about to relocate or had just done so. It would be no surprise, therefore to find that John's brother Richard and Richard's wife Ann were already settled in Currituck by 24 Jan 170$^3/_4$, according to Norfolk Co.,VA, Deed Book 7 [15 Sept 1703-15 May 1706], p. 24, and had sold the "Little Ridge," formerly acquired from brother John, to William Ballentine. This Richard died testate in Currituck between 20 Feb 173$^3/_4$ and 1 July 1740, NC Secretary of State loose wills, and also recorded in NC Land Grant Book 4, no. 111.

Although it is not unreasonable to assume that John of Norfolk and then later of Currituck was the decedent of Hyde precinct, Beaufort Co., NC, this has not yet been proved. William Doub Bennett in 1999 was commissioned to complete a research project on the descendants of John Bright. In this study, he revealed many of the errors in the research done by Mr. and Mrs. William M. Searcy of Wilmington, NC, in the 1940s and 1950s.

There is an excellent biography of Simon^2 Bright (and his namesakes for three generations) in William Powell's *Dictionary of North Carolina Biography*, vol. 1, *A-C*, pp. 225-227. All John's sons were bequeathed land near Matchapungo Creek.

The Children of John Bright and Elizabeth [__]:

[1] a. **Henry^2 Bright**.

[2] b. **Richard^2 Bright**, will dated 28 Nov 1731, Beaufort Co., NC, Old Will Book, p. 11; married [__].

[3] c. **Simon^2 Bright**, born *ca.* 1695, died intestate after 27 Feb 1773, Craven Co., NC, his last mention in the records, by Robert Hamilton in a petition to the court to resurvey a tract of land recently purchased from Simon Bright, Sr., according to Secretary of State, IX, Petitions for Resurvey of Land Grants, Dobbs County, SS.727.4, NC Archives, Raleigh; this Simon^2 probably married a sister of Francis Hodges, since his son is referred to in the petition as the nephew of Francis Hodges; Simon's son, **Simon^3** II, born *ca.* 1734, was Sheriff of Dobbs Co., 1770, and died testate between 23 Nov 1775 and 18 Jan 1777, Dobbs Co., NC, Secretary of State loose wills; married *ca.* 1730, Craven Co., NC, married **Mary**[5] **Graves**, sister to Richard[5] Graves, the testator of 3 May 1774, Craven Co., NC, Secretary of State loose wills; and daughter of Thomas[4] Graves and Sarah Turner, as seen in Fred Dorman's *Adventurers of Purse & Person*, 4th ed., vol. 2, *G-P*, pp. 152-53 and p. 195.

[4] d. **James^2 Bright**, died tesatate between 25 Mar and [--] 1735, Hyde Precinct, NC Secretary of State loose wills; married **Anne** [__].

[5]+ e. **William^2 Bright**, died testate between 12 Jan and Nov 1754, Craven Co., NC, NC Secretary of State loose wills; married **Ann** [__]

[6] f. **John^2 Bright**, married [__]; on 12 Jan 172^4/$_5$, John Bright of Hyde Precinct, Bath Co., Deed Book 1, p. 479, for love and affection plus £15, gave his son Henry^3 Bright 350 acres on the west side of Matchapungo River; Simon^2 Bright was a witness.

[7] g. **Mary^2 Bright**, married **William Wynn**.

[8] h. **Lydia^2 Bright**.

31. Edward Bryan of Nansemond Co., VA, according to evidence cited below, was born 1663, London, England, and died 1739, Craven Co., NC. He married

1690, Isle of Wight Co., VA, **Christian Council**, the daughter of Hodges^{A} Council and Lucy^{A} Hardy, who died 1743, Craven Co., NC. Hodges Council, in his will dated and recorded 10 Apr 1699, Isle of Wight Co., VA, Will & Deed Book 2, p. 409, named his daughter Christian the wife of Edward Bryan. Daughter Lucy Council the wife of Hodges Councill was named in the will of John^{B} Hardy of Isle of Wight Co., VA, according to Will & Deed Book 2, p. 146. Edward Bryan died testate in Craven, but his will has not survived. On 18 Mar 173^{8}[/$_{9}$], Christian Bryan, the widow of Edward Bryan, deceased came into court and made oath to an inventory of the estate of her deceased husband, according to Craven Co., NC, Court Minutes, 1730-1746, p. 73.

An entry in a website entitled "Notes for Hodges Council," reports the following contribution to the North Carolina Genealogical Society *News*, vol. 17, no. 3, p. 30:

> Discovery in Pamlico County, North Carolina... found in Scottstown near the Goose Creek in Pamlico, a 600- to 800-pound granite slab from an abandoned cemetery [reading:] "Edward Bryan, Born in London 1663, Emigrated to Nansemond County, Virginia, 1690, Moved to Craven 1700. Died 1739. Christiana, his wife, daughter of Hodges Council died 1743."

I have so far been unable to locate a copy of this issue, although there is nothing in the reported epitaph to inspire doubt. The list of his children below is proved by existing records—John^{2}, described as the heir of Christian (Council) Bryan, meaning the first born and eldest; Edward^{2}; Lewis^{2}; and Hardy^{2}, all four may safely be claimed as Edward's. Edward^{2} named brothers Hardy^{2} and Lewis^{2} in his 1745 will.

The Children of Edward Bryan and Christian Council:

[1] a. **John^{2} Bryan**, married [__]; according to the following deed, John^{2} was deceased by 20 Apr 1731: Isle of Wight Co., VA, Deed Book 4, p. 104, dated 20 Apr 1731; James^{3} Bryan yeoman of Lower Parish, and wife Joan, to Walter Bryan, yeoman of same, 200 acres adjoining Hodges Council, being part of a patent dated 1677 granted Mr. Hodges Council, Sr., as 941 acres, on 9 Aug 1669, which he willed to his daughter Christina Bryan wife of Edward^{1}; her heir John^{2} Bryan, Sr., willed [*sic*] it to said James; this suggests that John^{2} died testate, but that his will is now lost; however, a somewhat later deed in Isle of Wight Co., VA, Deed Book 5, p. 65, dated 19 Nov 1736, from Walter "Bryant," described the same chain of ownership without using the term "willed." Nevertheless, it seems certain that James^{3} was John^{2}'s heir, and that he remained on ancestral land in Isle of Wight for a while. On 20 Apr 1731, James^{3} Bryan, yeoman, of the

lower parish and wife Joan [__] sold this land to Walter Bryan, according to Isle of Wight Co., VA, Deed Book 4, p. 104.

[2] b. **Edward^{2} Bryan**, died testate between 28 Jan 1745 and 9 May 1746, probably in Craven Co, NC Secretary of State loose wills, naming therein brothers Hardy and Lewis; married **Anne (Depp) Hand**, the second wife of widower Peter Hand, who died testate between 1 Feb 1730 and 16 Mar $173^{0}/_{1}$, Craven Co., NC, Secretary of State loose wills; she was the daughter of immigrants Jean Depp and Penon [__]. An excellent study of the Depp family of Manikin Town and Craven Co., NC, was penned by Cameron Allen, "Jean Depp of Manakin Town, Virginia, and Bath/Craven County, North Carolina," in *The Genealogist*, vol. 15 no. 1 [Spring 2001], pp. 1-52; especially pp. 1-10, and pp. 20-23.

[3]+ c. **Hardy^{2} Bryan**, died testate between 28 Feb and May 1760, Craven Co., NC, Secretary of State loose wills; married **Sarah^{2} Bonner**.

[4] d. **Lewis^{2} Bryan**. There were several contemporary Lewis Bryans; however, they have not yet been unraveled.

32. Needham^{2} Bryan, reputedly (and mythologically) the son of a "William Bryan" of Isle of Wight and later of Pasquotank by a wife fancifully alleged to be one "Lady Alice Needham," was born 23 Feb 1690, Nansemond Co., VA, and died testate between 23 Sept 1767, the date of his will, and the 4th Tuesday in Mar 1770, according to Bertie Co., NC, Court Minutes, 1724-1772, p. 61. His will was recorded in Bertie Co., NC, Will Book A, p. 124. Research has revealed that Alice [__] Bryan, Needham's mother, was, however, Alice^{A} McCloud, the daughter of John^{B} McCloud, the testator of 1 June 1705, Isle of Wight Co., VA, Will & Deed Book 2, p. 473, whose will was proved 9 Nov 1705. John McCloud, who named his Bryant grandchildren, Needham^{2}, William^{2}, John^{2}, Mary^{2}, and Alice^{2}, is listed in the record erroneously as John "Marklond," which has caused untold confusion in the identification of his progeny. Other untold confusion has been caused by Emma Morehead Whitfield's *Whitfield, Bryan, Smith, and Related Families*, Book Two, *Bryan*[,] *Smith* (1950), pp. 6-7 [hereinafter Whitfield2], in which she stated that Needham's father William Bryan removed to Pasquotank Co., NC, and died there. Not only was this William not Needham's father, but according to Isle of Wight Co., VA, Deed Book 2, p. 265, even cited in Whitfield2, p. 6 (as proof that Needham had a brother named John), the **John^{A} Bryan** mentioned as deceased in that deed was the husband of Alice^{A} McCloud and the father of Needham Bryan(t) and his siblings, mentioned in John McCloud's will. The explanation for mention therein is that the children were fatherless in 1705. According to the deed cited above, dated 17 Feb 1713, Needham and his wife Anne, of the upper parish of

Nansemond Co., VA, sold 170 acres to James Noliboy of lower parish of Isle of Wight for love of his brother John Bryan, who now occupied the land, bounded by Edward Bryan and Mason. The land from which this tract was taken had been land granted to John[1] Bryan, deceased, then of Nansemond, on 20 Apr 1682. The patent for 470 acres, as recited therein, on the south branch of Nansemond River adjoined Robert Johnson and Thomas Mason, 150 acres of which patent had been granted Bryan on 8 Oct 1672, for seven headrights, one of whom was a William Goodman. This is taken from Virginia Land Patent Book No. 7, p. 133, abstracted in Nugent's *Cavaliers and Pioneers*, vol. 2, *1666-1695*, p. 231. According to Whitfield2, pp. 6-7, Needham Bryan(t) married first, 16 Nov 1711, **Anne** (said to be **Rambeau**—this is *extremely* unlikely as a surname; the next two are perfectly plausible), born 1695, died Mar 1730, Bertie Co., NC. He married second, 14 Aug 1732, **Susanna** (said to be **Harrell**), who died 14 June 1752, and third, 20 June 1753, **Sarah** (said to be **Woodward**), who died 19 June 1776, and who was named in Needham's will. Bryan witnessed land transactions in Bertie as early as Feb 172$^{2}/_{3}$, according to Bertie Co., NC, Deed Book A, p. 147. The birth and death dates for Needham and his spouses are taken from Whitfield2, pp. 6-7. *Caveat lector.* For reasons best known only to the gods themselves, Mrs. Whitfield attributed just two children to Needham Bryan, even though his will was available.

Estates Records for the division of Needham Bryan's property in Bertie included legacies to the following persons: Ezekiel Williams, Lewis Gardner, Joseph Jearnigan, William Bryan (son of the decd.), and Jacob Jearnigan; equal sums were also paid to the executors: Needham Bryan (son of the decd.), Rachel Whitfield (dau. of the decd.), and William Bryan (son of the decd.). It has been suggested that Needham[1] Bryan's gifts to his grandson William[3] Bryan were due to the fact that one of his unnamed daughters married [__] Bryan and left her only son as an heir. This is incorrect. In Bertie Co., NC, Deed Book L-2, pp. 76-87, dated 27 and 29 Jan 1767, Needham specifically identified this grandson as the son of William[2] Bryant. In Jan 1767, Needham Bryan, Sr., made a deed of gift of 640 acres to his son Needham[2] of Johnston Co., NC, according to Bertie Co., NC, Deed Book L-2, p. 75.

The Children of Needham Bryan and Anne [__]:

[1]+ a. **Rachel[2] Bryan**, born 10 June 1723, died Nov 1780; married, as his first wife, **William[2] Whitfield**, died testate 31 Mar 1795, Wayne Co., NC, loose wills. William and his first wife were buried at Seven Springs on the south bank of the Neuse River, Wayne Co., according to Susan Fergusson and Eleanor Powell, David Williams Chapter, DAR, Goldsboro, *Miscellaneous Records of Wayne County, North Carolina, Families and Some of the Their Ancestors*, p. 2 of 6.

[2] b. **William[2] Bryan**, born 31 Oct 1724, married **Elizabeth Smith**, which

is confirmed by a deed of gift from her father Col. John Smith, Sr., of St. Stephen's Parish, Johnston Co., NC, to his granddaughter Elizabeth^{3} Bryant, a 10-year old slave Milley, now in the possession of William Bryant, according to Johnston Co., NC, Deed Book D-1, p. 166, dated 10 July 1764.

[3] c. **Elizabeth^{2} Bryan**, married first, **James^{3} Williams**; second, as his first wife, **Henry^{3} King**, the son of **Michael^{2}** and Isabel [__] King.

[4] d. **Needham^{2} Bryan**, born 31 Oct 1726, died by 30 July 1776, Johnston Co., NC; married first, **Nancy Smith**; second, 5 Feb 1748, **Charlotte Moore**; an estate division for Needham^{2} Bryan was carried out by Henry Rains, Arthur Bryan and Philip Thomas for the following heirs, in order to make the distribution equal to what was advanced to Kedar^{3} Bryan: [1] Nathan Bryan, husband of Winifred^{3} Bryan; [2] Bryan Whitfield, husband of Nancy^{3} Bryan; [3] Charlottie^{3} Bryan; [4] Ridgon^{3} Bryan, according to Johnston Co., NC, County Court Minutes, 1767-1777, pp. 224-25. Theoretical daughter Esther Bryan, said to have married Christopher Curtis, on p. 11 of Emma Morehead Whitfield's *Whitfield, Bryan, Smith, and Related Families*, vol. 2, *Bryan—Smith*, was actually the daughter of William Hinton, whose representative Joseph Hinton of Chatham Co., on 20 Dec 1792, Johnston Co., NC, Deed Book S-1, p. 363, made a deed of gift to Christopher Curtis and wife Easter of Wake Co., stating that the land had been given by will to William's two daughters Sarah Hinton and Easther Hinton—to be equally divided.

[5] e. **[Daughter]^{2} Bryan**, married [__] **Jernigan**.

[6] f. **[Daughter]^{2} Bryan**, married **Lewis Gardner**.

33. James Bryant, Sr., was born *ca.* 1650 and died testate in Bertie Co., NC, between 11 Mar 1731 and Aug 1732, according to NC Secretary of State loose wills. He first resided in Isle of Wight Co., VA, as early as 28 June 1686, where he was listed as a debtor to the estate of Col. Joseph Bridger, recorded in Isle of Wight Co., VA, Will & Deed Book 2, p. 259. Bryant was in Albemarle/Chowan Co., NC, by 30 July 1717, as a witness to a deed recorded in Chowan Co., NC, Deed Book W#1, p. 194. He married **Elizabeth** [__], who died after 4 Feb 171$^{7}/_{8}$, Chowan Co., NC. There is some question concerning the validity of the list of his children below, but the language of James Bryant's will suggests that the persons named at the end of that document were his children and/or sons-in-law: John Dew, Richard Braswell, James^{2} Bryant, Thomas^{2} Bryant, Mathew Telar. Son and heir-at-law William^{2} was named separately and was bequeathed his father's land on the north side of the Maherrin River.

On 20 May 1740, Bertie Co., NC, Deed Book F, p. 136, William[2] Bryant of Edgecombe Co. sold to Thomas Uzzell 320 acres of land whereon James "Bryand," deceased, had lived, having been part of a tract granted Richard Braswell for 640 acres by patent dated 24 Nov 1706, and endorsed over to James Bryant in 1708, plus 100 acres which James, Sr., had purchased of John Dew, the latter of which sale occurred on 25 July 1730, Bertie Co., NC, Deed Book C, p. 361. The deed from William[2] recited somewhat unclearly that he himself might have purchased from John Dew, but the statement refers to actions of his father James[1] before James[1], Sr., himself died. The transfer (lacking a description of the land in question) from Braswell to James Bryant, Sr., is located in Chowan Co., NC, Deed Book W#1, p. 187, and dated 14 Mar 1708. On 24 July 1714, James Bryant, Sr., of Albemarle Co., sold 320 acres to John Dew, Chowan Co., NC, Deed Book W#1, p. 172. An earlier version of the deed from William[2] to Thomas Uzell of Nansemond mentions William's wife who signed with him, but neither the deed nor the Bertie Court Minutes contain her name.

The Children of James Bryant, Sr., and Elizabeth [__], probably:

[1] a. **William[2] Bryant**, married [__].

[2]+ b. **James[2] Bryant**, Jr., married **Sarah** [__].

[3] c. **Thomas[2] Bryant**.

[4] d. **[Daughter][2] Bryant**, married **John[2] Dew** of Northampton Co., NC, died testate between 2 Sept 1749 and 1762, Edgecombe Co., NC, Secretary of State loose wills.

[5] e. **Eleanor[2] Bryant**, married **Richard Braswell**; in Bertie Co., NC, Deed Book A, p. 113, dated 14 May 1723, Richard and wife Eleanor Braswell signed a deed witnessed by James and William Bryant.

[6] f. **[Daughter][2] Bryant**, married **Mathew Telar**.

34. James Bryant, Jr., the son of **James Bryant**, Sr., and Elizabeth [__], was born by 1680, and died after 12 June 1754, at which time, described as "Sr.," he sold a tract of 62 acres in the Catawiskey woods out of his 1723 patent [*i.e.*, granted to James Bryant, Jr.], according to Northampton Co., NC, Deed Book 2, p. 176. He was called "father-in-law" by John Drake in Drake's 172⁸/₉ will. He married **Sarah** [__], who appeared as a witness with him on a deed dated 27 Nov 1742 in Northampton Co., NC, Deed Book 1, p. 202. In Northampton Co., NC, Deed Book 1, p. 30, dated 15 May 1742, James Bryant is described as a shoemaker. His manor plantation was located on the Uraha Swamp in this same record. His earliest appearances were in Chowan wherein as James Bryant, Jr., with wife Sarah he sold land on 14 Oct 1720 to Thomas Futrall, according to Chowan Co., NC, Deed Book F#1, p. 92.

James[1] Bryant, Jr. [above], sold 400 acres of land purchased from the Braswells to his son Arthur[2] Bryant on 4 Dec 1754, according to Northampton Co., NC, Deed Book 2, p. 183, although there was no relationship mentioned. On 27 Aug 1755, according to Northampton Co., NC, Deed Book 2, p. 245, Arthur[2] and his wife Elizabeth sold the same tract, on the south side of the Uraha Swamp, to Robert Peele, carpenter, described as a tract sold to the grantor by the grantor's father James[1] Bryant. On 18 Sept 1756, the same Robert Peele, Jr., sold to Arthur[2] Bryant 125 acres of land on the north side of Catawiskey Swamp on Dawe's Branch, adjoining James Wood, in Northampton Co., NC, Deed Book 2, p. 367. On 24 Aug 1772, Northampton Co., NC, Deed Book 6, p. 286, Arthur[2] and wife Elizabeth Bryant sold almost all the land which they had acquired in Northampton: [1] 170 acres which Richard Sumner sold to Simon West between Cattawitske and Uraha Swamps, adjoining Peale; [2] 125 acres which were purchased of Robert Peele Jr., 18 Sept 1756; [3] 10 acres purchased from Joseph Jordan, 27 Aug 1768.

The Children of James Bryant, Jr., and Sarah [__]:

[1]+ a. **Sarah[2] Bryant**, born *ca.* 1705, married first, **John[1] Drake**, who died testate between 5 Jan 172$^8/_9$ and May 1729, Bertie Co., NC, Secretary of State loose wills; second, by 1736, **Benjamin[2] Bridgers**, who died after 1780, Nash Co., NC.

[2] b. **Arthur[2] Bryant** married, somewhat late in life, **Elizabeth[2] Peele**, born 7.9.1736, Rich Square Monthly Meeting, Northampton Co., NC, the daughter of **Robert[1] Peele** IV of Northampton Co., NC, who named her in his will dated 1 Jan 1782, Will Book 1, p. 253.

35. Lewis Bryant, the son of Robert[A] Bryant and Elizabeth [__], was baptized 24 Dec 1642, Bitton, Gloucestershire, and was a resident of Nansemond Co., VA, on 1 May 1689, according to Isle of Wight Co., VA, Deed Book 1, p. 17. In 1704, Lewis Brian was listed with 400 acres of land in Nansemond in Annie Laurie Wright Smith's *The Quit Rents of Virginia, 1704*, p. 13—this was his initial county of residence until the following notice in the Chowan records. Bryant's transportation rights for his family were recorded 15 Oct 1715, according to Chowan Co., NC, Deed Book B#1, pp. 12-14. This has served as a list of his children by wife **Elizabeth** [__]. Lewis Bryant died testate almost certainly in Nansemond well before 1 May 1735, Bertie Co., NC, at which time his son William of Pasquotank sold land in Bertie left him "by his father's will," Bertie Co., NC, Deed Book F, p. 193. Lewis Bryant's will, however, has not survived. What have survived, however, are the foolish notions that Elizabeth [__] Bryant was *née* Hunter and that their daughter was born Elizabeth Hunter

Bryant. Neither of these have any foundation in what might be termed "genealogical reality."

William[2] Bryant below has been placed among these children since he married in Pasquotank, a county where he resided for a while, and where his siblings all had strong connections. The brother Joseph Bryan whom William[2] named in his will, however, has not yet been placed, and does not occur among the children for whom Lewis Bryant sought importation rights. Joseph Bryan, the testator of 1770 in Craven, named a Bryan brother in his will, but the first name of that brother cannot be read in the original document. Another strike against Joseph as a sibling to this group is that all of these children were deceased by 1770. It is possible that Joseph Bryan was born after his putative parents Lewis[1] and Elizabeth had settled in Chowan, but that cannot be proved either.

Further connections among the siblings arise from the following facts: [1] Capt. Edward[2] Bryant named nephew David[3] Bryant, the son of Simon[2], in his will; [2] John Gray named not only his "brother" [Capt.] Edward[2] Bryan, but also his nephew Thomas[3] Whitmell in his will; [3] Simon[2] named brother Edward[2] in his will.

The Children of Lewis Bryant and Elizabeth [__]:

[1] a. **Symon[2] Bryant**, died testate between 26 Nov 1751 and May 1753, Bertie Co., NC, Secretary of State loose Wills; married first, *ca.* 1729, Pasquotank Co., NC, **Elizabeth (Bailey) Armour**, the widow of testator John Armour of Pasquotank, and the daughter of testator David Bailey of the same. He married second, **Anne** [__], whom he named in his will. Estates Records in Bertie for Symon revealed that Edward[2] and David[3] Bryan petitioned for a division; Edward[2] was appointed guardian of orphan Joseph[3] Bryan, 28 Jan 1757, and gave Henry Gibbon the right to take property of the deceased into his possession. According to Pasquotank Co., NC, Deed Book B, p. 84, dated 10 Mar 1748/9, Simon Bryan for love and affection gave to his children, David[3], Winnifred[3], and Joseph[3], 3 Negro girls, when children should arrive at age 21 or at marriage; Joseph[3] has been the only child of Symon[2] and Elizabeth to receive any formal attention in print, and his descendants are traced in Hathaway's *North Carolina Historical and Genealogical Register*, vol. 1, no. 4 [October, 1900], "Queries and Anwers," pp. 631-33. Joseph[3] Bryan was born 23 Sept 1742 and died 16 Apr 1807; he married **Mary[4] (Hunter) Coffield-Dawson**, the widow of Thomas Coffield and [__] Dawson, respectively, and the daughter of **Henry[3] Hunter** and **Sarah[2] Whitmell**.

[2] b. **William[2] Bryant** died testate between 12 Dec 1746 and June

1747, Craven Co., NC, Secretary of State loose wills; he named his brother Joseph in his will; he married 10 Jan 173$^{3}/_{4}$, Pasquotank Co., NC, as her second husband, **Anne^{2} (Delamare) Stoakley**, who died testate between 23 Oct 1767 and 9 Mar 1773, Craven Co., NC, Secretary of State loose wills, the widow of Joseph Stoakley. The births of two of William and Anne's eldest children were registered in the Pasquotank register: William^{3} Bryan, born 29 Sept 1734, and Elizabeth^{3} Bryan, born 6 Mar 173$^{5}/_{6}$.

[3] c. Capt. **Edward^{2} Bryant**, mariner, died between the signing of his will on 14 Mar 1761 and the date that the inventory of his estate was presented to court by his widow Martha Bryan, 14 July 1762, according to Bertie Co., NC, Administrators' Bonds, 1762-1769, p. 101; will recorded in Bertie Co., NC, Will Book A, p. 8; married **Martha^{3} West**, daughter of **Thomas^{2} West** and Martha (Blount); she died testate between 22 May and Aug 1777, Bertie Co., NC, Will Book B, p. 109. Estates Records in Bertie for Capt. Edward Bryan reveal that on 14 July 1762 a division included the following heirs: [1] Martha^{3} Bryan; [2] Elizabeth^{3} Bryan; [3] Ann^{3} Bryan; [4] Sarah^{3} Baker. On 22 Aug 1777, the following heirs were listed: [1] Thomas^{3} Bryan; [2] Jannet^{3} Hill; [3] Edward^{3} Bryan; [4] Winifred^{3} Bryan.

[4] d. **Janette^{2} Bryant.**

[5] e. **Mary^{2} Bryant.**

[6] f. **Joanah^{2} Bryant.**

[7] g. **Sarah^{2} Bryant.**

[8] h. **Ann^{2} Bryant**, married **John Gray**, surveyor,who died testate between 20 Sept 1745 and 16 Nov 1750, Bertie, NC Secretary of State loose wills.

[9] i. **Lewis^{2} Bryant**, removed to Craven Co., married [__]. On 14 Nov 1740, according to Bertie Co., NC, Deed Book F, p. 265, Lewis Bryan, then of Craven, sold land to his brother Edward^{2} which the grantor had received in the will of his father.

[10]+ j. **Elizabeth^{2} Bryant**, born 15 Sept 1694, died 18 Jan 1753; married first, *ca.* 1712, **Thomas^{2} Whitmel II**, born 16 Sept 1688, Charles City Co., VA, and died testate 24 Nov 1735, Bertie Co., NC, his will recorded in NC Land Grant Book 4, no. 22; married second, *ca.* 1736, as his second wife, **Robert^{2} Hunter**, who died testate between 3 June and Aug 1753, Bertie Co., NC Secretary of State loose wills.

36. John Bunn was born by 1690 and died testate after 20 Jan 1727, Bertie Co., NC, according to NC Secretary of State loose wills. As the testator's oldest son

John^2 was described as not quite 10 years old at the writing of this 1727 will, we may assume that Bun married *ca.* 1717, Isle of Wight Co., VA, **Eleanor Mandew**, the daughter of Thomas Mandew. This marriage is confirmed by a deed of gift from Thomas Mandew to his grandson Benjamin Bunn in Bertie, for 100 acres, Bertie Co., NC, Deed Book E, p. 17, dated 11 Aug 1737. Mandew died testate between 17 Apr and Aug 1736, Bertie, NC Secretary of State loose wills, and was married to wife Sarah [__] in Isle of Wight as early as 16 May 1690, according to Isle of Wight Co., VA, Deed Book 1, p. 36.

The Children of John Bunn and Eleanor Mandew:

[1] a. **John^2 Bunn**, born *ca.* 1720, died testate between 17 May and June 1760, Edgecombe Co., NC, Will Book A, p. 3; married [__].

[2]+ b. **David^2 Bunn**, born *ca.* 1722, will proved Feb 1785, Nash Co., NC, Will Book 1, p. 28; married [__].

[3] c. **Benjamin^2 Bunn**, born *ca.* 1724, died intestate in Edgecombe 1760-70; married **Mary^3 Fort**, according to the 1761 will of **George^2 "Foort"** which named daughter Mary Bunn, and which was witnessed by Benjamin Bunn.

[4] d. **Ann^2 Bunn**.

37. John Cake, Sr., was born by 1695 and died testate between 8 Dec 1770 and Mar 1771, Bertie Co., NC, Will Book A, p. 139. He married first, by 1720, Chowan Co., NC, **Ann** [__], still alive on 6 Nov 1742, according to Bertie Co., NC, Deed Book F, p. 383, as a witness with her husband to a deed of sale. John Cake married second, **Mary Fleetwood**, the daughter of William Fleetwood and Elizabeth [__], by Aug 1748, Bertie Co., NC, Deed Book G, p. 157, wherein Mary appeared as a witness with her husband to another deed of sale. Mary (Fleetwood) Cake was so named in the will of her father William Fleetwood, signed on 12 June 1769, recorded in Bertie Co., NC, Will Book A, p. 108. John Cake, Sr., purchased land in Chowan according to a deed dated 20 Apr 1720, Chowan Co., NC, Deed Book C#1, p. 49. The approximate date of 1720 was decided upon for John's first marriage since his son John^2 was listed as a witness to a deed dated 7 Apr 1750 as "Jr.," indicating that he was of age, and therefore born no later than 1729, Bertie Co., NC, Deed Book G, p. 290. Ann [__] Cake was almost certainly the mother of all of John Cake's children. On 16 June 1758, Bertie Co., NC, Deed Book I, p. 115, John Cake made a deed of gift of 120 acres on the Flat Swamp to his son Robert^2, land which adjoined Robert's sister Elizabeth^2 Carins. This demonstrates a first marriage for daughter Elizabeth^2 before she married [__] Hughes

A William Cake died intestate in Bertie, according to Estates Records, by 26 Oct 1756, and his estate was administered by Sarah Cake, presumably his widow, but his relationship to the above family has not yet been determined. In his will John Cake named the following grandchildren: William Cake^{3} Filgo, William^{3} Coward, and James^{3} Hughes.

The Children of John Cake and Ann [__]:

[1] a. **Robert^{2} Cake**.

[2] b. **Elizabeth^{2} Cake**, married first [__] **Carins**; second, [__] **Hughs**.

[3] c. **Mabel^{2} Cake**, married **John^{3} Coward** (John^{2}, William^{1}).

[4] d. **John^{2} Cake**, Jr., died testate between 19 June 1795 and May 1796, Bertie Co., NC, Will Book D, p. 329; married **Mary** [__].

[5]+ e. **Ann^{2} Cake**, married **Anthony Filgo**, died testate between 24 Oct 1776 and May 1777, Bertie Co., NC, Will Book B, p. 99. These two are ancestors of former vice-president Al Gore.

38. Moore Carter, almost certainly the son of Thomas^{A} Carter and Magdalin^{A} Moore, was born by 1680, Isle of Wight Co., VA. His putative father Thomas Carter died testate between 6 Feb and 10 Apr 1710, Isle of Wight Co., VA, Will and Deed Book 2, p. 499, and mentioned only his wife Magdalen, daughter Martha, and son Alexander Carter. Thomas Carter's wife Magdalen (Moore) Carter received a bequest of tobacco from her uncle Thomas^{B} Moore, the testator of 28 Sept 1696, Isle of Wight Co., VA, Will & Deed Book 2, p. 371. Moore Carter died intestate before 13 May 1740, Bertie Co., NC, at which time his widow Jane petitioned for administration of his estate, according to Bertie Co., NC, Court Minutes, 1724-1772, p. 148. His known wife was **Jane**, almost certainly the daughter of Samuel **Kindred**, the testator of 25 Jan $172^{8}/_{9}$, Isle of Wight Co., VA, Will Book 3, p. 166, who named daughter Jane but did not distinguish her (or any of his daughters) with a married name. Given the paucity of bequests in Jane's will, there is an excellent chance that she was a second wife whom Moore Carter married after $172^{8}/_{9}$, and the mother only of the children mentioned in her will—besides Susannah, who seems to have died early. This would certainly explain why her father referred to her as unmarried. Moore Carter, a patrilinear ancestor of former president Jimmy Carter, purchased from John Dickenson 210 acres of land on the north side of Catawhiskey Meadow on 10 Oct 1720, according to Bertie Co., NC, Deed Book A, p. 250. Jane Carter died testate between 27 Jan and Feb 1764, Northampton Co., NC, Will Book 1, p. 88. She named daughter Katherine^{2} Knight, son Kindred^{2}, son Isaac^{2}, and son-in-law William Knight.

This writer is uncomfortably aware of the two large assumptions he has made based on onomastic evidence alone. Nevertheless, he stands by his decisions to construct the family of this ancestor in this manner.

The unnamed Carter [daughter][2] who married Bryant O'Quin is referred to in Bertie Co., NC, Deed Book F, p. 207 [undated, but *ca.* May 1741], in which Briant O'Quin, Joseph Jones, and Frederick Jones promised to save Jane[2] Carter harmless from all of the estate of Patience[3] O'Quin, the granddaughter of Moor Carter deceased. In Bertie Co., NC, Deed Book F, p. 132, dated 24 July 1740, Jacob[2] Carter, heir at law to Moor Carter [and therefore his oldest son], granted his beloved brother Isaac[2] Carter a tract of land on the south side of Meherrin River, a part of a 400-acre patent granted father Moore Carter 1 Feb 1725. An estate division for intestate decedent Moore Carter, dated 30 Apr 1741, stipulated that the widow receive her thirds, and that the other heirs receive a division of the remaining 2/3 as follows: [i] *the widow*, received slaves Sam and Moll; [ii] *Kindred[2] Carter*, received boy slave Scipio; [iii] *Jacob[2] Carter*, personalty only, with £17; [iv] *Isaac[2] Carter*, received girl Jude; [v] *James Jones*, received slave Isabell; [vi] *Moore[2] Carter*, received livestock amounting to £17 in value; [vii] *Bryant O'Quin*, father of Patience[3] O'Quin, granddaughter of Moore Carter, personalty in the amount of £17; [viii] *Katherine[2] Carter*, received personalty in the amount of £17; [ix] *Susannah[2] Carter*, received £16 from Kindred[2] Carter and James Jones to be paid to Jane Carter, the mother of Susannah Carter.

Kindred[2] Carter married Mary [__] the widow of Walter Browne, who died testate between 17 Oct and Feb173$^{5}/_{6}$, Bertie Co., NC, Secretary of State loose wills. Walter mentioned his cousin Jesse Drake, although this turned out not to be a clue to Mary's identity. Walter was the son of Samuel Brown of Isle of Wight Co., VA, who in his will dated 7 Oct 1739, recorded 23 June 1740, named his grandson Jesse Drake, son of his daughter Mary, the wife of John Drake, Isle of Wight Co, VA, Will Book 4, p. 274.

An interesting deed in Northampton Co., NC, Deed Book 2, p. 381, dated 26 May 1757, recites that Kindred[2] Carter and Mary his wife, and Hardyman Pope and Sarah his wife, all of Edgecombe, sold land to John Hare of Bertie—100 acres in Northampton formerly belonging to Walter Brown and which descended to Mary as Walter's widow [now Kindred's wife], and to Sarah (Browne) Pope, as Walter's posthumously born daughter.

The Children of Moore Carter and [__]

[1] a. **[Daughter][2] Carter**, married **Bryant O'Quin**, daughter Patience[3].

[2] b. **Jacob[2] Carter**.

[3] c. **[Daughter][2] Carter** married **James Jones**, almost certainly the son of John Jones, Sr., who died testate after 17 Mar 173$^{5}/_{6}$, Bertie Co., NC, Secretary of State loose wills, and brother to Frederick and Joseph Jones, with whom he was associated in the records. John Jones, Sr., was originally from Isle of Wight Co., VA.

[4] d. **Moore[2] Carter**, died testate between 29 Dec 1800 and May 1805, Gates Co., NC, Will Book 1, p. 218; married **Elizabeth** [__].

The Children of Moore Carter and Jane Kindred, born after 1729:

[5]+ e. **Kindred[2] Carter**, will proved Oct 1777, Edgecombe Co., NC, Will Book A, p. 260; married after Feb 173$^5/_6$, Bertie Co., NC, **Mary [__] Browne**. Their daughter Priscilla[3] Carter married James Knight, whose will was dated 2 Nov 1786 and proved Feb 1794, Edgecombe Co., NC, Will Book C, p. 268; the Carter names came into the Knight family through this union rather than through that of Katherine[2] Carter and husband William Knight, both of whom remain untraced.

[6] f. **Isaac[2] Carter**, died intestate by 12 May 1800, Bertie; married **Nancy [__]**, named as his widow in her petition for dower in Bertie Estates Records.

[7] g. **Susannah[2] Carter**, *died before 1764.*

[8] h. **Katherine[2] Carter**, married by 1764, Northampton Co., NC, **William Knight**.

39. Edmund Chancey, Sr., council member in North Carolina, was born *ca.* 1640, and died testate in Albemarle Co. by 1677, although his will has been lost. There is an excellent biography of Edmund Chancey in William S. Powell's *Dictionary of North Carolina Biography*, vol. 1, *A-C*, pp. 353-54, by Mattie Erma Parker, although Mrs. Parker inserts a fourth fictional child into the family [see below]. Edmund's widow **Margaret [__]** married second,Valentine Byrd, whose estate she inventoried and then had appraised, 29 Mar 1680, according to *North Carolina Higher-Court Records, 1670-1696*, p. 10. She married third (in rapid succession), as his second wife, **John[3] Culpeper**. According to NC Secretary of State vol. 874.2, p. 24, dated 29 Mar 1680, "Mrs. Margaret Culpepper the relict applied to administer the estate of Edmond Chancey of Albemarle County." Margaret was dead by 23 Aug 1688, the date of Culpeper's third marriage to **Sarah[2] Mayo**.

On 2 Oct 1684, Thomas Burnby petitioned the court to receive the estate which would come to him by having married Hannah[2] Chancey, the daughter of Edmond Chancey, and ordered that a copy of the will be presented. Edmund[2], Jr., made choice of Thomas as his guardian. This may be found in *The Colonial Records of North Carolina, North Carolina Higher-Court Records*, 1670-1696, p. 350.

A daughter Elizabeth who married Samuel Nicholson has been suggested as a fourth (possible) child of Edmund, but she was Elizabeth[2] *Charles*, not Chancey [see below in the Charles sketch].

The Children of Edmund Chancey, Sr., and Margaret [__]:

[1] a. **Hannah[2] Chancey**, married 1684, **Thomas Burnby**, the son of John

and Elizabeth [__] Burnby, died testate between 12 May and 6 Oct 1687, Pasquotank Co., NC, Secretary of State loose wills; he named "brothers" Edmund[2] and William[2] Chancy.

[2]+ b. Hon. **Edmund/Edward[2] Chancey**, Jr., born *ca.* 1670, died testate between 15 Mar and July 1753, Pasquotank Co., NC, Secretary of State loose wills; married by Sept 1703, **Sarah Keile**, the daughter of Thomas Keile and Mary (Butler), who married second, Thomas Relfe. For more information about these relationships, please see John Anderson Brayton, "Rolfe/Relfe-Jennings: The Unclosed Case of anUnclosed Case," in *The North Carolina Genealogical Society Journal*, vol. 29, no. 1 [Feb 2003], pp. 3-43. On 8day.7mo.1703, Edmund and wife Sarah assigned a survey of land to Ann Pailin, Pasquotank Co., NC, Deed Book A, p. 12. There is no record in Pasquotank of the land in question; Edmund did not receive land grants in Pasquotank until 22 Nov 1714, NC Land Patent Book 8, p. 257, for 533 acres on Nobbs Crook Creek; on 4 Jan $171^4/_5$ in Book 8, p. 278, for 449 acres on Newbegun Creek adjoining Laurence Keaton; and again on 4 Jan $171^4/_5$, Book 8, p. 278, for 482 acres on Newbegun Creek.

[3] c. **William[2] Chancey**, died testate 2.28.1749, Pasquotank Monthly Meeting, his will dated 17 July 1746 and proved 4 Aug 1749, NC Secretary of State loose wills; married $11.2.170^0/_1$, Pasquotank Monthly Meeting, **Deborah Symons**, daughter of Jeremiah[1] Symons, who died 3.23.1718, Pasquotank Monthly Meeting.

40. William Charles was born say 1640-45, possibly in Rhode Island, and died 6 Aug 1677, Perquimans Co., NC. He married 14th [--] (*ca.* 1659), Rhode Island (registered in Perquimans), **Abigail[2] Bailey**, the daughter of **William[1] Bailey** and Grace [__] of Newport, Rhode Island. Abigail had a sister Mercy[2] who married John Stepney, according to the Perquimans registers, although the marriage was undated. Mercy was listed as the daughter of "Grace Baily of Rhode Island," although her sister was not so identified. Both of these daughters have been omitted from the list of William Bailey's children in John Osborn Austin's *The Genealogical Dictionary of Rhode Island*, pp. 9-11.

Abigail (Bailey) Charles married second, 21st [--], Perquimans, John Lacy of Perquimans, the testator of 1.10.1682 who named her in his will, filed among the NC Secretary of State loose wills. Abigail married third, in 1683, Perquimans Co., NC, Francis Toms of Perquimans, who died testate between 5 Sept and 7 Oct 1729, NC Secretary of State loose wills—she did not survive her third husband, and died 4 or 14 Mar 1687, Perquimans. Toms' will was also recorded in NC Secretary of state vol. 876, p. 201, and transcribed in *North*

Carolina Wills and Inventories, pp. 430-32. Abigail died between 1700 and 1707, Perquimans Co., NC. There is an excellent article by William Perry Johnson on the Baileys in *The Journal of North Carolina Genealogy*, vol. 13, no. 1 [Spring 1967], pp. 1835-40, which corrects the mistakes in Austin.

The Children of William Charles and Abigail Bailey, born Perquimans Co., NC:

[1] a. **William[2] Charles**, born 15 July 1661, will dated 7 Apr 1687, will proved 23 Sept 1687, NC Secretary of State loose wills; he married 8 Nov 1683, Perquimans, as her first husband, **Elizabeth[2] Kent**. She married second, 11 Aug 1687, Perquimans, **Giles Long**.

[2] b. **Daniell[2] Charles**, born 24 Dec 1666, will dated 17 Apr 1687, Perquimans, NC Secretary of State loose wills; named siblings.

[3] c. **John[2] Charles**, born 22 Nov 1668, died testate [--], Perquimans, NC Secretary of State loose wills.

[4] d. **Jane[2] Charles**, born 20 Jan 1670, died testate 12 July 1688, Perquimans, NC Secretary of State loose wills.

[5]+ e. **Elizabeth[2] Charles**, born 8 Jan 1671, married first, 16 Dec 1688, Perquimans, **Samuel[2] Nicholson**; second, as his second wife,10 June 1729, Perquimans, **Zachariah Nixon**, Sr., who died testate in Perquimans between 28 Sept and Oct 1739, NC Secretary of State loose wills; Elizabeth died testate between 19 Mar $174^{7}/_{8}$ and Jan $174^{8}/_{9}$, Perquimans, NC Secretary of State loose wills.

[6] f. **Samuel[2] Charles**, born 22 Mar $167^{4}/_{5}$, will dated 12 Mar $172^{7}/_{8}$, letters granted 18 Apr 1728, NC Secretary of State loose wills, recorded in NC Secretary of State voll. 876, p. 186; married **Elizabeth** [__].

[7] g. **Isaac[2] Charles**, born 12 Mar $167^{6}/_{7}$.

The Child of John Lacy and Abigail (Bailey) Charles, born Perquimans:

[8] h. **Sara Lacy**, born 15 Sept 1680.

The Child of Francis Toms and Abigail (Bailey) Charles-Lacy, born Perquimans:

[9] i. **Persillah Toms**, born 10 Dec 1684, married 20 Nov 1700, Perquimans, **John[2] Nicholson**, son of **Christopher[1]** and Hannah.

41. William Charlton was born by 1666 and was married well before 1698 since his son William, Jr., in Jan 1719 was old enough to patent land and to be distinguished legally from his father, according to Chowan Co., NC, Deed Book F#1, p. 7 (and was, therefore, of age). We might even assign William, Sr., a marriage date as early as 1688, since in 1711 he made a undated deed of gift to his daughter Sarah[2] and his son-in-law Luke Mizelle for land in Chowan, recorded in Chowan Co., NC, Deed Book W#1, p. 90. This land would eventually be cut off into Bertie at the formation of that county. William, Sr., died intestate after 28 Apr 1729, Bertie Co., NC—his last appearance with his son William, still designated as William, Jr., as found in Bertie Co., NC, Deed Book D, p. 116. He married **Susannah** [__], born *ca.* 1666, and died after 1710, Chowan Co., NC. According to Chowan Co., NC, Miscellaneous Papers, 1685-1744, p. 66, dated 11 June 1722, William Charleton was remunerated for having served as interpreter to the Tuscarora Indians. Wife Susannah was not *née* Smithwick. According to Caroline B. Whitley, *North Carolina Headrights, A List of Names, 1663-1744*, p. 166, on 11 July 1694, William Charleton petitioned for 250 acres for the transportation of himself, Lawrence, Bethinia, Luke, and Ellinor Mezaell, all, almost certainly, from Surry Co., VA. The four Mizelles were assigned to William by Lawrence Meazell.

His first patent of land was on 25 Feb 1696 for 240 acres in Chowan, adjoining John Porter, according to NC Patent Book 1, p. 54. From then on his principle holdings were on the Morattuck River in Chowan. William Charleton, Sr., made a deed of gift to Richard Swain and his wife Ann for love and affection, of land on Sothaca Creek and Roquist, called the "Meadow Tract," Bertie Co., NC, Deed Book B, p. 262, proved 6 June 1726. This deed of land may be interpreted to mean that Ann Swaine was *née* Charleton, and was a heretofore unknown daughter.

There was a John Charleton who owned land next to William Charlton, Sr., but he cannot be placed with this family.

The applicant who joined the OFFNC through William Charlton was descended through daughter Sarah[2] Mizell. As part of his proof, he apparently produced a 1736 document purporting to be the will of Luke Mizell, a testament which must have existed only in a private collection. Such a document has disappeared, but it is reasonable to deduce from it that Luke Mizell died *ca.* 1736, and that the deeds of gift enumerated below were granted by Luke[3] Mizell his son and heir: [1] Bertie Co., NC, Deed Book E, p.101, 200 acres in Kesia Neck adjoining Edward Collins and the Leggetts to daughter Susannah[4] Mizle; [2] 13 Nov 1749, Bertie Co., NC, Deed Book G, p. 233, 100 acres to daughter Martha[4] Mizell, land adjoining Richard Tomlinson, Legitt, and Edward Collins; [3] 13 Nov 1749, Bertie Co., NC, Deed Book G, p. 238, 100 acres to daughter Elizabeth[4], 100 acres adjoining Collins and Martha Mizell; [4] *ca.* Jan 1756, Bertie Co., NC, Deed Book H, p. 249, Luke and Luke[4], Jr., sold land to Charles Burch and wife Elizabeth.

The Children of William Charlton and Susannah [__]:

[1]+ a. **Sarah[2] Charlton**, born *ca.* 1686, Albemarle Co., NC, married by 1711, Chowan Co., NC, **Luke Mizell**. She appeared in the records as late as 13 Oct 1716, at which time she and her husband executed a

power of attorney to William Charleton for a sale of land to George Clark of Perquimans, according to Chowan Co., NC, Deed Book B#1, p. 402.

[2] b. **William[2] Charlton**, Jr., born *ca.* 1698, was of Craven Co., NC, when he sold 300 acres of land called "Indian Island," which his father William Charlton had purchased of the Indians, to Thomas Norcom of Perquimans, 1 June 1748, Bertie Co., NC, Deed Book G, p. 154. His first patent of land was on 3 Aug 1719, as "William Charlton, Jr.," for 490 acres in Chowan on the south side of Aligator Creek, adjoining Daniel McKay. He married **Mary** [__], according to Bertie Co., NC, Deed Book E, p.310 and p. 319, when she signed with him on deeds, both dated 6 May 1738, to William Jordan and Joseph Jordan, respectively. His activity in Craven commenced in the early 1740s; on 27 Mar 1763, Craven Co., NC, Wills, Deeds, Inventories, 1749-1777, p. 376; however, he gave all his land and chattels to his son William Meazell[3] Charleton.

[3] c. **Ann[2] Charleton**, married before 1726, **Richard[2] Swaine**, who died by 27 Feb 1761, Bertie Co., NC, according to Bertie Estates Records, the date of the presentation of his inventory to court by his widow Ann.

42. Robert Coleman, originally of Isle of Wight Co., VA, was born by 1645 and died testate between 9 July 1721 and 29 Mar 1725, Beaufort Co., NC. His will is found among the NC Secretary of State loose Wills and was also recorded in NC Secretary of State vol. 875, p. 346. In his will, he named wife **Mary** [__] **Odier-Eason**, who had been the widow of Dennis Odier and then of Henry Eason, both of Perquimans. The records for this are to be found in the Perquimans registers: "Denis Odeare the son of Denis Odeare and Mary his wife was born 8 Dec 1684." Mary [__] Odear married second, Henery Eason, 23 May 1687, Perquimans. According to the local probate information, Robert Coleman's will was also attested in Isle of Wight Co., VA. His first mention in those records was as an appraiser of the estate of Rev. Robert Bracewell/Braswell, dated 11 May 1668, Isle of Wight Co., VA, Will & Deed Book 2, p. 55. A discussion of the Reynolds branch of this family can be found in John Anderson Brayton, *Colonial Families of Surry and of Isle of Wight Counties, Virginia, Volume 9, The Family of George Williams, died 1672, of Isle of Wight Co., VA, with Corrections and Additions to* Adventurers of Purse and Person, *4th Ed., including the families of Reynolds, Hunt, and Parker*, p. 67.

David Dupuis, Sr., made a deed of gift dated 4 Apr 1704 to his children David, Jr., William, and Elizabeth in Beaufort Co., NC, Deed Book 1, p. 35 [94]. According to Craven Co., NC, Court Minutes, 1712-1715, p. 99, *ca.* 1713,

Christopher Gale granted a survey of 750 acres of land, on the sand banks between Bare Inlet and Brown's Inlet, to Sarah Dupuis, dated 20 Jan 171$^3/_4$ which her son and heir David Dupuis, in order to avoid any difficulties (and for £10), sold the back to Gale. This indicates that Sarah's husband was deceased. The identity of the children of Robert Coleman, especially [Daughter][2] (Coleman) Dupuis, is complicated by the fact that Lionell Reading, in some ways Robert Coleman's genealogical *doppelgänger*, wrote his will dated 12 July 1708, proved 18 Feb 1725, Beaufort Co., NC, NC Secretary of State loose wills, naming, among others, his [first] wife Mary, his daughter Sarah (Reading) Dupuis, and Sarah's husband David Dupuis. Letters of administration were granted to Reading's widow *Grace* Reading, whom he had married sometime between the signing of his will, 12 July 1708, and 18 Jan 171$^1/_2$, Norfolk Co., VA, according to Norfolk Co., VA Deed Book 9, part 2, Court Orders, p. 25, in which Lyonell Reading and his wife Grace, a legatee under the will of Thomas Butt, deceased, had given a power of attorney to John Hollowell to sue Richard Butt, the executor of the will. The case, however, was dismissed due to the inauthenticity of the power of attorney, and the will of Richard Butt has been lost. Lionell Reading's will was also recorded in NC Secretary of State vol. 876, p. 41. Why two seemingly unrelated men could both have wives named Mary and the same married daughter Dupuis puzzled this writer to no end. From these conflicting bits of data, a bizarre scenario presented itself in which [1] Reading and his wife Mary were divorced shortly after the writing of his will, and he married second, the much-married Grace (--)—for her marriages, see the sketch for Lyonel Readng in vol.2; [2] Mary Reading, a much married widow, immediately afterwards married Robert Coleman; [3] there were two women named Sarah Dupuis. But these were all completely unsatisfactory explanations. The only possible solution, given the fact that Sarah (Reading) Dupuis' son David came of age in 1709 (after the signing of Reading's will), was that Robert Coleman's [unnamed][2] daughter married by 1725, David Dupuis, Jr., the son of David Dupuis, Sr., and Sarah (Reading), and had a son David[3] Dupuis III named in Coleman's will.

It has been assumed by various persons, including this writer, that the Robert Coleman who died testate in Isle of Wight before Robert of Bath died was the latter's son and name-sake. This is a plausible conclusion, especially in view of the lack of any contradictory evidence. Robert Coleman, Jr., did mention his brother-in-law Christopher Reynolds without, however, specifying any relationship; but the testator left all his land to his "brother" Stevenson except for the land that a Richard Baton lived on. This land is not described, nor is Stephenson further identified. There is a patent dated 28 Sept 1667 to "Mr." Robert Coleman for 634 acres in Isle of Wight on the Cypress Branch, adjoining Mr. Driver's new land, Rutter's land, Ruffin's pocosin, Bennet and Smith: 300 acres by purchase of Ambrose Bennett, and 334 acres for transportation of himself and 6 other persons, VA Land Patent Book No. 6, p. 181. Then in VA Land Patent Book No. 6, p. 337, dated 4 May 1666, both William Ruffin and Robt. Coleman patented jointly 938 acres of land in Isle of Wight, adjoining Thomas Harris for the transportation of 19 persons. On 20 Apr 1684, Coleman received 530 acres of land on the west side of Reedy March, being a branch of Chuckatuck, adjoining Jeremiah Rutter and John Turner, formerly granted to Richard and Miles Lewis on 29 Jan 1667, and who sold land to Coleman, VA Land Patent Book No. 7, p. 378. On 21 Apr 1695, he patented 80 acres in Isle of Wight adjoining Thomas Jordan and Giles Driver, VA Land Patent Book No. 8, p. 422. Robert Coleman received a patent dated 28 Oct 1697 in Nansemond for 450 acres in the Upper Parish near Wickham Swamp, according to VA Land Patent Book 9, p. 109, for transportation of 9 persons. Significantly on 23 Oct 1703, Dennis Odier patented 119 acres on the Upper Parish of Nansemond, near South Key adjoining Robert Coleman, for transportation of Robert Coleman, among others, in VA Land Patent Book 9, p. 575. There is virtually no record of how Robert Coleman disposed of all these patents. We must assume that some land fell into Nansemond when the boundaries of the counties were adjusted. This notion is supported by Annie Laurie Wright Smith's *The Quit Rents of Virginia, 1704*, p. 20, on which Robert Coleman is listed with 1400 acres in Nansemond and 1500 acres in Isle of Wight.

The progeny and ancestry of Christopher Reynolds are discussed in Fred Dorman's *Adventurers of Purse and Person.*, 4th ed., vol. 3, *Families R-Z*, pp. 5-6.

The Children of Dennis Odear and Mary [__]:

[1] a. **Dennis Odear**, born 8 Dec 1684, Perquimans, died testate between 16 Feb 1746 and June 1747, Johnston Co., NC, NC Secretary of State Wills, as "Odyer;" married **Ann** [__].

The Children of Robert Coleman and Mary [__] Odear-Eason:

[2] b. **Ann[2] Coleman**, married first, **Christopher[4] Reynolds who** died intestate by 31 Dec 1741, Isle of Wight Co., VA, Will Book 4, p. 396; she married second, [__] **Hunt**.

[3] c. **Robert[2] Coleman**, Jr., died testate after 8 Mar 171$^{5}/_{6}$, Isle of Wight Co., VA, Will & Deed Book 2, p. 607.

[4] d. [**Daughter**][2] **Coleman**, married **David[3] Dupuis II**, son of David Dupuis I and **Sarah[2] Reading**.

[5]+ e. **Elizabeth[2] Coleman**, married **Christian[2] Isler**, who died testate between 4 Oct and 7 Nov 1747, Craven Co., NC, Secretary of State loose wills, recorded in Secretary of State vol. 878, p. 148.

[6] f. **Mary[2] Coleman**, married [__] **White**.

43. John Collins was most likely a native of Nansemond Co., VA, but immigrated to Chowan Co., NC, as early as 23 Mar 1723, according to NC Land Patent Book 3, p. 126, at which time he received 640 acres on the northeast side of the Chowan River. He married first, **Martha** [__], the mother of his children, whose last appearence in the records was on a deed with him dated 10 Aug 1742, Bertie Co., NC, Deed Book F, p. 378. He married second, **Mary** [__], named in his will. John Collins was born say 1700, Nansemond Co., VA, and died testate between 27 Dec 1749 and 18 Mar 1752, Bertie Co., NC. His will was filed in the collection of NC Secretary of State loose wills. A sketch of this family can be found in *Order of First Families of North Carolina, Ancestor Registry*, no. 1.

In Aug of 1742, according to Caroline B. Whitley's *North Carolina Headrights, A List of Names, 1663-1744*, p. 210: John Collins registered his imporation rights based on the following persons: Jno. Collins, Martha Collins, David Collins, Joseph Collins, Michael Collins, Damsey Collins, Jesse Collins, Absolom Collins, and the following slaves: Tony, Judith, Robin, Venus, and Rose.

The Children of John Collins and Martha [__]:

[1] a. **Martha**^{2} **Collins**, married [__] **Bryant**; on 8 Aug 1738, John Collins made a deed of gift to his daughter Martha^2 Bryant of a slave girl Hannah, Bertie Co., NC, Deed Book E, p. 339.

[2] b. **[Daughter]**^{2} **Collins**, married [__] **Keene**.

[3] c. **William**^{2} **Collins**, on 29 June 1752, sold 350 acres on the north side of Pelmell also called "Marbin Hills" to Jesse Collins, Bertie Co., NC, Deed Book H, p. 330, witnessed by Michael Collins.

[4] d. **John**^{2} **Collins**.

[5] e. **David**^{2} **Collins**.

[6] f. **Joseph**^{2} **Collins**, married **Rachel Bunch**, daughter of Henry Bunch, her will dated 21 Apr, proved Aug 1775, Bertie Co., NC, Will Book B, p. 34.

[7]+ g. **Michael**^{2} **Collins**, born 1728, married first, **Ann Perry**; second, 10 June 1773, Bute Co., NC (marriage bond, William Bridges, bondsman, Alexr. Muirhead, witness), **Elizabeth Drake**.

[8] h. **Dempsey**^{2} **Collins** married June 1753, **Elizabeth Downing**, daughter of William Downing, according to Estates Records in Bertie for Elizabeth [ ] Downing. William Downing died testate between 24 Feb 1748 and 7 Mar 174^8/$_9$, Tyrrell Co., NC, Secretary of State loose wills, naming wife Ann [__], daughters Mary and Elizabeth, and son Henry. William was the son of an older William Downing, who died testate between 1 and 6 Apr 1739, NC Secretary of State loose wills, naming wife Dorcas [__] and brother-in-law Ebeneezer

Slade.
[9] i. **Jesse[2] Collins.**
[10] j. **Absolum[2] Collins.**

44. John Cotton, a resident of Isle of Wight Co., VA, was born say 1660, and died testate between Oct 1727 and Mar 1728, Bertie Co., NC, his will filed among the collection of NC Secretary of State loose wills. In Annie Laurie Wright Smith's *The Quit Rents of Virginia, 1704*, p. 22, John Cotton was listed with 200 acres in Isle of Wight. He married, as her first husband, **Martha Godwin**, the daughter of William[A] Godwin and Elizabeth[A] Wright, born say 1670, Isle of Wight Co., VA. She married second, William Green, who died testate between 20 Dec 1760 and Mar 1761, Halifax Co., NC, Will Book 1, p. 22. John Cotton's first land grant in North Carolina was on 9 June 1719, according to NC Patent Book 1, p. 277. He received a grant of 640 acres in Chowan, on the southwest side of Ahoskey meadow. A sketch of this family can be found in *Order of First Families of North Carolina, Ancestor Registry*, no. 1.

The Children of John Cotton and Martha Godwin, ages and birth order approximate, born Chowan precinct, Albemarle Co., NC:

[1] a. **John[2] Cotton**, born *ca.* 1687, died testate 2 Feb 1741, Northampton Co., NC, his nuncupative will proved May Court 1742, NC Secretary of State loose wills; he married first, probably by 1710, **Judith** [__], who appeared on land sales with him until 1726; he married second, between Nov 1726—his last appearance with Judith—and 17 May 173$^5/_6$, Bertie Co., NC, when Anne was named in her father's will, **Anne Jones**, daughter of John Jones, Sr., of Bertie Precinct, NC, whose will was dated 17 Mar 173$^5/_6$, and proved May Court 1736, Secretary of State loose wills. Judith was almost certainly the mother of John's chidlren.

[2] b. **William[2] Cotton**, born *ca.* 1689, died after 1741, Northampton Co., NC, when he was executor to his brother John[2] Cotton's will; he married by 1729, as her second husband, **Sarah (Dew) Bridgers**, who died testate between 7 Dec 1753 and 28 Feb 1754, Northampton Co., NC, Secretary of State loose wills.

[3] c. **Samuel[2] Cotton**, born *ca.* 1691, died testate between 16 Jan and 18 May 1774, Northampton Co., NC, Secretary of State loose wills; he married first, **Elizabeth** [__]; second, **Lydia** [__] **Green-Ruffin-Howell/Ewell**, who died testate between 9 Jan and Apr 1783, Northampton Co., NC, loose Wills, also recorded in Will Book 1, p. 267.

[4] d. **Joseph[2] Cotton**, born *ca.* 1693, died testate by May 1772, Halifax

Co., NC, Will Book 1, p. 314; married [__].

[5] e. **Anne^{2} Cotton**, born *ca.* 1695, married **John Thomas**, who died testate between 18 March 1745 and May 1746, Northampton Co., NC, Secretary of State loose wills.

[6]+ f. **Patience^{2} Cotton**, born *ca.* 1697, married, as his first wife, Capt. **John^{1} Speir**, who died testate 20 Apr 1764, Greenville, Pitt Co., NC, Secretary of State loose wills.

[7] g. **Mary^{2} Cotton**, born *ca.* 1699, married **Richard Holland**.

[8] h. **Martha^{2} Cotton**, born *ca.* 1701, married **Frances Benton**.

[9] i. **Susannah^{2} Cotton**, born *ca.* 1703, *no further record.*

[10] j. **Alexander^{2} Cotton**, born *ca.* 1711, died Jan 1765, Hertford Co., NC; married first, **Ann Foster**; married second, **Elizabeth^{3} West**, the daughter of Peter West and Priscilla^{2} Williams, and the granddaughter of **Lewis^{1} Williams**.

[11] k. **Arthur^{2} Cotton**, born *ca.* 1712, died 20 May 1799, Hertford Co., NC; married **Elizabeth Rutland**.

[12] l. **Priscilla^{2} Cotton**, born *ca.* 1714, married [__] **Leonard**.

[13] m. **James^{2} Cotton**, born *ca.* 1716, died testate between 14 Jan and 28 Apr 1758, Bertie Co., NC, Secretary of State loose wills; married **Sarah** [__].

[14] n. **Thomas^{2} Cotton**, born *ca.* 1718, removed to Hertford Co., NC; married **Mary** [__].

45. William Coward, the son of James^{A} Coward and the widow Mary^{A} [__] Collige of North Farnham Parish, was born around 1689, Old Rappahannock Co., VA. The subject of his parents' marriage and the date thereof have received some discussion. James^{A} "Caward," listed in Annie Laurie Wright Smith's *The Quit Rents of Virginia, 1704*, p. 105, with 121 acres in the Richmond Co., VA, tax list of 1709, married Mary^{A} [__], the relict of Hezekiah Collige as early as 2 Feb $168^{7}/_{8}$, according to Old Rappahannock Co., VA, Order Book, 1687-1689, p. 51. On 27 May 1687, Old Rappahannock Co., VA, Deed Book, 1686-1688, pp. 353-54, Mary, still described as Mary Collige, made a deed of gift to the two children of her first marriage, Philip and Mary Collige. William Coward of Bertie died intestate between 4 Dec 1725—his last mention occurring in a purchase of 600 acres of land from John Harloe, Bertie Co., NC, Deed Book A, p. 418—and 9 Feb $17^{29}/_{30}$, in a deed from his son and heir John^{2} Coward for 100 acres out of that purchase to Joseph White wherein William^{1} is described as officially deceased, Bertie Co., NC, Deed Book C, p. 175. In addition, his (we may assume) widow **Mary** [__] presented an inventory of his estate to the court on 28 Mar 1728, NC Secretary of State vol. 876, pp. 166-67. William purchased 200 acres of land from Joseph Jessop of Perquimans in Chowan Co., NC, on 15

Apr 1718, Chowan Co., NC, Deed Book B#1, p. 564. There is a remote possibility that Mary^{A} [__] Collige was the daughter of John Alloway of Old Rappahannock Co., VA, but this has not been substantiated with available records. Robert J. Robinson, in his somewhat fanciful *Coward-Cowart Chronicles, 1650-1997*, p. 4, has attributed, reasonably, three other sons to William and Mary—James, Charles, and Edward—but this cannot be proved.

The Child of William Coward and Mary [__]:

[1]+ a. **John^{2} Coward**, died testate between 28 Mar and Aug 1737, Bertie Co., NC, Secretary of State loose wills; married **Elizabeth** [__].

Possibly:

[2] b. **James^{2} Coward**.

[3] c. **Charles^{2} Coward**.

[4] d. **Edward^{2} Coward**.

46. Robert Coxe, Sr., of Perquimans, died testate between 21 Feb $172^{5}/_{6}$ and 25 Nov 1730, Little River precinct, Chowan Co., NC. His will was filed among the NC Secretary of State loose wills. Robert Coxe married **Elizabeth** [__], named in his will. On 9 July 1722, Robert "Cock" of Perquimans Co., NC, purchased 100 acres of land from Zachariah Nixon, according to Perquimans Co., NC, Deed Book B, no. 318.

Two children of Thomas Weeks and Anne^{2} Cox are listed after the record of Anne's marriage to Thomas: Perquimans Court Minutes, 1688-1738, p. 165: [i] Miriam^{3} Weeks, born 8 July 1725; [ii] John^{3} Weeks, born 29 Sept 1727. John^{3} Weeks died testate between 4 Jan and Apr 1768, Perquimans Co., NC, Will Book C, p. 77, naming wife Sarah [__], children John^{4}, Shadreck^{4}, Thomas^{4}, Irenah^{4}, and Sarah^{4}, and naming brother Samuel^{3}.

The Children of Robert Cox and Elizabeth [__]:

[1]+ a. **Robert^{2} Coxe**, died testate before 5 June 1768, as "Cocks," Perquimans Co., NC, Will Book C, p. 82; married **Ann** [__].

[2] b. **Sarah^{2} Coxe**.

[3] c. **Achen^{2} Coxe**.

[4] d. **Anne^{2} Coxe**, married 2 July 1724, Perquimans Co., NC, "at the house of Robt. Cock her father," in Perquimans Court Minutes, 1688-1738, p. 165, **Thomas Weeks**. They were both still alive on 1 Aug 1744, at which time they sold 546 acres of land to Joseph Robenson, on the south west side of Little River, called "Pine Glade," according to Perquimans Co., NC, Deed Book D, no. 162. By 12 Sept 1763, Thomas was dead, and his sons John^{3}, Thomas^{3}, and Samuel^{3}

petitioned to have his property divided among them, with shares to minors James and Wilson Weeks, in Perquimans Co., NC, Deed Book G, no. 123. Thomas died testate between 2 Nov 1762 and Apr 1763, Perquimans Co., NC, Will Book C, p. 28, and mentioned wife Elizabeth (Wilson?) Barclift, obviously the mother of minors James and Wilson, and a widow with children Louraney and Joseph Barclift.

47. William Maunsell Crisp was born *ca.* 1700 and died testate after 14 Feb 1783, Martin Co., NC. Confirmation of his middle name, a rare onomastic occurrence in this time period, appeared in a deed from his son Ezekiel^2 to Godfrey Stancil, 6 Dec 1787, Martin Co., NC, Deed Book B, p. 46. Crisp's estate division occurred in Edgecombe Co., NC, dated 12 Dec 1800, according to Joseph Watson's *Estate Records of Edgecombe County North Carolina, 1730-1820*, p. 62, and named the children of both his wives (without separating them), referring to a will—the very odd document in the published abstracts of Martin Co., NC, Will Book 1, p. 107, called therein the will of "Frances Crisp." The recorded version in the actual will book is indeed the will of William *Chrisp*, as the surname is indexed in Mitchell; but this writer can see no reason whatsoever for such a bone-headed mistake on the part of the wills abstractor. William Crisp purchased land in Bertie Co., NC, Jan $172^8/_9$, according to Bertie Co., NC, Deed Book C, p. 82. Leading with a spectacular display of fertility, he married first, [__], the mother of the mother of John^2 Crisp, William^2 Crisp, Bray^2 Crisp, Mary^2 (Crisp) Wilkerson, Ann^2 (Crisp) Ross, Sarah^2 (Crisp) Edmundson (decd.), Susannah^2 (Crisp) Prescoat, and Martha^2 (Crisp) Flake. He married second, **Frances** [__],the mother of Winifred^2 (Crisp) Gibbs, Leda^2 (Crisp) Whitfield, Isabel^2 (Crisp) Whitley, Samuel^2 Crisp, Benjamin^2 Crisp, Sealey^2 (Crisp) Bullake/Bullock, Jesse^2 Crisp, and Ezekiel^2 Crisp, Elizabeth^2 (Crisp) Little (decd.), and son Francis^2 Crisp (decd.). If one seeks to compute reasonable dates of birth for the children, one must admit that the first child would have been almost 35-40 years younger than the last.

In his will, William Crisp enumerated the children of his "last" wife, which I supposed originally to mean his first wife, and not Frances. According to Edgecombe Co., NC, Estates Records, however, Frances [__] Crisp died intestate by 14 Mar 1801, and her estate was administered by son Samuel Crisp; the estate was divided, significantly, into 10 parts, indicating that it was Frances who had had ten children, and not the first wife.

A study of the Bertie Co., NC, land records reveals the following transactions which pertain to our William M. Crisp. In Bertie Co., NC, Deed Book G, p. 141, dated 9 Aug 1746, William Crisp and Frances Crisp (relationship not designated, but almost certainly his wife), sold 200 acres of land to Samuel Singleton, land on the north side of Roquis Islands at the edge of the Rocuis Posocon, adjoining Francis Hobson, and Robert Howell. Proceeding backwards in time, we find that this tract had been given to William Crisp from Francis Hobson in Jan $172^8/_9$, for "love good will and affection, for my loving William Crisp." Unfortunately the relationship between the two is undetermined.

According to Edgecombe Co., NC, Deed Book 9, p. 63, dated Aug 1798, William Crisp and his second wife Frances [__] were somehow the grandparents of William Lewis and Dillilah Lewis of Pitt Co., NC. The intervening generation has not appeared (yet) from the records.

For a transcript of the last will and testament of William M. "Chrisp," see the appendix.

The Children of William Maunsell Crisp and [__], in birth order from the will:

[1] a. **John² Crisp**.
[2] b. **William² Crisp**, died testate between 25 Aug and Nov 1819, Edgecombe Co., NC, Will Book E, p. 230; married [__]; according to his will, some of his children removed to Tennessee.
[3] c. **Bray² Crisp**.
[4] d. **Mary² Crisp**, married [__] **Wilkinson**.
[5] e. **Ann² Crisp**, married [__] **Ross**.
[6] f. **Sarah² Crisp**, *died before 1783*, married [__] **Edmundson**.
[7] g. **Susannah² Crisp**, married [__] **Prescoat**.
[8] h. **Martha² Crisp**, married [__] **Flake**.

The Children of William Maunsell Crisp and Frances [__]:

[9] i. **Winifred² Crisp**, married [__] **Gibbs**.
[10]+ j. **Leda² Crisp**, married first, **Joel Whitfield**; second, by 30 Dec 1797, Edgecombe Co., NC, Deed Book 8, p. 909, **Thomas Baden**.
[11] k. **Isabel² Crisp**, married [__] **Whitley**.
[12] l. **Samuel² Crisp**, died testate between 10 June and Nov 1829, Edgecombe Co., NC, Will Book F, p. 103; married [__].
[13] m. **Benjamin² Crisp**, died intestate by 29 Oct 1807, estate administered by Lewis Barlow, Edgecombe Co., NC, Deed Book 12, p. 150; Edgecombe Co., NC, Estates Records reveal his wife was **Nancy** [__].
[14] n. **Sealey² Crisp**, married **Josiah Bullock** of Martin Co., NC, according to Edgecombe Co., NC, Deed Book 8, p. 677, 23 Jan 1797; he died intestate 1799, according to Edgecombe Co., NC, Estates Records.
[15] o. **Jesse² Crisp**, Sr., died testate between 30 Dec 1829 and Aug 1831, Edgecombe Co., NC, Will Book F, p. 129; married [__].
[16] p. **Ezekiel² Crisp**.
[17] q. **Elizabeth² Crisp**, *died before 1783*, married [__] **Little**.

[18] r. **Francis[2] Crisp**, *died before 1783.*

48. Thomas Cullen, the son of Thomas[A] Cullen, Sr., and Jane[A] Loper, of St. Mary the Virgin, Dover, Kent, was baptized there, 9 Mar $161^{6}/_{7}$, and died intestate by 23 Oct 1689, Isle of Wight Co., VA, at which time an inventory of his estate was presented to court by Jeremiah Exum and Robert Lawrence, according to Isle of Wight Co., VA Will & Deed Book 2, p. 298. He married 26 Jan 1642, St. Mary the Virgin, Dover, Kent, **Sarah Alderstone**, the daughter of John[A] Alderstone and Mary[A] (Cook), born *ca.* 1622, St. Mary the Virgin, Dover, Kent, and died after her last appearance in the records on 10 Mar $167^{8}/_{9}$, Chowan Precinct, at which time Thomas Cullen made a deed of gift to wife Sarah and daughter Martha for the 640 acres he was first granted on Salmon Creek, in *North Carolina Higher-Court Records, 1696-1701*, pp. 31-32. A short biography of Thomas Cullen is given in William S. Powell's *Dictionary of North Carolina Biography*, vol. 1, *A-C*, p. 468, wherein it states that Cullen's first land grant was on Salmon Creek in Chowan, Oct 1669, mentioned in the above referenced deed of gift. He was apparently back and forth from Carolina to England, for on 16 Mar $168^{3}/_{4}$, John Gatlin sold to Thomas Cullen of Dover a tract of land on Rickahock Creek, according to *North Carolina Higher-Court Records, 1670-1696*, p. 452. The English ancestry of the Cullens of Dover, Kent, has been treated in the following article, John Anderson Brayton,"The Ancestry of Thomas Cullen," in *The North Carolina Genealogical Journal*, vol. 26, no. 4 [Nov 2000], pp. 376-92.

Sarah[2] Cullen's first husband Robert Cooper died by 9 Aug 1694, as demonstrated by Isle of Wight Co., VA, Court Orders, Oct 1693-May 1695, p. 47, in which Phillip Rayford sued John Williams and his wife Sarah[2], the administratrix of Robert Cooper, deceased. John Williams, the husband of Sarah[2] (Cullen) Cooper, was born no later than 1656, and died in Isle of Wight between his listing in the Quit Rents of 1704 and the deed of his son Arthur[3] (then of Albemarle Co., NC) to his brother John[3], dated 26 Sept 1719, Isle of Wight Co., VA, Deeds, 1715-1726, p. 300. All we know about John is that he had at least two sons, and that his land fell into Newport Parish, that part of Isle of Wight which did not become Southampton Co., VA. According to Annie Laurie Wright Smith's *The Quit Rents of Virginia, 1704*, p. 97, he was taxed on 971 acres, a combination of his two patents—one for 925 acres, 30 May 1678, VA Land Patent Book 6, p. 644; and one for 46 acres, dated 26 Apr 1698, VA Land Patent Book 6, p. 147—a clear indication that he had not thus far deeded away any of his land. After this, John and Sarah[2] disappeared from the records, presumably dying intestate.

The Children of Thomas Cullen and Sarah Alderstone, baptized St. Mary the Virgin, Dover, Kent:

[1] a. **John**[2] **Cullen**.

[2] b. **Richard**[2] **Cullen**.

[3] c. **Anne**[2] **Cullen**.

[4] d. **Christian**[2] **Cullen**.

[5]+ e. **Mary**[2] **Cullen** married first, by 1678, Albemarle Co., NC, **John Currer**, who died testate between 1 May 1681 and 5 Nov 1683, NC Secretary of State loose wills; she married second,**Thomas**[1] **Luten**, Sr., who died testate between 16 Feb 1729 and 31 Mar 1731, Chowan Co., NC. The only trace of his will (now lost) is an abstract which was produced in J. R. B. Hathaway, *The North Carolina Genealogical Register*, vol. 1, no. 1 [Jan 1900], p. 134.

[6]+ f. **Martha**[2] **Cullen** born 1 May 1663, Dover, Kent, married, first, after 1 May 1681, **Robert**[1] **West**, who died testate between 28 Mar 1689 and 4 Jan $16^{89}/_{90}$, Chowan precinct, Albemarle Co., NC, Secretary of State loose wills; she married second, 19 June 1690, Chowan Precinct, as his first wife, **Thomas Pollock**, died 30 Aug 1722, Chowan Co., NC, his will dated Feb, proved 20 July 1722, Secretary of State loose wills.

(Born most likely born in the colonies)

[7] g. **Sarah**[2] **Cullen** born *ca.* 1670, married first, *ca.* 1690, Isle of Wight Co., VA, **Robert Cooper**; she married second, by Aug 1694, Isle of Wight Co., VA, **John Williams**, "the [intestate] patentee of 1687."

49. John[3] **Culpeper**, the son of Thomas[A] Culpeper and Katherine[2] St. Leger, was baptized 4 Apr 1633, Hollingbourne, Kent, and died testate in that part of the Albemarle which would become Pasquotank Co., between 11 June 1691 and Feb $169^{3}/_{4}$. His will, however, has not survived. Culpeper married first, by 1671, **Judith** [__], who was with him in South Carolina after his appointment by the London proprietors as surveyor general of that state. By Nov 1673, Culpeper resided in the Albemarle, where, among his other duties, he settled the estate of his brother-in-law, Samuel Stephens. Mysteriously, Culpeper's Rebellion was named after our John Culpeper, although Culpeper himself was out of the country when it broke out. He married second, by 1680, **Margaret** [__] **Chancey-Byrd**, the widow of **Edmund Chancey**, Sr., and Valentine Byrd in rapid succession, respectively. According to NC Secretary of State vol. 874.2, p. 24, dated 29 Mar 1680, "Mrs. Margaret Culpepper the relict applied to administer the estate of Edmond Chancey of Albemarle County." His third marriage, 23

Aug 1688, Perquimans Register, to **Sarah**[2] **Mayo**, the daughter of **Edward**[1] **Mayo**, Sr., and Sarah Maggs, was the only union by which he would have known, surviving children. According to Caroline B. Whitley, *North Carolina Headrights, A List of Names, 1663-1774*, p. 8, Edward Mayo registered rights for the following thirteen importees: Edward Mayo, Sr., Edward Mayo, Jr., Sarah Mayo, Ann Mayo, Elizabeth Mayo, three Negroes, John Nixon, Em. Nixon, Ann Nixon, Affrica Pike, and Samuel Pike.

Sarah (Mayo) Culpeper married second, Patrick Henley, and third, 3.9.1699, Philadelphia Monthly Meeting, Matthew Pritchard. The will of Patrick Henley, dated 24 July 1696 and proved 1698, was filed, perplexingly, among the probate records of Philadelphia Co., PA, and was listed as follows: Patrick Henley, 1698, File 54, Administration Book A, p. 258 [see appendix]. Unfortunately, this will was not included in the abstracts of Philadelphia Co., PA, recorded wills. The testator named his "stepdaughter Sarah Culpeper," and left her £50 when she came of age, thus confirming not only her existence, but a direct relationship to her father John Culpeper.

The widow Henley, as stated above, married third, Matthew Pritchard of Pasquotank, brother of **Benjamin**[1]. An excellent sketch of John Culpeper can be found in William S. Powell's *Dictionary of North Carolina Biography*, vol. 1, *A-C*, pp. 470-72, although this was written before the discovery of Patrick Henley's will. Fred Dorman's chapter on the family of "St. Leger," in *Adventurers of Purse and Person*, 4th ed., vol. 3, *Families R-Z*, pp. 103-05, includes John Culpeper in the third generation, but does not attribute any children to him. We must credit OFFNC member **#244** for making available the Henley will. Katherine St. Leger's royal ancestry back to Edward III has been outlined in Gary Boyd Roberts' *The Royal Descents of 600 Immigrants*, p. 176

The Children of John Culpeper and Sarah Mayo:

[1]+ a. **Sarah**[2] **Culpeper**, born say 1689, married 9.2.1704, Pasquotank Monthly Meeting, NC, as his first wife, **Benjamin**[1] **Pritchard**.

[2] b. [possibly others].

50. George[(2)] **Cünys/Cunitz/Kuntz/Koonce**, the son of **Johan Cünys** and Alice [__], was born 6 Apr 1704, Craven Co., NC, and died 28 Jan 1778, Craven Co., NC, according to a family Bible record. He married *ca.* 1724, **Mary** [__]. George Koonce was the only member of his family to survive the Tuscarora Indian uprising 22 Nov 1711. John Koonce the father, according to Henry Z. Jones' *Even More Palatine Families, 18th Century Immigrants to the American Colonies and their German, Swiss and Austrian Origins*, vol. 2, pp. 1142-51, was a member listed on the "2nd Party London Arrivals List," taken at Walworth [Surrey], 27 May 1709. He was aged 33, identified as husbandman and vinedresser, and accompanied by an unnamed wife, sons aged 15 and 5, and a daughter aged 1. A copy of the Koonce family Bible is held in Heritage Place, Lenior Community College, Kinston, NC. Like the Kornegays, John Koonce was killed by the Tuscaroras on 22 Nov 1711.

The Children of George Koonce and Mary [__], born Craven Co., NC:

[1] a. **John**[2] **Koonce**, born *ca.* 1727, died testate between 6 Jan and May 1791, Jones Co., NC, Will Book A, p. 115; married **Catherine** [__].

[2]+ b. **Michael**[2] **Koonce**, born 6 June 1730, died testate 4 Aug 1782, Jones Co., NC, Will Book A, p. 15; married **Elizabeth** [__].

[3] c. **George**[2] **Koonce**, Jr., born *ca.* 1737, was dead by 5 July 1809, Jones Co., NC, Deed Book K, p. 327, in which his son Zenos[3] Koonce sold to brother Jarman[3] Koonce all his share in two tracts of land deeded by his father on 11 Nov 1805; married, possibly, **Susannah** [__], who witnessed with him the will of his brother Christian[2] Koonce; the deeds of Jones Co., NC, reveal the existence of George[2] Koonce's other children as well.

[4] d. **Christian**[2] **Koonce**, born *ca.* 1739, died testate after 24 Dec 1790, Jones Co., NC, Will Book A, p. 186; married **Philipena** [__].

[5] e. **Jacob**[2] **Koonce**, born *ca.* 1740, died testate June 1784, Jones Co., NC, Will Book A, p. 132; married **Martha** [__].

[6] f. **Tobias**[2] **Koonce**, born *ca.* 1742, married **Ann Gibson**.

[7] g. **William**[2] **Koonce**.

51. Johan[(1)] **Cünys/Koonce** was born *ca.* 1676 in either Germany or the German part of Switzerland, and died 23 Sept 1711, killed in battle by the Tuscarora Indians at Core Creek, Craven Co., NC. He married **Alice** [__], who was killed the same day, Craven Co., NC. The name "Cünys" was anglicized into Koonce. John Koonce, according to Henry Z. Jones, *Even More Palatine Families, 18th Century Immigrants to the American Colonies and their German, Swiss and Austrian Origins*, vol. 2, pp. 1142-51, was a member listed on the "2nd Party London Arrivals List," taken at Walworth, 27 May 1709. He was aged 33, identified as husbandman and vinedresser, and accompanied by an unnamed wife, sons aged 15 and 5, and a daughter aged 1. A copy of the Koonce family Bible is held in Heritage Place, Lenoir Community College, Kinston, NC.

The Children of Johan Cunys and Alice [__]:

[1] a. [**Son**][2] **Cunys**, *ca.* born 1694, died on or before 23 Sept 1711.

[2]+ b. **George**[2] **Cunys**, born 4 Apr 1704, Germany, died 28 Jan 1778, Craven Co., NC; married **Mary** [__].

[3] c. [**Daughter**][2] **Cunys**, born *ca.* 1708, died on or before 23 Sept 1711.

52. James Curry was born by 1700 and died testate between 22 Oct 1750 and May 1754, Bertie Co., NC, his will filed among the loose wills of that county. In 1762, according to Bertie Co., NC, Court Minutes, 1724-1772, p. 305, son John^2, aged fourteen, was bound out as an apprentice to Daniel Frazer. In his will, James Curry, or "Corree," singled out son James^2 as the son of **Mary Walker**, *suggesting* either a previous or a concurrent relationship with another woman other than his putative wife. James Curry purchased 100 acres of land on Wills Quarter Swamp from John Byrd on 1 Mar 1723, according to Bertie Co., NC, Deed Book A, p. 44. This land was bequeathed to his son James^2, Jr., and was said James' dwelling place for the rest of the eighteenth century. The parentage of Mary Walker has not been established.

The abundance of estates records in Bertie generated by the death of James Curry consisted almost entirely in a search for the whereabouts of an Isaac Butler, who owed the widow and executrix £15. Butler was still not located as late as 1764.

The Children of James Curry and [__]:
[1] a. **David^2 Curry**.
[2] b. **Margaret^2 Curry**.
[3] c. **Janet^2 Curry**.
[4] d. **John^2 Curry**, born *ca*. 1748.

The Child of James Curry and Mary Walker:
[5]+ e. **James^2 Curry**, married before 23 Aug 1782, Bertie Co., NC, Deed Book M, p. 547, **Joice Hawkins**, daughter of Thomas Hawkins, Sr., will proved Feb 1793, Bertie Co., NC, Will Book D, p. 214; Hawkins' wife was not named in his will, nor does her name appear in the Bertie deeds.

53. Robert Daniel I, Governor of the Northern Province of Carolina, was born *ca*. 1646, and died 1 May 1718, Albemarle Co., NC, although his will, dated 1 May and proved 12 May 1718, was recorded 14 May 1718, in South Carolina Miscellaneous [Probate] Records, 1711-1718, p. 55. He married first, by 1676, **Dorothy** [__], born *ca*. 1654, died 16 Oct 1711, St. Thomas Parish, Charleston, SC, according to Frank J. Klingberg, "Commissary Johnston's *Notitia Parochialis*" [reported by St. Philip's Parish], in *South Carolina Historical and Genealogical Magazine*, vol. 48 [1947], p. 31: "October 16, 1711, then departed this life, Colo. Daniels lady, St. Thomas Parish." This reference is impossibly garbled in York Wilson's work [see below]. Two days before her death, 14 Oct,

Dorothy signed a deed of gift to her grandson Marmaduke[3] Daniel, son of her son Robert[2] and his wife Sarah [__], according to [South Carolina] Records of the Secretary of the Province, 1714-1717, p. 43. Robert and Dorothy were certainly married by 14 June 1680, at which time Robert and Dorothy Daniel sold land to Jacob Guerard, in Proprietary Records of South Carolina, 1675-1696, pp. 153-54. Robert Daniel had formed a bigamous liaison of record by 8 Jun 1709 with **Martha Wainwright** [a rare colonial name] of Beaufort Co., NC, to whom (at which time) he deeded slaves for the sake of their son John[2], with residual benefits to their two daughters Sarah[2] and Martha[2] [Jr.], according to Beaufort Co., NC, Deed Book 1, p. 132. That these three children, during 1709, were all specifically described as "born of the body of Martha," in subsequent Beaufort deeds, pushes back Robert's connection with Martha to around 1704 at the latest. Martha Wainwright was, however, named as his wife in Robert's 1718 will. There is an excellent biography of Robert Daniel in William S. Powell's, *Dictionary of North Carolina Biography*, vol. 2, *D-G*, pp. 9-10, although Powell mistakenly ascribes husband *Charles* Logan to Martha[2] Daniel, Jr. Another treatment of this family can be found in Edgar and Bailey, *Biographical Directory of the South Carolina House of Representatives*, vol. 2, *The Commons House of Assembly, 1692-1775*, pp. 180-82. This SC volume does not address the issue of Robert Daniel's two wives. As a matter of fact, according to Brent Holcomb's *South Carolina Marriages, 1688-1799*, p. 154 [the other specific marriages noted in this sketch are from this same work], Col. George Logan [Sr.] of Berkeley Co., married 28 May 1719, "Martha Daniell, Sr., widow of Robert Daniel, late Deputy Gov[r]. of S.C." This information was taken from Books of the [SC] Secretary of the Province, 1714-1719, pp. 373-88. The will of George Logan [Sr.] of Berkeley Co., SC, dated 18 Mar $17^{19}/_{20}$, named wife Martha, according to SC Will Book 1721-1722, p. 86. The confusion comes from the fact that George Logan, Jr., married daughter Martha[2] Daniel, his stepsister, described [also] appropriately as "Jr."

The supposed royal ancestry of Dorothy Daniel, her supposed divorce from Robert Daniel, and her supposedly precipitous transatlantic return to and burial in England are all topics which are discussed without a *shred* of documentation by York Lowry Wilson in his *A Carolina-Virginia Genealogy*, pp. 6-20 (a compilation which seems to be more reliable in other chapters). Nowhere does the author cite authoritative proof that Dorothy Daniel was the daughter of Edmond Chamberlayne of Maughersbury, Gloucestershire. In fact, that very Edmond Chamberlayne of "Malgersbury," Gloucestershire, in his will dated 27 Aug 1675, proved 9 June 1676, PCC 1676, f. 61, named a daughter Dorothy and gave her £1000, but did not give her a married name. Thomas Fitz-Roy Phillipps' "Chamberlaine of Maugersbury in Stow," in his *Visitation of Gloucestershire, 1682-1683* (1884) pp. 37-38, listed Dorothy as the wife of "Edward Ridley, Steward to the Duke of Somerset." The will of Edward Ridley, gent., of Lincoln's Inn, Middlesex, dated 20 Oct and proved 18 Nov 1699, named wife Dorothy, his son Edward, and their four daughters. PCC, PROB11/453. Thus far, Dorothy [__] Daniel's identity is a mystery. Dorothy (Chamberlaine) Ridley's brother Thomas Chamberlaine, however, *did* come to Henrico Co.,Virginia, and a discussion of him and his descendants can be found in *Adventurers of Purse and Person*, 4th ed., *Families R-Z*, pp. 676-77.

It appears that York Wilson derived his Daniel genealogy from Worth S. Ray's excursus on the Daniel family in his normally helpful *Index and Digest to Hathaway's North Carolina Historical and Genealogical Register: with Genealogical Notes and Annotations*. The Daniel material is, unfortunately, some of the worst genealogical trash ever printed, and sadly Worth Stickley Ray has a deserved reputation for being highly unreliable.

There is a deed in South Carolina which establishes the existence of another daughter of Robert Daniel and Martha Wainwright who has heretofore escaped notice in any discussion of this family. SC Deed Book P-P, p. 455, dated 13 and 14 Dec 1731, recorded a marriage contract between Ann Daniel [described as the daughter of Hon. Robert Daniel and Martha Logan, Sr.] and Alexander Goodbee, which had been signed 8 and 9 Dec 1725 and concerned a tract of 340 acres located on the east side of the Cooper River in St. Thomas Parish, Berkeley Co., SC. According to SC Deed Book G-G, p. 63, dated 5 and 6 May 1749, Alexander Goodbee was deceased and his widow had married second, Daniel Conway. The Conways were at that time residents of Charleston. Ann was once again a widow by 1 Jan 1763, as recorded in SC Deed Book D-3, p. 524.

The Children of Robert Daniel and Dorothy [__]:

[1]+ a. **Robert**[2] **Daniel**, born *ca.* 1680, died *ca.* 1709; married **Sarah** [__], the sister of Ann [__] Chudleigh of England, named in her will, SC Will Book 1721-22, p. 21, will dated 28 July 1721; Sarah was buried 31 July 1721, Rev. Robert F. Clute, *Annals and Parish Register of St. Thomas and St. Denis Parish in South Carolina from 1680 to 1884*, p. 57.

The Children of Robert Daniel and Martha Wainwright:

[2] b. **Martha**[2] **Daniel**, "Jr.," married 30 July 1719, Christ Church Parish, Charleston, SC, **George Logan**, Jr.

[3] c. **Sarah**[2] **Daniel**, married Maj. **William Blakeway**. A sketch of Blakeway can be found in Edgar and Bailey, *Biographical Directory of the South Carolina House of Representatives*, vol. 2, *The Commons House of Assembly, 1692-1775*, pp. 83-84.

[4] d. **John**[2] **Daniel**, married 22 Jan 1736, Charles Town, SC, contained in the *South Carolina Gazette*, **Sarah Raven**, the daughter of William

Raven and Elizabeth Bedon. He died testate *ca.* 1763 in New Hanover Co., NC, as John "Daniell," his will recorded in Brunswick Co., NC, Deed Book A, p. 88. A sketch of John Daniel can be found in Edgar and Bailey, *Biographical Directory of the South Carolina House of Representatives*, vol. 2, *The Commons House of Assembly, 1692-1775*, p. 180.

[5] e. **Ann[2] Daniel**, born *ca.* 1710, married first, 9 Dec 1725, Parish of St. Thomas and St. Denis, SC, **Alexander Goodbee**; married second, by 5 May 1749, **Daniel Conway**.

54. Nicholas Daw was born by 1673 and died testate between 9 Jan and 2 July 1717, Hyde precinct, Bath Co., NC, his will recorded in Beaufort Co., NC, Deed Book 1, p. 282. He married *ca.* 1694, **Lidia[2] Windley**, named as (unmarried) daughter in the 1688 will of **Robert[1] Windley**. Nicholas mentioned but did not name his wife in his will. Lydia Daw, described as "widow of Hyde Precinct, Bath Co., and her son William[2] Daw sold land to John Clarke on 21 Mar $171^{6}/_{7}$, according to Beaufort Co., NC, Deed Book 1, p. 227. Nicholas Daw was listed as a headright 12 Apr 1694, when John Belman registered his rights for 650 acres due for the transportation of 13 persons, according to Caroline B. Whitley, *North Carolina Headrights, A List of Names, 1663-1744*, p. 161.

The Children of Nicholas Daw and Lidia Windley:

[1]+ a. **William[2] Daw**, born by 1695, will dated 20 Jan, proved Mar 1745, Beaufort Co., NC, NC Secretary of State loose wills; married **Dinah** [__].

[2] b. **Ann[2] Daw**, married first, *ca.* 1718, **William Stone**, who died testate between 29 Mar and 20 July 1720, Bath [Craven] Co., NC, his will recorded in NC Secretary of State vol. 875, p. 277; she married second, **Richard Harvey**, according to Carteret Co., NC, Deed Book B, pp. 83-85, dated 3 Mar $172^{3}/_{4}$, in which both she and her husband acknowledged inheritance of land from William Stone, deceased. On 4 Apr 1730, Beaufort Co., NC, Deed Book 2, p. 39, Richard Harvey made a deed of gift to his son Peter Harvey. No spouse signed, and there was no indication in the deed concerening Peter's age, although on 15 Feb $173^{3}/_{4}$, Peter Harvey witnessed a deed, Beaufort Co., NC, Deed Book2 , p. 109. He was possibly older than 13. Therefore, the maternity of Peter is still in question without further information concerning his age.

[3] c. **Priscilla[2] Daw**.

55. Francis Delamare, a French Huguenot, was born by 1660 and died intestate before 20 Oct 1713, Pasquotank Co., NC, at which time his second wife **Anne** was named as his widow and relict, according to Pasquotank Co., NC, Deed Book A, p. 63. An Isaac De La Mare received 150 acres for the transportation of himself, Francis Delamare, and Ephraim Coates on 11 July 1694, according to Caroline B. Whitley, *North Carolina Headrights, A List of Names, 1663-1744*, p. 157, although Isaac's precise relationship to Francis has not yet been determined. Francis married first, by 10 Oct 1694, **Susannah** [__] **Travis**, the widow of Daniel Travis of Pasquotank, at which time Francis and his (now) wife Susannah applied to administer the estate of her first husband. This is to be found in Wills, Administrations, Inventories, Deeds, 1677-1790, NC Secretary of State vol. 874.2 (1677-1701), p. 51. In Mar 169$^{7}/_{8}$, Francis "Le Mare" sought to be naturalized as a citizen of the colony. His petition stated that he was "by nation a French man and being a Protestant was compelled to fly from his Country upon account of his Religion, and hath been an Inhabitant of this Government for the space of eleven year…" giving him a record of early entry into the Albemarle—*ca.* 1686, just one year after the disastrous revocation of the Edict of Nantes. This document may be found in *North Carolina Higher-Court Records, 1697-1701*, p. 176. Francis married second, **Ann^{2} (Mayo) Pope**, the "Ann *Mays*, daughter of Edward and [--] *Mays*," baptized 26 Nov 1670, Christ Church Parish, Barbados [see sketch of **Edward^{1} Mayo**]. We know that Ann was *née* Mayo because she named her brother Edward Mayo II in her will. She was first the widow of Richard Pope, whose will was dated 23 June and proved 15 July 1701, NC Secretary of State loose Wills. By 8 July 1704 she was married, as his second wife, to Francis Delamare, according to Pasquotank Co., NC, Deed Book A, p. 5 and p. 62. She married third after 1713, Augustine Scarbrough (as mentioned in her will), and fourth, **John^{2} Jennings**, son of **William^{1}**. Her surviving children were Edward Pope, and the Delamare infants. The 1701 will of Richard Pope mentioned daughter Mary Pope, under 16 years of age, and she was left a bequest of a gold ring and £5 to buy a gown, in the will of Thomas Abington, dated 13 Nov 1707, NC Secretary of State loose wills. Ann Jennings' will, dated 20 Feb 17$^{19}/_{20}$ and proved 19 Apr 1720, was recorded in NC Secretary of State vol. 875, p. 224. Probably the Mary Reading named in her will was a daughter by her first husband. Ann very clearly named her children by her other marriages, although she did name Edward Pope and Mary Reading in the same clause.

The Children of Francis Delamare and Susannah [__] Travis:

[1]+ a. **Francis^{2} Delamare**, born *ca.* 1695, will proved Mar 1741, Craven Co., NC, Secretary of State loose wills, and also recorded in NC Land Grant Book 4, no.161; married **Susanah** [__].

The Children of Richard Pope and Ann Mayo:

[2] b. **Edward Pope**, died testate between 26 Jan $172^{1}/_{2}$ and 17 Apr 1722, Pasquotank, NC Secretary of State loose wills, also recorded in NC Secretary of State vol. 875, p. 337; married **Sarah** [__].

[3] c. **Mary Pope**, married [__] **Reading/Redding**.

The Children of Francis Delamare and Ann (Mayo) Pope-Scarborough:

[4] d. **Stephen[2] Delamare**, died testate Oct 1732, Pasquotank, NC Secretary of State loose wills; he did not marry, but named his sister Ann, then married to Stockley, and her children.

[5] e. **Isaac[2] Delamare**.

[6]+ f. **Anne[2] Delamare**, died testate between 23 Oct 1767 and 9 Mar 1773, Craven Co., NC, Secretary of State loose wills; married first, **Joseph Stoakley**, who died testate between 12 Dec 1729 and Jan $17^{29}/_{30}$, Pasquotank, NC Secretary of State loose wills; second, 10 Jan $173^{3}/_{4}$, Pasquotank Co., NC, **William[2] Bryan (Edward[1])**, who died testate between 12 Dec 1746 and June 1747, Craven Co., NC, Secretary of State loose wills.

56. John Dew II of Bertie, called "Sr.," the son of John[A] Dew I and Elizabeth[A] [__], was born 1676, Isle of Wight Co., VA, and died testate between 5 Sept 1740 and Nov 1744, Northampton Co., NC, his will filed in NC Secretary of State loose wills. John Dew II's age was revealed in a deposition taken 27 Jan 1712 in which he stated his age to be about 36 years. This can be found in *Calendar of Virginia State Papers and Other Manuscripts, 1652-1781*, vol. 1, p. 153. Jo hn[A] Dew I, whose will was dated 31 Jan $167^{7}/_{8}$, Isle of Wight Co., VA, Will & Deed Book 2, p. 167, named his son John. John Dew II married, as her first husband, **Susannah** [__], who married second, by 29 Nov 1745, Northampton Co., NC, according to Northampton Co., NC, Deed Book 1, p. 273, on which date there was "a marriage speedily to be solemnized," Joseph Washington.

There is a chance worthy of careful investigation that Susannah (--) Dew was the daughter of **Robert[1] Sherrer/Sherrod** who died testate after the signing of his will in Bertie on 27 Oct 1727. He named wife Elizabeth, sons Robert, Arthur, and John, and left his youngest children, "namely William, Sarah, and Prudence," with his daughter Susannah, naming John Dew and Arthur Williams as overseers of his will. The will was filed among the NC Secretary of State loose wills.

John Dew II removed from Isle of Wight Co., VA, to Chowan Co., NC, by 21 July 1714, at which time he purchased of James Bryant, Sr., of Albemarle Co., 320 acres, according to Chowan Co., NC, Deed Book W#1, p. 172. The following is a satisfactory genealogy of the Dew family: Ernestine Dew White, with the aid of Hugh Buckner Johnston, *Genealogy of Some of the Descendants of Thomas Dew, Colonial Virginia Pioneer Immigrant* (1937), although some of Mr. Johnston's conclusions about the extent of John Dew's children are not based on existing documents. John Dew named the following children in his will: John², Joseph², Patience², Spencer², William², Elizabeth² Clemments, and Mornen².

The Children of John Dew II and Susannah [__]:

[1]+ a. **John² Dew III**, born *ca.* 1704, died testate between 1 Aug 1759 and June 1760, Edgecombe Co., NC, Will Book A, p. 1; married [__]² **Bryant**, daughter of **James¹ Bryant**, who in his will dated 11 Mar 173¹/₂, named John Dew his son-in-law.

[2] b. **Joseph² Dew**.

[3] c. **Patience² Dew**.

[4] d. **Spencer² Dew**, in Nov 1757, he sold two tracts of land inherited from his father to William Baldwin, two 100-acre tracts on the north side of the Maherrin River, Northampton Co., NC, Deed Book 2, pp. 456-457; after these transactions, he and the entire family disappeared from the area, with the exception of John III and Sarah Bridgers.

[5] e. **William² Dew**.

[6] f. **Mornen² Dew**.

[7] g. **Elizabeth² Dew**, married [__] **Clements**.

[8] h. **Sarah² Dew**, died testate between 7 Dec 1753 and Feb 1754, Northampton Co., NC, Secretary of State loose wills; married first, **William² Bridger**, died testate between 11 Mar and Nov 1729, NC Secretary of State loose wills; second, **William² Cotton**.

57. John Dickinson was born by 1695 and died testate by Aug 1749, Northampton Co., NC. He married **Rebecca** [__], who died testate between 1 July 1750 and Feb 1753, Northampton Co., NC, both their wills filed in the NC Secretary of State loose wills. John Dickinson was in Chowan Co., NC, by 30 July 1717, at which time he sold land to John Dew, Chowan Co., NC, Deed Book W#1, p. 194.

The Children of John Dickinson and Rebecca [__]:

[1] a. **Isaac² Dickinson**, married **Priscilla** [__]; died testate between 21 Nov and Feb 1767, Northampton Co., NC, Will Boolk 1, p. 143, named silblings and nephews.

[2] b. **Daniel² Dickinson**.

[3] c. **John² Dickinson**, Sr., died testate between 12 June and Sept 1787,

Northampton Co., NC, Will Book 1, p. 381; married [__].

[4] d. **David[2] Dickinson**, died testate between 19 Mar and Dec 1783, Northampton Co., NC, Will Book 1 p. 279; married [__].

[5] e. **Sarah[2] Dickinson**, married [**John**?] **Daniel**, died testate between 13 Nov 1754 and Feb 1755, Northampton Co., NC, Secretary of State loose wills.

[6]+ f. **Elizabeth[2] Dickinson**, married **Thomas[2] Futtrell III**, born *ca.* 1717, Chowan, died testate between 27 Mar and June 1770, Northampton Co., NC, Will Book 1, p. 180.

[7]+ g. **Rebeckah[2] Dickinson**, married **Joel Newsom**; he died testate by Feb 1752, Northampton Co., NC, Secretary of State wills.

[8] h. **Charity[2] Dickinson**, married 6.1.1750, Perquimans Monthly Meeting, **Robert Peele IV**.

[9] i. **Mary[2] Dickinson**, died testate between 6 Oct and Nov 1753, Northampton Co., NC, Secretary of State loose wills.

58. John Drake, the son of Thomas[A] Drake of Isle of Wight Co., VA, who bought land in Chowan Co., NC, on 15 July 1717, according to Chowan Co., NC, Deed Book B#1, p. 478, was born say 1695, Isle of Wight Co., VA, and died testate between 5 Jan 172$^8/_9$ and May 1729, Bertie Co., NC, NC Secretary of State loose wills. He married, as her first husband, **Sarah[2] Bryant**, the daughter of **James[1] Bryant**, Jr., and Sarah [__]. In his will, John Drake identified James Bryant as his father-in-law. Sarah (Bryant) Drake married second, **Benjamin[2] Bridgers**, Sr. The relationship between the Drakes and the Bridgers was documented by John H. Wheeler in 1851, in his *Historical Sketches of North Carolina*, p. 274. John Drake's first appearance in Bertie Co., NC, was as a resident, 8 Oct 1725, Bertie Co., NC, Deed Book B, p. 84. A sketch of this family can be found in *Order of First Families of North Carolina, Ancestor Registry*, no. 1. Charles E. Drake published an excellent article on the Drake family tracing their ancestry back into Somerset in "Reconstructing an Immigrant Family from Fragile Clues," in *The National Genealogical Society Quarterly*, vol. 79, no. 1 [March 1991], pp. 19-32.

A partial Bible record for James Drake occurs in "The Benjamin M. Drake Bible," in Genealogical Publications of the Mississippi Genealogical Society, vol. 7 [Sept 1960], *Cemetery and Bible Records*, pp. 7-10, especially p. 8. Affia (Ballentine) Drake was named in the will of her father William Ballentine of Norfolk Co., VA.

The Child of John Drake and Sarah Bryant, born Bertie Precinct, NC:

[1]+ a. **James[2] Drake**, born 1725, died 1791, Richmond, VA, his will recorded in Nash Co., NC, Will Book 1, p. 249, will #236; he

married first, by 1746, Norfolk Co., VA, **Affia Ballentine**; second, by 1766, Halifax Co., NC, **Hartwell (Hodges) Davis**. James did *not* marry the fictional Sophia Valentine!

✠ **59.** Gov. **William Drummond** was born by 1610 in Scotland and was the first governor of the Albemarle. He was beheaded for treason on 20 Jan in 1677 at James Bray's home in Middle Plantation, VA. He married **Sarah Prescott** who died sometime after 1684. Drummond did not have descendants in Accomack Co., VA, and this particular descent has been disallowed, although he is perfectly eligible through his daughter Sarah^{2} Swann. His wife was buried in her son-in-law's family burial plot in Surry Co., VA, a possession of the Swann family. The only known (traceable) descendants of Gov. Drummond are in fact through daughter Sarah who married, as his first wife, Major Samuel Swann. There is an extensive biography of Gov. Drummond in William S. Powell's *Dictionary of North Carolina Biography*, vol. 2, *D-G*, pp. 107-08. A sketch of this family can be found in *Order of First Families of North Carolina, Ancestor Registry*, no. 1.

The Children of William Drummond and Sarah Prescott:

[1] a. **William^{2} Drummond**, born *ca.* 1650, married [__].

[2] b. **Sarah^{2} Drummond**, born 2 Mar 1654, died 18 Apr 1696, Perquimans Co., NC; she married 24 Mar 1673, as his first wife, Major **Samuel Swann**, born 11 May 1653, Surry Co., VA, died testate 14 Sept 1707, Perquimans Co., NC, Secretary of State loose wills.

[3] c. **Elizabeth^{2} Drummond**, said to have died in 1697, buried at Green Spring, VA, and whose tomb was "recently removed to the churchyard at Jamestown."

[4] d. **[Son]^{2} Drummond**, married, as her first husband, **Mary Hartwell**; she married second, [__] Marable, and had a son **John^{3} Drummond** by her first marriage, who is untraced.

60. Christopher Dudley was born *ca.* 1680, probably in Nansemond Co., VA, and died testate between 19 Mar 1744 and Apr 1747, Onslow Co., NC, his will filed among the NC Secretary of State loose wills. He married, first, **Ann** [__], who died before the writing of his will in 1747, and second, **Mary** [__], named as his executrix, who married second, Stephen Lee. Christopher Dudley was listed with 200 acres of land in Nansemond in Annie Laurie Wright's *The Quit Rents of Virginia, 1704*, p. 27. On 14 July 1709, John Church of Chowan gave Christopher Dudley his power of attorney to acknowledge a sale of land, Chowan Co., NC, Deed Book W#1, p. 116. Christopher's first wife Anne witnessed a deed on 14 July 1712 from Bethia Garrett to William Tomson, Chowan Co., NC, Deed Book W#1, p. 117. Anne's last mention in Chowan is on 30 July 1717, when she and her husband sold land to William Kelley of Nansemond, Chowan Co., NC, Deed book B#1, p. 558. On Apr 1713, Christopher Dudley purchased 250 acres of land on the north side of the Chowan River from Thomas Garrett, Jr., of Chowan and his wife Tomsin, Chowan Co., NC, Deed Book W#1, p. 144. By 25 July 1717, Christopher was a resident of Beaufort Co., NC, at which time he sold land to Robert Potter, Beaufort Co., NC, Deed Book 1 , p. 234.

One helpful monograph containing information on the Dudley family was P. W. Fisher's *One Dozen Pre-Revolutionary Families of Eastern North Carolina and Some of their Descendants*, pp. 274-78.

The Children of Christopher Dudley and Ann [__]:

[1] a. **Edward[2] Dudley**, died testate between 22 Jan and 3 Apr 1745, Onslow Co., NC, Secretary of State loose wills; married [__], mentioned but not named in his will.

[2]+ b. **Thomas[2] Dudley**, born *ca.* 1700, died testate between 13 May and June 1753, Carteret Co., NC, Secretary of State loose wills; married **Elizabeth[2] Jarrett**, named as daughter of testator **John[1] "Jarott"** of Carteret whose will was proved June 1745, NC Secretary of State loose wills.

[3] c. **Christopher[2] Dudley**, died testate 1764, New Hanover Co., NC, Will Book C, p. 64; married **Elizabeth Bishop**, daughter of George Bishop, Sr., and his wife Elizabeth [__], and the sister of George Bishop, Jr., whose will, dated 20 Dec 1743 at Wilmington and proved Sept 1744, NC Secretary of State loose wills, named his sister Betty Dudley.

[4] d. **Ann[2] Dudley** married first, **David Barry**, who died intestate by June 1736, Carteret Co., NC, according to Carteret Co., NC, Court Minutes, June Court 1736; she married second, according to that record, as his first wife, **Moses Houston**, who died testate in Jan 1774, Carteret Co., NC, NC Secretary of State loose wills; a deed of gift in Carteret Co., NC, Deed Book [A-C, E-F], p. 404, dated 27 Apr 1756, from Moses to his son-in-law James[3] Barry, son of David Barry, confirms this; Moses married second, Margaret [__]. Moses "Holston" came into court Mar $173^{5}/_{6}$, Carteret, and applied to be the guardian of his sister and brother Thomas and Elizabeth Houston.

[5] e. **William[2] Dudley**, died testate after 26 Mar 1772, Onslow Co., NC, Will Book 1, p. 88 [Zae Gwinn, vol. 1, p. 711]; he married **Elizabeth** [__], whom he named in his will.

[6] f. **John[2] Dudley**, died testate between 12 Sept 1748 and 30 Apr 1751, Craven Co., NC, Deed Book 5, p. 161; he married **Elizabeth** [__],

who died testate after 10 May 1770, Onslow Co., NC, Will Book 1, p. 87 [Zae Gwinn, vol. 1, p. 711].

61. George^{1} Durant was born 1 Oct 1632 in England—not 23 Aug 1623, the other of two birth dates indicated in the Durant Family Bible. Durant died testate 22 Jan $169^{4}/_{5}$, Perquimans Co., NC. He married 4 Jan $165^{8}/_{9}$, Northumberland Co., VA, **Ann Marwood**, born probably about 1640, who died testate 22 Jan 1694, Perquimans Co., NC. Durant was a resident for a time in Norfolk Co., VA, where he had a number of land transactions. Then by 1661, he was established as an important resident of the Albemarle. The George Durant Family Bible is preserved in the Southern Historical Collection, Wilson Library, University of North Carolina, Chapel Hill, NC. There is an extensive biography of both Ann (Marwood) and George Durant in William S. Powell's *Dictionary of North Carolina Biography*, vol. 2, *D-G*, pp. 122-125. Both their wills were filed in the NC Secretary of State loose wills, and Anne's was recorded in NC Secretary of State vol. 874.2, p. 58.

The Children of George Durant and Ann (Marwood), born Perquimans Precinct, NC:

[1] a. **George^{2} Durant**, born 24 Dec 1659, died 13 Sept 1671, Perquimans Precinct, NC.

[2]+ b. **Elizabeth^{2} Durant**, born 13 Feb $166^{0}/_{1}$, married first, say 1680, **Thomas Waller**, who died testate 2 July 1687, Perquimans Co., NC, Secretary of State loose wills; she married second, *ca.* 1687 [--], Perquimans, **John Harris**.

[3]+ c. **John^{2} Durant**, born 26 Dec 1662, died intestate 19 Jan $^{1699}/_{1700}$, Perquimans Co., NC; married 9 Apr 1684, Perquimans Prect., NC, **Sarah Cooke**, who married second, 1 Jan $170^{3}/_{4}$, Perquimans Co., NC, William Stephens/Stephenson.

[4] d. **Mary^{2} Durant**, born 11 Feb 1665, died before 1693 [not mentioned in her father's will].

[5]+ e. **Thomas^{2} Durant**, born 28 Aug 1668, died testate between 8 May 1728 and 15 Apr 1734, Perquimans Co., NC, Secretary of State loose wills; married **Elizabeth Gaskill**.

[6] f. **Sarah^{2} Durant**, born 17 Jan 1670, married 14 Aug 1690, Perquimans Prct., NC, **Elias/Isaac Rowden**.

[7] g. **Martha^{2} Durant**, born 28 Aug 1673, died after 1693 [mentioned in her father's will] *no further record.*

[8]+ h. **Perthenia^{2} Durant**, born 1 Aug 1675, married first, 18 June 1695, Perquimans Prct., NC, **Joseph Sutton**, who died testate between 11 Jan and 10 Mar $172^{3}/_{4}$, Perquimans, NC Secretaryu of State loose

wills, also recorded in Secretary fo State vol. 876, p. 19; she married second, 17 Mar 1726, Perquimans, **John Stevens**.

i. **Ann[2] Durant**, born 1 Apr 1681, married 6 Oct 1698, Perquimans Prct., NC, **William Bartlett/Barclift**, who died testate between 22 Mar 174$^7/_8$ and Jan 1748[/9], Perquimans Co., NC, Secretary of State loose wills.

62. John Edwards was born *ca.* 1680 and died intestate by Aug 1742, Bertie Co., NC, at which time he is referred to in a sale of land as being deceased, according to Bertie Co., NC, Deed Book F, p. 385. He married first, **Dorcas** [__], the mother of his children, who died after her last mention in 1722, Chowan Co., NC, Deed Book C, p. 169. He married second, by 1730, **Mary** [__], when he and his wife sold land to John Moore, Bertie Co., NC, Deed Book C, p. 326. John Edwards purchased 200 acres on the north side of Turkey Swamp near Horse Springs in Chowan Co., NC, in 1713, according to Chowan Co., NC, Deed Book W, p. 164. There is an excellent treatment of this family in David B. Gammon's, *Eastern North Carolina Families*, vol. 1, pp. 72-95.

The Children of John Edwards and Dorcas [__]:

[1]+ a. **John[2] Edwards**, Jr., died testate between 4 Dec 1764 and May 1765, Northampton Co., NC, Will Book 1, p. 122; married first, **Elizabeth** [__]; second, **Mary** [__].

[2] b. **Cordelia[2] Edwards**, married by 1718, Chowan Co., NC, **James Roberts**. John[1] Edward made a deed of gift of 320 acres, adjoining John Byrd, to his son-in-law Roberts on 8 July 1718, Chowan Co., NC, Deed Book B#1, p. 571. By 11 May 1734, Bertie Co., NC, Deed Book D, p. 60, Cordelia[2] and James had sold all of their "inheritance," and had disappeared from the Bertie records.

63. Robert Ellis died testate in the "Northwest Parish" of Bertie Co., NC, between 28 Jan 1740 and Feb 1743, his will filed among NC Secretary of State loose wills. He patented 640 acres of land on the north side of the Morratoke River, adjoining John Grey and William Reves, on 8 Sept 1722, according to NC Land Patent Book 3, p. 107. This land was cut off into the part of Bertie that would later become Northampton, and a "moiety" of this property was sold by the testator to Phillip Smith on 9 Feb 1740, Bertie Co., NC, Deed Book F, p. 122, indicating that son Robert[2], Jr., was already deceased (as indicated by the will). The name of the wife of Robert[1] Ellis, Sr., does not appear in the records, although the wife of Robert[2] Ellis, Jr., is probably the "Ellinor" mentioned in the will of Robert, Sr. If she were the widow of Robert[2], Jr., then she was still alive in 1766, at which time she and her son Robert[3] were mentioned in the will of Richard Brownen, dated 23 Nov 1766, proved Mar 1771, Northampton Co., NC, Will Book 1, p. 191. The grandsons of Robert Ellis[1], Sr., Robert[3] and John[3] Ellis, who were each bequeathed 160 acres and named in his will, died testate in Northampton Co., NC.

John[3] Ellis (Robert[2-1]) died testate between 6 Apr 1780 and Sept 1788, Northampton Co., NC, Will Book 1, p. 381, and named wife Mary [__], eldest son John[4] Ellis, other children (not named), and brother Robert[3] Ellis. Before his death, on 23 Jan 1762, John[3] Ellis sold his 160 acres to his brother Robert[3] Ellis, according to Northampton Co., NC, Deed Book 3, p. 157.

The Children of Robert Ellis and [__]:
[1] a. **John[2] Ellis**, *no further record.*
[2]+ b. **Robert[2] Ellis**, died by Feb 1740, married (probably) **Ellinor** [__].

64. Sir Richard Everard, the son of Sir Hugh[A] Everard and Mary[A] Brown, was baptized 24 June 1683, at Langleys in the parish of Much Waltham, Essex, and died testate 17 Feb 1733 at his home in Red Lion Street, Holborn, Middlesex, London. He was buried in Much Waltham, Essex. The will of Sir Richard Everard of St. Andrews Holborne, Middlesex, made bequests only to his wife Susanna, and was dated 7 June 1732, proved 21 Mar 1732, PCC Wills. Sir Richard married 13 June 1706, St. Alphage, London, **Susannah Kidder**, the daughter of the Right Reverend Richard[A] Kidder, Bishop of Bath and Wells, and his wife Elizabeth[A] [__]. Dame Susanna Everard, "Widow and Relict of Sir Richard Everard, baronet, deceased," resident of an unnamed parish in Somerset died testate between 6 Aug and 3 Oct 1739, PCC Wills. She made bequests to her daughter Susannah Mead, son Sir Richard Everard, Baronet, daughter Anne Everard, and son Hugh Everard. She named son Hugh and Robert Holliman as joint executors of her will. Sir Richard's father, Sir Hugh[A] Everard of Langleys, in the parish of Great Waltham, Essex, died testate between 28 May 1701 and 13 May 1707, PCC Wills, and named, among others, Richard[1] as his eldest son.

The Governor's family did not make a particularly good impression on the natives of the Albemarle. His "pack of rude children who gave offence daily" were the objects of special complaint, according to Marshall DeLancey Haywood's *Sir Richard Everard, Baronet, Governor of the Colony of North Carolina, 1725-1731, and his Descendants in Virginia*, pp. 7-8. Neither did the gov. garner any favors by being an ardent Jacobite, or by (according to report) having exclaimed at the death of George I: "Then *adieu* to the Hanover family, we have done with them!" In all fairness to the baronet, it must be conceded that neither the Albemarle nor the Everards were suited to or prepared for each other.

Sir Richard Everard was the last proprietary governor of North Carolina, and the only Lord proprietor to have descendants in this Order. A sketch of the governor appears in William S. Powell's *Dictionary of North Carolina Biography*, vol. 2, *D-G*, pp. 171-72. An extensive genealogy of Everard's wife's ancestry was published by the Rev. Edward Turner, "Richard Kidder, Bishop of Bath and Wells, and the Kidders of Maresfield," in *Sussex Archaelogical Collections*, vol. 9 [1857], pp. 125-38. But the maiden name of the Bishop's wife has not yet come to light.

Of Sir Richard's two sons and two daughters, only the daughters survived to have children: Susannah, who married David Meade in Virginia, and Anne, who married George Lathbury in England. Sir Richard's royal ancestry back to Edward III has been outlined in Gary Boyd Roberts' *The Royal Descents of 600 Immigrants*, pp. 47-49.

The Children of Sir Richard Everard and Susannah Kidder:

[1] a. **Richard^2 Everard**, born *ca.* 1708, *died childless.*

[2] b. Sir **Hugh^2 Everard**, died testate between 2 Mar 174^4/$_5$ and 31 Aug 1745, Great Waltham, Essex, PCC Wills; married **Mary** [__]; *died childless.*

[3]+ c. **Susannah^2 Everard**, married 1731, **David Meade**.

[4] d. **Anne^2 Everard**, married after 1739, **George Lathbury**.

65. Nathaniel Everitt was born by 1670, and died testate between 2 Nov and 13 Dec 1749, St. Andrew's Parish, Tyrrell Co., NC. He married between 1694 and 1700, **Mary** [__] **Harrison**, the widow of John Harrison, the testator of 18 Feb 169^3/$_4$, whose will was recorded in NC Secretary of State vol. 874.2, p. 43. It is extremely likely that Mary was *née* Mitchell, based on information carefully collected by Jane Stubbs Bailey and Vernon L. Everett, Jr., editors, *Nathaniel and Mary (Mitchell) Harrison of Tyrrell (Now Washington) County, North Carolina, and Some of their Descendants and Related Families*, 2 vols. Nathaniel made two wills, one dated 2 Sept 1720, recorded in Chowan Co., NC, Deed Book C#1, p. 4, and the other dated 2 Nov 1749, Tyrrell Co., NC, filed among NC Secretary of State loose wills. A sketch of this family can be found in *Order of First Families of North Carolina, Ancestor Registry*, no. 1.

The Children of Nathaniel Everitt and Mary (Mitchell) Harrison, all born Chowan Precinct, NC:

[1]+ a. **Mary^2 Everitt**, born *ca.* 1701, married *ca.* 1720, **Thomas Stubbs**, who died testate between 17 Jan 1735 and 10 Mar 1737, Beaufort Co., NC.

[2]+ b. **Elizabeth^2 Everitt**, born *ca.* 1703, married first, *ca.* 1718, **Benjamin^2**

Blount, who died testate between 1 Feb 1739 and June 1740, Tyrrell Co., NC, Secretary of State loose wills, the son of Capt. **Thomas**[1] **Blount** and Mary (Perry) Scott; second, *ca.* 1741, Tyrrell Co., NC, **William Ray**.

[3]+ c. **Sarah**[2] **Everitt**, born *ca.* 1705, died testate between 23 July 1780 and July 1783, Tyrrell Co., NC, Tyrrell loose wills; she married first, *ca.* 1725, **William Jordan**, who died testate between 4 July and 2 Nov 1732, Tyrrell Co., NC, Secretary of State loose wills; second, *ca.* 1734, **Richard Fagan**, who died testate between 29 Nov 13 George III and 1773, Tyrrell Co., NC, Tyrrell loose wills.

[4]+ d. **Nathaniel**[2] **Everitt**, born *ca.* 1707, died testate between 20 Feb and July 1782, Tyrrell Co., NC, Will Book 1, p. 150; married **Elizabeth** [__].

66. George Fort, almost certainly the son of Elias[A] Fort and Phillis[A] (probably Champion) of Isle of Wight and Surry counties, VA, married **Elizabeth Accabe Duckwood**, the very oddly-named indentured servant of William Foreman of Surry, as indicated by Surry Co., VA, Order Book 1691-1713, p. 152, dated 3 Mar 1695. George's father (there were no other Fort families in either county) Elias Fort died intestate by 10 Mar $167^8/_9$, according to Isle of Wight Co., VA, Administrations and Probates, p. 46, at which time his widow Phillis requested administration on his estate. Phillis married second, John Ducie of Surry Co., VA, and most of the records concerning these generations of the family are to be found, henceforth, in that county. Phillis Ducie administered the estate of her second husband John Ducie by 7 July 1691, Surry Co., VA, Order Book 1691-1713, p, 7. Her marriage to her second husband may be inferred by various deeds in Surry, notably one from William Baldwin to Elias Fort, Jr., as recounted by John Bennett Boddie's chapter on the family of "Fort," in *Southside Virginia Families*, vol. 1, p. 195-99 *et ff.* Boddie's analysis of the early generations of the Fort family is perfectly acceptable, and his citation of documents, appropriate; but he maddeningly cites the wrong record books of both Isle of Wight and Surry. We may assume that George Fort was born no later than 1679, given his first appearance in the Surry tithables in 1695, according to MacDonald and Slatten, *Surry County* [*Virginia*] *Tithables, 1668-1703*, p. 127. The will of George Fort was dated 15 May 1719 and proved 2 Oct 1719, Albemarle Co., NC, his will filed in the NC Secretary of State loose wills, and recorded in NC Secretary of State vol. 875, p. 154. His wife Elizabeth was named in his will. *A Family Called Fort: The Descendants of Elias Fort of Virginia*, Homer T. Fort (1920), is a very reliable and carefully done family genealogy, given its age.

The Children of George Fort and Elizabeth Accabe Duckwood:

[1] a. **Elias[2] Fort**, died testate between 14 Jan and Mar 1761, Edgecombe Co., NC, Will Book A, p. 27; married **Catherine** [__].
[2]+ b. **George[2] Fort**, died testate (as "**Foort**") between July and Dec 1761, Edgecombe Co., NC, Will Book A, p. 84; married **Mary** [__].
[3] c. **Benjamin[2] Fort**.
[4] d. **John[2] Fort**.
[5] e. **Samuel[2] Fort**.
[6] f. **Phillis[2] Fort**, married first, [__] **Fiveash**, who died *ca.* 1721, Bertie Co., NC; she married second, **Robert[1] Sims** of Nansemond, who died testate before 11 Feb 1729, Bertie Co., NC, Secretary of State loose wills. Around 1730, Phillis Fort, obviously a widow, sold 100 acres on the north side of the Morattuck River and Occaneche Swamp to Peter Jones, part of a patent granted William Braswell in $171^{1}/_{2}$, Bertie Co., NC, Deed Book C, p. 219.
[7] g. **Elizabeth[2] Fort**, married (probably) **William Boon**.
[8] h. **Alice[2] Fort**.
[9] i. **Catherine[2] Fort**.

67. John Freeman, Jr., was the son of John[A] and Hannah[A] [__] Freeman of Norfolk Co., VA, as proved by a deed in which his brother William[1] Freeman, for love and affection, gave his brother John 50 acres of land formerly patented by their father John Freeman on 6 June 1676, according to Norfolk Co., VA, Deed Book 9 (part 1), p. 179. Hannah [__] Freeman appeared with her husband on a sale of land dated 19 Feb $168^{3}/_{4}$ in Norfolk Co., VA, Book 4, p. 228. John[1] Freeman, Jr., was born *ca.* 1685, Norfolk Co., VA, and died testate between 19 Feb $17^{29}/_{30}$ and 6 May 1732, Chowan Co., NC, his will filed among the NC Secretary of State loose wills. John's father John[A], Sr., was born *ca.* 1650 and died *ca.* 1711, Norfolk Co., VA. Although it is clear that John Freeman married first, [__], our subject named wife **Mary** [__] in his will. Freeman was still a resident of Elizabeth Parish, Norfolk Co., VA, 16 July 1722, when John Goodwin and wife Mary of Chowan sold him 50 acres on the north side of Warwick Creek at the mouth of Walnut branch, adjoining Edward Wood and the Fox Branch, according to Chowan Co., NC, Deed Book C#1, p. 303. We may assume that John Freeman and his family removed from Norfolk to Chowan to settle permanently after that date. John Freeman and a Joseph Freeman witnessed the will of John Powell of Albemarle on 20 Feb $172^{3}/_{4}$, which was filed among the NC Secretary of State loose wills.

An interesting set of deeds in Chowan reveals the two marriages of John Freeman. Chowan Co., NC, Deed Book E, p. 167, dated 11 Sept 1746, recites that John Smith and wife Hannah[2], late Hannah Freeman; John Davison, Jr., and wife Edie[2], late Edie Freeman; Benjamin Hollyman and wife Elizabeth[2]

Hollyman, late Elizabeth Freeman, all of Bertie sold 250 acres of land to their brother John^2 Freeman, millwright of Bertie. Hannah, Edie, and Elizabeth called themselves sole heirs of Matthew^2 Freeman, their brother of the whole blood, and youngest son of John Freeman, deceased, late of Chowan. The same information is repeated in Chowan Co., NC, Deed Book E, p. 190, dated 31 Dec 1746, in which John Freeman sold the 250 acres just purchased to Patrick Hicks.

Merrill Hill Mosher's *John Freeman of Norfolk County, Virginia, His Descendants in North Carolina and Virginia* is an excellent example of diligent and competent genealogical analysis.

The Children of John Freeman and [__]:

[1]+ a. **John^2 Freeman**, Jr., born *ca.* 1711-20, Chowan, will proved May 1785, Bertie Co., NC, Will Book D, p. 27; married first, **Ann** [__]; second, **Elizabeth** [__]; third, **Sarah** [__] **Winborne-Rascoe**, the widow of Henry Winborne and James Rascoe, respectively.

[2] b. **James^2 Freeman**, died intestate after 1768, Bertie Co., NC, married [__].

The Children of John Freeman and Mary [__]:

[3] c. **Matthew^2 Freeman**, died intestate and childless by 1746, Chowan Co., NC.

[4] d. **Hannah^2 Freeman**, married **John Smith**.

[5] e. **Edie^2 Freeman**, married **John Davison**, who died testate between 10 Oct 1768 and 24 Mar 1772, Bertie Co., NC, loose wills.

[6] f. **Elizabeth^2 Freeman**, married **Benjamin Holloman**, who died intestate before 10 Feb 1752, Bertie Co., NC, Estates Records, 1753.

68. Thomas Futrell II, almost certainly the son of Thomas Futrell I and the widow Gillian [__] Alderman, was born by 1685 and died testate before 21 Sept 1748, Northampton Co., NC, although his will has been lost. On that date, Thomas' son Joseph^2 sold land to Enoch Lewis which had been bequeathed to him by the will of his father then deceased, Northampton Co., NC, Deed Book 1, p. 372. Thomas Futrell II appeared on the tax lists of Chowan Co., NC, in 1721 with 100 acres of land, according to Weynette Haun's *Old Albemarle County North Carolina, Miscellaneous Records, 1678 to ca. 1737*, p. 133, item 340. He married **Anne** [__], who appeared with him on a deed in Bertie Co., NC, 21 Jan 1741, for sale of land in Northampton precinct, Bertie Co., NC, Deed Book F, p. 329. There is an excellent discussion of the early generations of the Futrell family in Rebecca Leach Dozier's *Twelve Northampton County, North Carolina Families, 1650-1850*, pp. 83-174.

The Children of Thomas Futrell, Sr., and Anne [__]:

[1]+ a. **Thomas^2 Futrell III**, died testate between 27 Mar and June 1770, Northampton Co., NC, Will Book 1, p. 180; married first, **Elizabeth^2 Dickinson**; second, **Hannah** [__].

[2] b. **Joseph^2 Futrell.**

[3]+ c. **John^2 Futrell**, will dated 16 Nov 1786, proved Dec 1788, Northampton Co., NC, Will Book 1, p. 471; married **Martha** [__].

[4] d. **Benjamin^2 Futrell.**

[5] e. **William^2 Futrell.**

69. Henry Gibbs, Sr., was born by 1690, probably Norfolk Co., VA, and died testate between 8 Dec 1759 and Sept 1763, Hyde Co., NC, his will recorded in Hyde Co., NC, Orphan's Book 1756-1785, p. 74. He married by 1710, **Sarah** [__]. Henry Gibbs appeared on a Currituck tax list in William Doub Bennett's *Currituck County, North Carolina, Eighteenth Century Tax & Militia Records*, in 1714, p.4, and had a number of land transactions there.

According to VA Land Patent Book 7, p. 630, dated 21 Oct 1687, Capt. John Gibbs, Esq., received a patent for 3100 acres in Lower Norfolk, in "Corretuck precinct," being his seated plantation, adjoining land he bought of Jasper Lane, including Sampson's Island, adjoining Capt. Willoughby, Christopher Marchant, and Francis Jones: land due for the transportation of 49 persons, including "Capt. Jno. Gibbs, Madam Eliz. Gibbs, Mr. Jno. Gibbs, Jr., Mr. Henry Gibbs, Miss Gibbs," and others.

For further research: Norfolk Co., VA, Order Book 1675-1686, dated 15 May 1684: Whereas Capt. Jno. Gibbs and Henry Gibbs his brother Some time before this Sitting of this Court & afterwards the Court being sett did in the Court house yard draw their Swords in a quarrell beetweene them and others whereby much mischiefe might have Insued had It nott been prevented by the standers by, and the Capt. Jno. Gibbs being thereupon Seazed by the Sheriff drew a pistole out of his pockett. It is thereupon order that the sheff. take the sd Capt. Jno. Gibbs & Henry his brother and them disarme and In Safe prison to detayne untill they enter into bond with good security for their future good behaviour.

The Children of Henry Gibbs and Sarah [__]:

[1] a. **Henry^2 Gibbs**, born *ca.* 1715, witnessed some of his father's deeds in Currituck as Henry, Jr.

[2]+ b. **Joseph^2 Gibbs**, born *ca.* 1720, Currituck Co., NC, died by 1794, Hyde Co., NC; married **Mary Brinson**, born 1726, Princess Anne Co., VA.

[3] c. **William^2 Gibbs.**

[4] d. **Robert^2 Gibbs.**

[5] e. **Thomas^2 Gibbs.**

[6] f. **Benjamin^2 Gibbs.**

[7] g. **Mary^2 Gibbs.**

[8] h. **Rebecca^2 Gibbs.**

[9] i. **Sarah^2 Gibbs**, married by 28 Feb 1753, according to a deed of gift from her father, Hyde Co., NC, Deed Book A, p. 422 (310), **John Jennett**, who died testate between 20 Feb 1774 and June 1775, Hyde Co., NC, Will Book 1, p. 2.

[10] j. **Priscilla^2 Gibbs**, married by 23 Oct 1759, according to a deed of gift from her father, Hyde Co., NC, Deed Book A, p. 705, **Jacob Tuly**, according to Hyde Co., NC, Deed Book B, p. 202 (209), dated 24 Dec 1766, in which he appeared with her husband in a sale of land.

70. Rev. **Joseph Glaister**, a Quaker, the son of Robert^A Glaister and Elizabeth [__] (provided that she was his only wife), was baptized 24 Nov 1672, Holme Cultram, Cumberlandshire, and died testate 11.30.1718, according to the records of Pasquotank Monthly Meeting, NC. He married first, 16.1.$169^8/_9$, Pardshaw Monthly Meeting, Cumberland, **Sarah (Fearon) Robinson**, born 11.11.1665, Pardshaw Monthly Meeting, Cumberland, deceased before 1709, the daughter of John^A and Elizabeth^A (Fearon) Fearon, and the widow of John Robinson, all of Cumberland. Sarah had married Robinson *ca.* $168^6/_7$, and his burial was recorded 4.20.1689, Pardshaw Monthly Meeting. Joseph Glaister married second, 12.16.$17^{09}/_{10}$, Pasquotank Monthly Meeting, **Mary Clark**, born 1693, died testate 6.5.1740, Pasquotank Monthly Meeting, the daughter of John and Mary [__] Clark, the latter of whom were legatees under the 1695 will of Arthur Workman. Mary's Pasquotank will was dated 9 June and proved Oct 1740, NC Secretary of State loose wills. It is now clear that Rev. Glaister's first wife was the mother of his three daughters. Rev. Glaister's will was dated 27 Jan and proved 11 Feb $171^8/_9$, NC Secretary of State loose wills. It was also recorded in NC Secretary of State vol. 875, p. 142.

The Child of John Robinson and Sarah Fearon:

[1] a. **Sarah Robinson**, born 24.10.1688, Pardshaw Monthly Meeting, still alive in Pasquotank at the signing of her stepfather's 1719 will.

The Children of Joseph Glaister and Sarah (Fearon) Robinson, born Pardshaw Monthly Meeting, Cumberlandshire:

[2] b. **Ruth^2 Glaister**, born 7.12.1699, married 4.5.1729, Pasquotank Monthly Meeting, as his second wife, **Stephen Scott**, who died testate between 24 Nov 1752 and Jan 1753, Pasquotank Co., NC, Secretary of State loose wills.

[3] c. **Rachel[2] Glaister**, born 14.4.1702, buried 14.5.1704, Pardshaw, Monthly Meeting.

[4]+ d. **Sarah[2] Glaister**, born 5.11.1706, married 1.6.172$^8/_9$, Pasquotank Monthly Meeting, **Wyke Hunnicutt** of Surry Co., VA, who died by 1768, Burleigh, Prince George Co., VA; their children's births were registered at Blackwater Monthly Meeting, VA, and the notice of their father's death was registered among those records as well.

71. Cary Godbee/Godby died intestate before 22 Dec 1720, according to Chowan Co., NC, Deed Book C#1, p. 74, at which time his widow (specifically named as such) sold land to Thomas Pollock, Sr. Possibly a native of Norfolk Co., VA, where the name existed in the seventeenth century, Godbee married **Mary [__] Fox**, of Surry Co., VA, the widow of Richard Fox, according to a deed in Chowan, dated 8 Jan 1710, Deed Book W#1, p. 105, in which George Fox, still of Surry Co., VA, son of Mary Godbee, "now the wife of *Carew* Godby," sold 640 acres of land to her which she had seated. Richard Fox and Mary [__] were married as early as 1 Nov 1700, at which time, as residents of Perquimans, Richard and Mary Fox sold to Daniel Oneel Richard's right and interest in a patent, Perquimans Co., NC, Deed Book A, no. 183. Richard's land activity began in Perquimans, as a matter of fact, for on 22 May 1694, he was granted 200 acres on Perquimans River, according to NC Land Patent Book 1, p. 15. As late as 1714, in NC Land Patent Book 1, pp. 215-16, his land was still referred to as adjacent to other Perquimans patentees. Shortly afterwards, on 23 Nov 1700, they were residents of Chowan, selling 258 acres of land to John White, Jr. of Chowan, Deed Book W#1, p. 22.

Cary Godby received a land patent in Chowan on 5 Mar 171$^1/_2$, for 574 acres on Salmon Creek, NC Land Patent Book 1, p. 177. His land patents made him a neighbor of Thomas Pollock, and he was mentioned as such in several of the colonial land patents.

On 1 Mar 1711, Perquimans Co., NC, Deed Book A, no. 316, George Fox, then of Isle of Wight Co., VA, executed a complicated power of attorney to loving friend Richard Cheston to give permission to George's unnamed daughter to convey a parcel of land formerly in the possession of his deceased father Richard Fox—200 acres of land lying on the narrows of the Perquimans River—to William Bogue. On 20 Feb 171$^1/_2$, Mary (Marbury) Fox appeared as the relict of George Fox deceased, and relinquished her right of administration to Francis Maybury, Jr., according to Surry Co., VA, Orders 1691-1713, p. 388.

The Children of Richard Fox and Mary [__]:

[1] a. **George Fox**, died intestate by 19 Aug 1719, Surry Co., VA, Deeds, Wills, Etc., No. 7, p. 208; estate administered by Francis Maybury II,

married **Mary Maybury**, named as daughter in the will of her father Francis^{A} Maybury of Surry Co., VA, dated 22 Mar $171^{1}/_{2}$ and recorded 18 June 1714, Surry Co., VA, Wills, Deeds, Etc., No. 6, p. 106. Francis Maybury married, no later than 29 May 1688, Elizabeth^{A} (Gilliam) West, the widow of [__] West and daughter of John^{B} and Margery^{B} [__] Gilliam (who married second, Henry Briggs, Sr.), according to Surry Co., VA, Wills, Deeds, Etc., No. 4, p. 84.

The Children of Cary Godbee and Mary [__] Fox:

[2]+ b. **Cary^{2} Godbee II**, born *ca.* 1710, died testate between 17 Sept 1758 and 28 Feb 1759, Onslow Co., NC, Secretary of State loose wills; married first, **Elizabeth Coddell**, according to a deed in Carteret Co., NC, Deed Book D, p. 129, dated 13 Jan $173^{2}/_{3}$, in which she signed with him in a deed of sale; she was the daughter of Henry Coddell of Perquimans, Deed Book C, no. 90; he married second, **Anne** [__], whom he named in his will, and who was not the mother of his children.

[3] c. **Henry^{2} Godbee.**

[4] d. **Thomas^{2} Godbee.**

72. John Godley, blacksmith, was born *ca.* 1670 and died testate between 22 Jan $173^{1}/_{2}$, and May 1732, Bertie Co., NC, his will filed among NC Secretary of State loose wills. He married **Katherine** [__], whom he named in his will, and who executed along with John Edwards, cooper, of Roanoak. On 2 Aug 1729, John Godley received a patent of 167 acres of land in the northernly woods of the Morattock River, adjoining John Briggs and the south side of the Potecase Swamp, according to NC Land Patent Book 3, p. 217. Bertie Co., NC, Deed Book B, p. 297, dated 8 Aug 1727, however, showed a deed of sale from Thomas Kirby to John Godley—240 acres in the Pottakasie Woods, a tract which would adjoin his patent of 1729.

The Children of John Godley and Katherine [__]:

[1]+ a. **Nathan^{2} Godley**, born *ca.* 1710, Chowan, died after 28 Nov 1791, Beaufort Co., NC, Will Book A, p. 129; married **Mary** [__].

[2] b. **John^{2} Godley.**

[3] c. **Mary^{2} Godley.**

[4] d. **Amy^{2} Godley.**

[5] e. **Thomas^{2} Godley.**

73. Baron **Christopher de Graffenreid**, Landgrave of North Carolina, the son of Anton von Graffenreid and Catherine Jenner, was born 15 Nov 1661 in the village of Worb, in the Canton of Bern, Switzerland, and died 1743, Worb, Bern, Switzerland. He married 25 Apr 1684, Worb, Bern, Switzerland, **Regina Tscharner**, born 2 Dec 1655, died 1740, Bern, Switzerland, the daughter of Beat Ludwig Tscharner and Marguerithe Gueder. Baron de Graffenreid founded the city of New Bern, Craven Co., NC, in 1710. There is an excellent sketch of Baron de Graffenreid in William S. Powell's *Dictionary of North Carolina Biography*, vol. 2, *D-G*, pp. 327-28. De Graffenreid attempted to establish a colony on the Nuse and Trent Rivers and founded the town of New Bern, but the colony was almost wiped out by Indian attack. The Baron stayed in North Carolina from 1710 until 1713, but after the dreadful Tuscarora attack returned to live out his days in Switzerland. Christopher de Graffenried's ancestry is developed in Gary Boyd Roberts' seminal *The Royal Descents of 600 Immigrants*, in which, on pp. 521-22, the paternal line of the family is traced back to Bela I, King of Hungary, who died 1063. Thomas P. deGraffenried's *History of the deGraffenried Family, from 1191 A.D. to 1925*, is a very useful genealogy of the early family.

The marriage record of Christopher "Von Graffenried" and "jungfrau" Regina Tscharner can be found on p. 403 of the marriages of Worb, in the canton of Berne, Switzerland (FHL #2,005,841). It is always reassuring to know that a vital record long held to be accurate can be documented with an original. The marriage date for Christopher^2 has been taken from the deGraffenried genealogy and generally accepted to be true. Moreover, the marriage was confirmed in a set of depositions contained, improbably, in Lunenburg Co., VA, Deed Book 16, pp. 125-24. A transcription of those documents appear in the appendix. These consist of depositions taken in 1790 recalling events that took place in 1714, some 76 years past, *i.e.*, witnesses to Christopher's marriage with Barbara Tempest. The depositions were guaranteed by the seal of Charles Pinckney, the governor of South Carolina.

Unfortunately, the identity of Barbara Tempest has not been resolved by any indications in the colonies other than anecdotal ones. Whether or not she was *née* Needham remains to be discovered, most likely, in England.

The Child of Baron Christopher de Graffenreid and Regina Tscharner:

[1]+ a. **Christopher^2 de Graffenreid**, born 1685-90, died 27 Oct 1742, Amelia Co., VA; married 22 Feb 1714, Charleston, SC, **Barbara Tempest**, died 26 June 1744.

74. Thomas Grandy, Sr., born *ca.* 1675, Norfolk Co., VA, was the son of Charles^A Grandy and his wife [__] of Norfolk Co., VA, who in his will dated 14

Feb and proved 15 July 1687, Norfolk Co., VA, Will Book 5, p. 27, named sons William, John, Charles[1] and Thomas[1] Grandy. Thomas of Pasquotank died intestate before [--] Feb 1739, Pasquotank Co., NC, and married by 1700, **Elizabeth** [__]. Elizabeth Grandy died intestate after Feb 1739, Pasquotank Co., NC, at which time she recorded an extensive deed of gift to her children and grandchildren in Pasquotank Co., NC, Deed Book B, p. 334. She could only have done this as a widow. Thomas[1] and his brother Charles[1] described themselves as residents of the Albemarle when they sold 99 acres of land to Godwin Post on 16 Oct 1702, according to Norfolk Co., VA, Deed Book 7, p. 20a, although Charles disappeared from the deeds after the above sale. Thomas Grandy patented 385 acres of land in Pasquotank Co., NC, on 20 Oct 1727, according to Pasquotank Co., NC, Deed Book C, p., 272, wherein he and his wife sold land to James Williams.

The determination of Thomas' age has presented problems in sorting out his parentage. If we can assume that he and his brother Charles were of age when, already residents of the Albemarle, they sold their inheritance in Norfolk, then the assignment of birth dates between 1677-1680 would be appropriate for both of them. It has been posited that Thomas married Elizabeth Basnett, even thoughWilliam[A] Bass(n)ett, in his will dated 25 Mar and proved 17 May 1687, Norfolk Co., VA, Will Book 5, p. 22, named daughter *Mary* Grandy and her husband Thomas Grandy. Even if this can be proved to be a scribal error, this Thomas, who was married before 1687, seems to be of an older generation than ours.

Estates Records in Pasquotank indicate that brother Charles[1] Grandy died intestate by 10 Apr 1752 leaving wife Ann (Sawyer), with children Solomon[2] Grandy, Sary[2] Grandy, Mary[2] Grandy, Thomas[2] Grandy, and Charles[2] Grandy. Charles[2] Grandy was named as grandson in the will of John Sawyer of Pasquotank, dated 22 Dec 1713, proved 19 July 1720, NC Secretary of State loose wills.

The identity of the two wives of Thomas[2] Grandy, Jr., is deduced from two sources: [1] Pasquotank Co., NC, Deed Book D&E, p. 466, dated 15 June 1768, in which Davis[3] Grandy declared himself to be the heir at law of Dorothy Grandy, the daughter of Solomon Davis; [2] Pasquotank Co., NC, Deed Book D&E, p. 398, in which Thomas[2] Grandy and wife Ann sold her half of an inheritance left by her father Cornelius Jones to his two daughters Ann and Letitia. Therefore only Davis[3] Grandy seems to be the surviving issue of Thomas[2]'s first marriage to Dorothy. In his will, Thomas[2] also named brothers Caleb[2] and Absolum[2]. Daughter Sarah (Gregory) Grandy was named in the will of her mother Margaret Gregory, and Pasquotank Estates Records prove that she was indeed Absolum's wife. The identity of Absolum Grandy's wife is taken from Estates Records in Pasquotank for Margaret (Barcock—and later "Barco")

Gregory, dated 1756. I am grateful to genealogist Frederic Z. Saunders of Midvale, UT, for this discovery.

The Children of Thomas Grandy, Sr., and Elizabeth [__]:

[1] a. **Thomas**[2] **Grandy**, Jr., signed his will 7 Dec 1760, died after 12 Aug 1765, Pasquotank Co., NC, Will Book HIK, p. 1; married first, **Dorothy Davis**, daughter of Solomon Davis; second, **Ann Jones**, daughter of Cornelius Jones.

[2]+ b. **Absolum**[2] **Grandy**, married **Sarah**[2] **Gregory**, daughter of **Richard**[1] **Gregory** and **Margaret**[2] **Barcock** (Thomas[1]).

[3] c. **[Daughter]**[2] **Grandy**, married [__] **Wrichards**.

[4] d. **[Daughter]**[2] **Grandy**, married [__] **Jelico**.

[5] e. **Phillis**[2] **Grandy**.

[6] f. **Caleb**[2] **Grandy**.

75. Farnefold Green, the son of Timothy[A] Green and Ann[A] [__], was born 30 May 1674, St. Stephen's Parish, Northumberland Co., VA, and died testate after 26 Oct 1711, Bath Co., NC. His will, which because of the handwriting is extraordinarily difficult to read, was recorded in NC Secretary of State vol. 875, p. 10. He married *ca.* 1697, **Hannah**[2] **(Kent) Smithwick**, the widow of **John**[2] **Smithwick**, born 10 May 1673, Perquimans Co., NC, and died after the signing of her third husband's will—11 Apr 1730, Craven Co., NC. She was the daughter of **Thomas**[1] and Ann (Cornell) **Kent**, originally of Rhode Island, and the widow of John Smithwick of Archdale precinct, who died testate between 28 Aug 1696 and 6 Jan $169^6/_7$, NC Secretary of State loose wills, recorded in NC Secretary of State vol. 874.2, p. 93. Hannah was named in the will of her first husband. Hannah married third, after 1711, Richard Graves of Craven Co., NC, who, dying testate between 11 Apr and 16 Sept 1730—his will filed among NC Secretary of State loose wills—named Hannah and her children by her marriage to Farnefold Green therein. For the record, Hannah was not *née* Gonsalvo. There is an excellent sketch of Farnefold Green in William S. Powell's *Dictionary of North Carolina Biography*, vol. 2, *D-G*, p. 354, although his mother could not possibly have been *née* Farnefold. See John Anderson Brayton, "Did the Rev. John Farnefold Have Descendants?" in *The Virginia Genealogist*, vol. 48, no. 1 [January-March 2004], pp. 33-42. Farnefold Green was listed as a headright for Nicholas Tyler on 5 July 1697, according to Caroline B. Whitley, *North Carolina Headrights, A List of Names, 1663-1744*, p. 79.

The Children of Farnefold Green and Hannah (Kent) Smithwick:

[1] a. **Thomas**[2] **Green**.

[2] b. **John**[2] **Green**.

[3]+ c. **Elizabeth^{2} Green**, born *ca.* 1698, married 15 May 1715, Bath Co., NC, **Daniel^{1} Shine**, born *ca.* 1689, Ireland, who died testate in Craven Co., NC, between 5 May and Aug Court 1757, NC Secretary of State loose wills, also recorded in NC Secretary of State vol. 880, p. 191.

[4]+ d. **Farnefold^{2} Green II**, will dated 15 July 1749, Craven Co., NC, Wills, Deeds, Inventories, 1749-1777, p. 193; married **Sarah** [__].

[5]+ e. **James^{2} Green**, born *ca.* 1710, Bath Co., NC, will proved Dec 1788, Craven Co., NC, Will Book A, p. 183; married [__].

[6] f. **Titus^{2} Green.**

[7] g. **Jane^{2} Green.**

76. Richard Gregory of Pasquotank Co., NC, died testate between 17 May 1719 and 15 Sept 1720, at which time letters of administration were granted on his estate. His will was recorded in NC Secretary of State vol. 875, p. 235. If we are to trust implicitly the language of Richard's will, we must conclude that he married first, [__], by whom he had Richard^{2}, his "eldest," and then two sons James^{2} and John^{2}. He married second, **Margaret^{2} Barecock**, the daughter of **Thomas^{1} Barecock** and his second wife Margaret [__]. Thomas Barecock died testate between 1 and 17 Jan $172^{1}/_{2}$, his will filed among NC Secretary of State loose wills and also recorded in NC Secretary of State vol. 875, p. 303. Margaret Gregory survived her husband by more than thirty years, dying testate between 3 Feb $174^{6}/_{7}$ and July 1753, her will filed among the NC Secretary of State loose wills. Richard^{1} had earlier specified children Caleb^{2}, Mary^{2} and Margaret^{2} Gregory as the children of Margaret. Caleb^{2} Gregory was also named in the will of his grandfather Thomas Barecock.

As far as land patents are concerned, Richard Gregory is mentioned only twice in the provincial grants: [1] on 30 Mar 1721 as a neighbor of patentee Capt. John Sally, who received 196 acres on the north east side of the Pasquotank river, NC Land Patent Book 3, p. 63; [2] on 18 Dec 1716, as a neighbor of Griffith Jones who received 74 acres in Pasquotank on the north side of the River, NC Land Patent Book 8, p. 140. He appeared only once in the records of Pasquotank—as witness to a deed from Solomon Sawyer to John Sawyer, Deed Book A, p. 211, dated 22 July 1718. He is mentioned once in the colonial records, in *North Carolina Higher-Court Records, 1697-1701*, p. 374, on 2 Aug 1700 as a petitioner to receive recompense for having traveled to give evidence in court concerning the death of one Charles Wright. A puzzling reference to an actual patent granted Richard occurs in Pasquotank Co., NC, Deed Book B, p. 477, dated 15 Feb $174^{2}/_{3}$, in which his son John^{2} sold land to his brother Caleb^{2} Gregory which had been patented by his father on 1 Feb 1715. Such a patent cannot yet be located.

Determining the identity of Richard[2] Gregory's wives has proved complicated. Margaret [__] Browne-Peggs, the testatrix of 17 Feb 1729, NC Secretary of State loose wills, and widow respectively of John Browne and [perhaps Joseph?] Peggs, named daughter Mary the wife of Richard[2] Gregory.

The Children of Richard Gregory and [__]:

[1] a. **Richard[2] Gregory**, died testate between 7 Oct and Dec 1758, Currituck Co., NC, Secretary of State loose wills; married first, by 1729, **Mary Peggs**; second, [__].

[2] b. **James[2] Gregory**, died testate before 27 Sept 1776, Pasquotank Co., NC, Will Book HIK, p. 157; married **Ruth** [__].

[3] c. **John[2] Gregory**, married first [__]; second [__].

The Children of Richard Gregory and Margaret Barecock:

[4] d. **Caleb[2] Gregory**, died intestate by 1772, Pasquotank; married **Sarah** [__], his administratrix, according to Estates Records.

[5] e. **Mary[2] Gregory**, married **Christopher Humphries**.

[6] f. **Margaret[2] Gregory**, married **John Barber**.

[7]+ g. **Sarah[2] Gregory**, born *ca.* 1719, married **Absolum[2] Grandy**.

77. Jasper Hardison of "Albemarle County" died testate between 8 May and 5 Nov 1733, Perquimans Co., NC, and his will was filed among North Carolina Secretary of State loose wills. He married **Mary** [__], whom he named in his will. On 7 Jan 172²/₃, Jasper Hardison purchased 100 acres of land adjoining Browning, Thomas Lee and Cullen Pollock on Walches Creek, from William Morris, Chowan Co., NC, Deed Book C#1, p. 361.

Descent from this family (as far as the OFFNC has been concerned) has largely been through the Suttons and then through the descendants of Lemuel/Lam Hardy. All the research performed on this branch of the Hardys was taken on by the venerable Mewborn sisters of Wilson, NC, who left a remarkable legacy of accurately researched family history now housed in Heritage Place, Lenoir Community College, Kinston, NC. Unfortunately, the venerable sisters were genealogists of the type that, albeit scrupulously honest and fastidious in their virtuall door-to-door collection of data, neglected to leave behind any other confirmation of proof than their type-written and carbon-copied word. Anyone asking for the whereabouts of an original of a Bible record, for instance, would find him or herself rebuffed with the coldest of glares and an even stonier silence. Their typewritten word was, in their own opinion, their bond. *Sic transit gloria* evidence, in this world, at least.

Richard[2] Hardison was called, curiously, "godson" as the recipient of a deed of gift from [Governor] **Richard Everard**, gent., dated 17 Dec 1730,

Craven Co., NC, Deed Book 1, p. 233. The Carkeet connection to this family suggests a seventeenth-century New Hampshire connection, where there were Hardisons as well, but this has not yet been verified. An as of yet unidentified Charles Hardison was security for the will of Joseph Hudson (possibly of Perquimans), who died testate before Mar 1744, NC Secretary of State loose wills, naming wife Mary, and which will was witnessed by Benjamin Carkeet. John[2] Hardison was called "Capt." John Hardison in the will of Thomas Duggan of Tyrrell, who died testate between 9 May and June 1754, recorded in NC Secretary of State vol. 881, p. 110.

The Children of Jasper Hardison and Mary [__]:

[1] a. **John[2] Hardison**, died testate between 27 Nov 1778 and Sept 1780, Martin Co., NC, Will Book 1, p. 161; married **Olive** [__].

[2] b. **Mary[2] Hardison**, married [__] **Carkeet**.

[3]+ c. **Judith/Judah[2] Hardison**, married, as his second wife, **Thomas[3] Sutton**, the son of Joseph Sutton and **Perthenia[2] Durant**.

[4] d. **Jasper[2] Hardison**.

[5] e. **Joshua[2] Hardison**.

[6] f. **Thomas[2] Hardison**.

[7] g. **Richard[2] Hardison**.

[8] h. **Joseph[2] Hardison**, died testate between 29 Mar and June 1788, Martin Co., NC, Will Book 1, p. 143; married **Mary** [__].

78. John Hardy was born *ca.* 1650 and died after 1695, Chowan Co., NC. He married by 4 Oct 1672, Westmoreland Co., VA, **Charity Odgier/O'Dwyer**, born *ca.* 1655, the daughter of Capt. Gabriel[A] Odgier and Mary [__], who were in Northumberland Co., VA, as early as 20 Feb $165^{0}/_{1}$, at which time Gabriel[A] Odyer received a certificate for the importation of himself and wife Mary into the colony, Northumberland Co., VA, Record Book 1, p. 49. Capt. Odyer's inventory was presented to court on 20 Jan $16^{59}/_{60}$, Westmoreland Co., VA, Deeds, Wills, Etc., 1661-1662, p. 3a. John Hardy's marriage record to Charity is found in Westmoreland Co., VA, Deed, Patents, Etc., 1665-1677, p. 122a, in which John "Hardie" of Washington Parish, Westmoreland, acknowledged receipt of 5,970 pounds of tobacco from Charity[1] "Odgeas' " guardian, Capt. John Lord. On pp. 136a-137 of that same record, dated 26 Feb $167^{2}/_{3}$, Hardy named his wife's father as Gabriel[A] Odger, deceased. Charity's sister Mary[1] had been married to Nathaniel Butler, but by 19 Nov 1673, Mary[1] (Odger) Butler had died childless and her share of the Odger estate devolved onto Charity, according to Westmoreland Co., VA, Deeds, Patents, Etc., 1665-1677, p. 170. A list of John and Charity's children can be taken from his importation rights registered in court 7 Oct 1695, according to Caroline B. Whitley, *North Carolina Headrights,*

A List of Names, 1663-1744, p. 42: John Hardy for himself, Charity Hardy, William Hardy, Mary Hardy, John Hardy, Jr., Thomas Hardy, and Jacob Hardy. Brothers William, Jacob, and Thomas Hardy were all named in the will of John[2] Hardy, Jr.

Willliam[2] Hardy's last appearence in Bertie is in Deed Book G, p. 335, dated 2 Jan $175^0/_1$, in which Edward Rasor sold him 300 acres of land in the Middle Swamp of Salmon Creek. Later on in May, son Lamb[3] Hardy sold to Gov. Gabriel Johnston a tract of 270 acres on Salmon Creek which his father William[2] Hardy had conveyed to him as a deed of gift, according to Bertie Co., NC, Deed Book G, p. 357, dated 1 May 1751. Those are Williams' last two transactions, and we may assume that he died between Jan and May 1751.

The Children of John Hardy and Charity O'Dwyer, born Westmoreland Co., VA:

[1] a. **John[2] Hardy**, Jr., died testate between 19 Jan and 16 Mar 1719, Chowan Co., NC, Secretary of State wills, also recorded in NC Secretary of State vol. 875, pp. 232-33; married **Rebecca** [__].

[2]+ b. **William[2] Hardy**, of Scuppernong, died intestate between 2 Jan $175^0/_1$ and 1 May 1751, Bertie Co., NC; married **Edith[2] Batchelor**.

[3] c. **Thomas[2] Hardy**.

[4] d. **Jacob[2] Hardy**, married **Mary** [__], according to Chowan Co., NC, Deed Book F#1, p. 183, dated 20 Mar 1721.

[5]+ e. **Mary[3] Hardy**, married first, **John[1] Hinton**, who died testate between 21 June 1730 and Oct 1732, Chowan, NC Secretary of State wills, also recorded in NC Secretary of State vol. 876, p. 240; second, by 17 July1732, Chowan Co., NC, according to Chowan Co., NC, Court Minutes, 1730-1745, p. 27, in which William Hinton, one of the executors of the will of John Hinton (and his brother) declared that the widow had intermarried (rather quickly, I might add) with one **Thomas Holladay**. The order for Thomas to give security for the considerable estate of the Hinton orphans was delivered by one John White, who was told by Holladay that he would "split his Brains out if he [White] did not immediately leave." Mary (Hardy) Hinton-Holladay soon died and Thomas formed a relationship with Mary Hutson, with whom he had Hardy Holladay Hutson, Thomas Holladay Hutson, and John Holladay Hutson, all under age according to Thomas' will. In that document, dated 30 Aug and proved 1744, he named his daughter Elizabeth Burton [where was *she* from?] and made Mary Hutson his executrix, NC Secretary of State loose wills. Mary Hutson, in turn, married 10 Dec 1744, Chowan Co., NC (marriage bond, Mary "widow"), Walter Long/Lang, and so disappeared from our notice.

79. John Herring, Sr., the son of Anthony^{A} Herring, was born *ca.* 1680, Isle of Wight Co., VA, and died *ca.* 1754, Johnston Co., NC. He married **Catherine** [__]. Herring witnessed deeds in Chowan as early as July 1718, according to Chowan Co., NC, Deed Book B#1, p. 601. It has not been proved—and most likely never will be—that Catherine was *née* Morbe, but the source of this theory is found in a deed dated 18 Oct 1715, Chowan Co., NC, Deed Book B#1, p. 210, in which George Morbe and wife Catherine assigned to John Herring of lower parish of Isle of Wight a tract of 380 acres on the south side of the Bear Swamp. The lack of monetary stipulations in the deed and the repetition of the name Catherine are both coincidentally compelling, but not at all sufficient for proof. There is neither proof that John's father Anthony^{A} married Rebecca West, as stated in James Maurice Grimwood, *Herring Highlights III, 1642-1998*, p. 9 and p. 21, although that Herring genealogy is invaluable in many ways. One wishes that Mr. Grimwood had habit of providing actual documentary references for the many valuable records to which he continually alludes. On p. 21 of the aforementioned work is a reference to a promissory note dated 1 Jan 1753, located in the NC Archives, which named John^{2}, Jr., Simon^{2}, Benjamin^{2}, and Joshua^{2} Herring as sons of John^{1}, Sr.

The Children of John Herring and Catherine [__]:

[1] a. **John^{2} Herring**, Jr., born *ca.* 1705,died testate between 23 Oct 1773 and 1774, New Hanover Co., NC, Will Book C, p. 143; married **Rebecca Loftin**, the daughter of Cornelius Loftin, who gave his daughter Rebecca Herring, wife of John, a slave named Dido on 19 Dec 1743, Craven Co., NC, Deeds, Wills, Etc., 1743-1744, p. 14.

[2]+ b. **Simon^{2} Herring**, born *ca.* 1705, died *ca.* 1780, Wayne Co., NC; married **Ann** [__].

[3]+ c. **Benjamin^{2} Herring**, died testate after 28 Aug 1789, New Hanover Co., NC, Will Book C, p. 155; married **Mary** [said to be] **Bright**.

[4] d. **Joshua^{2} Herring**, born 23 Nov 1723, died Apr 1801, Moseley Hall, Lenoir Co., NC; married *ca.* 1750, Duplin Co., NC, **Elizabeth** [said to be] **Matchett**; on 31 Dec 1774, Duplin Co., NC, Deed Book 5, p. 32, Joshua Herring of Dobbs Co., NC, sold 160 acres of land to Jacob Langston.

Possibly, according to Grimwood:

[5] e. **Susanna^{2} Herring**, married **John Becton**.

80. Samuel Herring, who died testate between 22 Oct 1750 and 29 Mar 175$^{0}/_{1}$, Johnston Co., NC, was apparently the son of Anthony Herring of Isle of Wight

Co., VA. He married by 1716, as his second wife, **Anne**^{3} **Williams**, the daughter of **John**^{2} and Anne [__] Williams, who was born *ca.* 1696, Isle of Wight Co., VA. Ann's father John Williams made a deed of gift to her as Ann "Hearin" on 15 Oct 1716, according to Chowan Co., NC, Deed Book B#1, p. 395. Samuel's will, which did not name his wife, was filed among NC Secretary of State loose wills, and apparently recorded in Johnston Co., NC, Will Book A, pp. 23-24. A sketch of this family can be found in *Order of First Families of North Carolina, Ancestor Registry*, no. 2. See that work for this writer's reasoning that Anne Williams could not have been the mother of Anthony^{2} Herring.

The Child of Samuel Herring and [__]:

[1] a. **Anthony**^{2} **Herring**, born 1702-05, died testate between 13 Sept 1783 and Mar 1784, Wayne Co., NC, loose wills; he probably married **Bridget** [__], who appeared on a 1786 Wayne Co., NC, tax list after Anthony's death.

The Children of Samuel Herring and Ann Williams, born Isle of Wight Co., VA:

[2] b. **Stephen**^{2} **Herring**, born *ca.* 1717, died testate between 21 Sept and Oct 1797, Duplin Co., NC, loose wills; married **Sarah Bright**, the daughter of testator William Bright, who named his son-in-law Stephen Herring in his will dated 2 July 1762, Duplin Co., NC, Will Book A, p. 62.

[3]+ c. **Michael**^{2} **Herring**, born *ca.* 1722, died testate between 15 [--] 1805 and Nov 1808, Wayne Co., NC; married **Charity Graddy**, named as daughter in the will of John Graddy, dated 9 Feb 1773, proved Apr 1787, Duplin Co., NC, Will Book A, p. 152.

[4] d. **Barthena**^{2} **Herring**, *no further record.*

[5] e. **Kesiah**^{2} **Herring**, died testate between15 June and Dec Court 1801, Craven Co., NC, Wills, 1801-1809; married first, **John Connerley**, who died testate between 17 Oct 1751 and 9 Mar 175$^{1}/_{2}$, Johnston Co., NC, Craven Co., NC, Deed Book 5, p. 270; she married second, after July 1752, [__] **Jones**.

81. Robert$^{(3)}$ **Hill** was the son of Sion$^{(2)}$ Hill, Sr. [Robert$^{(1)}$], and Elizabeth [__] Spiltimber, the widow of John$^{(2)}$ Spiltimber [John$^{(1)}$]. Our Robert$^{(3)}$ died testate between 18 June 1762 and Apr 1765, Halifax Co., NC, Will Book 1, p. 159. He married before 21 Feb 1721, Surry Co., VA, Deeds, Wills, Etc., No. 7, **Tabitha** [__], which date is her first appearance in the records. Robert$^{(3)}$ Hill was born no earlier than 1687, Surry Co., VA, given that the Robert$^{(2)}$ Hill who appeared consistently in the tithable records with Sion$^{(2)}$ Hill, Sr., could not have been Sion's son. Therefore we must conclude that our Robert$^{(3)}$ became 16 years old after the posting of the last extant tithable list [1703] and never surfaced in the published records. This older Robert(2) Hill made his first appearance as [at least] a 16-year old with his (almost certainly brother) Sion(2) on the tithables of that county on 9 June 1688 (according to MacDonald and Slatten, editors, *Surry County* [*Virginia*] *Tithables, 1668-1703*, p. 87), and lived consistently near **George Fort**. He was therefore born by 1672. On 24 Mar 1725, our Robert(3) Hill, "Jr.," patented 235 acres of new land on the north side of Fountain's Creek in Isle of Wight, adjoining the older Robert(2) Hill's land, according to VA Land Patent Book 12, p. 466. According to Bertie Co., NC, Deed Book E, pp. 241-43, dated 30 Aug 1737 and 11 Mar 173$^{8}/_{9}$, Robert(3) Hill sold two 80-acre tracts of land on the south side of Fountain's Creek, which he had patented 22 Feb 1724.

Dr. Benjamin Holtzclaw contributed a perfectly sound chapter on the Hill family of Surry to John Bennett Boddie, *Southside Virginia Families*, vol. 2, pp. 164-69. There has been, however, as mentioned above, some difficulty in distinguishing our Robert with wife Tabitha from the older Robert(2) who married by 1694, Surry Co., VA, Elizabeth Marriott [see below], the widow of Luke Mizell, according to Surry Co., VA, Deeds, Wills, Etc., No. 5, p. 7. This elder Robert(2) was still married to Elizabeth on 15 Dec 1725 when in a deed to Joseph Pettiway he was listed as a resident of Isle of Wight Co., VA, according to Surry Co., VA, Deeds, Wills, Etc., No. 7, p. 619. Dr. Holtzclaw correctly identified this Robert(2) Hill as the uncle of our Robert(3) of Halifax. This older Robert(2) owned land adjoining Ansell Bayley, Richard Halleman, and George Fort. In fact, both Roberts removed from Surry to Isle of Wight at about the same time, where the older Robert(2) remained—the younger being listed as "Junior," according to the custom of naming the younger of-age member of a family thus to distinguish him from the elder member of the same family so named. The older Robert(2) died testate in Brunswick Co., VA, after 10 Apr and 4 Sept 1740, Will Book 2, p. 20.

Matthias Marriott died testate between 12 June 1705 and 2 Sept 1707, Surry Co., VA, according to Surry Deeds, Wills, Etc., No. 5, p. 374. He named daughter Elizabeth Hill therein, bequeathing to her and to her two sisters each a book of Divinity. This poor widow has been blamed on more Hills in Surry than almost any hapless daughter anywhere. When Luke Mizell died, his nuncupative will, dated 4 July 1693, Surry Deeds, Wills, Etc., No. 4, p. 308, named his wife, and two daughters, Elizabeth and Sarah. Obviously he was a young man with young children, and we might give both him and his wife dates of birth around 1665-1670. Sion(2) Hill, Sr., was already married to Elizabeth [__] Spiltimber in Feb of 1679, according to Isle of Wight Co., VA, Will & Deed Book 1, p. 428, which eliminates him from any Marriott ancestry. Only Robert(2) Hill, Sr., who did have a wife named Elizabeth, might qualify as the son-in-law of Matthias Marriott, principally because of timing.

In an almost throw-away remark in Isle of Wight Co., VA, Deed Book 1, pp. 326-27, dated 3 June 1696, in a deed from Edmund Wickins of Nansemond Co., VA, to Henry Baker, Wickins was identified as "ye sd Wickins father of Sion / Hill." Depending upon the whim of the clerk, Charles Chapman, the term "father" could have meant either that Wickins had married Sion's widowed mother, Mary [__] Hill, or that he was his (in modern terms) father-in-law. According to Isle of Wight Co., VA, Will & Deed Book 1, pp. 427-28, Edmond Wickins was in possession of a tract of land sold to Robert Hill, Sion's father, by George Archer in 1653. The deed was dated 9 Feb $167^{8}/_{9}$, and registered the formal sale of the tract from Sion, who had apparently come into the possesion of his father's property, to Wickins. The estate of Capt. Edmund Wickins, obviously father to the younger Edmond of Nansemond, was appraised on 8 May 1679, Isle of Wight Co., VA, Will & Deed Book 2, p. 201, and presented to court by George Moore in June of that year. Although it seems apparent that the younger Wickins of Nansemond married Mary [__], the widow of Robert$^{(1)}$ Hill, Sion's father, this cannot be true. I suspect that the scribe who penned the document has telescoped the generations and that Wickens the grantee of $167^{8}/_{9}$ married Mary [__] Hill.

The Children of Robert Hill and Tabitha [__]:

[1] a. **Sion^{2} Hill**, died testate between 29 Mar 1780 and 15 Sept 1783, Wake Co., NC, Will Book A, p. 155; married **Sarah** [__].

[2] b. **Abner^{2} Hill.**

[3] c. **Thomas^{2} Hill.**

[4] d. **Tabitha^{2} Hill**, married **David Chapman**, died testate in Chatham Co., NC, between 27 Jan 1779 and May 1780, Chatham loose wills. An abstract can be found in William Perry Johnson, "Chatham Co.: Abstracts of Unrecorded Wills, 1771-1793," *North Carolina Genealogy*, vol. 24, no. 2 [Summer 1967], p. 1877.

[5]+ e. **Agnes^{2} Hill**, born *ca.* 1727, died 1 June 1773, St. Bartholomew's Parish, Chatham Co., NC; married **Charles Harrington**, died 14 Aug 1797, Chatham Co., NC.

[6] f. **Lewraina^{2} Hill**, married [__] **Harrington.**

[7] g. **Ann^{2} Hill**, married [__] **Steed.**

[8] h. **Mary^{2} Hill**, married [__] **Bryant.**

[9] i. **Milbry^{2} Hill.**

[10] j. **Green^{2} Hill.**

[11] k. **William^{2} Hill**, died intestate in Chatham Co., NC; married [__]; one of his sons, William C.^{3} Hill died testate between 25 Jan and May 1803, Halifax Co., NC, Will Book 3, p. 398.

82. William Hilliard, the son of Jeremiah Hilliard and Elizabeth [__] (who married second, Capt. **Simon**[1] **Jeffreys**), was born *ca.* 1710, James City Co., VA, and died testate between 4 July 1754 and May 1756, Northampton Co., NC, his will filed among the NC Secretary of State loose wills, and recorded in NC Secretary of State vol. 880, p. 52. He married **Ann Newsum**, whose will was proved Sept 1771, Northampton Co., NC, Will Book 1, p. 204. She named cousin Isaac Newsom in her will.

A further division of the estate of Isaac[2] Hillliard occurred 20 May 1808, due to the deaths of sons Henry[3] and William[3], who died before coming of age, according to Nash Co., NC, Deed Book 5, p. 133.

The Children of William Hilliard and Ann Newsum:

[1] a. **William**[2] **Hilliard** had, according to will of his mother, a son named William Thomas[3] Roach.

[2] b. **James**[2] **Hilliard**, died testate between 12 Feb and Aug 1764, Northampton Co., NC, Will Book 1, p. 109; married [__].

[3]+ c. **Isaac**[2] **Hilliard**, born 28 July 1738, Edgecombe Co., NC, died 25 June 1790, Nash Co., NC, Will Book 1, p. 67; married 20 Apr 1765, **Leah Crafford**.

[4] d. **Elias**[2] **Hilliard**, died intestate by 31 July 1791, Northampton Co., NC, Guardian Accounts, 1781-1802, p. 126; **Lydia** [__], according to Northampton Co., NC, Deed Book 6, p. 134, dated 27 Dec 1776, in which she signed on a deed of sale from her husband to John Bridges.

[5] e. **Ann**[2] **Hilliard**, unmarried in Feb 1764.

83. Abraham Hobbs was born 1660-70 and died after 12 Apr 1715, Perquimans Co., NC, at which time his son Abraham[2], Jr., indicating the presence of an older person in the family by the same name (according to the OED), sold to Richard Leary a plantation of 400 acres adjoining Thomas Long, commonly called "Hobbs' Plantation," on the north east side of the Mill Swamp, Perquimans Co, NC, Deed Book B, no. 17. This is the last trace of the Sr.-Jr. designation, which indicated the existance of an older Abraham. Abraham's first entry in the records of Perquimans (apart from the birth of his son John) was on the second Monday in Apr 1697, wherein Abraham Hobbs, Leonard Loftin, James Oats, and Richard Nowell were appointed Overseers of the Highways, Perquimans Court Minutes, 1668-1738, p. 63. On 11 Mar 169$^7/_8$, Abraham recorded his livestock mark, Perquimans Court Minutes, 1688-1738, p. 76. In *The Colonial Records of North Carolina*, 2nd ser., vol. 4, *North Carolina Higher-Carolina Higher-Court Records, 1702-1708*, p. 11, we find that on 3 Apr 1702, Abraham Hobbs of the Precinct of Perquimans "not having the feare of god before his Eyes did on or about the 18 or 19th of day of November Last past… did feloniously with force and arms Kill and beare away one hogg of the Value of 18sh..." Although Hobbs plead not guilty, it was declared that he was indeed guilty and should be "banisht out of the Government for Ever." What happened to the perpetrator of this *porkicide* is not clear, but during July Court it was determined that even though Abraham had been banished from "this Government forever," it appeared that he still lurked about. He was thereupon ordered to be taken into custody. This can be found in *The Colonial Records of North Carolina*, 2nd ser., vol. 5, *North Carolina Higher-Court Minutes, 1709-1723*, p. 27. According to p. 29 of the same volume, on Oct 1712, appeared **Mary [__] Hobbs** praying administration as greatest creditor on the goods and chattels of David Wharton of Bath Co., deceased. In or about 1702, Mary Hobbs petitioned the court on behalf of her son Abraham[2], that, since her husband had received a survey of escheated land, the tract be repatented to her son, according to *The Colonial Records of North Carolina*, 2nd ser., vol. 7, *Records of the Executive Council, 1664-1734*, p. 392. What is interesting about these two records in which Mary acted as a "femme sole" is that Abraham was surely still alive; and as a married woman, without her husband's express permssion, Mary would have been unable to petition the court on her own without the help of a "next friend." Was Abraham in hiding, pretending to have vanished or to have died? Was his wife complicit in this, or simply acting on his advice to shift attention away from him?

Abraham Hobbs married **Mary** [__] by 1693-94, although they had only one of their children registered in the Perquimans birth records.

On 27 Mar 1714, John[2] Hobbs received a patent for 416 acres on the south side of the Fork Creek in Pasquotank, adjoining William Joy, the lake, and the creek, according to NC Land Patent Book 8, p. 236. On 15 Aug 1715, he received a patent for 80 acres on the west side of Moyock Creek in Currituck, adjoining John Stroud, the woods, a branch, and the creek. In Mar 1717, John[2] Hobbs was described at "late of Currituck," in *Colonial Records of North Carolina*, 2nd ser., vol. 5, *North Carolina Higher-Court Minutes, 1709-1723*, p. 152. Subsequent records will show that he settled in Pasquotank. According to Pasquotank Co., NC, Deed Book C, p. 286, Francis Hobbs *alias* Martin sold to William Williams, 12 July 1731, land formerly belonging to [her deceased husband] John[2] Hobbs, 360 acres on north east side of Pasquotank River.

Perquimans Co., NC, Deed Book C, no. 11, revealed that Thomas Blitchenden of Perquimans sold on 20 Jan 1728 to Thomas[2] Hobbs of Chowan 50 acres on the north west side of Perquimans River, adjoining James Field, and Moses Rountree. According to Chowan Co., NC, Deed Book G-1, pp. 21-26, dated 20 July 1753, Thomas[2] Hobbs made two deeds of gift—one to son Amos[3], for 175 acres in Chowan, and one to son Guy[3], for 96 acres. Chowan Co., NC, Deed Book E-1, p. 37, dated 10 Oct 1745 revealed that Thomas[2] Hobbs gave to son John[3] Hobbs 165 acres in Chowan.

On 5 Apr 1720, Abraham[2] Hobbs received a patent near Somerton for 166 acres, adjoining John Barefield and a swamp, according to NC Land Patent Book 3, p. 7.

The Children of Abraham Hobbs and Mary [__]:

[1]+ a. **Thomas[2] Hobbs**, born *ca.* 1695; married **Mary** [__].

[2] b. **John[2] Hobbs**, born 4 Dec 1696, Perquimans Register, died testate between 29 Oct 1728 and 14 Oct 1729, Pasquotank, NC Secretary of State loose wills; married, as her first husband, **Francis** [__], who married second, [__] Martin.

[3] c. **Abraham[2] Hobbs**, Jr., married **Millicent** [__].

84. John Hobson, the son of [__] Hobson and his wife Grace[A] [__], who married second, by 1716, Chowan Co., NC, **Edward[3] Smithwick** (Edward[2], Hugh[1]), was born by 1694, and died intestate before Dec 1736, Bertie Co., NC, at which time his widow made a deed of gift to her two children [see below]. A deed in Bertie reveals these relationships: in Deed Book E, p. 6, proved Aug 1736, Robert Anderson of Tyrrell Co., NC, sold to James Legatt 150 acres of land in Kesia Neck, a tract called "Frances," adjoining land of John Smithwick's which formerly belonged to Edward Smithwick, Jr., and left by his last will and testament to his wife Grace, given, in turn, by her to her sons Francis[1] and John[1] Hobson. The deed was witnessed by Grace[1] and William Kennedy.

John Hobson married **Sarah** [__]. He witnessed a deed on 19 Apr 1715 between his stepfather Edward[3] Smithwick and stepbrother John[4] Smithwick, according to Chowan Co., NC, Deed Book B#1, p. 88. On 10 Aug 1736, Sarah Hobson, for love and good will to her son and daughter, gave a slave named Seasor and kitchen utensils to her son Francis[2], and a slave boy named Pomp to her daughter Mary[2], according to Bertie Co., NC, Deed Book E, p. 9

John[1] Hobson had a brother Francis[1] Hobson who married first, Ann [__], according to Bertie Co., NC, Deed Book C, p. 224, dated 9 May 1730. He married second, Elizabeth [__], named in his will, and died testate in Bertie Co., NC, between 26 Feb 1766 and Sept 1768, Bertie Co., NC, Will Book A, p. 93. Francis mentioned his sister Grace[1] (Hobson) Kennedy/Cannaday and her children, as well as neice Mary[2] King and others, to each of whom he gave a shilling. Grace[1] Kennedy witnessed the will of Martin Cromen of Bertie, who died testate between 1 May and Aug 1733, NC Secretary of State loose wills, and made bequests to his brother Thomas Cromen of the village of Balart, Limerick, Ireland, his brother Timothy Cromen, and Grace's children William[2] Kennedy, Jr., and Francis[2] Kennedy.

The Children of John Hobson and Sarah [__]:

[1] a. **Francis[2] Hobson.**
[2]+ b. **Mary[2] Hobson**, died 14 Nov 1810, married **Michael King**, died 13 June 1805, Martin Co., NC, will proved 1811, Martin Co., NC, Will Book 2, p. 2. The exact dates of death were taken from the Bible record of William C.[3] King, son of this couple.

85. Robert Hodges, the son of Robert Hodges, Jr., and [__], was born *ca.* 1668, Isle of Wight Co., VA, and died testate between 30 Mar 1740 and Aug 1742, Bertie Co., NC, his will filed among the NC Secretary of State loose wills. Our Robert Hodges married by 1690, **Ann Branch**, the daughter of George[A] Branch, Sr., and Ann[A] England of Isle of Wight Co., VA (her father Francis[B] England named her and her three sons in his will dated 13 May 1677, Isle of Wight Co., VA, Will & Deed Book 1, p. 144), although they appeared together in the records for the first time as late as 5 Nov 1715, in a deed of land to Daniell Doyell, Isle of Wight Co., VA, Deeds, 1715-1726, p. 22. Robert Hodges purchased land in Bertie from William Gray on 7 Mar $172^6/_7$, according to Bertie Co., NC, Deed Boook B, p. 245. Ann Hodges was still alive 6 Dec 1751, at which time she made a deed of gift of a slave named Joe to her son Elias, Bertie Co., NC, Deed Book H, p. 102. Proof that she was *née* Branch is found in Isle of Wight Co., VA, Deeds, 1715-1726, p. 721, wherein on 25 Oct 1725 she and her husband Robert Hodges sold land which had belonged to her father George Branch.

The Children of Robert Hodges and Ann Branch:
[1] a. **Elias[2] Hodges.**
[2] b. **John[2] Hodges.**
[3]+ c. **Richard[2] Hodges**, will dated 3 Sept 1747, proved 16 Apr 1751, Beaufort Co., NC Secretary of State loose wills; married **Sarah** [__].
[4]+ d. **Ann[2] Hodges**, married **Joseph[1] Moore**, who died testate between 15 Feb 1753 and Feb 1757, Edgecombe Co., NC—his will was filed among the Secretary of State loose wills and also recorded in NC Secretary of State vol. 879, p. 211.
[5] e. **Olive[2] Hodges**, married [__] **Wiggins.**
[6] f. **Mathene/Martha[2] Hodges**, died testate between 31 Aug 1760 and [--] 1761, Johnston Co., NC, NC Secretary of State loose wills, also recorded in Johnston Co., NC, Will Book 1, p. 762; married **Isaac[3] Williams** (John[2-1]).
[7] g. **Sara[2] Hodges**, married **John Cain.**

86. Thomas Hoskins, Sr., was born by 1640 and died testate by Nov 1679, Albemarle Co., NC, in that section which would become Chowan precinct. Unfortunately his will did not survive. In this writer's transcription of William[2] Hoskins' $169^1/_2$ will, he noted that William made a bequest to a sister who might have been named Ann Hall. This caused a problem, since William[2] clearly had a blood sister named Ann[2] (Hoskins) Cox. The discovery of the probate for the now lost will of Thomas *Hodgkins*, dated Nov 1679, indicated that his widow and executrix married Roger Hall. This is, once again, a gift from William Perry Johnson, "Grimes Wills: Major Additions and Corrections," in *Journal of North Carolina Genealogy*, vol. 11, no. 4, pp. 1575-78, especially p. 1577, designated as NC Secretary of State File 874.2, Council Minutes, Wills and Inventories, 1677-1701, p. 153. It was worth considering, therefore, that our Thomas[2] was the son of this Thomas Hodgkins and his wife **Ann** [__] who married second, Roger *Hall*.

On 25 Sept 1663, Thomas Hodgkin received a patent of 1000 acres of land in a bay of the Carolina River, beginning at a small creek called Cannaughsaugh running up to a branch of Mattatomeck Creek, for the transportation of 20 persons, according to VA Land Patent Book 4, p. 93 (584). This was one of the first of the patents from Virginia in what would become Albemarle Co., NC. None of the names of the headrights, however, suggested any North Carolina pioneers. On 27 Sept 1670, Thomas Hoskins petitioned for and was granted administration on the estate of one John Alden, deceased, according to *North Carolina Higher-Court Records, 1670-1696*, p. 4. No connection has been made between the decedent and the *Mayflower* family.

The name of Hoskins' wife, or widow, was revealed in Caroline B. Whitley's *North Carolina Headrights, A List of Names, 1663-1744*, p. 195. On 29 Mar 1680, Ann Hall of Albemarle registered her importation rights for 200 acres for the transportation of 4 persons: John Benfeild, Thomas Twaight, Jno. Alexandr, and Thomas Hodgskins. On that same day, Roger Hall was awarded 100 acres for the transportation of 2 persons: Roger Hall and Ann his wife.

A deed in Chowan confirmed the connection between Thomas *Hodgkin* and Thomas Hoskins. According to Chowan Co., NC, Deed Book C#1, p. 66, dated [--] 1720, John Davis of Bath Co. and his wife Mary, the only daughter and heir of Roger Hall, deceased, of Albemarle Co., sold to Thomas Hoskins of Chowan, planter, 200 acres adjoining Edward Standing and Joseph Gilbert and a branch of Queen Ann's Swamp at Mattacomack Creek, formerly belonging to Roger Hall and now in the actual possession of the grantee. According to the will of Thomas' son William[2], Ann [__] Hoskins-Hall, widow of Thomas[1] Hoskins, was still alive in 1691.

The Children of Thomas Hoskins, Sr., and Ann [__]:

[1] a. **William[2] Hoskins**, died testate after $169^1/_2$, Chowan precinct.

[2]+ b. **Thomas**[2] **Hoskins**, born *ca*. 1670, married 19 Aug 1705, Bromley, Kent, **Mary Bowling**.
[3] c. **Ann**[2] **Hoskins**, married first, before 1691, **Daniel Cox**; second, by 1705, according to Chowan Co., NC, Deed Book W#1, p. 91, **William**[2] **Windley**.

The Children of Roger Hall and Ann [__] Hoskins:
[4] d. **Ann Hall**, died young.
[5] e. **Mary Hall**, married **John Davis**, removed to Bath Co.

87. Thomas Hoskins, Jr., the son of **Thomas Hoskins**, Sr., and Ann [__] who married second, Roger Hall, was born say 1670 in the Albemarle and died testate between 24 Oct 1733 and Apr 1734, Chowan Co., NC, his will filed among NC Secretary of state loose wills. According to J. R. B. Hathaway's *North Carolina Genealogical and Historical Register*, vol. 1, no. 3 [July, 1900], p. 475, Thomas traveled to the parish of Bromley, Kent, England, "the seat of his ancestors," to marry, 19 Aug 1705, **Mary Bowling**, who must have died before 24 Oct 1733, as she is not mentioned in Thomas' will. Thomas Hoskins was the younger brother of William Hoskins, whose NC Secretary of State loose will is so faded as to be almost impossible to decipher. In this will dated 20 Feb 169$^1/_2$, Chowan Co., NC, William Hoskins, of the northeast branch of Matocomack Creek, named the following persons: [1] his brother Thomas Hoskins; [2] his sister Ann who married first, Daniel Cox, and second, **William**[2] **Windley**, the son of **Robert**[1] **Windley**; [3] his nephew Daniel Cox; [4] and, without mentioning her name, the testator's mother [__]. The information concerning the Cox-Windley marriage is derived from a deed dated 8 July 1707 in Chowan Co., NC, Deed Book W#1, p. 84, in which Daniel Cox sold Samuel Patchett his plantation formerly conveyed to him by his father-in-law William Windley. A partial genealogy of the early Hoskins family is provided in "The Edenton Tea Party," in J. R. B. Hathaway, *The North Carolina Historical and Genealogical Register*, vol. 3, no. 1 [January 1903], pp. 116-24, especially the footnotes on pp. 116-17. Hathaway mistakenly identified Thomas Hoskins' Bromley wife as "Elizabeth Bowling," but she is clearly called "Mary" in the marriage register and earlier in vol. 1 [*vide supra*]. Unfortunately, there is no discernible trace of her in the North Carolina records.

On 1 Apr 1745, in Chowan Co., NC, Deed Book E-1, pp. 63-64, William[2] Hoskins made a deed of gift to his "loving" cousin John[3] Charlton, with reversion to John's brother William[3] in case of default of issue.

The Children of Thomas Hoskins and Mary Bowling:
[1] a. **Mary**[2] **Hoskins**, bapt. 8 Sept 1706, Bromley, Kent.
[2] b. **Thomas**[2] **Hoskins**, bapt. 12 Dec 1708, Bromley, Kent, died testate

after 2 Sept 17[--], Chowan Co., NC, Will Book A, p. 31; married **Mary** [__], died testate after 23 Apr 1783, Chowan Co., NC, Will Book A, p. 75.

[3] c. **Sarah^{2} Hoskins**, born *ca.* 1710, married **John Charlton**, who died testate between 13 May 1735 and 15 Apr 1736, Chowan Co., NC, Secretary of State loose wills.

[4]+ d. **Ann^{2} Hoskins**, born *ca.* 1711, married, as his first wife, **William^{2} Luten**, son of **Thomas^{1} Luten**; he married second, by 1744, Francis Hutchins.

[5] e. **Mathew[Martha]^{2} Hoskins**.

[6] f. **William^{2} Hoskins**, died testate after 7 Oct 1766, Chowan Co., NC, Will Book A, p. 36; married **Sarah^{4} Whedbee**, born 23 Jan 1717, Perquimans, daughter of Richard Whedbee and **Sarah^{3} Durant** (John^{2}, George^{1}).

88. William Hunter, weaver, originally of Upper Parish, Nansemond Co., VA, died testate between 4 and 18 Jan $173^{2}/_{3}$, Chowan Co., NC, his will filed among NC Secretary of State loose wills. His odd will mentioned property in Nansemond Co., VA, although it did not name all of his children. On 25 Apr 1701, William Hunter received 240 acres in Upper Parish of Nansemond Co., VA, on the southeast side of the Meherrin river, according to Virginina Land Patent Book 9, p. 309—this was for the transportation of himself, his wife, his daughter Alice, son Nicholas, and a Mary Cohoone. William Hunter married **Ann** [__], named in his will. Ann's will, dated 24 May 1749 and proved Oct 1751, Chowan Co., NC, in NC Secretary of State loose wills, was the document which revealed the married names of the Hunter daughters. According to Chowan Co., NC, Deed Book A#1, pp. 257-59, dated 16 Feb 1742, two of the heirs of William^{1} Hunter—sons Robert^{2} and Isaac^{2} Hunter—recited that their father had received a patent of land 21 Apr 1695 in that part of Nansemond Co., VA, which was cut off into Chowan. The two sons added that a second patent for 100 acres in Chowan had been registered to their father on 30 Aug 1714. The Virginia patent referred to is found in VA Land Patent Book 8, p. 431, dated 21 Apr 1695, to William Hunter, weaver, for 200 acres in the Upper Parish of Nansemond Co., on the east side of the main Cypress Swamp of Bennet's Creek, and on the south side of the further branch of Oysterland Neck, for the importation of four persons [Negro slaves]: Alla, Harry, Shambo, and Ned.

On 4 Feb 1745 in Chowan Co., NC, Deed Book E-1, pp. 87-89, Robert^{2} Hunter, then of Bertie, made a deed of gift to his son-in-law John Gordon, Jr. (who had married his daughter Mary^{3} Hunter) for 170 acres in Chowan, being part of 200 acres which his father William^{1} had left him in his last will and testament. The existence of son Nicholas^{2} Hunter came to light in a deed from

Nicholas' son Isaac[3] Hunter, Jr., to Isaac[2] Hunter, Sr., in Chowan Co., NC, Deed Book C#2, p. 45, dated 2 May 1739, in which the younger Isaac[3] sold his uncle 100 acres of land formerly patented by William[1] Hunter, deceased, and given to his son Nicholas[2] and by Nicholas[2] sold to Isaac[3], Jr. The land in question was on Bennet's Creek where the said Nicholas[2] formerly lived, obviously having been cut off into North Carolina from Nansemond. In the same deed, Isaac[3], Jr., also conveyed a tract of 164 acres formerly patented to Nicholas[2] Hunter and Thomas Davis of Perquimans, dated 9 Mar 1717; and, after having purchased Davis' portion, Nicholas sold the tract to Isaac[3], Jr. Another tract of 100 acres on Lassiter's Branch which had been sold by James Spivey and wife Maragaret of Upper Parish of Nansemond to Isaac[3] Hunter, Jr., "of the same," according to Chowan Co., NC, Deed Book C#1, p. 336, dated 25 Mar 1723, was included. This case of the Sr.-Jr. situation reveals that one must not always assume a father-son relationship.

There is a biography of Theophilus[4] Hunter, *ca.* 1727-1798, a Revolutionary leader, who was the son of Sarah (Hill) and Isaac[3] Hunter, Jr., the son of Nicholas[2] (William[1]), in William S. Powell's *Dictionary of North Carolina Biography*, vol. 3, *H-K*, p. 239. Nicholas Hunter and wife Rebecca [__] of Carteret Co., NC, have been incorrectly identified in several publications as members of this family.

The Children of William Hunter and Ann [__]:

[1] a. **Nicholas[2] Hunter**, of Nansemond Co., VA, married by 28 Apr 1711, according to a patent issued to him, his wife, and Francis Benton (an infant), in Nansemond for 148 acres, in VA Land Patent Book 10, p. 37, **Elizabeth** [__].

[2] b. **Allise[2] Hunter**, married **Edward Arnal/Arnold**. He is almost certainly the intestate decedent of 13 June 1777, Chowan Co., NC, whose estate was divided among William Arnell, Edward Arnell, John Arnell, Richard Arnell, Elizabeth Norfleet, Pleasant Knight, Mary Parker, Bathsheba Arnell, and Esther Arnell, according to Jonathan B. Butcher, "Probate Records in Chowan County, N.C., Bound Miscellaneous Papers, 1694-1799," in the *North Carolina Genealogical Society Journal*, vol. 7. no. 1 [February 1981], p. 19. The original record is listed as vol. 15, pp. 123-125.

[3] c. **William[2] Hunter**, died testate between 21 Mar 1749 and Apr 1750, Chowan, NC Secretary of State loose wills; married **Sarah** [__].

[4] d. **Robert[2] Hunter**, died testate between 3 June and Aug 1753, Bertie Co., NC Secretary of State loose wills; married first, [__]; married second, as her second husband, *ca.* 1736, **Elizabeth[2] (Bryan) Whitmel**.

[5]+ e. **Isaac[2] Hunter**, will dated 17 Apr, proved Apr 1752, Chowan Co.,

NC, NC Secretary of State loose wills, recorded in Secretary of State vol. 881, p. 100; married **Elizabeth Parker**, the daughter of Richard Parker, who died testate between 22 Sept 1749 and Apr 1752, Chowan Co., NC, Secretary of State loose wills. From Estates Records for Richard Parker, Jr., in Edenton District Loose Estates Papers, dated 20 Mar 1778, it appears that most of Richard Parker's property fell into Hertford Co., NC.

[6] f. **Epharim[2] Hunter**, was almost certainly the Ephraim with "now wife" **Ann** [__] who sold land to Robert Knite/Knight, 30 May 1747, Chowan Co., NC, Deed Book E-1, p. 255.

[7] g. **Judeth[2] Hunter**, married [__] **Bland**..

[8] h. **Ann[2] Hunter**, married [__] **Winborne**; he was possibly the William Winborne who died testate between 6 Aug 1748 and May 1761, Northampton Co., NC, Will Book 1, p. 44, naming children, wife Ann, and brothers Phillip and John Winborne.

[9] i. **Easter/Hester[2] Hunter**, married **Robert Knight**, although her married name was spelled "Knigh" in her mother's will; Robert Knight and wife Esther, on 1 Oct 1747, sold 258 acres of land to Thomas Norfleet of Nansemond, Chowan Co., NC, Deed Book E-1, p. 257.

[10] j. **Mary[2] Hunter**.

89. Nicholas Isler was born *ca.* 1661 and died after 1720, Craven Co., NC. According to Henry Z. Jones, *Even More Palatine Families, 18th Century Immigrants to the American Colonies and their German, Swiss and Austrian Origins*, vol. 2, p. 1103, and pp. 1121-22. Nicholas with his wife and five children were in the third Party Rotterdam Departure List, sailing from London 11 June 1709. At that time he was 48 years old, and was listed as a mason and a stonecutter, "Reformed," with sons 15, 8, and 6 years old, and daughters aged 5 and 1 year. The name of his wife is unknown. On 23 July 1713, he purchased from Dennis "Odia" [Odear] a tract of 220 acres on the south side of the Neuse River in Craven Co., according to Craven Co., NC, Court Minutes, 1712-1715, pp. 9-10, and p. 65.

The Children of Nicholas Isler and [__]:

[1]+ a. **Christian[2] Isler**, born *ca.* 1694, Germany, will dated 4 Oct, proved 7 Nov 1747, Craven Co., NC, Secretary of State loose wills, recorded in Secretary of State vol. 878, p. 148; married **Elizabeth[2] Coleman**.

[2] b. **Freidrich[2] Isler**, born *ca.* 1701, died testate *ca.* Sept 1784, Jones Co., NC, Will Book A, p. 38; married first, [possibly a daughter of] **Gillard**; second, **Sarah Bonner**, daughter of Thomas Bonner; she

married second, Thomas Worsley; third, Hardy Bryan; she died testate between 30 June and Sept 1796, Craven Co., NC, Will Book B, p. 12.

[3] c. **John**[2] **Isler**, born *ca.* 1703, died 1784.

[4] d. [**Daughter**][2] **Isler**, born *ca.* 1704.

[5] e. [**Daughter**][2] **Isler**, born *ca.* 1708.

90. Osborne Jeffrreys, the son of Capt. **Simon Jeffreys** and Elizabeth [__] Hilliard, was born say 1710 and died testate Dec 1793, Franklin Co., NC, Will Book A, p. 95. He married **Patience**[2] **Speir**, the daughter of **John**[1] **Speir** and **Patience**[2] **Cotton**, who was born 12 Nov 1725, Bertie Co., NC, and died Oct 1793, Franklin Co., NC. Osborne Jeffreys patented land in Chowan on 28 Feb 1725, 300 acres on the south side of Morratuck River, below the mouth of Fishing Creek, according to NC Land Patent Book 3, p. 242. A sketch of this family can be found in *Order of First Families of North Carolina, Ancestor Registry*, no. 1.

The Children of Osborne Jeffreys and Patience Speir:

[1] a. **William**[2] **Jeffrreys**, born *ca.* 1743, married 30 July 1773, Edgecombe Co., NC (marriage bond, Simon and James Gray, witnesses), **Mary Gray**.

[2]+ b. **Simon**[2] **Jeffrreys**, born *ca.* 1744, died intestate 11 Oct 1812, Franklin Co., NC; married **Sarah**[2] **Norfleet**, the daughter of **Marmaduke**[1] **Norfleet** and second wife Judith Rhodes, of Northampton Co., NC.

[3] c. **Osborn**[2] **Jeffrreys**, born *ca.* 1746, married 3 June 1778, Caswell Co., NC (marriage bond, Robert Dickson, wit.), **Sallie Taylor**.

[4]+ d. **David**[2] **Jeffrreys**, born *ca.* 1748, died testate after 24 Sept 1794, original will only, Franklin Co., NC; he married 3 June 1778, Wake Co., NC (marriage bond, David of Franklin Co., bondsman: John Hunt of Franklin Co., wit: Paul Jeffreys), as her first husband, **Barbara**[4] **Bell**, who married second, William Bowers. She was the daughter of Thomas Bell and Sarah[3] Hicks, granddaughter of Sarah[2] (Reeves) Hicks, and great-granddaughter of **William**[1] **Reeves** of Granville.

[5] e. **Mary**[2] **Jeffrreys**, born *ca.* 1749, died testate after 11 Aug 1811, Franklin Co., NC, Will Book C, p. 232; she married Capt. **John Hunt**, born 1754, died 9 Oct 1807, Franklin Co., NC.

[6] f. **Paul**[2] **Jeffrreys**, born *ca.* 1751, died July 1801, Person Co., NC; he married 10 Feb 1790, Wake Co., NC (marriage bond, Paul Tomkins, bondsman), **Susan Peters**.

[7] g. **Elizabeth**[2] **Jeffrreys**, died before her father, married **Charles Rust**

Eaton, who died testate between 23 Feb 1818 and Nov 1822, Granville Co., NC, Will Book 9, p. 141.

91. Simon Jeffreys, surveyor, whose ancestry is unknown, was born probably around 1680 and died intestate before 8 May 1733, Bertie Co., NC, at which time an inventory of his estate was presented to court by his widow. This record is found in Bertie Co., NC, Court Minutes 1724-1772, p. 43, and an estate division on p. 55, dated 13 Feb 173³/₄. The surviving records (of the following Virginia counties) indicate that Jeffreys spent most of his adult life in James City, Henrico, King and Queen, and Charles City before moving to Bertie Co., NC. On 12 July 1712, while still a surveyor in James City Co., VA, he gained some unwelcome notoriety by having to beg the governor of Virginia's forgiveness on bended knee for a serious slip of the tongue, according to the *Executive Journals of the Council of Colonial Virginia*, vol. 3, *1 May 1705-23 Oct 1721*, p. 313. No less outspoken in the new colony, particularly of Gov. Burrington, Jeffreys implied that the governor "had a commission to rob people," a remark found in Stephen Bradley's *Early Records of North Carolina*, vol. 9, *Colonial Court Records—Estates Papers, 1665-1775* [vol. 1], *A-Gibson*, p. 63. Simon married say 1710, James City Co., VA, **Elizabeth [__] Hilliard**, the widow of Jeremiah Hilliard of James City Co., VA, who had appeared in the Annie Laurie Wright Smith's *The Quit Rents of Virginia, 1704*, p. 44, with 225 acres. Elizabeth Jeffreys died testate between 20 June 1742 and Feb 174²/₃, Northampton Co., NC, Secretary of State loose wills. Elizabeth also left a nuncupative will (more like a codicil) dated 28 Jan 1742 and recorded in Land Grant Book 4, no. 142. Simon Jeffreys' first mention in the court records of Bertie was in July of 1727, according to the *Colonial Records of North Carolina*, vol. 2, *1713-1728*, p. 704 and p. 711. Most of the original research on the connections of Simon Jeffreys was undertaken by the late Mrs. Louise Jeffreys Andrew of Somers Point, New Jersey, who in 1984 wrote a monograph entitled *Marmaduke Norfleet Jeffreys, His Ancestors and Descendants*. A sketch of this family can be found in *Order of First Families of North Carolina, Ancestor Registry*, no. 1.

Elizabeth [__] Hilliard-Jeffreys named the following grandchildren in her will: (i) Jacob, son of Jeremiah; (ii) William, James, Isaac, and Elias, sons of William; (iii) John and Sarah, children of John; (iv) others, Robert, Mary, Sampson, and Jeremiah, who were not assigned to a specific Hilliard child. These children were named in the will of Robert Hilliard of Edgecombe, dated 13 Apr 1743. Jacob and Robert were sons of Jeremiah, deceased, as were Sampson, Mary, and Jeremiah, Jr.

As an addendum to the eternal search for Simon Jeffrey's origins, there has been found a reference to him in the York Co., VA, records. In York Co., VA, Deeds, Orders, Wills, Etc., 1711-1714, p. 169, dated 16 June 1712, Simon

Jeffreys, then of James City Co., was summoned as an wittness for William Smith against John Brookes.

The Children of Jeremiah Hilliard and Elizabeth [__], all born before 1710, James City Co., VA:

[1] a. **John Hilliard** died testate Nov 1748, Northampton Co., NC, Secretary of State loose wills; he married **Mary** [__], whom he named in his will.

[2] b. **Robert Hilliard**, died testate between 13 Apr 1743 and May 1751, Edgecombe Co., NC, Secretary of State loose wills; married, as her first husband,**Charity**[2] **Alston**.

[3]+ c. **Jeremiah**[1] **Hilliard**, died intestate $174^{1}/_{2}$, Edgecombe; married, as her first husband, **Mourning**[2] **Pope**, daughter of **Jacob Pope** and his first wife Mourning [__]. She married second, Joseph Thomas; third, William Pridgen; and fourth George Wimberley [see her sketch under **Jacob**[1] **Pope**].

[4]+ d. **William**[1] **Hilliard**, married **Anne Newsom** [see his sketch].

The Children of Simon Jeffreys and Elizabeth [__] Hilliard, born Henrico Co., VA:

[5]+ e. **Osborne**[2] **Jeffreys**, born 1710-1713, died testate Dec 1793, Franklin Co., NC, Will Book A, p. 95; married *ca.* 1742, Edgecombe Co., NC, **Patience**[2] **Speir**.

[6]+ f. **Elizabeth**[2] **Jeffrreys**, born *ca.* 1720, died after her mention in her brother's 1793 will; married first, **John Boddie**; second, after 1742, **John Pope**, who died intestate in Granville Co., NC.

92. Proprietary Governor **John Jenkins** was born by 1630 and died 17 Dec 1681, Perquimans Co., NC. He married **Johannah** [__], who married second, as his first wife,13 Apr 1682, Perquimans Co., NC, Thomas Harvey, the son of John[A] and [__] Harvey of Snitterfield Parish, Warwickshire, baptized 4 June 1643, Snitterfield, and died testate between 23 Mar and 2 Nov 1699, Perquimans, NC Secretary of State loose wills. Harvey married second, as her first husband, **Sarah**[2] **Laker**, by whom he did have issue.

Johannah [__] Jenkins-Harvey died 27 Mar 1688, Perquimans Co., NC. There is an excellent article on the Governor in William S. Powell's *Dictionary of North Carolina Biograpy*, vol. 3. *H-K*, pp. 277-78. A descendant of Henry Jenkins commissioned a very competent genealogist to determine whether Henry might possibly be a "lost" son of the governor. Neither the governor nor his widow left wills or estates records naming heirs, nor did Thomas Harvey mention Henry in any ancillary way at his own death. It seemed odd indeed that the son of a governor should escape notice so completely in an area of civilization that was quite finite and stable, and one especially containing a pool of individuals so well known to each other. The resesarch done by the genealogist was exhaustive and marshalled evidence of a circumstantial nature which was sufficiently convincing to this writer to persuade him to allow the filiation. Thus Henry has been accepted as a son of the governor.

The Children of John Jenkins and Johannah [__]:

[1]+ a. **Henry Jenkins**, born before 1669, Perquimans, died between 1725-1734, Nansemond Co., VA; married [__].

[2] b. **Joanna Jenkins**, married 9 Sept 1689, Perquimans Co., NC, as his second wife, **Robert Beasley**. There were no children of this marriage.

93. John Jennings, the son of **William Jennings** and Martha [__], was born by 150, Surry Co., VA, and died testate between 13 Aug 1718 and 16 June 1720, Pasquotank Co., NC. His first wife [__], who is unknown (and whom he must have married by 1670-75), was almost certainly the mother of his surviving children. She died before 1680 at which time John Jennings married second, **Dorothy [__] Relfe**, the widow of Dr. Thomas Relfe. He married third, **Ann (Mayo) Pope-Delamare-Scarbrough**, first the widow of Richard Pope, whose will was dated 23 June and proved 15 July 1701, NC Secretary of State loose Wills; by 8 July 1704 and before 23 Oct 1713 she was married, as his second wife, to **Francis**[1] **Delamare**, according to Pasquotank Co., NC, Deed Book A, p. 5 and p. 62. At some point after 1713 she married Augustine Scarbrough (as mentioned in her will), and then John Jennings. Her surviving children were Edward Pope, perhaps Mary Pope, and the Delamare infants. The will of Richard Pope mentioned daughter Mary, under 16 years of age, but Ann Jennings mentioned a Mary Reading, perhaps her now married daughter.

The Children of John Jennings and [__]:

[1] a. **William**[2] **Jennings**, born *ca.* 1672, married, first, *ca.* 1692, Pasquotank Co., NC, [__]; he married second, **Mary [__] Relfe**.

[2]+ b. **Mary**[2] **Jennings**, married **Thomas**[1] **Sawyer**, who died testate after 9 July 1720, Pasquotank Co., NC, Secretary of State vol. 875, p. 233.

[3] c. **Elizabeth**[2] **Jennings**, born *ca.* 1678, married by 1707, **Joseph Reding**.

The Child of John Jennings and Dorothy [__] Relfe:

[4] d. **Dorothy**[2] **Jennings**, born after 1680, *died young*.

94. William Jennings, the immigrant to Virginia, was born by 1625, and died testate between 24 Jan and Apr 1687, in that part of Albemarle precinct which would become Pasquotank Co., NC. His will was filed among NC Secretary of State loose wills. After a somewhat disastrous *début* in Surry Co., VA, he removed to that part of the Albemarle region of North Carolina which would eventually become Pasquotank Co., where he died, an imminently respectable citizen. Jennings entered into the colony of NC sometime between the registration of his land patent, 25 Sept 1663, and the recording of his land warrant, 30 Apr 1680. He married **Martha** [__] who died before the writing of his will in Jan $168^{6}/_{7}$. The Virginia records indicate that William was a cooper, and this trade was certainly one that existed in his family, throughout the generations.

There is a sketch of William Jennings in William S. Powell's *Y^{e} Countie of Albemarle in Carolina*, p. 46, footnote 3. In 1672 he was a member of the Council, and in 1677 a member of the Assembly. See also John Anderson Brayton, "Rolfe/Relfe-Jennings: The Unclosed Case of anUnclosed Case," in *The North Carolina Genealogical Society Journal*, vol. 29, no. 1 [Feb 2003], pp. 3-43.

The Children of William Jennings and Martha [__]:

[1] a. **Ann^{2} Jennings**, born *ca.* 1648, married, first, **William Seares**; second, after 1682, as his first wife, **Paul Lathum**.

[2] b. **Margaret^{2} Jennings**, born *ca.* 1650, married, as his first wife, **Ralph Garnet/Garner**.

[3]+ c. **John^{2} Jennings**, born by 1655, married, first, [__]; he married, second, by 1680, **Dorothy** [__] **Relfe**; he married, third, *ca.* Apr 1715, **Ann (Mayo) Pope-Delamare-Scarborough**.

[4]+ d. **[Daughter]^{2} Jennings**, born by 1660, married, as his first wife, **Thomas Barecock**, who died testate between 1 Jan 1721 and 17 Jan $172^{1}/_{2}$, Pasquotank Co., NC, Secretary of State loose wills.

95. John Jernigan, the son of Thomas Jernigan of Nansemond Co., VA, was born *ca.* 1670, and died testate between 10 Jan and Feb $173^{2}/_{3}$, Bertie Co., NC, his will filed among NC Secretary of State loose wills. He married **Temperance** [__], whom he named in his will. John Jernigan bought land in Bertie on the south side of Ahotsky swamp adjoining John Molton, Jr., from John Molton on 13 Feb 1722, Bertie Co., NC, Deed Book A, p. 32. Much work has been done on the Jernigan ancestry, and articles have appeared by Neil D. Thompson, "The Ancestry of Thomas Jernigan of Nansemond County, Virginia," in *The Virginia Genealogist*, vol. 48, no. 3 [July-September 2004], pp. 163-69, and by John

Anderson Brayton, "A Royal Descent for Thomas Jernigan," in *The Virginia Genealogist*, vol. 50, no. 1 [January-March 2006], pp. 73-74.

The Children of John Jernigan and Temperance [__]:
[1] a. **Henry**[2] **Jernigan**, married **Phebe** [__].
[2] b. **Thomas**[2] **Jernigan**, died 1769; married **Isobell** [__], who died testate between 9 Jan and Apr 1783, Wayne Co., NC, Will Book A, p. 25.
[3] c. **George**[2] **Jernigan** married **Lyda** [__], according to Wayne Co., NC, Deed Book 5, pp. 320-21, dated 14 Aug 1792, in which he gave his son Frederick[3] a tract of 170 acres and son William[3] a tract of 130 acres, both of which had been patented by George[2] on 18 Feb 1763, with the proviso that neither could have the tracts during the lifetime of George or during the eventual widowhood of Lydda. Mills[3] was another son, as evidenced by Wayne Co., NC, Deed Book 5-E, p. 46.
[4]+ d. **David**[2] **Jernigan**, born *ca.* 1700, Nansemond Co., VA, died *ca.* 1779, Wayne Co., NC; married **Patience** [__], alive 10 Oct 1795 when she made a deed of gift to her granddaughter Sallie[4] Bryan, Wayne Co., NC, Deed Book 5-E, p. 244.
[5] e. **James**[2] **Jernigan**.

96. Hannah Kent, the daughter of **Thomas**[1] **Kent** and Ann (Cornell), was born 10 May 1673, Perquimans Co., NC, and died before 11 Apr 1730, Craven Co., NC. She married, first, by 1690, **John**[2] **Smithwick**, the son of **Hugh**[1] **Smithwick** and wife Elizabeth [__], who died testate between 28 Aug 1696 and 6 Jan $169^{6}/_{7}$, NC Secretary of State loose wills. She married second, *ca.* 1697, **Farnefold**[1] **Green I**, the son of Timothy Green and Ann [__], born 30 May 1674, St. Stephens Parish, Northumberland Co., VA, and died testate after 26 Oct 1711, Bath Co., NC. Hannah married third, after 1711, **Richard Graves** of Craven Co., NC, who died testate between 11 Apr and 16 Sept 1730, his will filed among NC Secretary of State loose wills. She and her children by her marriage to Farnefold Green were named in Richard Graves' will. For the record, Hannah was not *née* Gonsalvo.

The Children of John Smithwick and Hannah Kent:
[1] a. **Sarah**[2] **Smithwick**, *died without issue.*
[2] b. **Ann**[2] **Smithwick**, will dated 5 Nov 1711, Craven Co., NC, Court of Pleas & Quarter Sessions, 1712-1715, p. 12, also NC Secretary of State loose wills.

The Children of Farnifold Green I and Hannah (Kent) Smithwick:

[3] c. **Thomas² Green**.
[4] d. **John² Green**.
[5]+ d. **Farnefold² Green II**, will dated 15 July 1749, Craven Co., NC, Wills, Deeds, Inventories, 1749-1777, p. 193; married **Sarah** (said to be **Graves**).
[6]+ e. **James² Green**, born *ca*. 1710, Bath Co., NC, will proved Dec 1788, Craven Co., NC, Will Book A, p. 183; married [__].
[7] g. **Titus² Green**.
[8]+ h. **Elizabeth² Green**, born *ca*. 1700, married 15 May 1715, Bath Co., NC, according to the Shine family Bible, **Daniel¹ Shine**, died testate in Craven Co., NC, between 5 May and Aug Court 1757, his will filed in the NC Secretary of State loose wills and recorded in NC Secretary of State vol. 880, p. 191.
[9] i. **Jane² Green**.

97. Thomas Kent was a resident of Portsmouth, Kent Co., Rhode Island, when he executed a letter of attorney to his son-in-law Laurence Gonzales (Gonsalles, Consalvo, etc.), 28 Mar 1672, to convey Kent's eight acres of land in Portsmouth to Witt Hall. The tract in question had originally been granted to a Stephen Wilcocks. This information is contained in Dorothy Worthington, editor, *Rhode Island Land Evidences*, vol. 1, *1649-1696, Abstracts*, f. 14, pp. 17-18. Kent was born by 1630 and died 2 June 1678, Perquimans Co., NC. He married, *ca*. 1650, **Ann Cornell**, the daughter of Thomas^A Cornell, Sr., and Rebecca^A Briggs, born *ca*. 1630, Saffron-Walden, Essex, England, and died after 1715, Beaufort Co., NC. Ann (Cornell) Kent married second, *ca*. 1679, Perquimans, Thomas Lepper, who died testate between 23 Oct 1715 and 20 July 1718, Craven Precinct, Beaufort Co., NC, his will filed among NC Secretary of State loose wills, also recorded in Secretary of State vol. 875, p. 163. That Rebecca (Briggs) Cornell died testate between 2 Sept 1664 and 1673, Portsmouth, RI, and that her will, found among unrecorded papers at the Portsmouth Town House, named her daughter Ann [__] and Ann's husband Thomas [__], are recorded in *The American Genealogist*, vol. 19, no. 3 [Jan 1943], p. 132. According to John Osborne Austin's *Genealogical Dictionary of Rhode Island*, pp. 54-55, Rebecca Cornell gave ten acres of land in Portsmouth to her "son and daughter Kent," 15 Aug 1659. There is an excellent article by William Perry Johnson on the Kent family in *The Journal of North Carolina Genealogy*, vol. 10, no. 4 [Winter 1964], pp. 1379-83, although Johnson was unaware of the now documented Rhode Island connection.

The Daughters of Thomas Kent and Ann Cornell:
[1] a. **Sarah² Kent**, married before 1684, first, as his second wife,

Lawrence Gonsalvo, Sr., who died testate after 25 Dec 1687, NC Secretary of State loose wills; second, 1 June 1689, Perquimans, **John Johnson**, who died testate between 10 Sept 1693 and 9 Apr 1694, NC Secretary of State loose wills, also recorded in Secretary of State vol. 874.2, p. 44; third, 6 Jan $169^{7}/_{8}$, Perquimans, **William Long**, who died testate between 2 Jan 1701 and the last Tuesday in July 1712, NC Secretary of State loose wills, also recorded in Secretary of State vol. 875, p. 54.

[2] b. **Rebecca**[2] **Kent**, married first, *ca.* 1675, **William Wyatt**; second, 7 Mar $168^{8}/_{9}$, Perquimans, **Thomas Long**, who died testate between 21 Sept and 10 Oct 1721, Perquimans, NC Secretary of State loose wills, also recorded in Secretary of State vol. 876, p. 136.

Born Perquimans:

[3] c. **Anne**[2] **Kent**, married 10 June 1679, Perquimans, **James Hogg**.

[4] d. **Elizabeth**[2] **Kent**, born 1 June 1667, married first, 8 Nov 1683, **William**[2] **Charles**, Jr.; second, 11 Aug 1687, Perquimans, **Giles Long**, who died testate between 12 Feb $169^{1}/_{2}$ and 13 Feb 1712, NC Secretary of State loose wills.

[5] e. **Mary**[2] **Kent**, born 14 Feb $16^{69}/_{70}$, married 30 July 1690, Perquimans, **Thomas Pierce**, born 7.8.1669, Perquimans Monthly Meeting, died testate 1732, Perquimans, NC Secretary of State loose wills, the son of John Pierce and Mary (Scott).

[6]+ f. **Hannah**[2] **Kent**, born 10 may 1673, married first, *ca.* 1690, **John**[2] **Smithwick**; second, *ca.* 1697, **Farnefold**[1] **Green I**; third, after 1711, **Thomas Graves**.

98. Michael King, Sr., was born by 1640, possibly in Norwich, Norfolk, England, and died testate, *ca.* 1700, in Nansemond, although there was an ancillary probate of his will in North Carolina. Neither will survived, but the North Carolina version was noted as having been proved in Perquimans on 29 Oct 1702 by William and John Early, according to *The Colonial Records of North Carolina, Higher Court Records of North Carolina*, vol. 2, *1697-1701*, p. 402. Michael King, Sr., is said to have married **Elizabeth** [ ]**ry**, whose last name is too faint in the family Bible to decipher correctly. His first patent of land was in the Upper Parish of Nansemond for 300 acres, dated 22 Apr 1667, adjoining lands of Symon Symmonds, Evan Griffith, Willm Pope, and Israel Johnson, according to VA Land Patent Book 6, p. 193. Next he was granted 600 acres of land which had escheated from Robt. Brashure, deceased, dated 18 Sept 1671, VA Land Patent Book 6, p. 479. Finally, he received, on 24 Feb $167^{5}/_{6}$, 900 acres in the Upper Parish of Nansemond, on the way to South Key at a place now called "Kingston," near the head of Somerton Swamp, adjoining John Winborne, Bream, and Robinson, VA Land Patent Book 6, p. 597.

Fortunately, in Henry Lee King's *A King Genealogy: Some Descendants of Michael King of Nansemond County, Virginia, 1667-1987*, pp. 1-2, a Bible record existing in the family of Solomon^{4} King (Charles^{3}, William^{2}, Michael^{1}), provides the origins for Michael, Sr., and the list of children below. William^{2} King and Michael^{2} King, Jr., patented 840 acres of land in the Upper Parish of Nansemond on 20 Apr 1694, on Battles Clear Ground, according to VA Land Patent Book 8, p. 331. Later on 23 Oct 1703, William^{2} patented 541 acres in the Upper Parish of Nansemond on "Kings" branch of the Cypress Swamp, according to VA Land Patent Book 9, p. 573. This land would soon (in 1728) be cut off into Chowan and eventually into Gates, decades later. As a matter of fact, William^{2}'s son Henry^{3}, after William's death, on 28 May 1728 patented the same 541 acres of Cypress Swamp, according to NC Land Patent Book 5, p. 83.

The Children of Michael King, Sr., and Elizabeth [ ]ry:

[1] a. **Nathan^{2} King**, mentioned in a patent to William Baker of Chowan, who received on 27 May 1728, 500 acres in Chowan on north side of Bennets Creek near Summerton Creek, and John Ellison *alias* Nathan King, NC Land Patent Book 3, p. 235. Did Nathan change his name?

[2]+ b. **William^{2} King**, born *ca.* 1673, Nansemond Co., VA, died intestate 1728, Chowan Co., NC; married [__].

[3] c. **Michael^{2} King**, Jr., died testate between 20 May and 29 Oct 1741, Bertie, NC Secretary of State loose wills; patented 84 acres in Nansemond adjoining a tract called "King Stone," taken up by "old Mr. King," dated 20 Apr 1694, VA Land Patent Book 8, p. 345; he married by 19 Apr 1721, **Isobel** [__], according to Chowan Co., NC, Deed Book F#1, p. 103; as a widow on 9 Aug 1742, Bertie Co., NC, Deed Book F, p. 381, she made a deed of gift to her son **Henry**^{3} of a Negro slave Cloe; later on 23 Sept 1742, she made a deed of gift of all the Negroes named in her husband's will to her children Michael^{3}, Henry^{3}, John^{3}, Cathrine^{3}, Isabell^{3}, Penelope^{3}, and Mary^{3}.

[4]+ d. **Henry^{2} King** of Nansemond Co., VA, died testate between 22 Feb 1714, and Apr 1716, NC Secretary of State vol. 875, p. 100; although he did not name his wife, he married by 1684, **Catherine** [__], who according to Chowan Co., NC, Deed Book B#1, p. 456, married second, by 4 Apr 1717, Gerard Lynch. While still a widow in 1716, Catherine/Katherine received a patent of 600 acres on the Middle Swamp of Salmon Creek, in Chowan, according to NC Land Patent Book 8, p. 130. See *Ancestor Biographies*, vol. 2, for a discussion of Catherine (Clarke) King.

[5] e. **John^{2} King**, patented 443 acres of land in the Upper Parish of

Nansemond, near head of Sumerton Swamp, adj. land of his father, Michael King, John Winbourn, and Wm. Breen, dated 31 Oct 1716, VA Land Patent Book 10, p. 309; he died testate between 5 Jan 174³/₄ and July 1749, Onslow Co., NC, Secretary of State vol. 877, p. 312; he married **Presilla** [__].

[6] f. **Elizabeth² King**.

99. George⁽²⁾ Kornegay, the son of **John George⁽¹⁾ Kornegay** and [__], was born *ca.* 1704 in the Upper Palatinate of the Rhine Valley, Germany, and died testate between 21 and 29 Nov 1773, Craven Co., NC, Craven loose wills. His entire family, save for him, was killed in the Tuscarora Indian Massacre on 22 Nov 1711. He is alleged to have married first, **Mary** [__] who must have predeceased him, but the wife he named in his will was **Susannah** [__], who married second, Charles Stevenson. On p. 28 of Jones Co., NC, Land Entries, 1779-1781, dated 24 June 1779, Martin Frank received a grant of 360 acres, described as on the north side of the Trent, and adjoining the land of Susannah Stevenson, wife of Charles Stevenson, who has died by 1792-1794, according to an undated lawsit in Jones Co., NC, Deed Book G, p. 388, in which his estate had to sell a Negro slave to pay debts.

A deed in Jones Co., NC, leads one to wonder whether George, Sr., had a wife named Mary at all. In Jones Co., NC, Deed Book G, , p. 113, dated 6 June 1792, Daniel² Kornegay sold to Samuel McCubbins all his right to a dividend of 320 acres of land, which was the "maidens land of his mother," Susana Stevenson, which at any time might become his own property by right of his mother.

The Children of John George Kornegay and [__], born Craven Co., NC:

[1] a. **John² Kornegay**, called "eldest son in father's will,"died testate between 26 Jan 1790 and Feb 1800, Jones Co., NC, Will Book A, p. 242; married **Rachel** [__], named in his will.

[2] b. **Daniel² Kornegay**, died testate between 23 Sept and Nov 1802, Jones Co., NC, Will Book A, p. 265; married **Matilda** [__], named in his will.

[3] c. **Elijah² Kornegay**.

[4] d. **Jacob² Kornegay**, married 19 July1777, Duplin Co., NC (marriage bond), **Mary Ward**.

[5]+ e. **George² Kornegay**, died testate between 31 Jan and Oct 1808, Duplin Co., NC, Will Book A, p. 266; married first, **Margaret** [__]; second, **Mourning (Stevens) Wiggins**.

[6] f. **William² Kornegay**.

[7] g. **Mary² Kornegay**, married **Edward Cornwallis DeBruhle**.

[8] h. **David[2] Kornegay**, died testate between 25 Apr and June 1784, Jones Co., NC, Will Book A, p. 34; married **Lettice** [__], who died testate between 1 Jan 1786 and Mar 1789, Jones Co., NC, Will Book A, p. 49; he mentioned brother Abraham[2] Kornegay in his will; she named sister Jane [__] Smith, wife of brother-in-law David Smith.

[9] i. **Joseph[2] Kornegay**.

[10] j. **Abraham[2] Kornegay**, died testate between 19 June 1809 and Mar 1810, Craven Co., NC, Will Book C [1810-1821], p. 5; he made bequests to the children of brothers John[2], Jacob[2], George[2], David[2], Daniel[2], and William[2]; he named nephew Daniel Simmons.

100. John George[(1)] Kornegay, husbandman and winedresser, was included on a list of poor Germans lately arrived from the Palatine (the Rhine River region) into England, around the parish of St. Catherine's, London. This document was labeled the "First Party List," and was dated 6 May 1709. John George was then aged 38, and therefore born *ca.* 1671; although his wife was listed with him, she was neither named nor assigned an age. Almost two years later, after having sailed to Craven Co., NC, in the "New World" with Baron Christopher de Graffenreid in Jan 1710, on 22 Nov 1711, the entire Kornegay family, except for son George[2], was killed in a raid by the Tuscarora Indians. Therefore, all Kornegays are descended from this surviving son. According to Henry Z. Jones, in *Even More Palatine Families, 18th Century Immigrants to the American Colonies and their German, Swiss, and Austrian Origins*, vol. 2, p. 809, and pp. 1022-36, especially pp. 1034-36, the name in Germany was originally *Gnäge*, which is actually closer to the way the name is pronounced in America (Kor-nĭ′-gē), than phonetically (Kor′-nuh-gay).

The Child of John George Kornegay and [__], born Upper Palatinate of the Rhine Valley, Germany:

[1]+ a. **George[2] Kornegay**, born 1704, died testate between 21 and 29 Nov 1773, Craven Co., NC, loose wills; married first, **Mary** [__]; second, **Susannah** [__], who married second, Charles Stevenson.

101. Benjamin Laker, the son of Thomas[A] Laker and Elizabeth[A] Swann, was baptized 13 Nov 1636, Dorking, Surrey, and died testate 21 Apr 1701, Castleton's Creek, Perquimans Co., NC, his will filed among the NC Secretary of State loose wills. He married in England, first, by 1662, **Elizabeth** [__], who died before 11 Feb 1686, Perquimans Co., NC. He married second, 11 Feb 1686, Perquimans Co., NC, **Jane** [__] **Dey**, who died 28 Feb 1695, Perquimans Co., NC. Laker married third and last, 17 Mar 1696, Perquimans Co., NC, **Juliana**

(**Hudson**) **Taylor**, who died 3 Dec 1738, Perquimans Co., NC, the daughter of Henry^{A} Hudson. All of Laker's children were by his first wife and were baptized at Betchworth, Surrey. He was in the Albemarle as early as 5 Jan 1693, according to old Albemarle Land Warrants and Surveys, 1681-1706. A sketch of this family can be found in *Order of First Families of North Carolina, Ancestor Registry*, no. 1. The late George Stevenson wrote an extremely informative article on Benjamin Laker's connection with the early Baptists in the *Dictionary of North Carolina Biography*,

The Children of Benjamin Laker and Elizabeth [__], born or baptized Betchworth, Surrey, England:

[1] a. **Elizabeth^{2} Laker**, baptized 4 Oct 1663, died 27 July 1685, Perquimans Co., NC.

[2] b. **Benjamin^{2} Laker**, baptized 18 June 1665, *died young*.

[3] c. **Mary^{2} Laker**, born 5 May 1667, died 26 Mar 1683.

[4]+ d. **Sarah^{2} Laker**, born 26 Oct 166[ ], married first, as his second wife, *ca*. 1687, Perquimans Co., NC, **Thomas Harvey**; second, as his first wife, 17 Jan 1702, Perquimans Co., NC, **Christopher Gale**.

[5]+ e. **Lydia^{2} Laker**, born 7 Feb 1672, married first, 21 Jan 1689, Perquimans Co., NC, **George Bleighton**; second, *ca*. 1704, Surry Co., VA, **Francis Clements**.

[6] f. **Lewesia^{2} Laker**, born 22 July 1675, *died young*.

[7] g. **Ruth^{2} Laker**, born 28 Sept 1679, married first, 16 Oct 1701, Perquimans Co., NC, **James Minge**; second, **Richard^{2} Sanderson**, Jr.

[8] h. **Deborah^{2} Laker**, born 4 May 1682.

102. Katherine [__] **Langston** was identified as the widow of **John Langston** who died before 20 Apr 1694, Nansemond Co., VA. On that date, "Catherine Langstone," widow of John Langston, was granted 380 acres of land in Nansemond Co., VA, on the Cypress branches of the Sarum Creek, for the importation of eight persons, in VA Land Patent Book 8, p. 335. Katherine died intestate after 6 June 1699, her last mention in the VA Land Patents, Book 9, p. 190, at which time John Nicholls was granted 249 acres of land in the upper parish of Nansemond, adjoining Katherine "Langstone," for the transportation of 5 persons. According to Chowan Co., NC, Deed Book E-1, pp. 255-57, in a deed dated 30 May 1747 from Ephraim Hunter and "now" wife Anne to Robert Knite, Katherine Langston's patent on the Cypress Creeks had been cut off into Chowan. Further inspection in Chowan Co., NC, Deed Book G-1, pp. 177-78, dated 15 Apr 1749, reveals that the land was located in Chowan as early as 30 July 1726, at which time John^{2} Langston repatented it.

The Child of John Langston and Katherine [__]:
[1]+ a. **John[2] Langston**, died after 10 Dec 1747, Nansemond Co., VA; married [__].

103. Robert Lanier was born *ca.* 1670, St. Michael's Parish, Barbados, and died testate between 20 Sept 1744 and Mar 174⁴/₅, Tyrrell Co., NC Secretary of State loose wills. He married **Sarah Barker**, the daughter of John[A] Barker of Surry Co., VA, who named her in his will dated 9 Oct 1713 and recorded 19 May 1714, Surry Co., VA, Deeds, Wills, Etc., No. 6, p. 191. John Barker's wife Grace[A] [__] also named her daughter Sarah Lanier in her will dated 10 June 1724, recorded 18 Aug 1725, Surry Co., VA, Deeds, Wills, Etc., No. 7, p. 599.

Robert Lanier appeared as a witness to a deed in Chowan on 24 Aug 1711 between William and Martha Bush to William Hooker in Chowan Co., NC, Deed Book W#1, p. 90. In Apr of 1711, Robert proved 11 rights, although the names have not appeared in any of the usual records, Chowan Co., NC, Deed Book W#1, p. 109. He purchased from Anthony Williams 150 acres of land on 21 July 1713, Chowan Co., NC, Deed Book W#1, p. 151. Finally, on 22 July 1719, Robert Lanier with wife Sarah sold 100 acres of land at the mouth of Horse Hung Branch to Isaac Zehenden, Chowan Co., NC, Deed Book B#1, p. 7.

Louise Ingersoll's *Lanier Family* has been a standard reference for Lanier genealogy since it was published, although it does not always contain the documentation for its material. The posterity of Robert Lanier is found on pp. 411-33 of that monograph. Ingersoll identifies this Robert as the son of Robert[A] Lanier, bapt. 22 May 1642, Greenwich, Kent [the son in turn of Clement[B] and Hannah[B] (Collett)], and his wife Rebecca[A] [__], who migrated to Barbados. Ingersoll further posits that our Robert was the brother of Lemuel and Clement Lanier, the latter of whom was baptized 21 Aug 1678, St. Michael's Parish, Barbados.

Robert Lanier named all his children in his will, but he did not list his married daughters' husbands by their names. Therefore, grandchildren John[3] Bryan, Adam[3] Lanier, Sarah[3] and Mary[3] Gilbert have not been assigned to their parents.

The Children of Robert Lanier and Sarah Barker:
[1] a. **Jean[2] Lanier**.
[2] b. **Sarah[2] Lanier**.
[3]+ c. **Elisebeth[2] Lanier**, died testate between 1 Mar and 9 June 1752, Tyrrell Co., NC Secretary of State loose wills; married **Thomas[2] Daniel (Owen[1])**, who died testate between 11 July and 14 Sept 1749, Tyrrell Co., NC Secretary of State loose wills.

[4] d. **Annanazah Christanah**[2] **Lanier**.
[5] e. **Grace**[2] **Lanier**, married [__].
[6] f. **Samarah**[2] **Lanier**, married [__].
[7]+ g. **William**[2] **Lanier**, born *ca*. 1710, died 17 Aug 1789, Beaufort Co., NC; married **Ann Martha Hill**.
[8] h. **John**[2] **Lanier**, married **Sarah** [__].

104. John[1] **Lee**, Sr., died testate by 1739 in that part of Bertie which would eventually become Hertford Co., NC, although his will has not survived. He received a land grant for 960 acres in Nansemond Co., VA, on the east side of the Sumerton Creek on 20 Apr 1694, according to VA Land Patent Book No. 8, p. 341. After William Byrd's 1728 survey, this land fell into Chowan Co., NC. The name of his wife does not appear in the records. He also received a land patent in Bertie on 26 Mar 1723 on Indian Creek, according to NC Land Patent Book No. 3, p. 128. The list of the 20 headrights in the 1694 land grant includes, among other names with an arguably Leceistershire origin—Goodale and Redfearn—the name of one *Dannit* Abney, rendered in most publications incorrectly as "Dennis." Dannett Abney, the fourth son of George Abney and Bathshua [__], was baptized 26 Feb 1660, St. Mary's, Leicester, Leicestershire, died testate after 5 Mar 1732 in Spotsylvania Co., VA, Will Book A, p. 209, and is said to have married *ca*. 1702, Mary Lee, daughter of Rev. Joseph Lee of Cotesbach near Lutterworth, Leicestershire, the headright's stepsister [see below]. Her mother Bathshua [__] Abney had married second, Rev. Joseph Lee. This Abney descent from Edward I is sketched out in Patrick W. Montague-Smith's (woefully undocumented) "An Unrecorded Line of Descent from King Edward I of England with some Early Settled American Descendants," in *The Genealogist*, vol. 5, no. 2 [Fall 1984], pp. 131-57, especially p. 151.

The will of Rev. Joseph Lee of the town of Leicester, dated 8 June 1691 and proved 27 July 1694 by his daughter Ann (Lee) Marriott, the wife of John Marriott, was recorded in the Prerogative Court of Canterbury (PCC 1694, vol. 123, f. 130) collection. The testator named the following persons: [1] his wife, the widow Bathshua [__] Abney-Lee, and mentioned a bequest left her by her late son Abraham Abney; [2] his eldest son Joseph Lee; [3] his second son Nathaniel Lee; [4] his daughter Ann Marriott; [5] his grandson Phillip Lee, son of Nathaniel Lee; [5] and his third son Samuel Lee. To his fourth son John Lee, he gave thirty pounds, "in case he shall survive and overlive me and my said Wife...." (A putative daughter Mary Lee was not named in Joseph's will, which may or may not be significant.) Executrix was daughter Ann Marriott, and overseers were the testator's following kinsmen: William Smith of Catthorpe, flaxman, William Orton of Leics, mercer, and Samuel Marshall of Leicester, mercer. It is probable that John Lee, the patentee of Nansemond, described in language indicating he was either distant or in parts (and condition) unknown, was this fourth son. Unfortunately, none of the names given John[1] Lee's colonial children reflect the Leicestershire ancestry. I am grateful to OFFNC member **#71** for the information concerning the Lee-Abney connection.

There is much information on the internet concerning the Abney family, some of which is even documented with real sources—*i.e.*, things that one can hold in one's hand—and some which is absolute garbage. One source states that Paul Abney, Dannett's brother, married Dannett's widow, a daughter of Rev. Joseph Lee, with no documentation. This would have been bigamy in Virginia even as late as the 1940s, and there would be scorching court records concerning that major religious infraction.

Information concerning the land of John Lee, Sr., and the names and testamentary disposition of his children have been taken from Henry Lee King, *Descendants of John Lee in Bertie and Edgecombe County, North Carolina, A Report for the Henry Lee Society* (1995). Proof of each child's relationship to the progenitor will be discussed briefly. Godrey[2] Lee came into possession of his father's 1694 patent. According to Bertie Co., NC, Deed Book E, p. 522, Joshua[2] Lee and wife Mary on 22 Aug 1739 sold land on Indian Creek in Bertie to William Battle, the land being described as patented formerly by John[1] Lee, deceased, and left in his last will and testament to Joshua[2] Lee. According to Sampson-Duplin Co., NC, Deed Book 1, p. 396, dated 14 Feb 1764, in a deed from Zebulon Hollingsworth to Henry Allen, Joshua[2] Lee was referred to as being deceased.

The Children of John Lee and [__]:

[1] a. **Richard[2] Lee**, died testate between 1 Apr and May 1756, Edgecombe Co., NC, Secretary of State loose wills, married [__].

[2] b. **Mary[2] Lee**, married **Thomas Thorne**, proved by Northampton Co., NC, Deed Book 1, p. 32, dated 23 May 1741, in which Thomas and Mary Thorne sold land bequeathed by her father John Lee, deceased, patented 1 Apr 1723.

[3] c. **Joshua[2] Lee**, died by 1764, Duplin Co., NC; married **Mary** [__].

[4] d. **[Daughter][2] Lee**, married [almost certainly] **Henry Gay**.

[5] e. **William[2] Lee**, died after 1752, Bertie Co., NC; married **Martha** [__], who signed with him on a deed of gift to his children Joshua[3], Francis[3], and Ann[3] Lee, dated 25 Jan 1752, Bertie Co., NC, Deed Book G, p. 509.

[6]+ f. **John[2] Lee**, Jr., died testate between 12 Mazy 1788 and 2 Apr 1789, Onslow Co., NC, Will Book 3, p. 22; married first, **Mary** (thought to be **King**); second, **Rachel Mashburn**.

[7] g. **Godfrey[2] Lee**, died 1748, Northampton Co., NC, married **Sarah** [__], mentioned with him on a deed dated 12 Nov 1739, Bertie Co., NC,

Deed Book E, p. 521, to Thomas Tarne.

105. John Lee, Jr., the son of **John Lee**, Sr., was born *ca.* 1705, Nansemond Co., VA, and died testate between 12 May 1788 and 2 Apr 1789, and recorded in Onslow Co., NC, Will Book 3, p. 22 (in Zae Gwynn's abstracts, vol. 1, p. 723). He named all his children except daughter Elizabeth^2, and only Penelope^2 Marshburn was identified as married. John Lee first purchased land in Onslow before June 1765, from George Brinson, according to a mutilated deed recorded in Onslow Deed Book H, p. 10. On 5 Feb 1770, he sold back to George Brinson 10 acres on Meeting House Branch on the New River and Evans' line, which had been part of a patent to Bringon dated 23 Apr 1761, according to Onslow Co., NC, Deed Book I, p. 30. He married first, **Mary** [__], and second, in Onslow Co., NC, **Rachel Mashburn**, the daughter of Daniel Mashburn. The will of Daniel Mashburn was dated 20 Jan 1783 and recorded in Onslow Co., NC, Will Book 3, p. 36. He named wife Elizabeth and daughter Rachel Lee, among others. The will of Henry Rhodes of New River in Onslow, dated 14 Sept, proved 4 Dec 1751, was recorded in Craven Co., NC, Deed Book 5, p. 206, named son-in-law Daniel "Mashbone" and granddaughter Elizabeth Mashbone. Rachel (Mashburn) Lee died testate 14 Oct 1800, leaving a nuncupative will recorded in Onslow Co., NC, Will Book A, p. 76 (in Zae Gwynn's abstracts, vol. 2, p. 1373). She named daughter Elizabeth Lee with John Gornto and Thomas Pitts swearing to the document's authenticity.

John Lee lived on his father's 1694 grant which had originally been for land in Nansemond, and which eventually became part of Hertford and then Gates Co., NC. This information is found also in Henry Lee King, *Descendants of John Lee in Bertie and Edgecombe County, North Carolina, A Report for the Henry Lee Society* (1995), p. 41. Information on the marriage of John and Mary's daughters can be obtained in Reba Shropshire Wilson and Betty Shropshire Glover, *The Lees and Kings of Virginia and North Carolina, 1636-1976*, p. 41. The chapter on this generation is fairly reliable, although the authors confused their Lees with the Leighs of Bath.

The Children of John Lee and Mary [__]:

[1]+ a. **Henry^2 Lee**, born *ca.* 1738, Edgecombe Co., NC, died testate 1808, Guilford Co., NC, Will Book A, p. 222; married **Sarah Sholar**, daughter of John Sholar of Bertie who died testate between 12 Aug 1791 and May 1792, Bertie Co., NC, Will Book D, p. 200.

[2] b. **Jacob^2 Lee**.

[3] c. **Sarah^2 Lee**, married 8 May 1800, Onslow Co., NC (marriage bond, "Grunto," Henry Mashburn, bondsman), **John Goronto**, who died testate between 2 June 1828 and Feb 1835, Onslow Co., NC, Will

Book B, p. 141 (Zae Gwynn's abstracts, vol. 2, p. 1389).

[4] d. **Mary^2 Lee**. She was said to have married John King in 1786, but a marriage bond for Mary *King* and John King exists in Onslow on that date.

[5] e. **Penelope^2 Lee**, married by 1788, **Joseph Mashburn**, who died testate between 7 Nov 1815 and Jan 1816, Onslow Co., NC, Will Book A, p. 84 (in Zae Gwynn's abstracts, vol. 2, p. 1374).

[6] f. **Agabail^2 Lee**, married 29 May 1797, Onslow Co., NC (marriage bond), **Kirkham Orrell.**

Child of John Lee and Rachel Mashburn:

[7] g. **Elizabeth^2 Lee.**

106. James Leigh, Sr., was born *ca.* 1670, according to a deposition taken in Accomack Co., VA, in Mar $169^4/_5$, found in Accomack Co., VA, Orders, 1690-1697, p. 147. Leigh died testate between 23 Sept and Oct 1728, Bath Co., NC, his will filed among the NC Secretary of State loose wills. Leigh's bequest of a tract called "Accomack Entry" to his son John Leigh provided his descendants with the clue which lead to the discovery of his origins. James Leigh married first, by Mar $169^2/_3$, Accomack Co., VA, **Sarah Helmot**, a servant of Col. John Wise, the former of whom in Feb $169^0/_1$ was brought into court for having had an illegitimate child named William [__], according to Accomack Orders, 1690-1697, p. 15. The clue which linked the Accomack colonist with the immigrant to Bath was Leigh's posting, on 7 Apr 1702, the news that he was removing from Accomack to North Carolina, Accomack Co., VA, Deeds, Wills, etc., 1691-1715, p. 287. Sarah (Helmot) Leigh was deceased by 1716, by which time James Leigh had married second, **Elizabeth (Rogers) Durham/Dereham**, the widow of the reprehensible Thomas Dereham, and the sister of Hannah (Rogers) Cockerham, who in Oct 1701 had made an entry of 640 acres for the transportation of James Leigh, his wife Sarah, and their children into North Carolina. This can be found in Caroline B. Whitley's *North Carolina Headrights, A List of Names, 1663-1744*, p. 204: James Leigh, 10 rights, land entry by Hannah Cockarum and since sold to Leigh: James Leigh, James Leigh, Jr., Sarah Leigh, Sr., Sarah Leigh, Jr., Mary Leigh, William Holeman, Patience Leigh, John Leigh, Eliz. Leigh, and Sarah Depee. On 18 July 1716, "Mrs. Elizabeth Dereham, now the wife of Jams. Leigh," was mentioned in a deposition by Martin Frank for the General Court, found in *The Colonial Records of North Carolina*, 2nd ser., *North Carolina Higher-Court Minutes, 1709-1723*, p. 124. The will of Thomas Dereham's daughter Elizabeth was dated 17 July 1716, Beaufort Co., NC, Deed Book 1, p. 276, and named, among others, father-in-law James Leigh, Patience Leigh, Elizabeth Leigh, and John Leigh. Further proof of these relationships can be found in the will of Joseph Rodgers of Bath County "in Pamplico Land," proved 2 Jan $170^4/_5$ and filed among the NC Secretary of State loose wills. Rodgers named, among others, wife Mary, his granddaughter Elizabeth "Dearam" and grandson Joseph Cockerum. Elizabeth (Rogers) Dereham was dead by 1720, and James married third, after Apr 1725, **Ann (Williamson) Durden**, who survived him. Ann (Williamson) Durden-Leigh of Beaufort Precinct, Bath Co., died testate between 9 Aug 1732 and Mar $173^2/_3$, her will filed among the NC Secretary of State loose wills. There were obviously no children by the third marriage. Ann Durden/Darden, *née* Williamson, was identified as the widow of Jacob Darden, in Allen Hart Norris, *Beaufort County, North Carolina, Deed Book 1, 1696-1729*, p. 160. Jacob Darden's will was dated 14 Apr and recorded 22 June 1719, Isle of Wight Co., VA, Will & Deed Book 2, p. 654, in which wife Ann was named. George Williamson, in his will dated 26 Apr 1721 and recorded 28 May 1722, Isle of Wight Co., VA, The Great Book, p. 118, named [orphaned] grandson Jacob Darden. Interestingly, on 19 Apr 1725, Ann "Dirden" was described in a deed from Maurice Moore as "late of Isle of Wight Co., VA," Beaufort Co., NC, Deed Book 1, p. 494. James Leigh was appointed Collector of her Majesty's Customs in Pamtico and Neuse Rivers in Bath County, by a commission dated 2 Nov 1703, according to Beaufort Co., NC, Deed Book 1, p. 23 (109). On 9 Apr 1724, a Commission of the Peace was issued for the precinct of Beaufort and Hyde to James Leigh, among others, according to *The Colonial Records of North Carolina*, 2nd ser., vol. 7, *Records of the Executive Council, 1664-1734*, p. 141.

On 17 July 1728, James Leigh, Esq., for love and affection gave his son-in-law Robert Purser, planter, 221 acres of land on the south side of Pamptico River in Bath Co., part of 442 acres formerly belonging to Charles Meagure, deceased, which for want of heirs was escheated to the Lords Proprietors, and then purchased from them by James Leigh as "nighest of kin," according to Beaufort Co., NC, Deed Book 1, p. 507. On the next page of that volume, on the same date, James Leigh for love and affection gave his son-in-law Thomas Underwood 221 acres out of the same tract, possibly because his daughter was deceased by that time.

The Children of James Leigh and Sarah Helmot, born Accomack Co., VA:

[1]+ a. **James[2] Leigh**, died testate after 24 Apr 1738, Beaufort Co., NC, Old Will Book, p. 53 (121A); married **Mary** [__].

[2] b. **John[2] Leigh**.

[3] c. **Lyonall[2] Leigh**, died intestate in Craven as Lionel/Lioney "Leeh," by 31 May 1749, according to the date of his estate appraisal, Craven Co., NC, Wills, Deeds, Inventories, 1749-1777, pp. 153-56. According to Craven Co., NC, Deed Book 4, p. 81, dated 5 Apr 1747, he married **Eleanor** [__], and he had at least one son, William[3]

Leigh, to whom he gave land on the north side of the Neuse River.

[4] d. **Sarah[2] Leigh**.

[5] e. **Patience[2] Leigh**, married **Robert Purser**, died testate between 10 May and 11 Sept 1733, Bath Co., NC, Secretary of State loose wills.

[6] f. **Elizabeth[2] Leigh**, married, as his first wife, **Thomas Underwood**, died testate between 22 Jan 1734 and Sept 1735, Beaufort Co., NC, Old Wills, p. 16; he married second, Clio [__].

[7] g. **Milly[2] Leigh**, married [__] **Durrham/Dereham**.

107. Alexander Lillington, the son of James[A] Lillington and Anne [__], was baptized 28 July 1644, All Hallows, Goldsmith Street, Exeter, Devon, and died 11 Sept 1697, Perquimans Co., NC. He married first, 11 June 1668, Perquimans Co., NC, **Sarah James** of Boston, who died by 1675, Perquimans. Henry F. Waters contributed to the *New England Historical and Genealogical Register*, vol. 30, no. 2 [April, 1876], p. 235, under "Notes and Queries," a small paragraph entitled "Lillington of Carolina," in which he provided an abstract of Essex Co., MA, Deed Book B4, p. 379, dated 3 Aug 1675: "Alexander Lillington of Albemarle Co., NC, being the husband of Sarah James, daughter of Thomas James late of sd. Carolina, deceased, but formerly of Salem in New England, which Sara is the only surviving child and rightful heir of the said Thomas James, etc." Unfortunately the two children of this marriage died young and Sara's progeny died out.

Alexander Lillingotn married second, 13 June 16[75], Perquimans Co., NC, **Elizabeth Cooke**, the daughter of Thomas Cooke and his wife Anne [__], who died 29 Sept 1695, Perquimans Co., NC. He married third, 19 Mar $169^5/_6$, Perquimans Co., NC, **Ann (Belliott) Elkes-Stuard**, the daughter of John Belliott and Bridgett [__] Foster-Belliott of Northampton Co., VA [see sketch of **Richard Elkes** in vol. 2] who died testate b etween 26 Jan 1724 and 1 Apr 1725, NC Secretary of State loose wills.

Ann was the widow, respectively of (1) Richard Elkes, whom she married 3 Apr 1671, Perquimans, and who died testate between 21 Sept and Oct 1678, Perquimans, NC Secretary of State loose wills. As Ann "Elles," she married second, 17 Sept 1688, Perquimans, John Steward. She married third, 19 Mar 1695, "Major" Alexander Lillington. Obviously I do not agree with the pattern of marriage attributed to Ann in the work which will be cited below. Argyll Simons named Ann Lillington as his "mother" in his will dated 13 Apr 1714, NC Secretary of State loose wills; and she, in turn, called his son John Simons her grandson in her 1725 testament. The name "Argyll" had to have come into the family through Ann Belliott's mother Bridgett, through her Northampton Co., VA, "Urmstone," Armstrong, and Foster connections, especially as Argyll named his cousin Francis Foster, the surname of Ann Belliott's mother's first husband.

According to Chowan Co., NC, Deed Book W#1, p. 43, dated 4 and 5 Oct 1703, Argyll and his wife Lydia sold land to Edward Norington. The relationship from John Simons to his grandmother Ann Lillington would have to be through this Lydia, who I suspect is an unrecorded daughter of Richard Elkes.

There is an excellent treatment of the descendants of Alexander Lillington in Allen Hart Norris, *Beaufort County, North Carolina, Deed Book 1, 1696-1729, Records of Bath County, North Carolina*, pp. 184-86, which was used in the compilation of this sketch.

The Children of Alexander Lillington and Sarah James, born Perquimans:

[1] a. **James[2] Lillington**, born 5 June 1671, died 15 Apr 1692.

[2] b. **Alexander[2] Lillington**, born 3 Aug 1674, died young, by 1693.

The Children of Alexander Lillington and Elizabeth Cooke, born Perquimans:

[3] c. **Elizabeth[2] Lillington**, born 17 June 1679, married first, 3 Jan $169^4/_5$, **John Fendall**, who died testate (20 Dec 1695, Perquimans) between 17 Dec 1695 and Apr 1696, NC Secretary of State loose wills; she married second, 19 May 1698, Perquimans Co., NC, **Samuel Swann**, who died testate between 12 Sept 1707 and Apr 1708, Perquimans, NC Secretary of State loose wills; married third, **Alexander Goodlatt**, "younger son to Abotts Haugh in Sterlingshire, Scotland," who died testate between 12 Oct 1710 and 1 Aug 1713, NC Secretary of State vol. 875, p. 4; she married fourth, say 1713, as his first wife, **Maurice Moore**, born *ca.* 1682, died 1743. Elizabeth had children by Samuel Swann.

[4] d. **Ann[2] Lillington**, born 1 June 1679, died 1712; married first, 20 Feb 1693, **Henderson Walker**, who died testate between 27 Oct 1701 and 4 July 1704, NC Secretary of State loose wills; she married second, **Edward Moseley**, who died testate between 20 Mar 1745 and Aug 1749, NC Secretary of State loose wills.

[5] e. **Sarah[2] Lillington**, born 20 Jan 1681, died 28 Feb $168^1/_2$.

[6]+ f. **Mary[2] Lillington**, born 22 Apr 1683, married first, **Samuel Swann**, Jr.; she married second, **Jeremiah[1] Vail**, who died intestate 10 Sept 1741, Chowan Co., NC

[7] g. **John[2] Lillington**, born 11 May 1687, died testate between 19 Mar $172^1/_2$ and 2 July 1723, Bath Co., NC Secretary of State loose wills; he married, as her first husband, **Sarah Porter**; she married second, Seth Pilkington, who died testate between 7 Oct 1751 and Mar 1754, Beaufort Co., NC, Secretary of State loose wills.

[8] h. **Sarah[2] Lillington**, born 16 Aug 1690, married first, **John Ismay**,

who died testate between 12 Jan 1729 and 5 Aug 1732, Chowan Co., NC, Secretary of State loose wills; second, as his third wife, Hon. **Christopher Gale**, who died testate between 17 Feb 1734 and 4 Dec 1735, NC Secretary of State loose wills.

[9] i. **George[2] Lillington**, born 10 Aug 1693.

108. William Lowe was born by 1650, Charles City Co., VA, the only son of Thomas[A] Lowe and [__][A] Wilson, the daughter of John[B] Wilson of Henrico, and died testate between 31 July 1720 and 17 Apr 1722, Chowan Co., NC. On 25 Feb 166³/₄, Thomas Lowe recorded a gift of cattle from his "father-in-law" John Wilson to Wilson's grandson William[1] Lowe, in Charles City Co., VA, Court Orders, 1655-1665, p. 458. William was still a resident of Prince George Co., VA, in 1704, according to Annie Laurie Wright Smith's *The Quit Rents of Virginia, 1704*, p. 57, with 1584 acres. His will was not only filed in the collection of NC Secretary of State loose wills, it was recorded in NC Secretary of State vol. 875, p. 336. He married **Anne** [__], whom he mentioned in his will.

The Children of William Lowe and Anne [__]:

[1] a. **John[2] Lowe**.

[2] b. **William[2] Lowe**.

[3] c. **Christiana[2] Lowe**, married **Robert Dixson**, died testate between 4 Apr and Aug 1727, Bertie Co., NC, Secretary of State loose wills.

[4]+ d. **Elizabeth[2] Lowe**, married **John[4] Pace**.

109. Thomas Luten was born say 1660 and died testate between 16 Feb 1729 and 31 Mar 1731, Chowan Co., NC. The only trace of his will (now lost) is an abstract which was recorded in J. R. B. Hathaway, *The North Carolina Genealogical Register*, vol. 1, no. 1 [Jan 1900], p. 134. He married the widow **Mary[2] (Cullen) Currer**, the daughter of **Thomas[1] Cullen** and Sarah Alderstone and the widow of John Currer, born say 1658, Dover, Kent. She died after the signing of her husband's 1729 will in Chowan. Thomas Luten was justice of the General Court and Chowan Precinct Court, an Assembly member, and provost marshall. He registered importation rights on 31 Mar 1697.

The length of child-bearing years for Mary (Currer) Cullen suggests that there may have been a second Mary Cullen, who was the mother of Thomas Luten's younger children. Several correspondents have offered various solutions to this problem.

The Children of John Currer and Mary Cullen:

[1] a. **Sarah[2] Currer**, born *ca.* 1677.

[2] b. **[Child][2] Currer**, born *ca.* 1681, *no further record.*

The Children of Thomas Luten and Mary (Cullen) Currer:

[3] c. **Esther[2] Luten**, born *ca.* 1686, married by 1713, Chowan Co., NC, **Robert Hicks**, who died testate between 25 Nov 1733 and Jan $173^{3}/_{4}$, Chowan Co., NC, Secretary of State, vol. 876, p. 297.

[4] d. **Mary[2] Luten**, born *ca.* 1698, married first, by 1716, **Jonathan Evans**, according to Hathaway, *The North Carolina Genealogical and Historical Register*, vol. 2, no. 2 [April 1901], p. 290; they had children registered in Perquimans; she married second, by 25 Nov 1725, **William Haughton**, who died testate between 17 Nov 1749 and Jan 1752, Chowan Co., NC, Secretary of State loose wills; she married third, by 1752, Chowan Co., NC, **Eli Griffin**, according to Chowan Co., NC, Miscellaneous Papers, 1694-1799, vol. 6, pp. 80-81, dated *ca.* July 1752; according to the same collection, vol. 7, p. 23, dated Apr 1753, she married fourth, **Thomas Barker**.

[5] e. **Thomas[2] Luten**, Jr., died testate after 21 Aug 1766, Chowan Co., NC, Will Book A, p. 259; he married **Hannah** [__].

[6]+ f. **William[2] Luten**, born *ca.* 1700, died after 1770, Orange Co., NC; married, first, by 1720, **Anne[2] Hoskins**; he married second, by 1744, **Francis Hutchins**, according to Chowan Co., NC, Deed Book 1755-1757, p. 81. William Luten qualified for the job of Sheriff according to Chowan Co., NC, Court Minutes, 1730-1745, p. 79, Apr 1741.

[7] g. **Constant[2]/Constance Luten**, married (possibly) **Elizabeth** [__].

[8] h. **Henderson[2] Luten**, died intestate by Oct 1744, Chowan Co., NC, Court Minutes, 1730-1745, p. 206; his estate was administered by his brother William[2] Luten and the court ordered the estate to be divided amongs the orphans [unnamed]; on p. 222 of the same volume, Jan $174^{4}/_{5}$, William Bonner declared that he had married one of Henderson Luten's daughters[3], *i.e.*, he married 21 Aug 1744, Chowan Co., NC (marriage bond), Sarah[3] Luten; on Jan 1746, Chowan Co., NC, Court Minutes, 1746-1748, p. 155, James Luten[3], orphan of Henderson[2], chose John Halsey as his guardian; on p. 172 of the same volume, Ephraim[3] Luten, orphan of Henderson[2], then 14 years old, chose William Bonner as guardian; in Jan 1750, Henderson[3] Luten chose his brother James[3] as his guardian, Chowan Co., NC, Court Minutes, 1749-1754, p. 223; Henderson[2] married [__]. On 17 July 1731, Henderson[2] Luten made a deed of gift to his mother Mary Luten, according to Chowan Co., NC, Court Minutes, 1730-1745, p. 14.

[9] i. **Christian[2] Luten**, married **Robert Beasley**; on 19 July 1735, Constance Luten of Bertie, and Robert Beasley and wife Christian of

Chowan sold 200 acres in Chowan to Thomas Luten of Chowan, formerly granted Major Thomas Luten, deceased, Chowan Co., NC, Deed Book W-1, p. 257; in the same volume, p. 353, dated *ca.* Nov 1737, William Cropley for love and affection gave Thomas[3] Beasley, the son of Robert and Christian, 400 acres on the Sound Side in Chowan.

[10] j. **Rachel[2] Luten**, married **James Farlee**, who, styled "gentleman," died testate between 12 and 17 Jan 1750, Chowan Co., NC, Secretary of State loose wills.

[11] k. **Ann[2] Luten**, married [__] **Brinn**, *no further record.*

[12] l. **Sarah[2] Luten**, born *ca.* 1710, married first, by 1728, **Edward Standing**, who died intestate by July 1738, Chowan Co., NC, according to Jonathan B. Butcher, "Probate Records in Chowan County, N.C., Bound Miscellaneous Papers, 1694-1799," in the *North Carolina Genealogical Society Journal*, vol. 7, no. 4 [November, 1981], p. 203; the estate generated paperwork up until Apr 1758, at which time Henderson Standing and Thomas Bonner stated that Edward's estate had never been divided between the widow and son, Thomas Standing; the four orphan children had arrived at full age by Oct 1752: Henderson[2], Edward[2], Sarah[2], and Mary[2]; she married second, by Feb 1743, Chowan Co., NC, **Joseph Creecy**, who had taken over the job of administrating the estate of Edward Standing from Sarah.

110. Daniel McDaniel was born before 1695 and died testate between 16 Apr 1733 and 2 May 1734, Bertie Co., NC, his will filed among NC Secretary of State loose wills. He married by July 1715, Chowan Co., NC, **Sarah[2] Brown**, whom he named in his will, daughter of **Thomas**[1] and Christian [__] **Brown** of Nansemond Co., VA (later Albemarle Co., NC). Thomas Brown of Albemarle Co., NC, in his will dated 1 Apr and proved 21 Oct 1718, NC Secretary of State loose wills, and recorded in NC Secretary of State vol. 875, p. 158, did name wife Christian but did not name daughter Sarah (Brown) McDaniel. However, Thomas Brown of Chowan with consent of wife Christian deeded his son-in-law Daniel McDaniel 100 acres of land on Old Tree Swamp, 19 July 1715, Chowan Co., NC, Deed Book B#1, p. 177. Sarah McDaniel appeared on a deed of sale with her husband on 10 Nov 1724, Bertie Co., NC, Deed Book A, p. 379.

The Children of Daniel McDaniel and Sarah Brown:

[1]+ a. **Daniel[2] McDaniel**, died testate between 5 June 1768 and Feb 1769, Edgecombe Co., NC, Will Book A, p. 169; married [__].

[2] b. **Archbell/Archibald[2] McDaniel**, died without issue [see below];

however, on 17 Aug 1743, his brother sold him 100 acres of land, part of a patent to James Castellow, which eventually descended to his brother Alexander, according to Edgecombe Co., NC Deed Book 5, p. 186.

[3] c. **Alexander[2] McDaniel**, probably the Alexander McDaniel of Bladen who, on 7 Oct 1769, Bladen Co., NC, Deed Book 1738-1779, p. 537, sold land on Buckhorn Swamp to John Legett, carpenter. On 10 May 1754, Alexander McDaniel, county unspecified, Edgecombe Co., NC, Deed Book 2, p. 23, sold 100 acres to John Bass, land which had belonging to his brother Archibald, who had died without issue, the inheritance having become the grantor's.

[4] d. **James[2] McDaniel.**

[5] e. **Mary[2] McDaniel.**

[6] f. **Ann[2] McDaniel.**

111. John Mann II, the son of John[A] Mann I and Dorothy[A] [__] MacRory, was baptized 6 June 1681, Christ Church Parish, Middlesex Co., VA, and died testate between 18 Feb $174^2/_3$ and May 1744, Tyrrell Co., NC, his will filed among the NC Secretary of State loose wills. He married, first by 1701, **Jane** [__], and second, **Margaret** [__], whom he named in his will. The maternity of John Mann's children is not absolutely clear, although he was still married to his first wife in 1703. John Mann II settled in that part of Currituck Co., NC, which would be cut off into Tyrrell Co., NC, by 2 Nov 1727, at which time he received a patent for 160 acres at the mouth of a small Creek and Mushoes Creek, according to NC Land Patent Book 3, p. 235. A sketch of this family can be found in *Order of First Families of North Carolina, Ancestor Registry*, no. 1.

The Children of John Mann and Jane [__], born Christ Church Parish, Middlesex Co., VA:

[1] a. **John[2] Mann**, born 1 May 1702, died young.

[2] b. **John[2] Mann**, born 25 Dec $170^4/_5$, named in his father's will.

[3] c. **William[2] Mann**, removed to Currituck.

[4] d. **Theophalas[2] Mann**, still alive 7 Mar 1764, Tyrrell Co., NC, Deed Book 4, part 1, p. 401, in which he sold land to Sussana Alexander, widow—this was his last appearance in the Tyrrell records.

[5] e. **Edward[2] Mann**, dead by 16 June 1755, Tyrrell Co., NC, Deed Book 4, part 1, p. 145, in which he was called deceased by his brother Joseph[2] Mann, in a deed mentioning Edward's property.

[6]+ f. **Thomas[2] Mann**, carpenter, born *ca.* 1717, died testate between 8 Nov 1766 and Mar 1767, Tyrrell Co., NC, Tyrrell loose wills; married **Hester** [__]; in his will, Thomas stated he was 49 years old.

[7] g. **Joseph[2] Mann**, died testate between 27 May 1765 and Aug 1770, Tyrrell Co., NC; married **Mary [__]**.
[8] h. **Dorothy[2] Mann**, married [__] **O'Neal**, mentioned in the will of her brother Joseph, 27 May 1765.
[9] i. **Elizabeth[2] Mann**.
[10] j. **Ann[2] Mann**, married [__] **Read**.

112. Thomas Mann II, the son of Thomas Mann I and Elizabeth [__] of Isle of Wight Co., VA, was born say 1666 in Nansemond Co., VA, and died testate between 30 Sept and Nov 1735, Bertie Co., NC, his will filed among the NC Secretary of State loose wills. He married by 1715, Chowan Co., NC, **Bridgett Hooker**, the daughter of William Hooker and his first wife Bridgett Foy of York and Surry counties, VA. She was named as Bridget Man in her father William Hooker's will, dated 8 Jan $171^6/_7$, and proved Oct 1717, NC Secretary of State loose wills, and also recorded in NC Secretary of State vol. 875, p. 143. A sketch of this family can be found in *Order of First Families of North Carolina, Ancestor Registry*, no. 1.

The Children of Thomas Mann and Bridget Hooker, born Chowan Precinct, NC:
[1] a. [**Daughter**][2] **Mann**, born *ca.* 1714, died before Sept 1735, married as his first wife, **Richard Williams**, who died testate between 28 Sept 1761 and Apr 1762, Bertie Co., NC, Will Book A, p. 1; son of George Williams, Sr., of Bertie Co., NC, and his wife Joannah [__].
[2] b. **John[2] Mann**, born *ca.* 1716.
[3]+ c. **Thomas[2] Mann**, born *ca.* 1718, died testate between 6 June and Nov 1792, Nash Co., NC, Will Book 1, p. 83; he married *ca.* 1745, **Elizabeth** (almost certainly **Denton**).
[4] d. **Bridgett[2] Mann**, married [__] **Griffin**.
[5] e. **Mary[2] Mann**, not 16 in 1735.

113. Joell Martin was born in Norfolk Co., VA, where he was left the bequest of a silver tankard formerly belonging to his father in the 24 Apr 1681 will of Robert Bray, Norfolk Co., VA, Will Book 4, f. 101. His father was mentioned therein as deceased but was not named. On 2 Nov 1692, Joel Martin identified himself as the son of John[A] Martin, deceased, and sold 200 acres of land called the Great Plantation to his brother-in-law Adam Keeling (who had married Joell's sister Ann), according to Princess Anne Co., VA, Deed Book 1, p. 28. Joell Martin died testate between 24 Oct 1715 and 3 July 1716, Bath Co., NC. He married **Elizabeth[2] Alderson**, named in his will, which was not only filed among NC Secretary of State loose wills, but also recorded both in NC Secretary of State vol. 875, p. 131, and in Beaufort Co., NC, Deed Book 1, p. 269, as Joel "Marten." Elizabeth was the daughter of Eleanor [__] and **Simon**[1] **Alderson**, Sr., the testator of 9 Jan $171^{2}/_{3}$, Bath Co., NC. Although the name "Joell Martin" would by itself prove unusual enough to link this ancestor with Norfolk Co., VA, the fact that an entire group of Virginians, connected to him and his children by blood, removed from Norfolk to Bath Co., NC, only serves to confirm his identity as an early resident of Norfolk. It has not yet been proved that Joell's mother was *née* Keeling, but descendants would love to discover the location of the silver tankard mentioned above.

A suit of ejectment filed in Pitt Co., NC, July 1790, in the Court of Pleas and Quarter Sessions, enumerates the children of John Snoad with their married names: Henry[3] Snoad; Mary[3], wife John Lane; Ann[3], mother of James[4] Bonner; Elizabeth[3], wife of Henry Bonner and mother of Henry Snoad[4] Bonner. Depositions concerning the descent of the Snoad children were contained in depositions taken in 1792.

The Children of Joell Martin and Elizabeth Alderson:

[1] a. **Joel**[2] **Martin**, died before 24 Oct 1715, Bath Co., NC.

[2] b. **Mary**[2] **Martin**, married **Henry Woodard**, who died after 1715, his nuncupative will, now lost, mentioned in his son's will, Beaufort Co., NC.

[3] c. **John**[2] **Martin**.

[4] d. **William**[2] **Martin**, died testate between 23 Aug 1745 and 18 Feb $174^{5}/_{6}$, St. Thomas Parish, Beaufort Co., NC, Secretary of State loose wills; married, as her first husband, **Mary** [__]; she married second, Henry Lucas, and died testate between 24 Mar and Apr 1761, Beaufort Co., NC, Secretary of State loose wills.

[5]+ e. **Ann**[2] **Martin**, married, as his first wife, **John**[1] **Snoad**, who died testate 30 June 1744, Beaufort Co., NC, his will recorded in NC Land Grant Book 4, no. 145.

[6] f. **Elizabeth**[2] **Martin**, married, as his second wife, **John Penny**.

[7] g. **Francis**[2] **Martin**, died before 1750, married **Foster Jarvis of** Currituck, who died testate between 5 Dec 1750 and Jan $175^{0}/_{1}$, NC, Secretary of State loose wills.

114. William Martin died testate between 8 Apr 1735 and Aug 1736, Bertie Co., NC, his will filed among the NC Secretary of State loose wills. He married **Else** (most likely **Alice**) [__], whom he named in his will. William Martin, Sr., received a land grant of 520 acres on Potekasey Creek adjoining Robert Paterson, John Dickenson, and John Lane on 26 Mar 1723, according to NC Land Patent

Book 3, p. 145. On 10 Nov 1725, according to Bertie Co., NC, Deed Book B, p. 50, William Martin sold his patent of 520 acres to Francis Pugh of Chowan.

Only son Richard[2] Martin was not described in his father's will as being under age. Puzzlingly, a William Martin, Jr., not named in the will of this William, received a patent on 26 Mar 1723 for 190 acres on the south side of Potokasey Creek, adjoining William Martin "the Older" and John Lane, according to NC Land Patent Book 3, p. 146. Were they father and son, or more likely, uncle and nephew?

William was in no way elated to **Joell Martin** above.

The Children of William Martin and Alice [__]:

[1] a. **Richard[2] Martin**, born *ca* 1710.

[2] b. **Moses[2] Martin.**

[3] c. **Thomas[2] Martin.**

[4]+ d. **John[2] Martin**, Sr., died intestate Northampton Co., NC, before 1 June 1794; married **Lucy** [__], will dated 17 Dec 1808, proved Dec 1816, Northampton Co., NC, Will Book 3, p. 183.

[5] e. **Mary[2] Martin.**

[6] f. **Else/Alice[2] Martin.**

115. John Mason, Sr., born by 1680, died testate between 15 Feb 173$^7/_8$ and Sept 1741, and signed his will curiously as a resident of Hyde precinct, Currituck Co., NC, although the probate occurred in Hyde. He married **Mary** [__], whom he named in his will. His first notice in provincial North Carolina was as a petitioner on a document in Wickham precinct, Bath Co., NC, which was undated but which had to have been created between 1708 and 1711. This petition sought to form a court in Wickham precinct distinct from that of Bath, which the petitioners stated was too distant to be convenient for the transaction of business. This document, including members of the Tyson family, can be found in *The Colonial Records of North Carolina*, 2nd ser. vol. 7, *Records of the Executive Council, 1664-1734*, p. 430.

An insidious genealogical rumor has been spread for many years that Mary [__] Mason was *née* "Winfield," due to a missreading of John Mason's will. Legatee "Linkfield," who was *not* named "Winfield," may have been named for the following family of headrights assigned by John Barras to Henry Eborne on 29 July 1702, according to Beaufort Co., NC, Deed Book 1, p. 13 (42): Francis, Mary, and John Linfield, and Edward Hogg. Could Mary [__] Mason have been a relative (*i.e.*, either a daughter or sister) of Francis Linfield? Francis "Linkfield" and Thomas Gettings/Giddings received a patent of 4060 acres [*sic*!] in New Curratuck, Bath Co., in Hyde precinct, on the east side of Matchapungo River, adjoining Frank's Bay, the Pamplico River, Bell's Bogg and

Creek, and Jarvis Creek, according to NC Land Patent Book 2, p. 330. By himself, Francis Linfield received a patent of 180 acres of land in Bath Co., on the Bear River, adjoining the head of Oyster Creek, the Great Gum Swamp, and Bells Creek, on 2 Aug 1726, according to NC Land Patent Book 2, p. 239. This land is mentioned in the deeds of Hyde Co., NC, which begin in 1736; most of Linfield's land was sold to a John Avery.

However, the actual wording of John Mason's will is a bequest to his sons "Thomas and John Mason and Linkfield." Three possibilities arise: [1] was "Linkfield" the name of a Mason son? [2] was "Linkfield" a son-in-law, the husband of an unnamed Maron daughter? [3] was he simply appointed to help execute John Mason's will? The will itself does not help in any way, nor do the records themselves, such as are available to the researcher, give any clues about his relationship to the Mason family.

The Children of John Mason and Mary [__]:

[1] a. **Mary^2 Mason**.

[2]+ b. **Sabra^2 Mason**, married **Thomas^2 Tyson**, who died before 1755, Beaufort Co., NC

[3] c. **Roger^2 Mason**, died testate between 23 Dec 1754 and June 1756, Hyde Co., NC Secretary of State loose wills; he married **Mary** [__].

[4] d. **Margaret^2 Mason**.

[5] e. **Thomas^2 Mason**.

[6] f. **John^2 Mason**.

Possibly:

[7] g. [**Daughter**]^2 **Mason**, married [__] **Linkfield**.

116. Edward Mayo, Sr., born by 1640 and deceased after 1700, left very few records of himself in the Albemarle, although it is clear that he immigrated first to colonial South Carolina from the island of Barbados. According to the Proprietary Records of South Carolina, vol. 1, p. 161, 1675-1695, dated 12 Mar 1682, he was identified as a Deputy Register of the [South Carolina] Province. On pp. 66-67 of the same volume, he received a bequest from the 1682 will of Thomas Stanyarne, a Quaker from Barbados. One of his first notices in the records of South Carolina was 30th.2mo.1679, whereon a John Jennings of Barbados addressed him a letter concerning a letter originally written by Mayo to Jennings, same volume, p. 33.

Edward Mayo married first, 2 Sept 1666, Christ Church Parish, Barbados, **Sarah Maggs**, although they are listed as Edward *Mays* and Sarah *Meggs*. In the collection *Genealogies of Barbados Families, from Caribbeana and the Journal of the Barbados Museum and Historical Society*, G. Andrews

Moriarty has an extremely helpful article entitled "A Letter from Barbados, 1672," pp. 567-69. He noted the mistake in spelling of the Mayo-Maggs marriage, and quoted a letter form George[A] Maggs to his kinsman John Clifford of Essex Co., MA. Without identifying them further, Maggs mentioned his Uncle Francis Carter and his Uncle "Tiss," apparently from Gloucestershire. (An inspection of probate indices from the Archdeaconry of Gloucestershire revealed no Maggs testators.) Sarah Maggs was the daughter of Quakers Ann[A] [__] and the aforementioned testator George[A] Maggs of St. Michaels Parish, Barbados, the latter of whom died between 14 and 25 June 1677, Barbados, Wills and Administrations, RB6/13, p. 413, in which he named the children of his daughter Sarah Mayo: Sarah[2], Ann[2], Elizabeth[2], and Edward[2]. The will of an Edward Mayo, "late of the Liberty of London," dated 23 Oct 1653 and proved 22 Nov 1656, London, named the following siblings: Robert Mayo, Sarah Mayo, Virtue [female] Mayo, Grace Mayo, Hester Mayo, Will Mayo and wife, Thomas Mayo, and testator's wife Katherine Mayo. No similarly-named brother or son Edward was mentioned therein, Barbados, Wills and Administrations, RB6/14, p. 439. "Brother" Robert Mayo is possibly the Robert who appeared in the South Carolina records about the same time as Edward, our immigrant. Abstracts of these two wills were obtained from Joanne McRee Sanders' *Barbados Records, Wills and Administrations*, vol. 1, *1639-1680*, p. 230 (Maggs) and p. 238 (Mayo). The marriage itself is found in Joanne McRee Sanders, *Barbados Records, Marriages 1643-1800*, vol. 1, p. 325.

According to Caroline B. Whitley, *North Carolina Headrights, A List of Names, 1663-1774*, p. 8, on the first Monday of Feb, 169$^3/_4$, Edward Mayo registered rights for the following thirteen importees: Edward Mayo, Sr., Edward Mayo, Jr., Sarah Mayo, Ann Mayo, Elizabeth Mayo, three Negroes, John Nixon, Em. Nixon, Ann Nixon, Affrica Pike, and Samuel Pike. These names were entered during Feb 169$^3/_4$ in Perquimans County Court.

Hugh B. Johnson and William Perry Johnson, joint authors of "The Mayo Family of North Carolina," in *North Carolina Genealogy*, vol. 17, no. 1 [Spring/Summer, 1971], pp. 2617-22, found the last record pertaining to Edward Mayo, Sr., in an inquisition into the property of William Mowbray, deceased, taken at the home of Mr. Richard Pope in Pasquotank, dated 13 June 1700. Edward Mayo married second, **Emma [__] Pike-Nixon**, the widow first of John[A] Pike of St. Mary Aldermary, London, and second of John Nixon of Pasqauotank, the latter of whom had died testate between 4 Feb 168$^7/_8$ and 1 Aug 1692, NC Secretary of State loose wills. Emma was also the mother of Samuel[1] and Africa Pike. For further information concerning the children and marriages of Edward[2] Mayo, Jr., see Hugh B. Johnson and William Perry Johnson, "The Mayo Family of N. C.," in *North Carolina Genealogy*, vol. 19, no. 2 [Fall/Winter, 1973], pp. 2875-91.

John[A] Pike married Emma [__] by 1667, died 1 Oct, and was buried 2 Oct 1681, St. Mary Aldermary, London, his intestate estate probated in the Deanery of the Arches, held at Lambeth Palace. Their first child, Katherine, was baptized 25 July 1668, St. Giles Cripplegate, and the remaining children were baptized (and buried) at St. Mary Aldermary, London. Two survived: the immigrants Africa Pike, bapt. 3 June 1671, and Samuel Pike, bapt. 29 Oct 1678. With the exception of their first daughter, the vital records of the Pike family occur in *Publications of the Harleian Society. Parish Register Series*, vol. 5. *The Parish Registers of St. Mary Aldermary, London, Containing the Marriages, Baptisms, and Burials from 1558 to 1754*, Joseph Chester, ed., (London 1880).

Emma [__] Pike married, second, 1 Jan $168^{3}/_{4}$, Temple Church, London, John "Nickson," which information can be found in *Publications of the Harleian Society*, New Series, vol. 1, *The Register of the Temple Church, London, Baptisms, 1629-1853, Marriages, 1628-1760*, p. 82.

The Children of Edward Mayo, Sr. and Sarah Maggs, born Christ Church Parish, Barbados:

[1]+ a. **Sarah[2] Mayo**, born *ca.* 1668, married first, as his third wife, 23 Aug 1688, Perquimans Register, **John[1] Culpeper**; she married second, **Patrick Henley**, and third, 3.9.1699, Philadelphia Monthly Meeting, **Matthew Pritchard**.

[2]+ b. **Ann[2] Mayo**, almost certainly "Ann Mays, daughter of Edward and [--] Mays," baptized 26 Nov 1670, Christ Church Parish, Barbados, married first, **Richard Pope**, whose will was dated 23 June and proved 15 July 1701, NC Secretary of State loose Wills; she married second, as his second wife, 8 July 1704, **Francis[1] Delamare**, according to Pasquotank Co., NC, Deed Book A, p. 5 and p. 62; she married third, after 1713, **Augustine Scarbrough** (as mentioned in her will); she married fourth, as his third wife, **John[2] Jennings**. See Joanne McRee Sanders, *Barbados Records, Baptisms, 1637-1800*, p. 269.

[3] c. **Elizabeth[2] Mayo**, born *ca.* 1672, married first, *ca.* 1698, **Stephen Scott** of Pasquotank, who died testate between 12 Mar 1711 and 10 Sept 1716, NC Secretary of State loose wills, also recorded in Secretary of State vol. 875, p. 106; second, 1712, **Henry Keaton**, who died testate betwee 20.7.1715 and 19.8.1715, NC Secretary of State loose wills. The widow Keaton appointed her "beloved brother" Edward Mayo executor of her late husband's estate.

[4] d. **Edward[2] Mayo**, Jr., born *ca.* 1674, will dated 12day.8mo, proved 20 Oct 1724, Pasquotank, NC Secretary of State loose wills, also recorded in NC Secretary of State vol. 876, p. 17; married first, *ca.*

1702, [--], whose name does not appear with the births of their children; second, 2.[--].1709, Perquimans Monthly Meeting, as her first husband, **Mary**[2] **Clare**, who made a final deed of gift to her children, dated 12 July 1726, Perquimans Co., NC, Deed Book B, p. #243, in which she mentioned her upcoming marriage to Joseph Newby whom she married second; Newby died testate between 22 Jan 1726 and 21 Apr 1735, NC Secretary of State loose Wills.

The Child of John Nixon and Emma [__] Pike:
[5] e. **Ann Nixon**, born *ca.* 1684.

117. Charles Merritt was born 1652, according to an extremely informative deposition taken 1707 in which he stated his age to be 55 years. This can be found in *The Colonial Records of North Carolina*, 2nd ser., vol. 7, *Records of the Executive Council, 1664-1734*, p. 415. The deposition revealed that Charles Merritt came to Virginia about 1666 (although it does not specify from where, or where specifically in the colonies he first landed, or under whose "aegis"—Charles does not appear as a headright in the Virginia land patents), and lived for 20 years on the south side of James River, residing on the plantation of Col. Benja. Harrison on Blackwater "within call of the Weyanoake Indian Fortes." As a matter of fact, on 3 Feb 1697, Mr. Benj[a]. Harrison was awarded £9.12.4 from the estate of Charles Merritt, according to Surry Co., VA, Order Book 1691-1713, p. 190. Aside from a couple of lawsuits with the Foremans, there are no substantive (genealogical) records of this Merritt family in Surry Co., VA. As Charles "Meret" he signed his will [--] Apr 1718, and on 21 Oct 1718 it was proved, Chowan Co., NC, Secretary of State loose wills. He married by 1680, **Eleanor** [__], whom he mentioned but did not name in his will. Eleanor appeared as a grantee with her husband in a deed from Peter Evans, carpenter, dated 10 Mar 1707, Chowan Co., NC, Deed Book W#1, p. 112.

According to Caroline B. Whitley, *North Carolina Headrights, A List of Names, 1663-1774*, p. 64, on 27 Aug 1714, Henry Bradley received 640 acres on the west shore of Chowan for a warrant surveyed and dated 29 Aug 1712. The headrights were as follows [commas added by writer]: Henry Bradly, Kath. Bradly, Kath. Bradly Junior, Rt. Bradly, Joseph Bradly, Waltr. Konrell, Chas. Merit, Ellenr. Merrit, Jno. Merritt, Michll. [*sic*] Merritt, Chas. Merritt Junior Jno. Early, Mary Early.

Charles[2] Merritt, Jr., appeared as a grantor in Edgecombe Co., NC, Deed Book 3, p. 228, dated 29 Mar 1748, in which he sold 240 acres of land on the south side of Morratock River and the north side of Deep Creek to John Lamon of Northampton Co., NC. Merritt had obtained this land in an undated sale (*ca.*

1745) from David Hopper of Northampton, according to Edgecombe Co., NC, Deed Book 5, p. 391.

The Children of Charles Merritt and Eleanor [__]:

[1] a. **Charles**[2] **Merritt**, born *ca.* 1680, married **Mary** [__].

[2] b. **Anne**[2] **Merritt**.

[3]+ c. **Nathaniel**[2] **Merritt**, born 1685-90, died testate, as "Merit," between 10 Apr 1735 and Feb $173^5/_6$, "Bertie Precinct in Roanoke," Secretary of State loose wills; married **Mary** [__], who died testate between 2 June 1761 and Oct 1765, Halifax Co., NC, Will Book 1, p. 177.

[4] d. **Sarah**[2] **Merritt**.

[5] e. **John**[2] **Merritt**, born *ca.* 1690, died testate between 13 Jan and Nov 1757, Edgecombe Co., NC, NC Secretary of State loose wills, and recorded in NC Secretary of State vol. 882, p. 133; married **Mary** [__].

[6] f. **Hardy**[2] **Merritt** (daughter), married, almost certainly, **William**[2] **Reeves**, Jr., with whom she sold land on 23 Sept 1741, Edgecombe Co., NC, Deed Book 5, p. 19, to Mary [__] Merritt.

[7]+ g. **William**[2] **Merritt**, born *ca.* 1700, died testate between 10 Aug 1778 and Feb 1784, Halifax Co., NC, Will Book 3, p. 54; married **Elizabeth** [__].

118. Matthew Midyett , the son of John[A] and Catherine [__] Midyett of James City Co., VA, was born 10 Apr 1676 and died testate between 21 Dec 1734 and 1 July 1735, Body Island, Currituck precinct, Albemarle Co., NC. His will was filed in the collection of NC Secretary of State loose wills, and in that document he named his wife "**Jude**." He removed from Virginia to Anne Arundel Co., MD, where he married, 13 July 1702, **Judith White**, born 3 Aug 1681, died 26 Sept 1744, Currituck Co., NC, the daughter of Samuel[A] White of Anne Arundel. Matthew Midgett, on 16 Apr 1712, patented 360 acres on the northwest side of Alegator Creek in Chowan precinct, adjoining William Raphell and Creek Marsh, according to NC Land Patent Book 1, p. 183. On 30 Oct 1715, Matthew and his wife Judith sold this tract to John Mixon, according to Chowan Co., NC, Deed Book B#1, p. 580. On 7 Feb 1712, he patented 341 acres on the south side of Albemarle Sound, called White Oak Island, according to NC Land Patent Book 1, p. 199. Midyett's pattern of migration from Chowan back up to Currituck is most unusual but can be substantiated by the records.

The will of Samuel[A] White of Anne Arundel Co., MD, was dated 17 June and proved 9 July 1703 in MD Prerogative Court vol. 11, p. 313. Although the published abstract names only "the wife of Matthew Miggett," the recorded copy names "my Daughter Judith Wife of Mathew Miggitt." For the actual Midyett Bible records, see *High Tides*, vol. 8, no. 1 [Spring 1982], pp. 22-24.

The Children of Matthew Midyett and Judith White, born Ann Arundel Co., MD:

[1]+ a. **Samuel**[2] **Midyett**, born 6 Dec 1704, died 29 Jan 1790, Body's Island, Currituck; married 8 June 1723, Ann Arundell Co., MD, **Mary Paine**, born 30 Dec 1707, died 20 May 1778, Currituck Co., NC.

[2] b. **John**[2] **Midyett**, born 10 Feb $170^6/_7$, died 1735, Currituck; married 1 May 1728, **Sarah Paine**.

born on Body's Island, Currituck Co., NC.

[3] c. **Joseph White**[2] **Midyett**, born 16 May 1709, died testate between 24 Jan and June 1771, Currituck Co., NC, Will Book 1, p. 60; married 3 Aug 1730, **Elizabeth Margery Neal**.

[4] d. **Ann**[2] **Midyett**, born 30 Mar 1712, married **George Pugh**.

[5] e. **Matthew**[2] **Midyett**, Jr., born 16 Apr 1715.

[6] f. **Catherine**[2] **Midyett**, born 10 Oct 1716, married 2 July 1736, **Ezekiel Hooper**.

[7] g. **Thomas**[2] **Midyett**, born 14 Nov 1717, married *ca.* 1737, **Bethaney [__]**.

[8] h. **Judith**[2] **Midyett**, born 12 Aug 1719, married 30 Sept 1738, **William Daniels**.

[9] i. **Dinah**[2] **Midyett**, born 10 June 1721, married 19 July 1740, **Thomas Morris**.

119. Joseph Moore, the son of Gov. James[A] Moore and Margaret[A] Berringer of South Carolina, was born *ca.* 1703, Goose Creek, Berkeley Co., SC, and died testate between 15 Feb 1753 and Feb 1757, Edgecombe Co., NC—his will was filed among the Secretary of State loose wills and also recorded in NC Secretary of State vol. 879, p. 211. He married by 1728, **Ann**[2] **Hodges**, the daughter of **Robert**[1] **Hodges** and Ann Branch of Isle of Wight Co., VA and later of Bertie. On 11 May 1724, Joseph Moore purchased land on Little Roquiss Swamp, as recorded in Bertie Co., NC, Deed Book A, p. 333. Ann (Hodges) Moore, although described as of Halifax Co., NC, died testate between 22 Feb 1774 and Jan 1776, Martin Co., NC, Will Book 1, p. 27.

The Children of Joseph Moore and Ann Hodges:

[1]+ a. **James**[2] **Moore**, born 14 Nov 1729, Bertie Co., NC, died *ca.* 1785, Sampson Co., NC; married **Ann Thompson**, whose Moore children were named in the will of her brother John Thomson of Duplin, who died testate between 3 May 1781 and July 1786, Duplin Co., NC,

Will Book A, p. 464. The Sampson Co., NC, Court Minutes, 14 May 1804, contain a record of the death of Mrs. Anne Moore as former executrix of Col. James Moore and an order to divide the Negroes among the children.

[2] b. **Hodges**[2] **Moore**, died testate after 15 Sept 1795, Martin Co., NC, Will Book 1, p. 322; he married **Mary** [__].

[3] c. **Jesse**[2] **Moore**.

[4] d. **Ezekiel**[2] **Moore**, died testate between 7 June and Sept 1780, Martin Co., NC, Will Book 1, p. 63; he married **Elizabeth** [__].

[5] e. **Ann**[2] **Moore**, married **William McGee**, according to Sampson-Duplin Co., NC, Deed Book 5, p. 263, dated 21 Oct 1776, wherein she signed with her husband; apparently William was dead by 9 Oct 1779, as Anne McGee made a deed of gift to her sons James[3], Lewis[3], and Moore[3], and daughters Elizabeth[3] and Celia[3] McGee, in Sampson-Duplin Co., NC, Deed Book 6, p. 366.

[6] f. **Martha**[2] **Moore**, married **Micajah Hinton**, whose nuncupative will was dated 5 Oct 1756 and proved Jan 1757, Bertie Co., NC, Secretary of State loose wills.

[7] g. **Cealia**[2] **Moore**.

[8] h. **Millia**[2] **Moore**.

[9] i. **Joseph**[2] **Moore**, married **Ann** [__]; died testate between 6 Oct 1775 and Jan 1776, Edgecombe Co., NC, Will Book A, p. 240.

120. John Morris, Quaker, the son of John Morris/Morrison and **Damaris**[2] **Page**, was born 3.31.1680, as recorded in Pasquotank Monthly Meeting, and died testate 9.20.1739, Pasquotank Monthly Meeting, his will filed among NC Secretary of State loose wills. Names (perhaps those ending in "s") such as Stevens and Morris were often rendered indiscriminately as Stevenson and Morrison, which explains the significance of the marriage between Henry[(2)] White and Damaris *Morrison*. John Morris married 9.4.1703, Pasquotank Monthly Meeting, **Mary**[2] **Symons**, born 12.4.1687, Pasquotank Monthly Meeting, died 8.14.1745, Pasquotank Monthly Meeting, the daughter of **Thomas**[1] **Symons** and Rebecca West. A deed of gift, including a tract out of a patent dated 25 Sept 1663, from Henry[(2)] White, Sr., of Pasquotank to his "son-in-law" John Morris, dated 18 Apr 1704, recorded in Pasquotank Co., NC, Deed Book A, p. 6, is explained by Damaris' second marriage to White. John Morris made a deed of gift out of this same tract, containing 50 acres, to his son Aaron[2] Morris on 14 Jan 1729, Pasquotank Co., NC, Deed Book C, p. 236.

The Children of John Morris and Mary Symons, born Pasquotank Monthly Meeting:

[1] a. **Aaron^2 Morris**, born 7.14.1704, married 6.20.1724, Pasquotank Monthly Meeting, **Mary^2 Pritchard**.

[2] b. **Elizabeth/Bette^2 Morris**, born 9.6.1707, married 6.5.1725, Pasquotank Monthly Meeting, **William Symons**.

[3] c. **Sarah^2 Morris**, born 9.6.1712.

[4]+ d. **Joseph^2 Morris**, born 12.4.1709, married 10.2.1731, Pasquotank Monthly Meeting, **Elizabeth^2 Pritchard**.

[5] e. **John^2 Morris III**, born 12.21.1716, married 3.2.1745, Perquimans Monthly Meeting, **Sarah Peirce**.

[6] f. **Mary^2 Morris**, born 11.24.1719, married 1.2.173$^7/_8$, Pasquotank Monthly Meeting, **John Robinson**.

[7] g. **Zachariah^2 Morris**, born 9.23.1722, married 11.1.1752, Perquimans Monthly Meeting, **Anne Williams**.

[8] h. **Hannah^2 Morris**, born 12.23.1726, married 10.6.1750, Pasquotank Monthly Meeting, **William Bundy**.

121. John Nelson, Sr., miller, was born *ca.* 1639, according to a deposition giving his age in Nov 1689, Accomack Co., VA, Wills and Orders, 1682-1697, p. 171. He was transported by his son John Nelson, Jr., into North Carolina 28 Oct 1702, a fact found in Caroline B. Whitley's *North Carolina Headrights, A List of Names, 1663-1744*, pp. 40-41. John, Sr., died after 1708, probably in Craven Co., NC. The name of his first wife [__] does not appear in the records, but he married second, **Joan** [__]. Joan [__] Nelson was accused of murdering her stepson Bowles^2 Nelson, as indicated by a trial in Accomack reported 6 Aug 1691 in Accomack Co., VA, Orders, 1690-1697, p. 37. The details of what exactly happened have never come to light, but she was not convicted by the Grand Jury, which reported that "Joane, by her foolish, unadvised and rash acting hath been the cause of the said Bowles Nelsons's death." She was exonerated from the charge of murder, but John Nelson was responsible for the court costs, which were ruinous.

John Nelson, Jr., on 28 Oct 1702, according to Beaufort Co., NC, Deed Book 1, p. 31 [85], petitioned for 12 rights on a land entry for the following persons transported various numbers of times: John Nelson, Jr., John Nelson, Sr., Judith Woddis, William Capps, John Nelson, Sr., Joan Nelson, Eliz Nelson, and Mary Nelson. In fact, on 5 Jan 170$^3/_4$, John Nelson, Jr., and wife Ann sold to John Nelson, Sr., a tract of land purchased of William Handcock on Old Town Creek, adjoining Mr. Jones' plantation, according to Beaufort Co., NC, Deed Book 1, p. 32 [88]. Later they were in Craven Co., as appears by this record: Craven Co., NC, Court Minutes 1712-1715, p. 146, dated 12 July 1716: John Nelson, Esq., acknowledged a conveyance of 640 acres near Bear Inlett to Capt. Thomas Lee; Ann Nelson, wife of Capt. John Nelson, relinquished her right of dower. John[2] Nelson, Jr., besides having been distinguished with the honorifics "Capt.," and "Esq.," also served as Judge for a time, according to Craven Co., NC, Deeds, 1713-1715 (C.028.40001), p. 622, dated 14 Aug 1714.

The Children of John Nelson, Sr., and [__]:

[1] a. **Bowles[2] Nelson**, died by Aug 1691, Accomack Co., VA.

[2]+ b. Capt. **John[2] Nelson**, Jr., died intestate before Mar 1755, Craven Co., NC; married first, **Ann [__]**; he married second, **Mary** [__].

122. James[(2)] Newby, the son of **John[(1)] Newby** and **Magdalene** [__], was born say 1675, and died testate between 29 Nov 1739 and Jan 1743, Pasquotank Co., NC, NC Secretary of State loose wills. His mother Magdalen married second, Matthew Calley, who died testate between 16 Apr 1697 and 16 Jan 1699, Pasquotank, NC Secretary of State loose wills, leaving his stepson James property in Pasquotank Co. Magdalen was still alive at that time. James married first, 5.5.1699, Perquimans Monthly Meeting, **Sarah[2] Nicholson**, born 15 Aug 1682, Perquimans, died by 1719, Pasquotank Co., NC, the daughter of **Christopher[1] Nicholson** and Ann Atwood. James married second, at Little River Meeting House, 5.18.1719, Pasquotank Monthly Meeting, **Elizabeth[(3)] (White) Davis**, the widow of James Davis and the daughter of Henry[(2)] White, who had been married 4.6.1690, Pasquotank Monthly Meeting (at the house of Henry White). Elizabeth's marital history was revealed in a deed dated 8.25.1719, Pasquotank Co., NC, Deed Book A, p. 233, in which James Newby pledged himself to the upkeep of his son-in-law (*i.e.*, stepson) Robert Davis, the son of James Davis, until he came of age. James Davis died testate after 22 Apr 1715, Pasquotank Co., NC, his will filed in NC Secretary of State loose wills, and recorded in NC Secretary of State vol. 875, p. 179. On 6.7.1729, James Newby was dismissed from the Pasquotank Co. Friends for reasons which were not revealed. It could mark the date of his decision to marry "out of unity." He married third, **Hannah** [__], whom he named as his executrix, and who survived him. James and Hannah were married by 13 Oct 1729, according to Pasquotank Deed Book C, p. 226, in which he and his wife sold land to James' son Benjamin[2] Newby. The maternity of his last four children has not been absolutely determined, but it would be reasonable to assume that they were considerably younger and therefore the product of James' last marriage.

In Pasquotank Co., NC, Deed Book C, p. 100, dated 25 Apr 1752, Jacob[2] Newby, "singleman," with his mother Hannah, sold land his father had lived on to Charles Taylor.

The Children of James Newby and Sarah Nicholson, born Pasquotank Monthly Meeting, except for [1];

[1] a. **James^{2} Newby**, born 4 Aug 1702, Perquimans Register, *died young*.
[2]+ b. **Samuel^{2} Newby**, born 8.23.1704, married 9.11.1725, Perquimans Monthly Meeting, Lower Meeting House, **Elizabeth^{2} Albertson**.
[3] c. **Benjamin^{2} Newby**, born 6.25.1707, died testate 9.28.1739, Pasquotank Monthly Meeting, NC Secretary of State loose wills; he married 12.16.1731/2, "at the house of James Griffin in Chowan," registered in Perquimans Monthly Meeting, **Susannah Griffin**, who married second, 12.5.$174^{0}/_{1}$, Pasquotank Monthly Meeting, James Overman, who died testate between 20 Mar $174^{5}/_{6}$ and July 1746, NC Secretary of State loose wills, Pasquotank Co., NC.
[4] d. **Ann^{2} Newby**, born 11.1.1708, married 11.5.1726, Pasquotank Monthly Meeting, **Francis Mace** of Nansemond Co., VA, who died testate between 7 Feb 1748 and 1 Aug 1749, NC Secretary of State loose wills.
[5] e. **James^{2} Newby**, born 7.14.1710, died 11.1.1760, Pasquotank Monthly Meeting; married 5.12.1732, Pasquotank Monthly Meeting, **Naomi White**, daughter of Henry, died 11.9.1771, Pasquotank Monthly Meeting, aged 68 years; a son of theirs, James^{3} Newby, removed to Core Sound Monthly Meeting and married 2.12.1769, Carteret Meeting House, Sarah Stanton.
[6] f. **Hannah^{2} Newby**, born 1.31.1713.

The Children of James Newby and Hannah [__]:
[7] g. **Jacob^{2} Newby**.
[8] h. **Sarah^{2} Newby**.
[9] i. **Magdalene^{2} Newby**, married **Charles Markham**.
[10] k. **Mary^{2} Newby**.

123. John$^{(1)}$ Newby, whose origins are thus far unknown, was born *ca.* 1650 and died by 1697, Perquimans Co., NC. He married **Magdalene** [__], who married second Matthew Calley, although the Quaker records listed him as "Collins." In Calley's will, dated 16 Apr 1697 and proved 16 Jan 1699, Pasquotank Co., NC, Secretary of State loose wills, were named his wife's four children: James^{2}, Elizabeth^{2}, John^{2}, and Rebecca^{2} Newby. James^{2} was to have his stepfather's plantation, John^{2} was to have one, and Rebecca^{2} Newbey was to have the plantation whereon her stepfather lived. Calley's will was also recorded in NC Secretary of State vol. 874, p. 123.

The Children of John Newby and Magdalene [__], born Pasquotank Monthly Meeting:
[1] a. **Elizabeth^{2} Newby**, married 11.14.1696, Little River, Pasquotank

Monthly Meeting, **John White**.

[2]+ b. **James[2] Newby**, born *ca.* 1675, married first 5.5.1699, Perquimans Monthly Meeting, **Sarah[2] Nicholson**, born 15 Aug 1682; married second, Little River Meeting House, 5.18.1719, Pasquotank Monthly Meeting, **Elizabeth[(3)] (White) Davis**, the widow of James Davis and the daughter of Henry[(2)] White; married third, **Hannah** [__], whom he named as his executrix.

[3] c. **John Newby**.

[4]+ d. **Rebecca[2] Newby**, married 10.7.1699, Pasquotank Monthly Meeting, **Jacob[2] Overman II**.

124. Nathan[(2)] Newby, Quaker Minister, identified as the son of **William[(1)] Newby** of Chuckatuck Monthly Meeting, Nansemond Co., VA, was a resident of Nansemond when he married, 10.13.1687, Chuckatuck Monthly Meeting, Nansemond Co., VA, **Elizabeth Hollowell**, born 7.9.1662, Chuckatuck Monthly Meeting, Nansemond, listed as the daughter of Thomas[A] Hollowell and Alice[A] [__]. She died before 1706. Nathan Newby, "late of Nansemond, VA," married second, 8.1.1720, Perquimans Monthly Meeting, NC, **Mary Toms**, and he died testate between 1 Apr and July 1735, Perquimans Co., NC, his will filed among NC Secretary of State loose wills. As a resident of Nansemond, however, he still owned land there as late as 1704, wherein he was taxed on 850 acres, according to Annie Laurie Wright Smith"s *The Quit Rents of Virginia*, 1704, p. 65. He must have inherited this land from his father as there are no earlier pertinent Newby patents before this date. He continued to increase his holdings: on 23 Dec 1714, he received a patent of 485 acres of new land in Nansemond, plus 176 acres adjoining his own land. His neighbors were listed as Thomas Norfleet, Dyor, Joseph Booth, Thomas Price, Jonathan Belch, and Thomas Robert. This land was obtained through the imporation of 10 persons, according to VA Land Patent Book 10, p. 218.

Mary (Toms) Newby married second, 11.2.1744, Perquimans Monthly Meeting, Samuel Moore, the son of William Moore and Elizabeth, born 23 Dec 1707, Perquimans. Samuel died testate between 25 Oct 1751 and Jan 1752, Perquimans, NC Secretary of State loose wills, although he did not name the daughter which he had by Mary Toms. Perhaps she had died.

While Nathan Newby did not mention daughter Rachel Pearson in his will, Peter Pearson in his will, dated 15 Mar 1734, proved 21 Apr 1735, NC Secretary of State loose wills, named brother Nathan Newby.

The Children of Nathan Newby and Elizabeth Hollowell:

[1]+ a. **Rachel[2] Newby**, born *ca.* 1690, died testate between 25 June 1750 and Jan 175$^{0}/_{1}$, NC Secretary of State loose wills; she married *ca.*

1709, **Peter[1] Pearson**, Quaker Minister.

The Children of Nathan Newby and Mary Toms, born Perquimans:

[2] b. **Thomas[2] Newby**.

[3] c. **Francis[2] Newby**, died unmarried but testate between 8 Jan and July 1752, Perquimans, NC Secretary of State loose wills; he named mother Mary Moore, brothers Nathan[2], Thomas[2], and brother-in-law John Robinson.

[4] d. **Nathan[2] Newby**.

[5] e. **Mary[2] Newby**, married 1.4.17$^{39}/_{40}$, Perquimans Monthly Meeting, **John Robinson**.

The Child of Samuel Moore and Mary (Toms) Newby, born Perquimans:

[6] f. **Mary Moore**, born 15 July 1739.

125. Samuel[(3)] Newby, the son of **James Newby** (John[1]) and **Sarah Nicholson**, was born 8.23.1704, Pasquotank Monthly Meeting, and died 12.16.1770, "a worthy minister many years," Pasquotank Monthly Meeting. He married 9.11.1725, Perquimans Monthly Meeting, at the Lower Meeting House, **Elizabeth Albertson**, the daughter of **Nathaniel Albertson** and **Abigail Nicholson**.

The Children of Samuel Newby and Elizabeth Nicholson, born Pasquotank Monthly Meeting:

[1]+ a. **Miriam[2] Newby**, born 6mo.1726, married 12.6.1750, Perquimans Monthly Meeting, **William Lamb**, died testate between 4 Dec 1757 and Apr 1758, Perquimans Co., NC, Secretary of State loose wills; after William's death, Miriam Lamb was "liberated" to marry Abraham Elliott on 3.7.1759, Perquimans Monthly Meeting, but it was reported on 4.4.1759 there that the wedding did not take place.

[2] b. **William[2] Newby**, born 7.22 or .23.1727, requested to remove to Perquimans Monthly Meeting on 4.1.1749; he married 7.6.1749, Perquimans Monthly Meeting, **Jemima Newby**.

[3] c. **Hulde[2] Newby**, born 4.16.1729, died by 1755, Pasquotank Monthly Meeting; married, as the second of his four wives, 8.6.1752, Pasquotank Monthly Meeting, **Joshua Morris**, died 2.14.1777, aged 51, Pasquotank Monthly Meeting. Hulde and Joshua had one son Benjamin[3] Morris, born 5.26.1754, Pasquotank Monthly Meeting.

[4] d. **Darcas[2] Newby**, born 10.4.1730, married 8.3.1751, Pasquotank Monthly Meeting, **John Sanders**.

[5] e. **Mary[2] Newby**, born 7.28.1732.

[6] f. **Joseph^{2} Newby**, born 9.2.1734, died 8.2.1739.

[7] g. **Demcy^{2} Newby**, born 12.20.1736, married 3.6.1760, Pasquotank Monthly Meeting, **Mary Ross**; on 8.23.1764, Pasquotank Monthly Meeting, Demcy was disowned from the Friends.

[8] h. **Elizabeth^{2} Newby**, born 10.30.1738.

[9] i. **Pleasant^{2} Newby**, born 3.2.1740.

[10] j. **Ruth^{2} Newby**, born 3.20.1743, died 3.2.1752.

[11] k. **Samuel^{2} Newby**, born 6.8.1746, was condemned on account of his behavior, 1.20.1768, Pasquotank Monthly Meeting.

126. William$^{(1)}$ Newby was born by 1630 and died before 1704, Perquimans Co., NC, although he was a resident of Chuckatuck Montly Meeting in Nansemond as early as 1687. He was married first to **Isabel** [__] by 1665, the approximate year in which their son Gabriel^{2} was born. He is almost certainly the William Newby who married second, according to Perquimans Co., NC, Deed Book A, no. 173, dated 12 Aug 1701, **Jean** [__] **Moore-Loadman-Byer**. Upon her marriage to William Newby, Jean gave all of her estate to her son William Moore who could take possession of it only after her and her latest husband's decease. William Newby the elder was distinguished from his grandson William^{3} (Gabriel^{2}), as late as 1704, the date at which surviving heir Nathan^{2} was listed as the only Newby land holder in Nansemond according to Annie Laurie Wright Smith"s *The Quit Rents of Virginia*, 1704, p. 65. William's marriage to "Jane Byer" was recorded in Perquimans Monthly Meeting minutes, 7.3.1701.

Son Nathan^{2} Newby and daughter Dorothy^{2} Newby were both identified as children of William in their marriage records at Chuckatuck Monthly Meeting. Son Gabriel^{2} was likewise identified as a son of William but in his marriage record in Perquimans Monthly Meeting.

Jean [__] married first, [__] Moore, and second, [__] Loadman. As Jane "Loedman," she married third, [--] Jan $168^{2}/_{3}$, Perquimans, Richard Bier. Then she married fourth, 7.3.1701, Perquimans Monthly Meeting, William Newby [Sr.]. In Feb $169^{3}/_{4}$, Perquimans Court, Jean's son James Loadman registered rights for the following importees: Hubbart Lambert, Jeane Buyard his mother, and James Loadman (himself), according to Caroline B. Whitley's *North Carolina Headrights, A List of Names, 1663-1744*, p. 9. A more complicated list follows: on the second Monday in Apr 1696, Jan Byer proved transportation rights for 9 persons and assigned two of them to Timothy Clare—herself, Richard Byer, Lawrence Nogell, Jan Byer, Robert Bote, William Boyd, Margaret Boyd, William Moore, and James Loadman. The mention of Lawrence Nogell recalls what might be the first marriage of Richard Byer to Jane Nogell on 8 Oct [--], Perquimans.

An excellent, definitive article by Paul C. Reed on Levin Bufkin has appeared in *The American Genealogist*, vol. 84, no. 1 [January 2010], pp. 29-45: "The English Ancestry of Leven[1] Bufkin of Nansemond County, Virginia: With Some Account of his Royal Descent."

The Children of William Newby and Isabel [__]:

[1]+ a. **Nathan[2] Newby**, died testate between 1 Apr and July 1735, Perquimans Co., NC, Secretary of State loose wills; married first, 10.13.1687, Chuckatuck Monthly Meeting, **Elizabeth Hollowell**; he married second, "late of Nansemond, VA," 8.1.1720, Perquimans Monthly Meeting, NC, **Mary Toms**

[2] b. **Gabriel[2] Newby**, born *ca*. 1665, died 12.25.1735, Perquimans Monthly Meeting, aged 70, as recorded in Pasquotank Monthly Meeting; married 4.1.1689, Perquimans Monthly Meeting, "at a Quaker Meeting at the house of Ann Nicholson," **Mary Tomes**, died 11.26.1738, aged *ca*. 70 years, Pasquotank Monthly Meeting.

[3] c. **Dorothy[2] Newby**, married first, 2.17.1688, Chuckatuck Monthly Meeting, **Levin Bufkin**, the immigrant, who spent two years as a hostage of the Barbary pirates. He was baptized 13 Oct 1634, Barcombe, Sussex, the son of Levin Bufkin and his first wife Anne Walthall, a cousin of the immigrant to Henrico Co., VA, William Walthall. Their son Leven[3] was born 12.8.1688, registered in the records of Chuckatuck Monthly Meeting. Dorothy married second, as his first wife, 7.6.1699, Chuckatuck Monthly Meeting, **Mathew[3] Jordan**, born 11.1.1676, Chuckatuck, the son of Thomas[2] and Margaret (Brasseur) Jordan. Dorothy was dead by 3.17.1702, at which time Mathew married second, at Levy Neck Meeting House, Isle of Wight Co., VA, the widow Susanna (Bird) Bressy. The maternity of Mathew's children is somewhat uncertain.

127. Christopher Nicholson, the son of Edmund[A] Nicholson and Elizabeth[A] Simpson of Lynn, Essex Co., MA (who married second, [__] Brown), was born say 1638, Essex Co., MA, and died 8 Dec 1688, Perquimans Co., NC. He married first, 22.8.1662, Lynn, Essex Co., MA (Vital Records, vol. 2, p. 279), **Hannah Redknap**, the daughter of Joseph[A] and Sarah [__] Redknap of Lynn. He married second, as her first husband, 11 Apr 1680, Perquimans Co., NC, **Ann Atwood**, daughter of Thomas[A] Atwood of Middlesex, England. The widow Ann (Atwood) Nicholson married second, 26 June 1690, Perquimans Co., NC, Richard Dorman, by whom she had at least two more children. She married third, 12.11.1711, Perquimans Monthly Meeting, Richard Cheston, Jr. Records of her death have not been located. For more information concerning the Rednap family, see John Anderson Brayton, "Nicholson and Redknap Families of Massachusetts and North Carolina," in *The North Carolina Genealogical Society Journal*, vol. 30, no. 2 [May 2004], pp. 173-197, especially editor Winslow's excellent addendum.

The Children of Christopher Nicholson and Hannah Redknap, born Perquimans:

[1] a. **Deliverance² Nicholson**, born *ca.* 1663, died 10 Apr 1700; married first, *ca.* 1678, Perquimans Co., NC, **Joseph² Sutton**; second, 7 Oct 1697, **Andrew Reed**.

[2]+ b. **Samuel² Nicholson**, born 1.12.1665, died testate 29 Mar 1728, Perquimans, NC Secretary of State loose wills; married as her first husband, 16 Dec 1688, Perquimans, Co., NC, **Elizabeth Charles**, who died testate between 19 Mar $174^7/_8$ and Jan $174^8/_9$, Perquimans; she married second, 10 June 1729, Zacharian Nixon.

[3] c. **Hannah² Nicholson**, born 1.4.1667, married first, 5 July 1685, Perquimans, Co., NC, **John Gosbey**, who died 24 Aug 1693, Perquimans; second, 14 Aug 1694, Perquimans Co., NC, **Francis Foster** of Accomack Co., VA.

[4] d. **Joseph² Nicholson**, born 7.26.1670, died testate between 12.6.1679 [*sic*, for 1697] and 10 Jan 1697/8, Perquimans, Secretary of State vol. 874.2, p. 95; married 7 June 1693, Perquimans Co., NC, **Hannah Albertson**, who died 2 Jan $169^4/_5$, Perquimans.

[5] e. **John² Nicholson**, born 10.17.1671 [or 1673], died testate between 26 Apr 1710 and 12 Aug 1712, Perquimans; married as her first husband, 20 Nov 1700, Perquimans Co., NC, **Presila Toms**; she married second, 23.6.1711, Perquimans Monthly Meeting, John Kinsey, who died testate between 8 Oct 1718 and 14 Apr 1719, Perquimans.

[6] f. **Nathaniel² Nicholson**, born 10.7.1675, died testate between 12 mar $173^1/_2$ and July 1737, Perquimans; married 8^{th}mo.1704, Perquimans, **Sarah Harris**.

[7] g. **Benjamin² Nicholson**, born 9.26.1678, died testate after 19 Jan 1712, Perquimans.

The Children of Christopher Nicholson and Ann Atwood, born Perquimans:

[8] h. **Elisabeth² Nicholson**, born 11.13.1680, died 11 Sept 1682.

[9]+ i. **Sarah² Nicholson**, born 6.15.1682, died 13.3.171, Perquimans Monthly Meeting; married 5.5.1695, Perquimans Monthly Meeting, as his first wife, **James⁽²⁾ Newby**; he married second, 18.5.1719, Symons Creek Monthly Meeting, Elizabeth (White) Davis.

[10] j. **Elizabeth² Nicholson**, born 11 Mar $168^3/^4$, died before 1713, Perquimans; married, as his first wife, 6.11.1707, Perquimans

Monthly Meeting, **John Newby**; he married second, Elizabeth Barrow.

[11]+ k. **Christopher^2 Nicholson**, born 2 Nov 1685, will proved 23 July 1723, Perquimans; married, as her first husband, 12 Nov 1707, Perquimans, **Mary Poole**; she married second, William Bundy; third, William Low.

[12] l. **Thomas^2 Nicholson**, born 7 Feb 168$^7/_8$, died 4 Mar 168^7[$/_8$].

[13] m. **Ann^2 Nicholson**, born 8 Feb 168$^8/_9$, married 11 May 1721, Pasquotank Register, **Samuel Bundy**.

128. Marmaduke Norfleet, the son of Thomas^A Norfleet, Jr., of Nansemond Co., VA, and Perquimans Co., NC, inherited a portion of a patent granted his father on 19 Jan 171$^5/_6$ for 100 acres in Perquimans adjoining William Brin, according to NC Land Patent Book 8, p. 294. Marmaduke's father Thomas died about 1721 in Nansemond Co., VA, probably never having lived in the Albemarle, and Marmaduke certainly installed himself on his own portion shortly after his father's death. His father's Nansemond land was cut off into Perquimans, as demonstrated by Perquimans Co., NC, Deed Book G, No. 188, dated 26 Apr 1766, in which Marmaduke Norfleet sold to George Washington and Fielding Lewis "of the Colony of Virginia, gentlemen," two parcels of land called "White Oak Springs:" one given by his father Thomas Norfleet, deceased, which was half a tract purchased of William Jones for 225 acres on 5 Apr 1707; and the other, of 40 acres, purchased from Charles Drury on 26 July 1721. By 30 Mar 1769, however, according to Perquimans Co., NC, Deed Book H, no. 61, Norfleet had removed to Northampton Co., NC. Our subject was born *ca.* 1700, Nansemond Co., VA, since he stated in his will (dated June 1774) that he was "upwards of seventy-four years of age." Norfleet died testate between 28 June 1774 and Mar 1775, Northampton Co., NC, Will Book 2, p. 210. He married first, **Elizabeth Gordon**, who was dead by 1751, Perquimans, the daughter of John^A Gordon of Perquimans Co., NC. John^A Gordon was born 25 Sept 1705, Perquimans, and died testate between 25 Apr 1754 and Apr 1758, Perquimans, NC Secretary of State loose wills. In his will, Gordon named his grandson Marmaduke^2 Norfleet [Jr.]. Marmaduke is said to have married second, by 1750, **Judith Rhodes**. The chapter, "The Norfleet Family of Nansemond Co., VA, and Gates and Bertie Counties, NC," which was compiled from the records of the late Stuart H. Hill, W. A. Graham Clark, Fillmore Norfleet, and C. T. Smith, Jr., in John Bennett Boddie, *Southside Virginia Families*, vol. 1, pp. 333-37, seems perfectly reasonable, save for the fact that no proof is provided for Norfleet's second marriage, which may have occurred in Nansemond.

Information on the birth date of Judith[2] Norfleet and the second marriage of Reuben[2] Norfleet have been taken from David B. Gammon's *Eastern North Carolina Families*, vol. 1, p. 16 and pp. 98-99, respectively.

The Children of Marmaduke Norfleet and Elizabeth Gordon:

[1] a. **Marmaduke[2] Norfleet**, married [__].

[2]+ b. **Reuben[2] Norfleet**, born *ca.* 1730, died testate between 13 Apr 1799 and May 1801, Bertie Co., NC, Will Book E, p. 120; married, first **Lucy (Smith) Langley**; second, after 1777, Northampton Co., NC, **Mary (Figures) Exum**, the widow of Matthew Exum, who died testate between 6 Jan and Mar 1777, Northampton Co., NC, Will Book 1, p. 396; and daughter of Richard Figures of Hertford Co., NC.

The Children of Marmaduke Norfleet and Judith Rhodes:

[3] c. **Judith[2] Norfleet**, born 1752, died 14 Feb 1812, Gates Co., NC, according to the 6 Mar 1812 edition of the *Raleigh Register*; married **William[3] Baker**, who died testate after 10 Mar 1803, Gates Co., NC, Will Book 1, p. 240.

[4]+ d. **Sarah[2] Norfleet**, married **Simon[3] Jeffreys**, who died intestate 11 Oct 1812, Franklin Co., NC.

129. John[4] Pace, the son of Richard[3] Pace, Sr., and Mary [__] of Bristol Parish, Henrico and Charles City counties, VA, was born say 1667-69, Charles City Co., VA, and died testate between 21 Mar $172^6/_7$ and Aug 1727, Bertie Co., NC. He married by 1700, **Elizabeth[2] Lowe**, the daughter of **William[1]** and Ann [__] **Lowe**, originally of Charles City and Prince George counties, VA, and later of Chowan. Elizabeth married second, [__] Moore. The first six generations of the Pace family are covered in John F. Dorman's *Adventurers of Purse and Person*, 4th ed., vol. 2, *Families G-P*, pp. 764-69.

The Children[5] of John Pace and Elizabeth Lowe:

[1] a. **Mary[2] Pace**, married [__] **Melton**.

[2] b. **John[2] Pace**, married **Sarah** [__].

[3] c. **William[2] Pace**, married, as her first husband, **Mary** [__], who married second, John Corlew.

[4] d. **George[2] Pace**, married **Obedience** [__], who married second, Robert Cade.

[5] e. **Frances[2] Pace**.

[6] f. **Ann[2] Pace**.

[7] g. **Elizabeth[2] Pace**.

130. Richard[4] Pace, Jr., the son of Richard[3] Pace, Sr., and Mary [__] of Bristol Parish, Henrico and Charles City counties, VA, was born *ca.* 1665, Charles City Co., VA, and died testate between 13 Mar $173^{6}/_{7}$ and Feb $173^{8}/_{9}$, Bertie Co., NC. He will was filed among the loose wills of the NC Secretary of State Collection. He married **Rebecca** [__]. On 22 Nov 1706, Richard Pace, Jr., patented 640 acres on the Morratoke River in Chowan Precinct, according to Chowan Co., NC, Deed Book C-1, p. 75. The first six generations of the Pace family are covered in John F. Dorman's *Adventurers of Purse and Person*, 4th ed., vol. 2, *Families G-P*, pp. 764-69.

The Children[5] of Richard Pace and Rebecca [__]:

[1] a. **William[2] Pace**, married **Celia Boykin**.
[2] b. **Thomas[2] Pace**, married **Amy** [__].
[3] c. **Richard[2] Pace**, married **Elizabeth Cain**.
[4] d. **Ann[2] Pace**, married [__] **Steward**.
[5]+ e. **Rebecca[2] Pace**, married first, **John Bradford**; second, after 1736, Brunswick Co., VA, **William Aycock**, died by 1765, Orange Co., NC.
[6] f. **Amy[2] Pace**, married [__] **Green**.
[7] g. **Frances[2] Pace**, married [__] **Green**.
[8] h. **Tabitha[2] Pace**, married **John Moore**.
[9] i. **Mary[2] Pace**, married [__] **Johnson**.
[10] j. **Sarah[2] Pace**, married [__] **House**.

131. Francis Parrott, formerly and mistakenly thought to be the posthumously born child of Francis Parrott, Sr., and Sarah [__] of Calvert Co., MD, was born *ca.* 1670. An article by Harald Reksten and Wayne Parrott entitled "A Reexamination of the Relationships among the Parrott Families in the American Colonies in the 17th Century," published in the *Magazine of Virginia Genealogy*, vol. 47, no. 2 [May 2009], pp. 129-47, revealed that the Chowan descendants of Francis have different DNA from the descendants of the various Maryland branches. The unborn child of Francis of Calvert Co., MD, has been identified as, more likely in fact, a Francis Parrott who died *ca.* 1710 in Queene Anne's Co., MD.

Our Francis Parrott died intestate before 21 Apr 1715, Chowan Co., NC. He married, as her first husband, **Frances Johnson**, said to have been born 2 Feb $168^{0}/_{1}$, and died testate between 20 Apr 1747 and 17 Dec 1748, Bertie Co., NC, the daughter of [__] and Susannah [__] Johnson, her will filed among the NC Secretary of State loose wills. Frances (Johnson) Parrott married second, Edward

Frederick Rasor. Francis Parrott was in North Carolina as early as 1694, at which time he appeared in court and was reimbursed for travel. On 21 Apr 1715, Susannah Johnson of Chowan made a deed of gift to her grandchildren, the children of Francis Parrott, lately deceased, according to Chowan Co., NC, Deed Book B#1, p. 178. Francis Parrott was also a Justice of the Peace for Chowan in Apr 1711, as found in Hathaway, vol. 3, p. 441.

Francis (Johnson) Parrott-Rasor named her daughter Elizabeth^2 Hardy and her granddaughter Frances^3 Hardy in her will, among others.

The Children of Francis Parrott, Jr., and Frances Johnson, born Chowan:

[1]+ a. **Jacob^2 Parrott**, Sr., born 8 May 1696, died testate between 3 Nov and Nov Court 1738, Bertie, NC Secretary of State loose wills; married **Martha** [__].

[2] b. **Susanna^2 Parrott**.

[3]+ c. **Elizabeth^2 Parrott**, born *ca*. 1702, Chowan, died 1800, Bertie; married first, **Lemuel/Lamb^3 Hardy**, died 1750, Bertie; second, **Martin Frederick Rasor**.

The Children of Edward Frederick Rasor and Frances (Johnson) Parrott:

[4] d. **Edward Rasor**, married **Elizabeth** [__].

[5] e. **Christena Rasor**, married [__] **Bell**.

132. Jonathan Pearson, the son of Rev. **Peter Pearson** and **Rachel Newby**, was born 11.10.1711 or 2, Perquimans Monthly Meeting, and died at Contentnea Monthly Meeting, between 1780 and 1783. He married first, 9.6.1745, Perquimans Monthly Meeting, **Rebeckah Elliott**. He married second, Pasquotank Monthly Meeting, 1.2.1766, **Sarah (Bogue) Bundy**, widow of Joseph Bundy. He probably married third, 9.9.1780, Contentnea Monthly Meeting, **Sara Peele**, daughter of Joseph Peele. She married second, 3.9.1783, Contentnea Monthly Meeting, Frederick Loving, at Great Contentnea Meeting House.

Tragically, because of the lack of probate material, or of loose estates papers for Jonathan^1 Pearson, only the following proved children can be listed for his family. *Please* do not trust Mrs. Winslow on this matter.

Proved Children of Jonathan Pearson and Rebeckah Elliott, born Pasquotank Monthly Meeting:

[1]+ a. **Ichabod^2 Pearson**, married 10.5.1774, Pasquotank Monthly Meeting, **Miriam^3 Lamb**, the daughter of William Lamb and **Miriam^2 Newby**; the births of their children were registered in Contentnea Monthly Meeting.

[2] b. **Rhoda[2] Pearson**, born 4mo.1750, married 11.15.1785, Contentnea Monthly Meeting (identified as daughter of Jonathan), **Reuben Peele**.

The Children of Jonathan Pearson and Sarah (Bogue) Bundy:

[3] c. **Elizabeth[2] Pearson**, born 7.15.1767, married 3.13.1784, Contentnea Monthly Meeting, **Richard Ratcliff**, died 5.22.1839, Henry Co., IN.

133. Rev. Peter Pearson, the son of Christopher[A] Pearson and Eleanor[A] Fearon of Ullock in the parish of Dean, Cumberlandshire (who were married 4.9.1670 at Pardshaw Crag Monthly Meeting), was born 12.21.1679, Ullock Dean, and died testate 21 Apr 1735, Perquimans Co., NC, his will proved the same date and filed among the NC Secretary of State loose wills. The Cumberland Quaker information is taken from the *Digest of the Society of Friends*, Cumberland, SPEC JAC film #823, D/FCF/5/14 (for births), and D/FCF/5/16 (for marriages and burials), viewed at the Cumbria Record Office, Carlisle. Peter married by 1709, Perquimans Co., NC, **Rachel[2] Newby**, who was born 1690, Isle of Wight Co., VA, died testate between 25 June and Jan $175^{0}/_{1}$, Perquimans Co., NC, the daughter of **Nathan[1] Newby** and Elizabeth Hollowell.

Mrs. Watson Winslow, in her *History of Perquimans County*, p. 399, misread the specific bequest in Rachel (Newby) Pearson's will to daughter "Betty Bagley" [rendered curiously by Dr. Stephen Bradley as "Batty,"], as "Betty Bailey," having assumed that this child was a Pearson *son* by a former marriage. Mrs. Winslow also assumed that Rachel's failure to name son Nathan[2], who was named in Peter Pearson's will, indicated the same [unsubstantiated] earlier marriage. A testator or testatrix may specifically number children to insure that they alone are included in the division of specific property. Jonathan K. T. Smith's *A Genealogical Memoir, Peter and Rachel Pearson of Nansemond County, Virginia*, pp. 1-8, is an excellent study of the Pearson family both in the colonies and back into Cumberlandshire.

The Children of Peter Pearson and Rachel Newby, born Perquimans Monthly Meeting:

[1] a. **Peter[2] Pearson**, born 6.19.1711, reported to have married "out of society," Perquimans Monthly Meeting, 11.2.1763.

[2] b. **John[2] Pearson**, born 9.22.1714, died intestate before 7 June 1760; married 11.3.$173^{8}/_{9}$, Perquimans Monthly Meeting, **Elizabeth Croxton**. He was dismissed from "unity," 6.4.1739.

[3] c. **Rachal[2] Pearson**, born 11.16.1716, married 8.4.1738, Perquimans Monthly Meeting, **Robert Bogue**.

[4] d. **Nathan[2] Pearson**, born 12.6.1718.

[5] e. **Mary[2] Pearson**, born 11.20.1720, married first, 9.20.1740, registered in Perquimans Monthly Meeting, but married near Levin Buffkin's house in Nansemond Co., VA, **John Winslow**, son of Thomas; married second, 1755, **Joshua Moore**.

[6]+ f. **Jonathan[2] Pearson**, born 11.10.1711 or 1712, Perquimans Monthly Meeting, married first, 9.6.1745, Perquimans Monthly Meeting, **Rebeckah Elliott**; married second, Pasquotank Monthly Meeting, 2.2.1766, **Sarah (Bogue) Bundy**, widow of Joseph Bundy.

[7] g. **Betty[2] Pearson**, married 5.1.1747, Perquimans Monthly Meeting, **William Bagley**.

134. Robert Peele I was born by 1630 and died after 1694, probably in Nansemond Co., VA. He was granted 350 acres of land on the southwest side of the "Pasbetanke" River, between Dr. Relfe and John Battle, in North Carolina on 25 Sept 1663, according to Virginia Land Patent Book 4, p. 96 (588). This land would eventually fall into Pasquotank Co. On 30 Apr 1679, Robert Peele, Sr., and Robert[2] Peele, Jr., jointly patented 179 acres in Nansemond Co., VA, at the head of Mr. Bennett's Creek, half of which was an ancient patent granted to one More and Welton, which escheated to Samll. Granberry, and was conveyed to the said Peele, according to VA Land Patent Book 6, p. 678. Robert Peele's last definite appearance was as a Justice of the Peace for Nansemond Co., VA, on 13 Nov 1694, wherein he witnessed a power of attorney from James Alexander of Nansemond to **Alexander Lillington**. The name of his wife does not appear. Robert Peele's land in Nansemond was eventually cut off into North Carolina.

The Child of Robert Peele I and [__]:

[1]+ a. **Robert[2] Peele II**, married **Sarah [__] Jarrat**.

135. Robert Peele II, the son of Robert Peele I and [__], was born by 1650 and died before 1704. He married **Sarah [__] Jarrat**, the widow of Thomas Jarrat. On 24 Apr 1703, Robert "Peale" was granted 134 acres in the Lower Parish of Nansemond Co., VA, on the east side of the Nansemond River, near the Sleepy Hole and John Peters, in Belson's line. This land had been granted to Richard Russell, 27 Aug 1653, who sold it to Edward Dence, from whom it escheated to Thomas Jarrat, 6 Apr 1671, who bequeathed it to his wife Sarah, who intermarried with the said Peale. This concatenation of events can be found in VA Land Patent Book 9, p. 512.

The list of children below is based on Hugh Buckner Johston's altogether reasonable treatise on the Peele family of Nansemond and Northampton, found among his typescripts at the Wilson County [NC] Public Library. Mr. Johnston obviously examined the records of *The Vestry Book of the Upper Parish of Nansemond County*, which would be the parish bordering the Virginia-North Carolina line, and extracted the names of the other males with the surname of Peele. This is not a completely "unscientific" deduction, but is based on the conclusion that Robert Peele II was the only offspring of Robert I, and that other males owning land near his would have to be his children, and not of other heretofore unknown siblings.

The Children of Robert Peele II and Sarah [__] Jarratt:
[1] a. **William² Peele**, born *ca.* 1679.
[2]+ b. **Robert² Peele III**, born *ca.* 1681, married **Judith** [__].
[3] c. **Ephraim² Peele**, born *ca.* 1685.
[4] d. **Joseph² Peele**, born *ca.* 1687.

136. Robert Peele III, the son of Robert Peele II and Sarah [__] Jarratt, was born *ca.* 1681, Nansemond Co., VA, and died intestate there about 1748. He was listed with 275 acres of land in Annie Laurie Wright Smith's *The Quit Rents of Virginia, 1704*, p. 68. After his death, his Quaker family sold their land and removed to the Rich Square area of Northampton Co., NC. His wife **Judith** [__] died testate between 22 June and Aug Court 1756, Northampton Co., NC, Secretary of State loose wills.

The bracketed dates of birth below have been taken from Hugh Buckner Johnston's chapter on the Peele family, and cannot be proved. The volume in question is not presently available at the Wilson County Public Library. Children mentioned in the will of Judith Peele are marked with the symbol "§."

The Children of Robert Peele III and Judith [__]:
[1]§+ a. **Robert² Peele IV**, born 6.29.1709, married first, *ca.* 1729, **Elizabeth** [__], and second, **Charity² Dickinson**.
[2] b. **Edmund² Peele**, born [11 Dec 1710].
[3]§ c. **Sarah² Peele**, born 11.22.1712, married **John Duke**, who died testate between 30 Jan 1783 and June 1787, Northampton Co., NC, Will Book 1, p. 464.
[4]§ d. **Joseph² Peele**, born [16 Feb 1715].
[5] e. **John² Peele**, born [27 Jan 1717], died *ca.* 1725.
[6]§ f. **Joshua² Peele**, born [5 Feb 17¹⁹/₂₀].
[7] g. **James² Peele**, born [5 Apr 1721].
[8]§ h. **Josiah² Peele**, born [20 Oct 1723].
[9]§ i. **John² Peele**, born [2 Aug 1729].
[10]§ j. **Mary² Peele**, born [16 Nov 1731], married **William Granberry**, who died tstate between 24 Feb 1787 and Mar 1790, Northampton

Co., NC, Will Book 1, p. 390.

137. Robert Peele IV, the son of Robert Peele III and Judith [__], was born 6.29.1709, Nansemond Co., VA, and died testate 13 July 1782, Rich Square Monthly Meeting, Northampton Co., NC. His will was recorded in Northampton Co., NC, Will Book 1, p. 172. He married first, *ca.* 1729, **Elizabeth** [__] of Nansmond, who died *ca.* 1749. According to Hugh Buckner Johnston's treatise on the Peele family, supposedly located in the Wilson County [NC] Public Library, Peele's first wife was Elizabeth Edgerton, the possible daughter of Patrick and Mary Edgerton of Nansemond, but I can find no proof of this. Robert Peele IV married second, 6.1.1750, Perquimans Monthly Meeting, **Charity**[2] **Dickinson**, the daughter of **John**[1] and Rebecca [__] Dickinson of Northampton.

The children of both wives of Robert Peele IV are recorded on p. 225 of William Wade Hinshaw, *Encyclopedia of American Quaker Genealogy*, vol. 1, *North Carolina*, although Hinshaw confused Charity the wife with Charity the daughter. On p. 252 of that same volume, in confirmation of Hinshaw's mistake, daughter Mary is listed in her 1760 marriage as the daughter of "Elizabeth deceased." Hinshaw also confused first wife Elizabeth with daughter Betsy. Elizabeth [__] Peele was clearly not alive just prior to her putative death date on 4.26.1763, as Hinshaw states.

The Children of Robert Peele IV and Elizabeth [__], births recorded Rich Square Monthly Meeting, Northampton Co., NC:

[1]+ a. **Robert**[2] **Peele**, Jr., born 9.15.1730, married 5 Sept 1753, Northampton Co., NC, **Margaret B. Jossey**.

[2] b. **Isaac Passco**[2] **Peele**, born 7.29.1733.

[3] c. **Elizabeth**[2] **Peele**, born 7.9.1736, married **Arthur**[2] **Bryant**, the son of **James**[1] **Bryant**, Jr.

[4] d. **Mary**[2] **Peele**, born 2.2.1742, married 12.7.1760, Rich Square Monthly Meeting, **Thomas Hollowell**.

[5] e. **Sarah**[2] **Peele**, born 7.30.1746, died 6.11.1813, Contentnea Monthly Meeting; married by 1764, **David Newsom**, who died testate between 20 Oct 1815 and Feb 1816, Wayne Co., NC, RD-3, p. 339.

The Children of Robert Peele IV and Charity Dickinson, born Rich Square Monthly Meeting, Northampton Co., NC:

[6] f. **David**[2] **Peele**, born 10.10.1751, died testate 4.25.1807, Contentnea Monthly Meeting, his will proved Feb 1808, Wayne Co., NC, Will Book B, p. 416; married 2.9.1794, Contentnea Monthly Meeting, **Priscilla Fletcher**, who died testate between 9 Nov 1807 and July

1808, Wayne Co., NC, RD-1, p. 88. David Peele, on 4.7.1773, Rich Square Monthly Meeting, requested a certificate to join Contentnea Monthly Meeting.

[7] g. **Judith[2] Peele**, born 10.24.1754, married 4.19.1777, Rich Square Monthly Meeting, **Josiah Cox**; the births of their children were registered at Contentnea Monthly Meeting.

[8] h. **Jeremiah[2] Peele**, born 6.9.1756, married 1.20.1776, Rich Square Monthly Meeting, **Elizabeth Daughtry**.

[9] i. **Anna[2] Peele**, born 5.4.1756, married 5.15.1773, Rich Square Monthly Meeting, **Cornelius Outlaw**.

[10] j. **Charity[2] Peele**, born 5.27.1759, died 6.5.1777, Rich Square Monthly Meeting.

[11] k. **Abba[2] Peele**, born 3.1.1761, married [__] **Jennett**.

[12] l. **Betsey[2] Peele**, born 6.18.1762, died 12.13.1779, Rich Square Monthly Meeting.

[13] m. **Rachel[2] Peele**, born 12.1.1764, died 3.13.1816, Contentnea Monthly Meeting, married 12.13.1783, Contentnea Monthly Meeting, **Robert Fellow**.

[14] n. **Selah[2] Peele**, born 8.4.1766, married 2.14.1784, Contentnea Monthly Meeting, **Zachariah Morris**; the births of two of their children were registered at Contentnea.

138. Jacob Perry, Sr., was born *ca.* 1695, possibly in Nansemond Co., VA, and died testate between 4 Mar 1775 and Oct 1777, Perquimans Co., NC, Will Book C, p. 234. He married first, by 1724, Perquimans Co., NC, **Hepzibah[2] Clare**, the daughter of **Timothy[1] Clare** and third wife Hannah (Lawrence) Snelling, born 2.14.1702, Perquimans Monthly Meeting, NC. Jacob Perry married second, **Anne** [__]. On 14 July 1724, Perquimans Co., NC, Deed Book B, no. 119, William Moore sold 400 acres of land to Jacob Perry on the northeast side of the River adjoining Thomas Lilly and the grantor. On 11 Sept 1727, Perquimans Co., NC, Deed Book B, no. 275, Jacob sold 200 acres of that tract to Benjamin Perry, whose relationship to the grantor has not yet been revealed by the records.

On pp. 401-402 of her *History of Perquimans County North Carolina*, Mrs. Winslow concocted a lively narrative connecting Jacob Perry of Perquimans with the family of a much, much older Phillip Perry and wife Grace [__] of Isle of Wight Co., VA. One reason for believing this assertion is the list of importees registered by one John Perry in May 1742 [referred to later in this sketch as "John of 1742"], according to Caroline B. Whitley's *North Carolina Headrights, A List of Names, 1663-1744*, p. 207: John Perry, Sarah Perry, Nichs. Perry, Jacob Perry, Isaac Perry, Benja. Perry, Sarah Perry, Grace Perry, James Perry, Anne Perry, Josiah Perry, Saml. Thomas, and six Negro slaves. The name Grace would certainly be unusual enough at this time to suggest a relationship with the Virginia family.

John Perry of 1742 with wife and headright Sarah, above, was in Bertie as early as 13 June 1737, according to Bertie Co., NC, Deed Book E, p. 334. None of the names included in the list of headrights corresponds with the family of John[2] of Perquimans and later Martin counties [see below], although in Chowan Co., NC, Deed Book B#1, p. 5, dated 28 July 1719, a Jacob Perry, probably ours, did witness the sale of land from a James Perry of the Upper Parish of Nansemond to a John Perry of the same—that was Jacob's last appearance in the Chowan records. The grantee in this record, John Perry, was the same person who with wife Sarah sold land in Bertie, noted above. According to Chowan Co., NC, Deed Book F#1, p. 123, on 17 Apr 1721, Edward Howcott sold land to John "Parry" of the Upper Parish of Nansemond, the same tract which John and Sarah later sold above. Mrs. Winslow's thesis is engaging, but at this point not proveable. And we must conclude that the list of headrights belonged to John and Sarah Perry of Chowan and Bertie, not John[2] the 1789 testator of Martin County.

Phillip[(A)] Perry, the progenitor of this family, died testate between 26 Nov 1667 (then aged about 70) and 9 Oct 1669, Isle of Wight Co., VA, Will & Deed Book 2, p. 77. His wife Grace [__], obviously much younger than he, married second, before 1 May 1674, Phillip's former overseer, Ralph Channell, according to Isle of Wight Co., VA, Will & Deed Book 1, p. 312. The testator mentioned only "eldest" son Phillip[(B)], not yet 21, and "youngest" son John[(B)], (who was of age when he mentioned his mother and step-father—therefore born *ca.* 1653), but this comparison of adjectives seems merely a quirk of grammar—there is no suggestion of any other children.

We must skip a generation (at least) and consider the importation rights of John Perry in 1742, listed above. It is genealogically reasonable to assume that John of 1742 might be a grandson of Phillip and Grace the progenitors, but this is only logical finger-painting. Nor is it unreasonable to theorize that Phillip and Grace were the grandparents of our Jacob[1] and his (possible) brother or cousin Phillip[1] Perry, the latter of whom died testate between 5 July and Oct 1751, Perquimans Co., NC, Secretary of State loose wills, naming brother John (of 1742), and executor Jacob Perry so of John Perry.

For reasons that are not clear, daughter Mary[2], who married Pritlow Elliott, possibly as his third wife, was not mentioned in her father's will.

The Children of Jacob Perry and Hepzibah Clare:

[1] a. **Elizabeth[2] Perry**, married 2.6.1743, Perquimans Monthly Meeting, **Isaac Willson**.

[2] b. **Jacob[2] Perry**, will proved July 1790, Perquimans Co., NC, Will Book C, p, 414; married **Mary** [__].

[3] c. **Israel^2 Perry**, will proved 27 May 1779, Perquimans Co., NC, Will Book C, p. 224; married [__].
[4] e. **Reuben^2 Perry**, married 11.6.1754, Perquimans Monthly Meeting, **Esther Winslow**.
[5] d. **Dempsey^2 Perry**.
[6]+ f. **John^2 Perry**, born *ca.* 1730, died between 27 Nov and Dec 1789, Martin Co., NC, Will Book 1, p. 153; married **Sarah** [__].
[7] g. **Priscilla^2 Perry**, married **Dempsey Welch**.
[8] h. **Mary^2 Perry**, married 7.4.1759, Perquimans Monthly Meeting, **Pritlow Elliott**, who died testate between 5 July and Oct 1787, Perquimans Co., NC, Will Book C, p. 354.
[9] i. **Hepzibah^2 Perry**, married **Hardy Stallings**.
[10] j. **Ann^2 Perry**, married 11.1.1769, Perquimans Monthly Meeting, **Caleb Winslow**.

139. Robert Peyton II, the son of Robert Peyton, Sr., [see below] and [__], was born *ca.* 1680, Gloucester Co., VA, which birthplace was revealed in the 1746 will of his son Benjamin^2, who bequeathed 350 acres in Gloucester Co., VA, to his own son-in-law Henry Snoad. According to Annie Laurie Wright Smith's *The Quit Rents of Virginia, 1704*, p. 70, our Robert Peyton was taxed on 680 acres of land in Kingston Parish, Gloucester Co., VA. Robert Peyton died testate between 3 Jan 1733 and 10 Sept 1754, Beaufort Co., NC, according to NC Secretary of State loose wills. His will was also recorded in NC Secretary of State vol. 881, p. 104. He married after 17 May 1703, the date at which her first husband's will was proved, according to VA Land Patent Book 9, p. 588, **Mary** [__] **Long**, the widow of Abraham Long of Kingston Parish, Gloucester Co., VA [see below].

Robert Peyton was engaged in a lawsuit in colonial North Carolina in Mar 1722 with Thomas Swann who spoke "divers false and Scandalous Words," concerning Peyton's service on a jury in Currituck, according to *The Colonial Records of North Carolina*, 2nd ser., vol. 5, *North Carolina Higher-Court Minutes, 1709-1723*, pp. 267-68. Unfortunately, Peyton did not win the suit and had to pay court charges. Robert Peyton was appointed a Justice of the Peace for Beaufort in 1724, according to *The Colonial Records of North Carolina*, 2nd ser., vol. 7, *Records of the Executive Council, 1664-1734*, p. 141.

The surviving records of Gloucester Co., VA, provide some startlingly concise records for Robert Peyton II. In vol. 2 of Polly Cary Mason's *Records of Colonial Gloucester County Virginia*, p. 45, is given the following information, contained in the "Berkeley Family Papers:" on 29 June 1714, Robert Peyton of Kingston Parish acknowledged his indebtedness to Edmund Berkeley of Middlesex in the sum of £290 sterling. The consideration was that Robert Peyton must produce the last will and testament of his father and declare that he, the grantor, had no right to the land sold to Berkeley in King & Queen Co., VA, on 18 June 1714. The previous abstract from the Berkeley collection was dated 17 June 1714 and was a deed from Robert Peyton of Kingston parish to Edmund Berkeley of Christ Church Parish of Middlesex for 350 acres of land, formerly in the possession of Ralph Green in 1662, who sold it to Col. Richard Dudley, Sr., of Gloucester, who, in turn, sold it to Robert Peyton the father in 1680, whose will was recorded in Gloucester in 1695.

The second record of interest was a deed from Robert and Mary Peyton of Kingston Parish, Gloucester, to Edmund Berkeley of Christ Church Parish, Middlesex Co., VA. Mary, formerly the wife of Abraham Long, had a life interest in a plantation in Kingston Parish, formerly the land of Abraham Long containing 350 acres, and formerly granted to Sarah Long and Mary Shipley, daughters of Abraham English, deceased, 1/3 part of which belonged to Ann Forrest as sister and coheiress of the said Abraham Long, and by her sold to Robert Peyton by deed dated 1707. These cited records do not, unfortunately, provide quite enough information to sort out all these implied relationships. Elizabeth Peyton, the sister of Robert, Sr., of Gloucester, married Col. Peter Beverley, which explains the presence of Peyton transactions in the Berkeley papers. See reference to Hayden, below.

William Bell of Currituck married 30 May 1722, Norfolk Co., VA (marriage bond, surety Solomon Wilson, wit: Tabitha Wilson), Eleanor Corprew. See Elizabeth B. Wingo, compiler, *Marriages of Norfolk County Virginia ,1706-1792*, vol. 1, p. 4. From Dr. Stephen E. Bradley, Jr., compiler, *Early Records of North Carolina*, vol. 9, *Colonial Court Records—Estate Papers, 1665-1775, A-Gibson*, item 32, pp. 17-18: the petition of Benja[2]. Peyton, admr. of William Bell, decd., to the Precinct Court of "Carrotock," 13 July 1723; listed in his petition were noted the orphans, Ellenor the widow of William Bell who had since married sd. Benj[a]. [Peyton]; the petition of Joseph Sanderson to General Court in behalf of Sarah Bell and Keziah Bell orphans and children of William Bell committed to his "tuition;" also for John Woodhouse in behalf of Jane Bell, another orphan, who stated that Benj[a]. Peyton of Bath Co. had taken administration of the estate and refused to pay sd. orphans their portions. Eleanor (Corprew) Bell-Peyton continued to reside in Bath, eventually Beaufort Co., NC, until she died testate. She bequeathed to son William Bell land that Capt. Henry Snoad took up on the head of Durham's Creek, adjoining Mr. Thomas Bonner on the south side of Horse Pond; she named the following daughters: Elenor[3] Peyton, Grace[3] Peyton, and made son William Bell her executor.

The Rev. Horace Edwin Hayden, in his *Virginia Genealogies, A Genealogy of the Glassell Family…*", proposed the English ancestry of Robert[A] Peyton, Sr., pp. 463-67, connecting him to Thomas[B] Peyton and first wife

Elizabeth[B] Yelverton of Rougham Hall, Norfolkshire. Hayden was a talented researcher, who, although proficient in disovering "secondary" genealogical and heraldic resource material which proved more often than not to be especially reliable—such as visitations and other such pedigrees—and generally acceptable, did not try to obtain primary research data such as parish records and probate which would have proved beyond a doubt his findings. He was, however, practically the first Virginian to investigate the English roots of the Virginia Cavalier classes on a semi-professional basis and his work has served as an extremely useful spring-board for more in-depth studies.

I hired a colleague in England to search the parish registers of Rougham, Norfolk, for traces of the Peyton family, and the following results were had: Thomas Peyton and his wife Elizabeth [Yelverton] had the following children baptized in the parish of Roughan: [*i*] Thomas, bapt. 4 Jan 163$^7/_8$, buried 2 Apr 1638; [*ii*] Elizabeth, bapt. 25 May 1639, buried 5 July 1640; [*iii*] William, bapt. 18 Apr 1640; [*iv*] Robert, bapt. 6 Sept 1641; [*v*] John, bapt. 5 Sept 1642; [*vi*] Jane, bapt. 28 Aug 1643. Elizabeth Peyton was buried there 6 June 1668. Transcripts of the registers at the Society of Genealogists, London (Microfilm #4069), were inspected. Elizabeth Peyton, obviously with her husband's permission, signed her will on 20 Feb 1664 which was proved 9 Feb 1669, PCC Wills [FHL# 2,262,380]. There were apparently more children born and buried after the six listed above, given the many gaps reported in the registers: named in her will were daughter Ann, and sons Charles, Robert, and Yelverton. None of her sons were yet 25 years old. Thus we have the immigrant Robert Peyton's baptismal date.

The pedigree proposed by Hayden, and also the royal descent included in Gary Boyd Roberts' *The Royal Descent of 600 Immigrants*, seem to be entirely reasonable, and this writer sees no reason not to accept them. Hayden, on pp. 470-71, located a birth record for William[2] Peyton, and had many interesting records on the North Carolina branch of the family.

The Children of Robert Peyton and Mary [__] Long, born Bath Co., NC:

[1]+ a. **Benjamin[2] Peyton**, will proved Sept 1746, Beaufort Co., NC, Old Will Book p. 166 (375 A&B); married **Eleanor** (**Corprew**) **Bell**, daughter of John Corprew of Norfolk and widow of William Bell of Currituck Co., NC, born *ca*. 1702, Norfolk Co., VA, her will dated 9 Oct 1751, proved Dec 1753, Beaufort Co., NC, Old Will Book, p. 43.

[2] b. **Thomas[2] Peyton**.

[3] c. **Robert[2] Peyton** of St. Thomas Parish, will dated 16 May 1759, Beaufort Co., NC, Old Will Book, p. 196 (445). He made bequests to his niece Celea[3] Peyton and to loving cousin John[3] Peyton, two children of his brother William[2] Peyton.

[4] d. Capt. **William[2] Peyton**, baptized 3 July 1718, Kingston Parish,

Gloucester Co., VA, said to have died *ca.* 1792, Bourbon Co., KY, aged 74 years; married [__] **Patterson**, a native of New Jersey.

[5] e. **Ambross² Peyton**.

[6] f. **Sarah² Peyton**.

[7] g. **Dorothy² Peyton**, married first, **Joshua Porter**; second, [__] **Finch**.

140. Samuel Pike II was the son of **Samuel Pike** I, and Jean [__], named in his father's will dated 11 Nov 1716 in Pasquotank (filed in NC Secretary of State loose wills), and his wife Jean[A] [__], who married second, 4.9.1720 (recorded in Pasquotank Monthly Meeting), at Little River Meeting House, Arnould White. Samuel II was born say 1712, Pasquotank Co., NC, and died before 1790, Contentnea Monthly Meeting, Dobbs Co., NC. He married first, 2.7.1737, Pasquotank Monthly Meeting, **Sarah⁴ Overman**, born 1.12.1722, Pasquotank Monthly Meeting, died before 1763, Pasquotank Monthly Meeting, the daughter of Ephraim Overman and **Sarah³ Belman**, married at Pasquotank Monthly Meeting, 3.13.1708. On 10.1.1730 and on 4.4.1741 Samuel and his family requested a certificate for removal to "Opecking" Monthly Meeting [Hopewell], in Virginia. On 2.2.1742, Samuel and his wife Sarah requested removal from Pasquotank to Cape Fear; on 6.5.1760, to Carver's Creek Monthly Meeting; on 2.4.1762 to Cane Creek; and on 1.20.1773, to Rich Square Monthly Meeting. Samuel married second, 2.3.1763, Pasquotank Monthly Meeting, **Tabitha Scott**. He married third, Rich Square Monthly Meeting, 4.16.1774, **Anne Jucely**. There were no children by these last two marriages.

In the minutes of Pasquotank Monthly Meeting, Ann² Pike, "now Boles," was dismissed for marrying out of faith. This is confirmed by Pasquotank Co., NC, Deed Book D&E, p. 429, in which she signed a sort of pre-nuptial agreement with her soon-to-be husband.

The Children of Samuel Pike and Sarah Overman, born Pasquotank Monthly Meeting:

[1] a. **Patience² Pike**, born 2.17.1738.

[2] b. **Ann² Pike**, born 2.28.1740, married *ca.* 7 July 1768, Pasquotank Co., NC, **David Boles**.

[3] c. **Miriam² Pike**, born 12.5.1742, married 11.5.1761, Pasquotank Monthly Meeting, **Benjamin White**.

[4] d. **Elizabeth² Pike**, born 12.9.1747, married 3.20.1771, Pasquotank Monthly Meeting, **Samuel Collier**.

[5] e. **Mary² Pike**, born 2.27.1749.

[6] f. **Susanna² Pike**, born 5.12.1752, married 7.15.1772, Pasquotank Monthly Meeting, **Joshua Copeland**.

[7] g. **Rhoda² Pike**, born 2.22.1758.

[8]+ h. **Nathan[2] Pike**, born 8.22.1760, married 8.15.1781, Contentnea Monthly Meeting, **Rachel Mauldin**.

141. Jacob Pope, the son of Henry Pope and Sarah Watts of Chuckatuck Monthly Meeting, was born *ca.* 1695, Isle of Wight Co., VA, and died testate at a considerable age between 1 Mar 1770 and May 1772, Edgecombe Co., NC, Will Book A, p. 189. He married first, say 1715, **Mourning** [__], as proved by deeds in Isle of Wight Co., VA, wherein on 172$^1/_2$ Jacob and wife Mourning [already residents] of Chowan Co., NC, sold land which Jacob's brother William had patented in 1715, Isle of Wight Co., VA, Deeds, 1715-1726, p. 185, and p. 482. Pope had two early grants for land: [1] an undated one for 245 acres on the south side of Morattock River in about 1721, according to NC Land Patent Book 3, p. 86; [2] another on 7 Nov 1723 for 240 acres in Bertie on south side of Morattock River adjoining Looking Glass pocoson, according to NC Land Patent Book 3, p. 179. Jacob married second, by 1 Feb 1743, Edgecombe Co., NC, **Tabitha** [__], who appeared on a deed of gift with Jacob to Jacob Sikes, the son of John Sikes, according to Edgecombe Co., NC, Deed Book 5, p. 218. Jacob married third, **Jane** [__], thought to be the widow Jane (Braswell) Williams, named in the will of Samuel Williams, who died testate between 18 Nov 1748 and Feb 174$^8/_9$, Edgecombe, NC Secretary of State loose wills. Actual "widow" Jane Williams was the daughter of Richard Braswell of Isle of Wight Co., VA, who named her in his will dated 28 Jan 172$^4/_5$, The Great Book, p. 174. Jane Pope's identity as a Williams widow can neither be disproved nor confirmed, although the chronology and onomastic evidence fits for her to have been Samuel's relict. Sorting out the descendants of the Popes has been made difficult by the existence of several contemporary Jacob Popes: Jacob Pope, son of William (who died 1749, Edgecombe), died intestate in 1752, had a wife Patience; Jacob Pope, Jr., died intestate by 1744, and was probably the son of Jacob just mentioned.

Daughter Mourning[2] Pope is placed as a product of the first marriage for onomastic reasons. Identifying Mourning's children has been a study in the perils of rapid-fire serial monogamy, given the fact that each of her husbands in his will did not name any stepchildren by his present wife. On 22 Nov 1744, Edgecombe Co., NC, Court Minutes, an allowance was granted Joseph Thomas "who intermarried with the widow of Jeremiah Hilliard, decd., for the maintenance of the orphans." Fortunately we have the will of Jeremiah's brother Robert Hilliard who died testate between 13 Apr 1743 and May 1751, Edgecombe Co., NC, Secretary of State loose wills, and named the children of his deceased brother: Jacob[3] Hilliard (died testate 1764, Edgecombe), Robert[3] Hilliard, Jeremiah[3] Hilliard, Sampson[3] Hilliard, and Mary[3] Hilliard. It is perfectly reasonable to assume that Mourning was also the mother of the children of Joseph Thomas of whom she was appointed guardian: Charity[3] Thomas, and

Mourning[3] Thomas, according to Edgecombe Co., NC, Estates Records. The fact that George Wimberley's son George, Jr., married 1 Sept 1764, Charity[3] Thomas, Edgecombe Co., NC, Williams and Griffin, *Marriages of Edgecombe County North Carolina, 1733-1868*, p. 177, supposes that he married his stepsister and not his half sister. Therefore, we may also assume that Mourning did not have children by her last marriage. On p. 40 of the same volume of Edgecombe marriages, we have a marriage bond dated 19 Nov 1770 for Jacob Dickinson and Mourning[3] Thomas, witnessed by George Wimberley.

Daughter Rebecca[2] Sikes appeared as a witness with John Sikes to a deed from Jacob Sikes of New Hanover Co., NC, to John Watkins of Edgecombe, dated 27 Nov 1761, according to Edgecombe Co., NC, Deed Book 1, p. 262. Pilgrim[2] Pope is placed as a son of Jacob and Jane because he was called "their son" in a deed of gift dated 27 Sept 1762, Edgecombe Co., NC, Deed Book 1, p. 366. Jacob and Jane gave him 150 acres on the north bank of the Tar River, which was part of a patent to Jacob dated 1730. Pilgrim[2]'s wife Olive [__] appeared with him on a deed in Edgecombe, Deed Book 3, p. 508, dated 2 Oct 1779.

The Children of Jacob Pope and Mourning [__]:

[1]+ a. **Mourning[2] Pope**, born say 1715, married first, **Jeremiah[1] Hilliard**, who died intestate, $174^1/_2$, Edgecombe; second, **Joseph Thomas** of Edgecombe, who died testate between 24 Oct 1757 and June 1758, NC Secretary of State loose wills; third, as his second wife, **William Pridgen** of St. Mary's Parish, Edgecombe Co., NC, died testate between11 May and June 1762, Edgecombe Co., NC, Will Book A, p. 98; fourth, as his second wife, **George Wimberley**, who died testate between 26 May 1764 and May 1768, Edgecombe Co., NC, Will Book A, p. 165.

The Children of Jacob Pope and Tabitha [__]:

[2] b. **Elijah[2] Pope**.

[3] c. **Rebeccah[2] Pope**, married **John Sikes**.

[4] d. **Mary[2] Pope**, married [__] **Surringer**.

The Children of Jacob Pope and Jane (Braswell) Williams:

[5] e. **Pilgrim[2] Pope**, married **Olive** [__].

[6] f. **Sampson[2] Pope**.

142. George[(2)] Powell, the son of **John[(1)] Powell** and **Marian[2] Smith**, was born *ca.* 1694, Norfolk Co., VA, and died testate between 24 Mar $173^5/_6$ and May 1736, Bertie Co., NC, his will filed among the NC Secretary of State loose wills.

He married **Ann** [__]. His first record in Chowan was a purchase of land, 16 Apr 1720, from Richard and Jane Church, according to Chowan Co., NC, Deed Book F#1, p. 18. Although George did not mention a wife in his will, her existence was confirmed by a deed in Bertie Co., NC, Deed Book A, p. 30, dated Feb 1722, in which she relinquished her dower in a sale to Dennis McClendon.

The Children of George Powell and Ann [__]:
[1]+ a. **Kader/Cader[2] Powell**, married (possibly) **Anna** [__].
[2] b. **George[2] Powell.**
[3] c. **Lewis[2] Powell.**
[4] d. **Moses[2] Powell**, under age in $173^5/_6$.

143. John[(1)] Powell, the son of Richard[A] Powell and Susannah[A] Clement, was born $167^0/_1$, according to a deposition, Norfolk Co., VA, and died *ca.* 1747-49, Perquimans Co., NC. He married first, **Miriam[2]** or **Marian Smith**, the daughter of **Thomas[1] Smith II** and wife Alice [__] of Norfolk Co., VA. John and Marian Powell appeared in court in Williamsburg 1 May 1714 in order to prevent Thomas Etheridge from seating a patent formerly due to Matthew Nicholas, late of Norfolk Co., because they had paid for part of it. This information can be found in H. R. McIlwaine, editor, *Executive Journals of the Council of Colonial Virginia*, vol. 3, *1 May 1705--23 Oct 1721*, p. 373. He married second, prior to 1734, **Esther** or **Hester** [__]. John Powell, on 8 Oct 1723, styled as "of the Upper parish of Nansemond Co., VA," purchased 250 acres on the southwest side of the Perquimans River, adjoining Timothy Clare and Thomas Roundtrees, from Daniel Smith and his wife Sarah, according to Perquimans Co., NC, Deed Book B, no. 144. Powell received a patent of 300A on the west side of the Perquimans River, adjoining the side of a branch and the said river, on 1 Feb 1725, according to NC Land Patent Book 3, p. 230.

Rev. Silas Lucas' woefully unindexed *Powell Families of Norfolk and Elizabeth City Counties, Virginia and their Descendants*, provides a somewhat rambling explanation of the connections between the Powells, the Bowles, and the Smiths, which in themselves are remarkably confusing, but that author did expertly resolve the relationship between Marian Powell and her parents (to this writer's great satisfaction). This will be discussed in vol. 2 of the *Ancestor Biographies*, wherein the sketch of **Thomas Smith II** will appear. Alice [__] Smith married second, by 16 Jan $169^3/_4$, Norfolk, William[A] Powell, an uncle of John[1] Powell, according to Norfolk Co., VA, Record Book 5, p. 237. William[1] Powell, brother of John[1] Powell, named his nephew Lemuell[2] Powell in his will, in Norfolk Co., VA, Will and Deeds 9, p. 456. Thomas Smith II, father of Marian Powell, died intestate, 1693, in Currituck.

The Children of John Powell and Miriam Smith:

[1] a. **Lemuel^{2} Powell.**

[2] b. **John^{2} Powell.**

[3]+ c. **George^{2} Powell**, died testate between 24 Mar $173^{5}/_{6}$ and May 1736, Bertie Co., NC, Secretary of State loose wills; married **Ann** [__].

[4] d. **Robert^{2} Powell.**

[5] e. **Elizabeth^{2} Powell**, married **John Wimberly**. A deed in Perquimans Co., NC, Deed Book C, no. 131, dated 15 Apr 1734, recited that John Wimberly and wife Elizabeth, with the consent of John Powell, sold 125 acres of land on the southwest side of the Perquimans River, to Nicholas Stallings.

[6] f. (possibly) **Francis^{2} Powell**, of Nansemond Co., VA.

144. Kader/Cader$^{(3)}$ Powell, the son of **George$^{(2)}$ Powell** and Ann [__], was born *ca.* 1715, Chowan Co., NC, and died *ca.* 1785, Hertford Co., NC. His wife's name may have been **Anna** [__], but due to the destruction of Hertford's early records this is not completely certain. A 1742 deed in Chowan recites the chain of descent of land from his grandfather John$^{(1)}$ Powell to his father George$^{(2)}$ and uncle Robert Powell, according to Chowan Co., NC, Deed Book A#1, p. 227.

There exists a family history of the later Powells, penned by Jesse^{3} Powell (Lewis^{2}) when the author was 68 years old, descibing his father, grandfather, and part of his mother's Cotton ancestry. However, not much information is given concerning his own generation due to the author's tearful lapses into the details of a morose religious ephiphany which inspired him to hope that his brief flirtation with deism (and that a somewhat more lingering one with whiskey) would not consign him to the flames of eternal damnation, etc., etc.

The Children of Kader Powell and Anna [__]:

[1]+ a. **Lewis^{2} Powell**, born *ca.* 1743, died 1778, Hertford Co., NC; married, as her first husband, **Helen^{3} Cotton** (Arthur^{2}, John^{1}); she married second, Moses Tyler.

[2]+ b. **Willis^{2} Powell**, born *ca.* 1750, Bertie, died before 1810, Bertie Co., NC; married 17 Jan 1782, **Celia Averett**, daughter of Henry Averett, Jr. (son, in turn, of testator Henry, Sr.), the former of whom (Henry, Jr.) died testate after 28 Oct 1771, Bertie Co., NC, Will Book A, p. 144, leaving wife Millea/Mildred [__].

145. George Powers was born about 1691, according to a deposition taken in Pasquotank Co., NC, dated 16 Mar 173$^{1}/_{2}$, in which he described himself as about 40 years of age. This is found in Pasquotank Co., NC, Deed Book B, pp. 523-24. George Powers appeared on a list of tithables in Pasquotank in 1717, and died testate between 27 Mar 1754 and June 1755, his will filed among NC Secretary of State loose wills. He collected taxes for the tithables in his district on the Northwest River in Jan 172$^{0}/_{1}$, according to William Doub Bennett's *Currituck County, North Carolina Eighteenth Century Tax & Militia Records*, pp. 62-63. He was again listed in Currituck in 1726 and 1727, at which time he was identified as a Quit Rents collector for that county, as recorded in The *Colonial Records of North Carolina*, 2nd ser., vol. 7, *Records of the Executive Council, 1664-1734*, p. 553. Powers married around 1720, **Isabel**^{2} **Bateman**, the daughter of **William**^{1} **Bateman** of Currituck and [__]. Isabel died testate between 23 Nov and 20 Dec 1757, her will filed among NC Secretary of State loose wills, and recorded in NC Secretary of State vol. 880, p. 233. George Powers was, mysteriously, the sole beneficiary of a Robert Irving, merchant tailor of Currituck precinct, who died testate between 16 Feb 173$^{5}/_{6}$ and 5 Apr 1737, NC Secretary of State loose wills.

The same children were named in both wills of their parents, with the exception that daughter Abigail had married by 1757. The Etheridge husbands have been assigned as listed in Dr. Benjamin Holtzclaw's chapter "Etheridge of Norfolk County, Virginia, with related families...," in Mrs. John Bennett Boddie, *Historical Southern Families*, vol. 14, pp. 151-55.

The Children of George Powers and Isabel Bateman:

[1] a. **William**^{2} **Powers**, died testate between 30 Dec 1794 and 12 Jan 1796, Currituck Co., NC, Will Book 2, p. 65; married [__].

[2] b. **George**^{2} **Powers**, died testate between 9 Dec 1794 and 26 Mar 1795, Currituck Co., NC, Will Book 2, p, 42; married **Mary** [__].

[3] c. **Caleb**^{2} **Powers**.

[4] d. **Mary**^{2} **Powers**, married **Caleb**$^{(4)}$ **Etheridge** [John$^{(3)}$, Marmaduke$^{(2)}$, Thomas$^{(1)}$], and died intestate *ca.* 1773-75, Currituck Co., NC.

[5]+ e. **Isabel**^{2} **Powers**, married **John**^{2} **Bright**, died testate between 29 July 1777 and 16 Dec 1780, Currituck Co., NC, Will Book 1, p. 162

[6] f. **Lydda**^{2} **Powers**, married (probably) **Richard**$^{(4)}$ **Etheridge** [Henry$^{(3)}$, John$^{(2)}$, Thomas$^{(1)}$], who died testate between 9 Mar 1789 and 3 July 1794, Currituck Co., NC, Will Book 2, p. 27.

[7] g. **Jean**^{2} **Powers**, married, as his first wife, **Willis**$^{(4)}$ **Etheridge** [John$^{(3)}$, Marmaduke$^{(2)}$, Thomas$^{(1)}$], died *ca.* 1812, Currituck Co., NC; he married second, Lydia [__], the widow of Capt. Hilary White.

[8] h. **Abigail**^{2} **Powers**, married 1754-1757, **Peter Poyner**, who died testate between 7 May and 20 Oct 1796, Currituck Co., NC, Will Book 2, p.

92.

146. Benjamin Pritchard was born by 1680, perhaps in Philadelphia, PA (depending upon when the family actually arrived in the colonies), and died intestate 7.21.1739, Pasquotank Monthly Meeting. Benjamin[1] Pritchard and his brother Matthew[1] were sons of Thomas[A] Pritchard, cordwainer, of Philadelphia Monthly Meeting, and his wife Barbara[A] [__], both of whom died testate in Philadelphia. The will of Thomas Prichard, whose death was recorded 2.2.1698, Philadelphia Monthly Meeting, was dated 29 Jan and proved 1 Nov 1698, Philadelphia Co., PA, Will Book A, p. 419. Thomas' land in Strawberry Alley was mentioned. The will of his wife Barbara was dated 30 Sept 1699 and proved 10 Feb $^{1699}/_{1700}$, Philadelphia Co., PA, Will Book B, p. 32, and her death was recorded 8.3.1699, Philadelphia Monthly Meeting. They both named the following children: Mathew[1]; Benjamin[1]; John, died 10.10.1738, Philadelphia Monthly Meeting; Mary, buried 9.8.1690, Philadelphia Monthly Meeting; Ann, married 11.26.1699, Philadelphia Monthly Meeting, John Jones; Jane; and Martha. Brothers Benjamin and Matthew Pritchard joined the Quakers of Pasquotank on 1.4.1701, after having produced a letter of request from Philadelphia Monthly Meeting dated 9.18.1700, according to Hinshaw, vol. 1, p. 162. Benjamin Pritchard married first, 9.21.1704, Pasquotank Monthly Meeting, **Sarah[2] Culpeper**, born *ca.* 1690, died 10.25.1723, Pasquotank Monthly Meeting, the daughter of **John[1] Culpeper** and **Sarah[2] Mayo**. Benjamin married second, 7.6.1729, Pasquotank Monthly Meeting, **Isabell[3] (Newby) Henley**, the widow of John Henley, the latter of whom died testate in Pasquotank between 1.21.1726 and July 1728, NC Secretary of State loose wills, and recorded in NC Secretary of State vol. 876, p. 146. Isabell married third, 7.4.1744, Pasquotank Monthly Meeting, Thomas Peirce of Perquimans. She was a widow, once again, on 12.7.1757, Perquimans Monthly Meeting, at which time she was criticized for "detaining a bond [*meaning unclear*]." "Zibell" or Isabell Newby, the daughter of Gabriel[2] Newby, married John Henley "at the dwelling house" of her father, 11.9.1716, Perquimans Monthly Meeting. Isabell Peirce's will was dated 3day.4mo.1755, Chowan Co., NC, and named the following children: John Henley, Benoni Pritchard, Mary Ricks, Hannah Pritchard, Mattthew Pritchard, Peninnah Willson, husband (then still alive) Thomas Peirce, and specified the following children as her five youngest: Jesse Henley, Peninnah Wilson, Matthew Pritchard, Hannah Pritchard, and Benoni Pritchard. A copy of her will was located in the Hayes Collection (item 324), Microfilm Reel 2, 1694-1770, items in year 1755, Southern Historical Collection, Wilson Library, University of North Carolina, Chapel Hill, NC. A transcription of this will can be found in the appendix of this book.

The Children of Benjamin Pritchard and Sarah Culpeper, born Pasquotank Monthly Meeting:

[1] a. **Mary[2] Pritchard**, born 7.28.1707, died 10.12.1791, Pasquotank Monthly Meeting, married 6.20.1724, Pasquotank Monthly Meeting, **Aaron[2] Morris**.

[2]+ b. **Elizabeth[2] Pritchard**, born 1.19.1710, married 10.2.1731, Pasquotank Monthly Meeting, **Joseph[2] Morris**.

[3] c. **Martha[2] Pritchard**, born 11.11.1712, died 5.19.1788, Pasquotank Monthly Meeting, married first, 3.2.1734, Pasquotank Monthly Meeting, **Nehemiah White**; second, 3.1.1753, Pasquotank Monthly Meeting, **Joseph Overman**.

[4] d. **Joseph[2] Pritchard**, born 9.1.1712, married first, 1.4.$174^0/_1$, Perquimans Monthly Meeting, **Elizabeth[5] White**; second, **Elizabeth Newby**; third, **Sarah Barrow**.

[5] e. **Benjamin[2] Pritchard**, born 2.[--].1719.

[6] f. **Sarah[2] Pritchard**, born 10.10 or 12.1723, married 8.1.1747, Pasquotank Monthly Meeting, **William Albertson**.

The Children of Benjamin Pritchard and Isabel (Newby) Henley, born Pasquotank Monthly Meeting:

[7] g. **Matthew[2] Pritchard**, born 2.7.1732, died 11.2.1778, Pasquotank Monthly Meeting, married first, 6.7.1759, Pasquotank Monthly Meeting, **Rosannah Benston**, daughter of James Benston; he married second, as her first husband, 4.7.1763, Pasquotank Monthly Meeting, **Sarah Low**; she married second, 2.26.1783, Pasquotank Monthly Meeting, at Newbegun Creek Meeting House, John Overman.

[8] h. **Hannah[2] Pritchard**, born *ca.* 1734.

[9] i. **Benoni[2] Pritchard**, born *ca.* 1736, married, as her first husband, Pasquotank Monthly Meeting, 2.4.1762, **Miriam Winslow**; she married second, 9.29.1774, Pasquotank Monthly Meeting, at Symons Creek Meeting House, John Symons.

147. Col. **Francis Pugh** of Nansemond Co., VA, was born by 1695 and died testate between 5 July 1733 and 4 Oct 1736, Bertie Co., NC, his will filed among the NC Secretary of State loose wills, and recorded in NC Land Grant Book 4, no. 34. He married 8 Sept 1722, Elizabeth City Co., VA (Elizabeth City Co., Deeds & Wills, 1737-1749, p. 74), **Pheribee[4] Savage**, the daughter of Thomas Savage and Alicia[3] Harmonson of Northampton Co., VA. Pheribee (Savage) Pugh married second, by 11 May 1744, Bertie Co., NC, as his first wife, Thomas Barker, who was born 17 Feb $171^2/_3$, Pembroke, MA, and died testate after the dating of his will, 17 Oct 1786. Descendants of this couple have been traced in

Adventurers of Purse and Person, 4th edition, vol. 3, *Families R-Z*, pp. 125-41, with the exception of daughter Ferebee[2] and her husband John Williams who were parents of Gov. Benjamin[3] Williams.

The odd will of Francis Pugh names only sons Thomas[2] and John[2] Pugh and wife Pheribee. On 5 Jan 1750, Bertie Co., NC, Deed Book G, p. 329, John[2] Pugh sold 157 acres of land to his brother Thomas[2] Pugh, land which had formerly belonged to their father Francis Pugh. Daughter Ferebee[2] Pugh, still unmarried, witnessed a deed from her stepfather Thomas Barker to John Jameson, dated 24 Aug 1741, Bertie Co., NC, Deed Book F, p. 404. In Bertie Co., NC, Court Minutes, 1724-1772, p. 177, dated 10 Nov 1741, Thomas Barker proved his importation rights with the following persons: Thomas Barker, Ferribe Barker, Jno.[2] Pugh, Thos.[2] Pugh, Fras.[2] Pugh, Pheribe[2] Pugh, Peggy[2] Pugh, Mary[2] Pugh, and Negroes: Mark, Crowell, Pat, Affra[,] Sebina, Rachel, Sarah, Hannah, Rose, Priss, and Shake. On 11 Dec 1765, Mary (Whitmel) Pugh made a gift of Negro slaves to her three sons, Thomas Whitmell[3] Pugh, Francis[3] Pugh, and John[3] Pugh, Bertie Co., NC, Deed Book L-2, p. 91.

In Craven Co., NC, Deed Book 4, p. 52, dated 18 Dec 1746, Cornelius Loftin, planter, for £5 sold to John Williams 25 acres on the south side of the Nuse River, adjoining the Stoney Branch of John Williams, and the land of the grantor. The deed was witnessed by "Farabe" Williams, James Williams, and William Nunn, and places the family of John Williams and Ferebee[2] Pugh specifically in Craven. They have always been thought to be the parents of Gov. Benjamin[3] Williams.

The Children of Francis Pugh and Pheribee Savage:

[1] a. **John[2] Pugh**, died by May 1754, Bertie Co., NC; married **Elizabeth** [__], died before Aug 1754, Bertie Co., NC; his estate was divided among his siblings.

[2] b. **Thomas[2] Pugh**, born 6 Aug 1726, died testate 15 Jan 1806, Bertie Co., NC, Will Book F, p. 26; married **Mary Scott**. According to Bertie Co. Estates Records for Thomas[3] Pugh, Jr., his widow Esther deposed that Thomas[3] Pugh, Jr., died 3 Feb 1799.

[3] c. **Francis[2] Pugh**, died intestate before Oct 1762, Bertie Co. ,NC, Court Minutes 1724-1772, p. 305; married, as her first husband, **Mary[2] Whitmel**, who died testate between 10 June and Aug 1807, Bertie Co., NC, Will Book F, p. 38; she married second, **Hezekiah Thompson**, died testate between 25 Jan and Mar 1771, Bertie Co., NC, Will Book A, p. 132.

[4]+ d. **Margaret[2] Pugh**, born 1729, married, as his first wife, Col. **Benjamin Wynns**, who died in the 1780s, Hertford Co., NC.

[5] e. **Mary[2] Pugh**, married **James[3] Luten**, who died testate after 24 Sept 1766, Chowan Co., NC, Will Book A, p. 251.

[6] f. **Ferebee[2] Pugh**, married 1741-46, **John Williams** of New Bern, Craven Co., NC.

The Children of Thomas Barker and Pheribee (Savage) Pugh:
[7] g. **Elizabeth Barker** died testate between 17 June and Nov 1803, Bertie Co., NC, Will Book 3, p. 218; married **William Tunstall**, said to have died *ca.* 1791, Pittsylvania Co., VA.

148. William Reed was born say 1670 in England and died late in the evening between 11 and 12 Dec 1728, Pasquotank Co., NC. Gov. Reed's date of death can be found in a deposition by George Allyn, dated 4 May 1731, to whom the Governor's illness had already been communicated by the second Mrs. Reed, and who (the deponent) went to call on the invalid. Unfortunately, George Allyn arrived on 13 Dec 1728, the day after Mr. Reed had died, according to *The Colonial Records of North Carolina*, 2nd ser., vol. 7, *Records of the Executive Council, 1664-1734*, p. 193. William Reed married, first, **Christian** [__], who appeared on a deed with her husband 21 Oct 1701, Pasquotank Co., NC, Deed Book A, p. 15. He married second, **Jane** [__], who signed with William Reed on a deed to Thomas Sawyer, dated 20 Oct 1719, Pasquotank Co., NC, Deed Book A, p. 232. Reed served as acting Governor of North Carolina from 7 Sept 1722 to 15 Jan 1724, was President of the Council, and served as Deputy Proprietor from 1712 until his death. An excellent biography of William Reed is found in William S. Powell, *Dictionary of North Carolina Biography*, vol. 5, *P-S*, pp. 187-88. All of William Reed's children married descendants of **George[1] Durant**.

The Children of William Reed and Christian [__]:
[1] a. **Christian[2] Reed**, married by Jan 1738, **Mary[4] Durant**, born 2 Dec 1718, the daughter of George[3] Durant (John[2], George[1]).
[2]+ b. **Joseph[2] Reed**, died 7 May 1765, Perquimans; married **Elizabeth[4] Durant**, the daughter of George[3] Durant (John[2], **George[1]**).

The Children of William Reed and Jane [__]:
[3] c. **William[2] Reed**, Jr., married, as her first husband, 18 Mar 1735/6, Perquimans, **Elizabeth[4] Hatch**, born say 1714; she married second, MacRora Scarbrough; third, as his second wife, Joseph Blount; she was the daughter of Anthony Hatch and Elizabeth[3] Durant (John[2], **George[1]**).

149. William Reeves was born by 1685 and died testate before 3 Dec 1751; his will was filed among the loose wills of Granville Co., NC. He married first, by

1706, [__], the mother of all of the children named in his will, except possibly for son Burgess and the two [then] unmarried daughters. He married second, **Margaret** [__], said to have been *née* Burgess. There is a useful treatment of this Reeves family in Jonathan Floyd Reeves and Emma Barrett Reeves, *The Reeves Review, Compiled by a few Descendants of William Reeves of Granville County, N.C. (1690-1751)*, pp. 1-2.

William Reeves' first purchase of land was on 30 Sept 1718 from Robert Smith, according to Chowan Co., NC, Deed Book B#1, p. 638, for 150 acres on the Morattock River. He sold part of this land as a resident of Edgecombe on 8 Aug 1739 to Robert Harris of Bertie as recorded in Bertie Co., NC, Deed Book E, p. 504. William Reeves' origins have not yet been determined, although various writers have attempted to connect him, unsuccessfully, with the *Rives* family.

A John Reeves, not named in William Reeves' will, has traditionally been appended to this group of children. Although there is a John Reeves in the area of Edgecombe which would later become Granville, he appears in connection to the Reeves family once, and then only as a witness to a deed from William Reeves, Sr., to James Reeves, "Jr." [*sic*?], Edgecombe Co., NC, Deed Book 4, p. 12, dated 31 Dec 1750.

Other internet information has given Isaac Reeves a death location in Rowan Co., NC, but the deeds and estates records revealed nothing about him. Another site has attributed a second marriage to Elizabeth (Reeves) Hodges with a Parham, but that information did not pan out.

The Children of William Reeves and [__], born Bertie Co., NC:

[1] a. **William[2] Reeves**, Jr., born *ca.* 1707, married almost certainly **Hardy[2] Merritt**; he witnessed a deed from his father as "William, Jr.," dated 8 Feb 172$^{8}/_{9}$, Bertie Co., NC, Deed Book C, p. 117. William must have died before 19 Jan 1787, at which time Thomas Thomason and wife Anna made a deed to Hardy, Granville Co., NC, Deed Book O, p. 488. The William Reeves who lived to be almost 100 years old and died in South Carolina *ca.* 1823 might have been a son of this couple.

[2] b. **James[2] Reeves**, will proved Aug 1781, Guilford Co., NC, Will Book A, p. 302; married **Millicent** [__], named in his will; she also signed with him on a deed dated 7 Nov 1763, Granville Co., NC, Deed Book F, p. 425, to Malachy Reeves, "Jr." They were married as early as 20 Aug 1754, when she signed with him on a deed in Edgecombe Co., NC, Deed Book 2, p. 77. Malachi[3] Reeves, Jr., was the son of this couple, so called, no doubt, in deference to his uncle[2].

[3] c. **Benjamin[2] Reeves**.

[4] d. **Isaac[2] Reeves**, bought land in Edgecombe on 14 Aug 1749 from Peter

Bruce, 100 acres adjoining Smith and the Marsh Swamp, witnessed by William Reeves, Edgecombe Co., NC, Deed Book 3, p. 371. This is virtually his only appearance in the records.

[5] e. **Malachiah[2] Reeves**, said to have died *ca.* 1789, York Co., SC; married **Elizabeth** [__], who signed with him on a deed of sale, dated 1 Nov 1787, Granville Co., NC, Deed Book O, p. 591.

[6]+ f. **Sarah[2] Reeves**, born *ca.* 1722, died testate between 19 Feb 1797 and Aug 1806, Granville Co., NC, Will Book 6, p. 294; she married *ca.* 1745, Edgecombe Co., NC, **Robert Hicks**, born 1 May 1713, Flushing, Long Island, Queens Co., NY, died testate between 15 Apr 1788 and May 1792 in Granville Co., NC, Will Book 2, p. 290.

[7] g. **Elizabeth[2] Reeves**, married [__] **Hodges**.

[8] h. **Mary[2] Reeves**, married [__] **Carpenter**.

The Children of William Reeves and Margaret [__] (possibly):

[9] i. **Burgess[2] Reeves**, born 10 May 1746, Granville Co., NC, died testate between 6 Mar and June 1811, Pendleton District, SC, his will recorded in Anderson Co., SC, Will Book A, p. 130; married **Frances Mauldin**, and named his wife Fanny, and children John[3], Mauldin[3], Leathy[3], and William[3] Reeves. He is listed in the *DAR Patriot Index*, vol. 3, p. 2430.

[10] j. **Ann[2] Reeves**.

[11] k. **Olive[2] Reeves**.

150. Isaac[(3)] Ricks, the son of Isaac[(2)] Ricks (born 6.17.1669. Chuckatuck Monthly Meeting) and Sarah [__], was born 27.12.1702, Chuckatuck Monthly Meeting, Isle of Wight Co., VA, and died testate between 15 Apr and Dec 1760, Edgecombe Co., NC, Will Book A, p. 9. He married **Elizabeth Skinner** of Nash Co., NC, the sister of Samuel Skinner. She married second, Jacob Barnes of Nash Co., NC, who died testate between 25 Jan 1780 and Oct 1781, Nash Co., NC, Will Book 1, p. 21. Elizabeth returned to Edgecombe and died testate there between 6 June 1789 and May 1794, Edgecombe Co., NC, Will Book C, p. 175, naming her brother Samuel Skinner and his son Theophilus. Samuel and Theophilus Skinner cannot, however, be connected with the Skinners of Perquimans. On 10 Nov 1724, William Ricks, almost certainly Isaac's brother, and his wife Esther, sold to Isaac 240 acres on Kirby's Creek and the Reedy Branch. Part of this land on Reedy Branch was bequeathed in Isaac's 1760 will to his son James[2].

Published Ricks genealogy is mostly a mess. The old Ricks genealogy compiled by Guy Scoby Ricks, *History and Genealogy of the Ricks Family of American*, cannot be trusted in the third generations; and Boddie's compilation in

Seventeenth Century Isle of Wight, around pp. 233-34, is even more moronic. The statement made in Boddie that James Ricks married first, Mary Crudup, cannot be substantiated; and James' children not mentioned in Phebe Ricks' will applied for a division of their part of her estate, indicating that they were her heirs as well. Phebe's ancestry has not yet been determined.

The Children of Isaac Ricks and Elizabeth Skinner:

[1]+ a. **James^2 Ricks**, died testate between 13 Mar and May 1792, Edgecombe Co., NC, Will Book C, p. 187; married **Phebe** (said to be **Horn**), who died testate between 22 Oct 1806 and May 1812, Edgecombe Co., NC, Will Book E, p. 36.

[2] b. **John^2 Ricks**, married **Esther** [__] **Ross**, the widow of Andrew Ross, Jr., who died before his father Andrew Ross, Sr., signed his will on 14 Apr 1761, Edgecombe Co., NC, Will Book A, p. 63.

[3] c. **Sarah^2 Ricks**, married **Daniel Ross**, who died testate between 3 July and Aug 1781, Edgecombe Co., NC, Will Book B, p. 76.

151. Edward Salter, cooper, the ancestor of the Pitt County family, was born by 1700 and died testate between 6 Jan and 5 Feb $173^4/_5$, Beaufort Co., NC, his will recorded in NC Secretary of State vol. 876, p. 356. Edward Salter patented 80 acres of land in the fork of the Pamticough River adjoining the land of Samuel Boutwell on 3 Dec 1720, according to NC Land Patent Book 2, p. 299. On 26 Sept 1721, Salter purchased two ½-acre lots in the town of Bath from Henry Rowell, according to Beaufort Co., NC, Deed Book 1, p. 443. His first wife was almost certainly **Mary** [__], because of her presence as a witness to the following transaction: Beaufort Co., NC, Deed Book 2, p. 8, dated 12 June 1729, Edward Salter to Robert Canpain, 570 acres on south side of Pamlico River, on west side of Broad Creek, *alias* Goode Creek, adjoining William Jones' land, granted to John Snoad by patent dated 4 Apr 1720, and by Snoad sold to grantee, per deed dated 7 July 1724, and by Campaign sold to Salter by deed dated 12 Nov 1726.

Edward Salter married second, as her second husband, 12 June 1731, Perquimans Co., NC [*What* was he doing up there?], "Madam" **Elizabeth (Cole) Harvey**, daughter of Samuel Cole and widow of Thomas Harvey, the latter of whom named wife Elizabeth in his will dated 10 Apr 1729, filed among NC Secretary of State loose wills.

Elizabeth married third, [probably *John*] Caldom, whose family has been said to be related to the Readings and the Churchills; she was also said to have been buried beside her husband Salter in 1761. In Beaufort Co., NC, Deed Book 2, p. 245, dated 30 May 1740, Elizabeth Caldom as administratrix presented the inventory of John Caldom, deceased, to the court, and the same was recorded 12 Oct 1741. By 29 July 1748, Beaufort Co., NC, Deed Book 2, p. 540, she was a resident of Perquimans, and gave her power of attorney to her son John Harvey to transact for her in Beaufort concerning any undisposed property. In Perquimans Co., NC, Deed Book F, no. 201, on 15 July 1756, Elizabeth "Calldrom" and John Harvey confirmed a deed to John Morris, son of Richard Morris, now deceased, for land bequeathed to her by her father Samuel Cole, and which she and her then husband Thomas Harvey, now deceased, had sold to Richard Morris during his lifetime. Edward Salter's roots are unknown, although a possible South Carolina origin has been proposed for him due to his purchases of land from wealthy natives of that colony.

Edward[2] Salter made deeds of gift to two of his children before his death: [1] to son Robert[3] Salter, Pitt Co., NC, Deed Book C, p. 44, dated 20 Feb 1764, tracts of 326 acres and 350 acres; he married **Cleare[2] (Speir) Hardee**; [2] to son Edward[3] Salter, Jr., Pitt Co., NC, Deed Book C, p. 219, dated 20 Feb 1765, 300 acres formerly belonging to Lewis Duvall. Son Thomas[3] Salter was identified as one of his sons in Pitt Co., NC, Deed Book D, p. 134, dated 3 Oct 1770, in a land sale to Jacob Palmer. John[(3?)] Salter sold land in 1770 to William Judgkins which was identified as having belonged to Edward Salter, although no relationship was stated, Pitt Co., NC, Deed Book D, p. 132.

The existence of posthumously born daughter Hannah[2] Salter was revealed in a deed from Edward[2] Salter, Jr., to Thomas Respass, dated 15 June 1758, Beaufort Co., NC, Deed Book 3, p. 774. The deed itself is an astonishing example of the recital of a chain of ownership involving some dozen persons. For a consideration of £260, Virginia money, Salter sold to Respass, merchant of Beaufort, 400 acres in Bath Town Creek adjoining Brick-House plantation, late in the possession of Joshua Porter, and then purchased by Messrs. Robins and Elsy from John Linington [Lillington]. Linington sold the property to Maurice Moore, who sold it to James Robins, who sold it to Robert Cawper [Champain], who sold it to Edward[1] Salter, Sr., who by his last will and testament bequeathed it to his unborn child, "should it live." (Why should the French be considered such experts in obstetrics? this writer wonders while he considers the following statement.) In this deed, Edward[2], Jr., described his half-sister as having been *en ventre de sa mère*, and outlined the sale of the property from Hannah Salter and her husband William Baker of Virginia to him. An additional 55 acres were included in the sale, which by the last will and testament of Tobias Knight had been devised to Elizabeth Swann, who with her husband John Swann sold the land to Hannah[2] Salter, described in that deed as a "spinster." Hannah[2] married soon after, wherby she and her husband sold this land to Edward[2] Salter, Jr. She was left a bequest of slaves named Moll and Sampson for her lifetime in the will of her half-brother Thomas Harvey, dated 21 Nov 1748 and proved Jan $174^{8}/_{9}$, Perquimans, NC Secretary of State loose wills.

On 18 May 1731, Edward Salter, along with others, was appointed Justice of the Peace for the precincts of Beaufort and Hyde, according to

Colonial Records of North Carolina, 2nd ser., vol. 7, *Records of the Executive Council, 1664-1734*, p. 210.

The Children of Edward Salter and [__], born Beaufort precinct, Bath Co., NC:

[1]+ a. **Edward² Salter**, died by 28 July 1768, Pitt Co., NC, Deed Book C, p. 19, in which his son Edward³ sold land formerly belonging to his father, deceased; married **Ann² Bonner**, named as daughter in the will of her father **Thomas Bonner**, dated 1 Nov 1764, Beaufort Co., NC, Will Book A, p. 285A

[2] b. **Sarah² Salter**.

[3] c. **Mary² Salter**, married by 17 Mar 1753, Beaufort Co., NC, **Caleb Grainger**, who died testate between 1763 and 31 Oct 1765, New Hanover Co., NC, gent., requesting a masonic funeral; he named only son Cornelius Harnett³ Grainger and daughter Mary³ Grainger; the marriage was revealed in Beaufort Co., NC, Deed Book 3, p. 131, in a sale of land from Caleb and Mary Grainger to Walter Dixon, dated as above, tract of 306 acres called Mt. Calvert deeded to Mary 24 Nov 1733 and bequeathed to her by her father.

[4]+ d. **Susannah² Salter**, married **Edward² Vail**, according to according to Beaufort Co., NC, Deed Book 3, p. 278, dated 14 Apr 1756, in which Edward Vail and wife Susannah, both of Chowan, sold 510 acres on the Pamptico to Simon Jones, land bequeathed her by the last will and testament of her father.

The Child of Edward Salter and Elizabethy (Cole) Harvey, born Beaufort precinct, Bath Co., NC:

[5] e. **Hannah² Salter**, born 1735, married by 1758, **William Baker**.

152. Hon. **Richard Sanderson** was born *ca.* 1641, according to a deposition made in 1711 [which this writer cannot locate], and died testate 171⁸/₉, Currituck Co., NC. His will, however, was declared invalid because it was suspected of forgery by his second wife, found to be in cahoots with the clueless William Alexander, "Collector of Currituck," according to Saunders' *Colonial Records of North Carolina*, vol. 2, *1713-1728*, p. 401, dated 29 July 1719. Richard Sanderson married first [__], whose name does not appear in the records, and who was the mother of his children. He married second, by 19 Sept 1711, **Demaris [__] Coleman**, the widow of Ellis Coleman of Philadelphia, PA, who as widow applied on that date to administer the estate of her first husband, according to NC Secretary of State, Deeds, Wills, and Inventories, 1695-1712, vol. 874.1, p. 30. She married third, Col. Thomas Swann. An excellent biography of Richard Sanderson appears in William S. Powell, *Dictionary of*

North Carolina Biography, vol. 5, *P-S*, pp. 282-83. A biography of his son Richard, Jr., appears on pp. 283-84 of the same volume. As Richard Sanderson became older (in Apr 1712), he showed "his uneasiness in his travels and stay at Councils and Assemblys," impelling the President to force Sanderson's hand in the matter and possibly replace him with someone more willing to leave home. This can be found in *The Colonial Records of North Carolina*, 2nd ser., vol. 7, *Records of the Executive Council, 1664-1734*, pp. 15-16.

According to Norfolk Co., VA, Deed Book 9, p. 290, Richard[2] Sanderson, Jr., identified therein as a resident of North Carolina, was married to Elizabeth [__] Mason, the widow of Thomas Mason by 19 Feb 1713. He married third, after 29 Apr 1724, Perquimans, when she was still listed as the "unremarried" relict of James Minge, according to Perquimans Co., NC, Deed Book B, p. 191, **Ruth[2] (Laker) Minge**, born 28 Sept 1679, Betchworth, Surrey, England [see Laker]. Richard[2] Sanderson obviously gave his third wife permission to write her own will, dated 4 Sept 1726 and proved 29 July 1727, before his death in 1731. She called herself the "wife" of Richard Sanderson, and made bequests to members of her own family, exclusively. Therefore Grace Woodhouse had Sanderson children between the years 1694 and 1713, while Elizabeth [__] Mason had Sanderson children between the years 1713 and 1724.

Joseph Church's will was dated 28 Feb 172²/₃ and proved 9 Apr 1723, NC Secretary of State loose wills. His widow Julian married second, Joseph[2] Sanderson, both of whom died testate. There is some difference of opinion concerning the meaning of the word "brother-in-law" employed by Richard Sanderson, Jr., in his will, in reference to Henry[4] Woodhouse. The relationship with the Woodhouses was most likely through his first wife's family. Richard Sanderson, Jr., in his 1733 will, identified his sister as Susanna[2] Erwin, and stated that she was living on his plantation in Perquimans.

There were other Sandersons in the records of about the same age and standing as Richard, Sr.: Basil, a mariner, from the Isle of Antigua, according to Chowan Co., NC, Deed Book C#1, p. 195 (dated 1 June 1721), and Robert Sanderson, both of whose connections to this family are unknown.

The Children of Richard Sanderson and [__]:

[1] a. **Richard[2] Sanderson**, Jr., died tesatate between 17 Aug and 15 Oct 1733, Perquimans Co., NC, Secretary of State loose wills; he married first, between 24 Apr 1693—Princess Anne Co., VA, Deed Book 1, p. 45, at which time her father John[3] Woodhouse named her (as yet unmarried) in his will—and 2 May 1704, Princess Anne Co., VA, Deed Book 1, p. 416 (at which time she was identified as his wife), **Grace[4] Woodhouse**, the daughter of John[3] Woodhouse and Ruth Cason; he married second, by 1713, Norfolk Co., VA, **Elizabeth [__] Mason**, widow of Thomas Mason of Norfolk, who died testate

between 9 Jan 17$^{10}/_{11}$ and 15 June 1711, Will Book 9, p. 60; third, after 29 Apr 1724, Perquimans Co., NC, **Ruth**[2] **(Laker) Minge**, the daughter of **Benjamin**[1] **Laker** and the widow of James Minge.

[2]+ b. **Joseph**[2] **Sanderson**, died testate between 13 Jan 174$^{3}/_{4}$ and Oct 1746, Currituck Co., NC, NC Secretary of State loose wills; married **Julian [__] Church**, the widow of Joseph Church; she died testate in Currituck, between 31 July 1749 and 17 Apr 1752, NC Secretary of State loose wills.

[3] c. **Susanna**[2] **Sanderson**, married first, [__] **Tully**; second, by 17 Aug 1733, [__] **Erwin**.

153. Caleb[2] **Sawyer**, the son of **Thomas**[1] **Sawyer** and **Mary**[3] **Jennings**, was born *ca.* 1697, Pasquotank Co., NC, and died testate 1758, Pasquotank Co., NC, as demonstrated by his estate division among his wife and heirs recorded 2 Nov 1758, Pasquotank Co., NC, Court minutes, 1754-1777, ff. 1-3. His will, however, has not survived. He married **Susanna** [__], included in the estate division as his widow.

After Caleb's death, on 8 Sept 1759, the following was recorded in Pasquotank Co., NC, Deed Book F&G by John[2] Sawyer, Caleb's son and heir-at-law who made deeds of gift to his male siblings: [1] p. 333, to brother Elisha[2], land which Caleb bought of Dennis Sawyer, adjoining Lemuel Sawyer, John Scott, and Solomon Sawyer; [2] p. 334, to brother Lemuel[2] Sawyer, land Caleb bought of John Cook, adjoining John Sawyer, Thomas Sawyer, and William Jennings; [3] p. 335, to Silvanus[2] Sawyer, land near John Sawyer (son of Solomon), Thomas Sawyer, Robert and Henry Sawyer, and land given by will from Robert to Dennis Sawyer; [4] p. 337, to brother Demsey[2] Sawyer, land their father bought of Robert Spence and Thomas Sawyer, adjoining Richard Sawyer, Edward Williams, Caleb Koon, James McDaniel.

There is a good biographical sketch of Caleb Sawyer in Jesse Forbes Pugh's *Three Hundred Years Along the Pasquotank, A Biographical History of Camden County*, pp. 45-47. He was the first resident of Pasquotank Precinct, Albemarle Co., NC, to petition the governor to form a separate district in order to have its own votes in the House of Commons. The petition was promptly vetoed by the governor who did not wish to extend to these residents of the Northeast Parish [later Camden County] any more voting power than they already had.

The Children of Caleb Sawyer and Susanna [__], born Pasquotank Co., NC:

[1] a. **John**[2] **Sawyer**, born say 1720, said to have married **Eleanor Lynch**.

[2] b. **Miriam**[2] **Sawyer**, married 4 Feb 1741, Pasquotank Co., NC, **Henry Pailin**, who died testate between 9 July 1768 and [--], Pasquotank Co., NC, Will Book HIK, p. 322.

[3]+ c. **Thomas[2] Sawyer**, born say 1725, married, as her first husband, 14 Sept 1749, Plymouth, Plymouth Co., MA, **Margaret[(4)] Cotton**, born 27 Jan $17^{29}/_{30}$, Plymouth, Plymouth Co., MA, the daughter of Josiah[(3)] Cotton and Hannah Sturtevant; she married second, say 1769, Pasquotank Co., NC, John Sawyer, and had one child by her second husband.

[4] d. **Elisha[2] Sawyer**, born say 1730.

[5] e. **Lemuel[2] Sawyer**, born 24 Dec 1734, married 4 July 1755, Pasquotank Co., NC, **Mary Taylor**, the daughter of Thomas Taylor and Elizabeth Woodley, born 15 Mar $173^{8}/_{9}$, Pasquotank.

[6] f. **Sylvanus[2] Sawyer**, married **Mary Jones**, daughter of Griffith Jones, who made to them the gift of a Negro slave Stephen on 9 Sept 1762, Pasquotank Co., NC, Deed Book D&E, p. 202.

[7] g. **Mary[2] Sawyer**, married **Josiah Nash**, who died testate 14 Apr 1766, Pasquotank Co., NC, Will Book HIK, p. 359.

[8] h. **Lidia[2] Sawyer**.

[9] i. **Dempsey[2] Sawyer**.

154. Thomas[1] Sayer/Sawyer, originally thought to be a son of John Sawyer, the Pasquotank testator of 1713, was almost certainly related to that family, but our Thomas' ancestry is unknown. The other Thomas (son of John) was still alive on 26 May 1730, at which time he sold part of his inheritance from his father John Sawyer to Charles Sawyer, Pasquotank Co., NC, Deed Book C, p. 268. This Thomas Sawyer was known as Thomas, Sr., in subsequent records.

Thomas[1]' undated will was proved 19 July 1720, NC Secretary of State vol. 875, p. 233, Pasquotank Co., NC, by his wife, according to Pasquotank Co., NC, Deed Book A, p. 238, dated 1 Jan $17^{19}/_{20}$, in which Mary Sawyer, as executrix of Thomas Sawyer, confirmed a deed from her late husband to Edward Williams. Thomas married **Mary[3] Jennings**, the daughter of **John[2] Jennings** and his unknown first wife, and the granddaughter of **William[1] Jennings** and Martha [__].

Dr. Stephen E. Bradley's *Early Records of North Carolina*, vol. 4, *Wills, 1663-1722*, p. 76, mistakenly identifies Richard Hastings as Thomas Sayer's "brother-in-law." The recorded copy of his will clearly describes him as "son-in-law."

The Children of Thomas Sawyer and Mary Jennings:

[1] a. **Stephen[2] Sawyer**, born *ca.* 1695, was designated "heir apparent" of Thomas[1] Sawyer, decd., according to Pasquotank Co., NC, Deed Book A, p. 309, dated 21 Apr 1724, at which time he agreed with his brother Caleb to sell some of the land and plantation he had inherited.

The language of his father's will indicates that Stephen was infirm in some way. It is unlikely that Stephen had issue.

[2] b. **Dancy[2] Sawyer**, born *ca.* 1697, married (almost certainly) **Henry McDonell**, a surname, which in Pasquotank, was interchangeable early on with "McDaniel." Thomas Sawyer transferred to Henry McDaniel 100 acres out of a 400-acre patent on 9 Dec 1713, Pasquotank Co., NC, Deed Book A, p. 105. Later, on 11 Oct 1732, James *McDonnell* and Will McDonnell his son sold the same tract back to Caleb[2] Sawyer, Pasquotank Co., NC, Deed Book C, p. 389.

[3]+ c. **Caleb[2] Sawyer**, born *ca.* 1699, died 1758, Pasquotank Co., NC; married **Susanna** [__].

[4] d. **[Daughter][2] Sawyer**, born *ca.* 1701, married **Richard Hastings**.

[5] e. **Thomas[2] Sawyer**, born *ca.* 1703, was bequeathed 100 acres at the North River.

[6] f. **Mary[2] Sawyer**, born *ca.* 1705, with her sister **Ann[2]** was to have part of a patent surveyed by David Wilkins, 225 acres between them.

[7] g. **Ann[2] Sawyer**, born *ca.* 1707.

[8] h. **Richard[2] Sawyer**, born *ca.* 1708, was bequeathed 100 acres adjoining Richard Hastings. As of Feb 1760, according to Pasquotank Co., NC, Deed Book F&G, p. 422, he was a resident of Perquimans, and with his wife Ann, sold a plantation on the northeast side of Pasquotank River, containing 100 acres. He married **Ann** [__].

[9] i. **Hannah[2] Sawyer** born *ca.* 1709, was bequeathed 105 acres aout of the "Wilkins" patent.

155. Rebecca Sebrell, the daughter of Anthony[A] and Martha [__] Sebrell, was born 12mo.1695, York Co., VA, and died 4.6.1772, Surry Co., VA, her will recorded in Surry Co., VA, Will Book 10a, p. 252. She married 23.9.1701, Perquimans Monthly Meeting, **Thomas Pretlow** (formerly Pricklove), born 12mo.1675, died 9.12.1754, Surry Co., VA, whose will was recorded in Surry Co., VA, Will Book 10, p. 4. Thomas cannot be connected genealogically with John Pretlow, the son of Samuel and Rachel (Lawrence) Welsh, but both John and Thomas married Sebrell sisters, a compelling reason to suppose they were related in some way. In his will, Thomas named a sister Ann Nail.

The Children of Thomas Pretlow and Rebecca Sebrell, taken from the Joel Cook Pretlow manuscript, which was said, in turn, to have been copied from an old registry:

[1] a. **Martha[2] Pretlow**, born 2nd mo.1707, *no further record.*

[2] b. **Joseph[2] Pretlow**, born 13.3.1713, died 7th mo.1740, married 2.9.1738, Pagan Creek Monthly Meeting, as her first husband, **Sarah**

Scott.

[3] c. **Mary^{2} Pretlow**, born 21.9.1714, died 10th mo.1753; married 3.9.1743, Pagan Creek Monthly Meeting, **Thomas Newby**.

[4] d. **Thomas^{2} Pretlow**, born 24.4.1717, died testate 5th mo.1787, Southampton Co., VA; married 17.11.174$^{4}/_{5}$, **Mary Ricks**.

[5]+ e. **Joshua^{2} Pretlow**, born 11.1.1719, died 11.2.176$^{1}/_{2}$, Sussex Co., VA; married 2 June 1753, Henrico Monthly Meeting, VA, **Ann Crew**.

[6] f. **John^{2} Pretlow**, born 15.1.1722, died testate 2.10.1788, Isle of Wight Co., VA; married **Mary Bracey**.

[7] g. **Samuel^{2} Pretlow**, born 12.6.1726, will dated 11.14.1781, recorded 23 Apr 1782, Surry Co., VA, Will Book 11, p. 235; married first, 1.18.1753, Black Water Monthly Meeting, Surry Co., VA, **Mary Bailey**; he married second, 7.5.1780, Perquimans Monthly Meeting, **Kezia (Pierce) Newby-Nixon.**

156. Matthew Sellers was born by 1696 and died intestate by Feb 1740, Bertie Co., NC, at which time his son Benjamin^{2} Sellers of Edgecombe sold 50 acres of land (in Bertie) on which his mother then lived and part of which his father Matthew had patented, according to Bertie Co., NC, Deed Book F, p. 195. Matthew married **Katherine** [__], who petitioned to administer his estate in Aug 1740, Bertie Co., NC, Court Minutes, 1724-1772, p. 151. She exhibited an inventory of her husband's estate in Nov of that year, p. 155, and died sometime after her mention therein. Matthew Sellers purchased land in Chowan on the Reedy Swamp, 15 July 1717, from Benjamin Foreman, Sr., according to Chowan Co., NC, Deed Book, B#1, p. 471, and received a patent of 170 acres on the south side of the Maherine River on 26 Mar 1723, recorded in NC Land Patent Book 3, p. 136.

The Child of Matthew Sellers and Katherine [__]:

[1]+ a. **Benjamin^{2} Sellers**, will dated 3 Jan 1761, Edgecombe Co., NC, Will Book A, p. 25; married **Sarah** [__].

157. Thomas Sessums was born *ca.* 1677, Surry Co., VA. He and his wife **Elizabeth**, in a deed dated 2 May 1699, sold 250 acres of land in Southwark Parish to Nathaniel Harrison, according to Surry Co., VA, Deeds, Wills, Etc., No. 5, p. 204. Thomas was the son of testator Nicholas^{A} Sessums by his first wife [see below], with whom he appeared on the 1693 Surry Titlable list, in Edgar MacDonald and Richard Slatten's *Surry County* [*Virginia*] *Tithables, 1668-1703*, p. 113. By 1698, Thomas Sessums was appearing by himself (p. 147). Nicholas^{A} Sessums died testate in Surry, naming wife Katherine [__], between 8

Oct 1715 and 21 Oct 1716, Surry Co., VA, Deeds, Wills, Etc., #7, p. 33, but he did not mention Thomas—only daughters, grandchildren, and sons-in-law. Thomas settled definitely in Chowan before 17 Apr 1711 at which time his wife Elizabeth prayed for letters of administration on his estate, according to Chowan Co., NC, Deed Book W#1, p. 109. Thomas Sessums married, as her first husband, **Elizabeth Smith**, who married second, probably as his second wife, James Boone. She died after 1735, having executed her second husband's will dated 8 June 1733, proved 31 Mar 1735, Bertie Co., NC, filed among NC Secretary of State loose wills. Son-in-law Cullmer[2] Sessums was the only stepchild named in James Boone's will. Son Richard[2] Sessums was deeded land by his uncle Nicholas Smith on 8 Feb 1729, Bertie Co., NC, Deed Book C, p. 129—100 acres adjoining Richard Killingsworth and John Gray. James Boone made three sales of land to Nicholas Sessums in Oct of 1718, Chowan Co., NC, Deed Book W#1, pp. 187-88.

Testator Richard[A] Smith of Surry Co., VA, in his will dated 24 Feb 1712, proved 20 May 1713, Deeds, Wills, Etc., No. 7, p. 144, made bequests to Elizabeth "Boun" and Richard[2] Sessums. Richard[A] Smith had married first, Margery[A] [__], the widow of George Blow. Richard married second, *ca.* 4 Mar 1678, acco rding to Surry Co., VA, Deeds, Wills, Etc., No. 2, p. 199, Mary [__] Twyford, the widow of decedent John Twyford. Dr. Claiborne Smith's *Smith of Scotland Neck*, pp. 3-5, must not be used for this family without careful location of documentation for the statements made concerning Thomas and Elizabeth Sessum's children.

Witness the following prime example of genealogical finger-painting in order to explain the surname "Culmer," which appeared mysteriously in the third generation of this family. On 6 Nov 1662, Thomas[B] Culmer of Surry Co., VA, made a deed of gift to his daughter Hannah[A], the wife of Robert Lane, according to Surry Co., VA, Deed Book 1, p. 198. The deed consisted of land which came to Culmer by default from a lawsuit in which Culmer had acted as surety for **William[1] Jennings**, who had fled from the tidewater to escape creditors and to learn the art of impulse control in the Albemarle. Culmer gave his daughter Hannah[A] 300 acres on the Upper Sunken Marsh in Southwarke Parish. Virginia Land Patent Book No. 4, p. 18 (27), dated 1 Feb 1655, revealed that this patent was originally obtained by William Jennings, but escheated to Culmer, and was renewed by Robert Lane on 18 Mar 1662. Robert Lane disappeared from the Surry Co. tithable lists around 1670, and no further trace of either him or his father-in-law can be found in the Surry records after that time. On 8 Jan 1685, Nicholas[A] Sessums with [first] wife Hannah[A] of Lawnes Creek parish sold 330 acres of land at Blackwater in Southwarke parish, adjoining Sessum's own land, Richard Blow, Pigeon Swamp, and William Edwards, described as being part of a patent dated [--]. This is located in Surry Co., VA, Deeds, Wills, Etc., #3, p. 47. Fourteen years later, on 2 May 1699, Thomas[1] Sessums and wife Elizabeth of Lawnes Creek sold to Nathaniel Harrison 250 acres known as "*Lanes*" bounded by the James River, Harrison, Charles Goring, and Walter Flood, according to Surry Co., VA, Deeds, Wills, Etc., #5, p. 204.

My interpretation of this concatenation of events is that Nicholas[A] Sessums married *ca.* 1670 the widow Hannah[A] (Culmer) Lane, who died after having one child—Thomas[1] Sessums, named after his grandfather—and the dower land which Thomas[B] Culmer had given to his daughter descended to Thomas Sessums, now provided for, rendering it unnecessary for him to be mentioned in his father's will—which left everything to his new wife and *their* children. Where Thomas Culmer and Robert Lane died has not been revealed.

The Children of Thomas Sessums and Elizabeth Smith:

[1]+ a. **Cullemiar/Culmer[2] Sessums**, married first, **Mary Wynns**, the daughter of George Wynns and Rose (Bush), the former of whom died testate between 2 Feb and May 1751, Bertie Co., NC, Secretary of State loose wills; he married second, **Jennit** [__], according to Bertie Co., NC, Deed Book H, p. 276, in which he and (presumably) wife Jennit witnessed a deed dated 15 Feb 1755, in which William Wright of Perquimans sold land originally purchased of George Wynns.

[2] b. **Richard[2] Sessums**, died testate between 22 Apr and May 1769, Edgecombe Co., NC, Will Book A, p. 171; married **Sarah** [__]

[3]+ c. **Nicholas[2] Sessums**, born by 1697, died testate between 28 May and Oct 1764, Edgecombe Co., NC, Will Book A, p. 141; married **Elizabeth (Hooker) Sizemore**, widow of Samuel Sizemore, and daughter of William Hooker, Sr., of Chowan, whose will was dated 8 Jan 171$^6/_7$ and proved Oct 1717, NC Secretary of State loose wills, also recorded in Secretary of State vol. 875, p. 143. Hooker named his son-in-law Samuel Sizemore and his daughter Elizabeth, Samuel's wife.

Possibly and logically, but unproved:

[4] d. **Mary Sessums**.
[5] e. **John Sessums**.
[6] f. **Samuel Sessums**.
[7] g. **Thomas Sessums**.

158. The remarkably peripatetic **Darby Sexton** was born *ca.* 1635 and died intestate *ca.* 1700, Perquimans precinct, Albemarle Co., NC. He married first, between 25 Jan 1654 and 15 Sept 1658, Norfolk Co., VA, **Deborah Richards**, named as stepdaughter in the will of Thomas Cheley, who had died testate between 20 Aug 1653 and June 1654, Norfolk Co., VA, Record Book C, p. 122b.

Thomas Cheley had married second, Joane [__], the widow of [__] Richards. According to Norfolk Co., VA, Record Book D, p. 165, dated 15 Sept 1658, Darby Sexton, who had married the "daughter" of Thomas Cheeley, sued John Henley who had married Cheeley's widow. Other records have revealed that Col. Thomas Cheley had a first wife who was the subject of two different escheat actions in Nansemond earlier in the 1650s, althouth they were not recorded until the 1670s. In a long running series in the *Virginia Genealogist*, "Inquisitions on Escheated Land, 1665-1670," particularly in vol. 20, no. 1 [January-March, 1976], pp. 21-22, it appeared that Margaret the wife of Col. Thomas Cheley had been married twice before: first to John Rogers who died intestate leaving her with 300 acres which was granted to her by patent in 1655; then she married John Garrett, who also died testate seized of 400 acres and devised the tract to Margaret. But as she died without heirs, both tracts escheated.

Darby Sexton's residence in Lower Norfolk was not always happy, indicated by the fact that as an indentured servant he ran away from his master Henry Woodhouse. This was reported on 23 May 1655, Norfolk Co., NC, Record Book C, p. 157b—he received 20 lashes for this infraction. Darby Sexton was transported into Maryland "from the Southward of Virginia," in 1665, according to MD Liber 17, f. 490, found in Gus Skordas, *The Early Settlers of Maryland*, p. 412. Sexton married second, by 1680, as her first husband, **Dorothy** [__], who was listed as the mother of their daughter Sarah[2] at her marriage to Esay Albertson. On 29 Mar [--], probably in the 1690s, Darby Sexton applied for 300 acres due him for the transportation of six persons into the Albemarle. Out of the six, due to the mutilation of the record, are named only Darby Sexton, Dorathy his wife, Edw. German, and Tho. French, according to Caroline B. Whitley, *North Carolina Headrights, A List of Names, 1663-1744*, p. 83.

Dorothy [__] Sexton married second, William Simson. The will of William Simson of Albemarle, dated 15 Jan and proved 17 Apr 1694, NC Secretary of State loose wills, named wife "Dority," their children Hannah, William, and John, and in addition her children by her first marriage: William[2] Sexton and Sarah[2] Sexton, to whom were bequeathed cattle in Pasquotank.

Andrew[2] Sexton's first appearance in the Talbot Co., MD, Deeds, was as a witness to a sale of land, dated 26 Oct 1682, from George Collinson and wife Elizabeth to James Dowdell, Talbot Co., MD, Deed Book 4, p. 319. His widow Catherine purchased land, 100 acres in Talbot adjoining land of John Glandening and Col. Henry Coursey, from Edmund O'Dwyer, dated 18 Mar 1688, Talbot Co., MD, Deed Book 5, p. 225. A deed was recorded from Katherine [__]

Sexton-Murphey to her underage son Andrew[3] Sexton on 11 June 1705, Talbot Co., MD, Deed Book 9, p. 320.

The Child of Darby Sexton and Deborah Richards, born Norfolk Co., VA:
[1]+ a. **Andrew[2] Sexton**, born by 1660, died intestate between 1682-88, Talbot Co., MD; married **Katherine** [__], who married second, [__] Murphey, and died testate as a widow between 21 Apr 1703 and 4 Jan 1704, Talbot Co., MD, Prerogative vol. 3, p. 349.

The Children of Darby Sexton and Dorothy [__], born Perquimans Co., NC:
[2] b. **Sarah[2] Sexton**, born *ca.* 1680, married 7 Jan $170^0/_1$, Perquimans, **Esay[2] Albertson** (Albert[1]).
[3] c. **William[2] Sexton**.

159. Thomas Sharbo was born *ca.* 1700 and married first, 9 Apr 1725, Perquimans Co., NC, **Barbara Lacey**, born *ca.* 1701, the daughter of William Lacey and Grace Davis, married at Perquimans 1 Mar 1684. He married second, **Rebecca** [__], who signed with him on a deed in Perquimans, dated 29 Apr 1742, Perquimans Co., NC, Deed Book C, no. 69. Thomas was certainly dead by Oct 1748, because Rebecca Sharber submitted a petition to the court of Pasquotank at that time, which petition was "quashed;" she would never have been able to do that if her husband had been alive. This may be found in Pasquotank Co., NC, Court Minutes, 1747-1753, p. 55. Rebecca was still alive on 11 Jan 1758, at which time she sold land to Robert Murden, Pasquotank Co., NC, Deed Book F&G, p. 154.

Thomas Sharbo's first appearance in Perquimans is in a purchase of land from John Flowers, shoemaker, and wife Mary, for 100 acres on the northeast side of the river adjoining Ralph Fletcher and William Lacy, according to Perquimans Co., NC, Deed Book B, no. 211, dated 30 July 1725. Thomas Sharbo was deceased by 7 Jan 1753 at which time his son Jonathan sold land where his father had formerly dwelled, Perquimans Co., NC, Deed book F, no. 261.

The sequencing of Thomas Sharbo's wives, and particularly the births of his children, provides an interesting study in either multiple marriages or early polygamy. There is no indication in the records of Perquimans that there was an older or contemporary Thomas Sharbo; and unless one posits a first wife Elizabeth, followed by Barbara Lacey, a third wife Elizabeth, and a fourth wife Rebecca, one is at a loss to explain in any other reasonable fashion the entries in the Perquimans register. Possibly the simplest explanation is that Thomas had a liaison with the same Elizabeth [__], then married Barbara Lacey, had another liaison with the same Elizabeth, and then married Rebecca [__], after the death of his other wife Barbara Lacey. It is unlikely that an unmarried partner would sign on a deed with her mate. And then, common law marriages have always been uncertain ground in the early colonial period. This writer is not an expert in that field, either practically or theoretically.

According to Weynette Parks Haun, *Old Albemarle County North Carolina, Pasquotank Precinct (Count) Births, Marriages, Deaths, Brands and Flesh Marks, & County Claims, 1691-1833*, p. 54, at different times both Thomas Sharber and Rebecca, then of Pasquotank, registered flesh marks for two of their "children." On 19 Aug 1746, [Thomas] registered on for his "son" Thomas, and on 10 Dec 1748, Rebecca registered one for her "daughter" Elizabeth. Each child was specifically designated as a child of the grantor. After this point, the family took up its permanent residence in Pasquotank.

The Child of Thomas Sharbo and Elizabeth [__], born Perquimans:
[1] a. **Thomas[2] Sharbo**, born 30 Sept 1730.

The Children of Thomas Sharbo and Barbara Lacey, born Perquimans:
[2]+ b. **Jonathan[2] Sharbo**, born 1 Jan 1734, will dated 4 Nov 1771, filed among Chowan Co., NC, loose wills; estate division by 22 Nov 1788, Pasquotank; married, as her first husband, **Miriam Richardson**; she married second, David Nichols, who died testate after 7 Nov 1779, Pasquotank Co., NC, Will Book HIK, p. 461.
[3] c. **William[2] Sharbo**, born 4 July 1738.

The Child of Thomas Sharbo and Elizabeth [__], born Perquimans:
[4] d. **Elizabeth[2] Sharbo**, born 8 Jan 1740.

160. Alexander Sherrod, the son of John[A] Sherrod (Sherrer) and [__] of Isle of Wight Co., VA, and brother to **Robert[1]**, was born there by 1684 and died testate in Bertie Co., NC, as "Alexander Shirod" between 10 July 1731 and May 1734, his will filed in the NC Secretary of State loose wills. John[A] Sherrod named son Alexander as his executor (there is no indication that Alexander was not of age) in his will dated 23 Jan 1705, Isle of Wight Co., VA, Will & Deed Book 2, p. 480. Alexander married **Mary** [__], whom he named in his will. He was a resident of Chowan Co., NC, by 12 Feb 171$^8/_9$, at which time he purchased land from John Councill, according to Chowan Co., NC, Deed Book B#1, p. 694. The name Sherrod has undergone many incarnations: Sherrer, Shearrer, Shearin, Serer, Sherwood, and Sherrod.

The Children of Alexander Sherrod and Mary [__]:
[1] a. **Martha[2] Sherrod**.

[2] b. **Esther[2] Sherrod.**
[3] c. **Catrain[2] Sherrod.**
[4] d. **Alexander[2] Sherrod**, born *ca.* 1713, was bequeathed his father's plantation in Virginia at the age of 21; he sold this on 23 Aug 1734—100 acres, part of a patent to John Sherrar for 500 acres—to George Goodrich of upper parish of Isle of Wight, Deed Book 4, p. 358.
[5] e. **Aaron[2] Sherrod.**
[6]+ f. **John[2] Sherrod**, died testate between Dec 1779 and Mar 1780, Martin Co., NC, Will Book 1, p. 59; he married **Mary** [__].
[7] g. **Elisabeth[2] Sherrod.**

161. Robert Sherrod, the son of John[A] and [__] of Isle of Wight, and brother to **Alexander**[1], was born by 1690, Isle of Wight Co., VA, and died testate as "Robert Shearer," after the signing of his will on 7 Oct 1727, Bertie Co., NC, which was filed among the NC Secretary of State loose wills. Under the terms of his father's will, Robert received 100 acres in Isle of Wight adjoining John Britt. Robert married **Elizabeth** [__], whom he named in his will, although he signed his will as Robert *Shearrer.* The name Sherrod has undergone many incarnations: Sherrer, Shearrer, Serer, Sherwood, and Sherrod. He was a resident of Chowan on 4 May 1719 at which time he purchased land on the south side of the Meherrin River from John Blackburn and his wife Martha, Chowan Co., NC, Deed Book B#1, p. 707.

The Children of Robert Sherrod and Elizabeth [__]:
[1]+ a. **Robert[2] Sherrod**, died testate between 13 Sept 1775 and Mar 1779, Martin Co., NC, Will Book 1, p. 55; married **Lydia** [__].
[2] b. **Arthur[2] Sherrod**, married by 3 June 1740, Bertie Co., NC, Deed Book F, p. 183, **Mary** [__]; his cousin Elizabeth and her father Thomas[1] Sherrer (Arthur's uncle) received a gift from John[A] Sherrer, Sr., on 16 Mar 1701, for Arthur and Elizabeth sold that tract on 25 Mar 1734 to Richard Blunt—one tract of100 acres in upper parish adjoining the land of his late uncle Thomas Sherrod, and another of 105 acres formerly granted to Thomas Sherrod, Isle of Wight Co., VA, Deed Book 4, p. 331. It is possible that Arthur remained in Southampton Co., VA.
[3] c. **John[2] Sherrod**, sold two tracts of land to John Nicholson of Surry Co., VA, in Bertie on 6 Feb 1740, Bertie Co., NC, Deed Book F, p. 227: 100 acres, part of a patent to Henry Wheeler in 1714, by virtue of a devise in will of his father Robert Sherrod; p. 228: 100 acres purchased of Emperor Wheeler on south sideof Meherrin River.

[4] d. **Susannah[2] Sherrod** (possibly married **John[1] Dew II**).
[5] e **William[2] Sherrod**.
[6] f. **Sarah[2] Sherrod**.
[7] g. **Prudence[2] Sherrod**.

162. Daniel[1] Shine was born about 1689 in Ireland, and died testate in Craven Co., NC, between 5 May and Aug Court 1757, his will filed in the NC Secretary of State loose wills and recorded in NC Secretary of State vol. 880, p. 191. According to the Shine family Bible, he married 15 May 1715, Bath Co., NC, **Elizabeth[2] Green**, the daughter of **Farnefold[1] Green** and **Hannah[2] (Kent) Smithwick**, born *ca*. 1700, Bath Co., NC.

According to Craven Co., NC, Deed Book 2, p. 331, dated 10 May 1758, James Reed and wife Hannah[2] of Craven for £30 sold to Francis Mackilwean, planter, 150 acres on the south side of Stony Town Creek, lately the inheritance of Francis Stringer, deceased, late husband of Hannah Reed.

The Children of Daniel Shine and Elizabeth Green:
[1] a. **Hannah[2] Shine**, born 16 July 1718, married first, **Francis Stringer**, surgeon, who died testate between 8 Jan 1749 and 30 Mar 1753, Craven Co., NC, Deed Book 5, p. 297; married second, **James Reed**.
[2] b. **Elezabeth[2] Shine**, born 19 Feb 1721, married [__] **Vaughan**.
[3] c. **Mary[2] Shine**, born 11 July 1724, died young.
[4]+ d. **John[2] Shine**, born 25 Nov 1725, married 22 Mar 1752, Craven Co., NC, **Sarah McIlwean**.
[5] e. **Mary[2] Shine**, born 29 Dec 1727.
[6] f. **Daniel[2] Shine**, born 10 Feb 1729.
[7] g. **James[2] Shine**, born 9 Jan 1732.
[8] h. **Sarah[2] Shine**, born 7 Feb 1732.
[9] i. **Thomas[2] Shine**, born 1 Oct 1736.
[10] j. **Francis[2] Shine**, born 1 June 1739.
[11] k. **William[2] Shine**, born 25 Mar 1741.

163. John Shine, the son of **Daniel Shine** and **Elizabeth[2] Green**, was born 25 Nov 1725, Bath Co., NC, according to the Shine family Bible. He died 12 Dec 1783, Dobbs Co., NC, and married 22 Mar 1752, Craven Co., NC, **Sarah McIlwean**, born *ca*. 1727, the daughter of surveyor James McIlwean.

The Children of John Shine and Sarah McIlwean:
[1] a. **James[2] Shine**, born 30 Juan 1753.
[2] b. **Eleazabeth[2] Shine**, born 24 Sept 1756.

[3]+ c. **Eleanor[2] Shine**, born 24 Sept 1756, married, as his second wife, 22 June 1775, Dobbs Co., NC, **Samuel Caswell**.
[4] d. **John[2] Shine**, born 22 Nov 1758, married **Clarissa(5) Williams**, the daughter of James(4) Williams [Theophilus(3), John(2-1)], and Sarah Brice, according to Jones Co., NC, Deed Book 1, p. 346, dated 31 Mar 1795.
[5] e. **Francis[2] Shine**, born 24 Mar 1760.
[6] f. **Hanah[2] Shine**, born 18 June 1762.
[7] g. **Mary[2] Shine**, born 11 Dec 1763.
[8] h. **Eleasabeth[2] Shine**, born 7 June 1765.
[9] i. **William[2] Shine**, born 26 Sept 176[--]
[10] j. **Daniel[2] Shine**, born 23 July 1771.
[11] k. **Nancey[2] Shine**, born 14 Oct 1772.

164. Robert Sims was born *ca.* 1695, and died testate before 11 Feb 1729, Bertie Co., NC, his will filed among the NC Secretary of State loose wills. On 11 Nov 1720, Robert Sims, as a resident of Chowan Co., NC, purchased from James Anderson 100 acres on Cypress Swamp on the Morattock River, adjoining William Boon, which was part of a patent granted William Braswell dated 4 mar 171$^1/_2$, according to Chowan Co., NC, Deed Book C#1, p. 145. He married **Phillis[2] (Fort) Fiveash**, the daughter of **George[1] Fort** and Elizabeth Accabee Duckwood, the latter of whom was mentioned as wife but not named in George Fort's will. Robert Sims named his brother John Sims in his will, and deed activity in Chowan related him also to Henry (with wife Grace) and Joseph Sims (with wife Sarah), almost certainly his brothers. In the 1720 tax list for Chowan, Robert Sims was identified as Constable, according to Weynette Parks Haun's *Old Albemarle County North Carolina Miscellaneous Records, 1678 to ca. 1737*, p. 125, item #330. He is, in fact, also listed therein next to the same Joseph Sims and Henry Sims.

Around 1730 an undated deed was recorded in Bertie Court wherein Phyllis Sims had sold to Peter Jones 100 acres on the north side of Morratuck River and Occaneche Swamp, which was part of a patent granted to William Braswell in 171$^1/^2$, Bertie Co., NC, Deed Book C, p. 219. This is the exact same land purchased by Robert Sims in 1720. A witness to this transaction was Joseph Sims.

The Children of Robert Sims and Phillis (Fort) Fiveash:
[1]+ a. **Robert[2] Sims**, born *ca.* 1725, Bertie, will proved Apr 1791, Wayne Co., NC, Will Book A, p. 244; married **Mary[2] Barnes**, daughter of **Edward[1]**.
[2] b. **Thomas[2] Sims**, bequeathed 100 acres on Oachoneeche Neck

adjoining William Boon.

[3] c. **James[2] Sims**, bequeathed 100 acres on Conoconara Swamp adjoining Matthew Caps.

165. Nicholas Smith, the son of Richard Smith[A] and second wife Mary[A] [__] Twyford, was born *ca.* 1682, Surry Co., VA, and died testate before 19 Feb 1744, Edgecombe Co., NC, according to Edgecombe Co., NC, Court Minutes [unpaged]. His will, however, has not survived. He married after 1711, **Mary Drew**, the daughter of John[A] Drew and Elizabeth[A] Swann (Matthew[B]) of Surry Co., VA. According to NC Land Patent Book 3, p. 172, dated 4 Aug 1723, Nicholas Smith was granted 390 acres on the west side of Elk Marsh. A sketch of this family is given in *Colonial Families of Surry and of Isle of Wight Counties, Virginia*, vol. 2, *The Descendants of Robert Harris of Isle of Wight County, Virginia.*

Both Bryant sons-in-law of Nicholas Smith were sons of John Bryant of Edgecombe, who died testate between 14 Sept 1734 and May 1735, his will filed among NC Secretary of State loose wills, and also recorded in NC Land Grant Book 4, no. 4. John Bryant's wife was mentioned in his will but not named.

The most pressing issue of this sketch concerns the marriages of Capt. James[2] Smith, and the ancestry of his second wife, Millea Turner. A "troubling" [*i.e.*, difficult to interpret in light of later, anecdotal information] land patent was located in the Virginia Land Patents in Patent Book 34, p. 811, dated 14 Feb 1761: a grant of 360 acres in Isle of Wight to James Smith, on the side of a large swamp formerly called the Head of New Town Haven River, being the head of Chuckatuck Creek, down the Cooper's Swamp, adjoining Thomas Howell, Joseph Matthews, Thomas Pinner, and Samuel Bradley.

Even more puzzlingly, on 27 Nov 1761, James Turner and wife Ann of Southampton Co., VA, with James[2] Smith and wife Milley of Halifax Co., NC, sold to James Pedin of Isle of Wight, 360 acres on the north side of Newtown Haven River, being the head of Chuckatuck adjoining Thomas Howell, John Matthews, Thomas Penner, the Coopers Swamp, Samuel Bradley, and the head of Chuckatuck, according to Isle of Wight Co., VA, Deed Book 11, p. 10. It has long been assumed that James Turner and Milley Smith were the children of *Thomas* Turner (**Henry**[1]), the intestate Edgecombe decedent of 1749, but this has yet to be proved. There were many Thomas Turners in the Edgecombe area—one of Isle of Wight, and the another possibly a son of **Henry**[1]. The records do not reveal how James Turner and James Smith came into possession of the 1761 patent, nor is James Smith listed on the patent as being a resident of North Carolina.

Incidentally, grantor James Turner of Southampton died testate between 18 July 1763 and 12 May 1768, Southampton Co., VA, Will Book 2, p. 237, bequeathing land in Northampton Co., NC, to his sons Jacob and William Turner. On 13 Oct 1766, James Pedin of Nansemond sold the above 360 acres of land to Samuel Bradley of Suffolk Parish in Nansemond, according to Isle of Wight Co., VA, Deed Book 12, p. 94, and the land passed out of our interest.

Finally, it seems almost certain that James[2] Smith married second, Milly *Turner*, but her paternity cannot be exactly determined from the records. Were it not for the given name "Turner" appearing among the descendants of this couple, one might as easily imagine a sibling relationship between James Smith and Ann Turner, or even between Ann Turner and Millie Smith.

Information on the Ruffin connections to the family were taken from John Bennett Boddie, *Virginia Historical Genealogies*, pp. 265-66.

The Children of Nicholas Smith and Mary Drew:

[1] a. **Richard[2] Smith**, born *ca.* 1716, married, as her first husband, **Anne** [__], who married second, Francis Bythell Haynes. There has been something of a controversy about Anne [__] Smith's second marriage— after the publication of my *Robert Harris* genealogy, I received an extremely abusive letter from a very irate woman, which I quite naturally relocated to the "circular file;" according to Joseph W. Watson's *Estate Records of Edgecombe County, North Carolina, 1730-1820*, p. 246, Richard Smith died intestate before 21 Aug 1751, and his administratrix Anne divided his property between Francis Bythel Haynes and the brothers[2] [*i.e.*, Smith] of the deceased. Drew[2] Smith bequeathed to his daughter Ann[3] the plantation on which Francis Bythel Haynes then lived, part of Drew's inheritance from his brother now being "enjoyed" (in the words of David B. Gammon) by Richard's widow Anne and her second husband. Anne [__] Smith has been identified, reasonably, as the daughter of testator Christopher Dicken of Edgecombe, who died testate between 13 May and Nov 1779, Edgecombe Co., NC, Will Book B, p. 32. Dicken named daughter Ann and grandson Christopher Haynes. However, I am not totally convinced that Christopher Haynes, who would have to have been born after 1751, would have witnessed a will in 1759 (Thomas Wilkins, Halifax Co., NC, Will Book 1, p. 53), notwithstanding the laxity in age requirements for that particular public service. According to Halifax Co., NC, Inventories of Estates, 1773-1779, p. 88, recorded Feb Court 1775, Christopher Haynes filed a guardian's account for the orphans of Francis Bithell Haynes for the years 1770 through 1774: Bithell, Christopher, Mary, Lucy, Thomas, Hannah, and Francis. The maiden name of Ann [__] Smith-Haynes depends upon which Christopher was named as grandson of Christopher Dicken in his 1779 will.

[2] b. **Drew[2] Smith**, born *ca.* 1718, died testate between 22 Feb and Mar 1762, Halifax Co., NC, Will Book 1, p. 57; married **Elizabeth** [__]; he also bequeathed property to Nicholas[3] and Nathan[3] Bryant, the sons of his sister Mary[2] by Arthur Bryant.

[3] c. **James[2] Smith**, born *ca.* 1720, died testate between 4 Oct 1809 and Feb 1811, Halifax Co., NC, Will Book 3, p. 514; according to family legend recounted in Claiborne Smith's *Smith of Scotland Neck*, he married 5 times; he married first *ca.* 1744, (said to be) **Mary Edwards**—one daughter Lucy[3] Smith was born of this marriage; second, *ca.* 1747, **Milly Turner**, born Mar 1729, died 27 July 1766, according to the James Smith Bible; 5 children were born of this union: [i] Pheraby[3], died young; [ii] Nancy[3], died young; [iii] Turner[3]; [iv] James[3]; [v] Mary[3], died young; James married third, by 1770, Halifax Co., NC, **Anne** [__], whose only mention was a deed wherein she signed with her husband James Smith in a sale of 200 acres of land to Thomas Hunter, dated 26 Mar 1770, Halifax Co., NC, Deed Book 12, p. 70; fourth, [__], theorized to have been Mourning Dixon (Crudup) Thomas of Nash who had indeed married second, a James Smith. Capt. Micajah Thomas died testate in Edgecombe between 4 Dec 1769 and Feb 1770, Edgecombe Co., NC, Will Book A, p. 178, leaving widow Mourning, who died testate, as Mourning Smith, between 12 May 1778 and July 1781, Nash Co., NC, Will Book 1, p. 8. Since she named Smith children who were clearly not named by James Smith in his will, we may conclude that she married a different James from ours; fifth, bef. 30 Apr 1796, **Sarah (Hill) Ruffin**, widow of William[5] Ruffin (nephew of Robert[4] Ruffin below) and daughter of Capt. Richard Hill of Sussex Co., VA and Margery Gilliam.

[4] d. **Mary[2] Smith**, born *ca.* 1721, married **Arthur Bryan(t)**.

[5] e. **Sarah[2] Smith**, born *ca.* 1722, married **William Bryant**, who died testate between 14 Mar and Nov 1761, his nuncupative will recorded in Edgecombe Co., NC, Will Book A, p. 77.

[6]+ f. **Arthur[2] Smith**, born 14 Nov 1732, died testate between 7 Feb and May 1789, Halifax Co., NC, Will Book 3, p. 169; married **Anne[3] Ruffin**. On 22 May 1745, 14-year old orphan Arthur[2] Smith, son of Nicholas[1] Smith, chose his brother Drew[2] Smith as his guardian, Edgecombe Co., NC, Court Minutes, 1744-1746. Anne Smith died testate between 8 Jan 1800 and Aug 1801, Halifax Co., NC, Will Book 3, p. 362. Ann[5] Ruffin was the daughter of Robert[4] Ruffin and **Ann[2] Bennet** (Capt. **William[1]**).

166. Robert Smith died testate between 26 Jan and May 1726, Bertie Co., NC, his will filed among NC Secretary of State loose wills. He married, as her first husband, **Mary** [__], whom he named in his will. An interesting inventory of his estate, dated *ca.* Nov 1726, appears in Bertie Co., NC, Deed Book B, p. 201. In his will, Robert Smith bequeathed to eldest son Robert[2] 150 acres purchased of Berreby Melton, and to daughter Elizabeth[2], 200 acres also purchased of Melton. No such transactions can be located either in the records of Chowan or of Bertie. There is, however, a deed dated 30 Sept 1718, Chowan Co., NC, Deed Book B#1, p. 638, from **William[1] Reeves** of Chowan, planter, to Robert Smith, for 150 acres adjoining the Widow *Molton*, the Main Road and Reeves, witnessed by Thomas Smith, and John *Molton*. On 1 Feb 1725, Robert Smith received a patent of land for 181 acres on south side of Morratuck River in Bertie, adjoining Thomas Whitmel, and *Berry Melton*, NC Land Patent Book 3, p. 192.

In Feb of 1742, someone proved importation rights for Robert Smith, *i.e.*, Robert Smith, Mary Smith, John Smith, Elizabeth Smith, James Smith, Anne Smith, and William Smith, according to Caroline B. Whitley, *North Carolina Headrights, A List of Names, 1663-1774*, p. 211. Interestingly, both Robert, Sr., himself, and Robert, Jr., were already deceased by the time this list was submitted.

Mary [__] Smith married second, Capt. **John[1] Spann**, who presented to court the inventory of Robert Smith's estate, according to Bertie Co., NC, Inventories of Estates, 1728-1744, p. 42, dated 24 Jan $172^7/_8$. This "working hypothesis" can be supported by the bequest in James[2] Smith's will of one Negro man named Ben to "Sarah the wife of John Spann," John[2] Spann being almost certainly the son of Capt. John Spann and his wife Mary [__] Smith-Spann, and a half-relation to James Smith.

Robert Smith's Surry Co., VA, connections have been located in a deed dated 18 Feb 1739, Surry Co., VA, Deeds, Wills, Etc., #9, p. 123, from Samuel Norwood and wife Mary, and Thomas Bradford and wife Elizabeth of the colony of Carolina to John Jones of Prince George Co., VA, for the sale of 100 acres on the north side of Blackwater Swamp, adjoining the land of John Jones, formerly belonging to Robert Smith, father of the above Mary and Elizabeth, who inherited as coheirs. Previously, according to VA Land Patent Book 10, p. 274, dated 23 Mar 1715, for 10 shillings, Robert Smith of Surry received a patent of 100 acres of new land in Southwark Parish, on the north side of the Main Blackwater Swamp, adjoining James Jones' line. There is, unfortunately, only one almost negligible mention of Robert Smith in the Surry court minutes, and that only as a defendant in a law suit—there is no genealogical information contained therein whatsoever, and Robert does not surface in the land records at all, even as a witness to a deed.

The Children of Robert Smith and Mary [__]:

[1] a. **Robert[2] Smith**, died intestate and childless by 1737, as his 150-acre bequest from his father was divided between his two sisters, Bertie Co., NC, Deed Book E, p. 182.

[2] b. **Elisabeth[2] Smith**, died by 14 Nov 1754, Edgecombe Co., NC; married, as his first wife, **Thomas[(3)] Bradford**, the son of Richard[(2-1)] Bradford (and Frances Taylor the daughter of Richard Taylor and Sarah Barker—the division of Richard Taylor's estate occurred Oct 1684, Charles City Co., VA, Court Orders, 1676-1695, p. 149) of Charles City Co., VA, who sold land his father bequeathed him in Westover Parish, Charles City Co., VA—200 acres, according to Charles City Co., VA, Wills and Deeds, 1725-1731, p. 215, dated 3 Dec 1728. Elisabeth (Smith) Bradford had inherited land from her father, according to Edgecombe Co., NC, Deed Book 1, p., 14, dated 20 Nov 1732, in which Thomas and wife Elisabeth Bradford sold 180 acres of land in Edgecombe to Philip Mulky, land on south side of Moratock river, adjoining Thomas Whitmel and Beary Melton, patented by Robert Smith on 1 Feb 1725. Later, Thomas Bradford, his wife Elisabeth, and Samuel Norwood and wife Mary sold 150 acres of land to Barraby Melton, land formerly granted to William Reeves for 440 acres, dated 13 Mar 1721, according to Bertie Co., NC, Deed Book E, p. 182, dated 3 Sept 1737. Thomas Bradford, "Sr.," married second, as her first husband, Mary [__] by 14 Nov 1754, when they sold land to John Rozar, Edgecombe Co., NC, Deed Book 2, p. 300; Thomas died testate between 23 May 1761 and Nov 1762, Northampton Co., NC, Will Book 1, p. 75; Mary [__] Bradford married second, Benjamin Wallis, and with her stepson Thomas[3] Bradford were of Craven Co., SC, according to a deed dated 7 Feb 1775, Halifax Co., NC, Deed Book 13, p. 284. Elizabeth[2] (Smith) Bradford was the mother of all of Thomas'children.

[3] c. **James[2] Smith**, died testate between 3 Jan and June Court 1762, Halifax Co., NC, Will Book 1, p. 70; married **Frances [__] Bundy**. The testator mentioned children by a Jeremiah Smith, but he is thus far unidentified.

[4]+ d. **Mary[2] Smith**, married by 1737, **Samuel Norwood**, will dated 21 Oct 1795, proved Nov 1795, Halifax Co., NC, Will Book 3, p. 28.

[5] e. **William[2] Smith**, died testate between 20 Dec 1760 and May 1761, Northampton Co., NC, Will Book 1, p. 47; he married **Mary** [__], whom he named in his will; all his children were under age.

[6] f. **John[2] Smith**.

167. Hugh Smithwick was born *ca.* 1610 and died testate between 1674 and 1680, Shaftesbury Precinct, Albemarle Co., NC, although his will has been lost. This information is taken from NC Secretary of State, vol. 874.2, Council Minutes, Wills, and Inventories, 1677-1701, p. 28, in which son and executor Edward reported that his father's will had been "miscarried," and that he wished to be appointed administrator of the estate. Hugh Smithwick was listed as a headright in a patent for one William Eyres, 23 May 1642, who received a grant for 750 acres in Upper Norfolk Co., VA, according to VA Land Patent Book 1, part 2, p. 777. In 1694, orators Edward[2] and John[2] "Smithweck," sons and heirs of Hugh Smithwick late of Chowan, deceased, stated that their father had arrived in the colonies 35 years hence (*ca.* 1659), according to *North Carolina Higher-Court Records, 1670-1696*, p. 71. Hugh married **Elizabeth** [__], who married second, [__] Ward, and died after May 1694. Proof of Elizabeth's second marriage can be found in *Warrants and Surveys*, p. 14, in which, on 25 May 1694, as Elizabeth Ward she assigned over her importation rights to her son Edward[2] Smithwick. Hugh Smithwick is reputed to have been the first settler in Edenton Bay, about 1659, [possibly even predating **George Durant**!]. In 1669 Hugh Smithwick listed himself, his wife Elizabeth, his sons Edward, Hugh, and Ralph, his daughter Elizabeth, and an Elizabeth Bembridge as headrights to obtain 400 acres of land. William Doub Bennett's *Hugh Smithwick Descendants* is an adequate treatment of the later generations of the Smithwick family, although Mr. Bennett missed the high drama of the fourth Mrs. Smithwick's precipitous flight from the stifling bonds of matrimony with Herman Joyner in Isle of Wight.

The age of Edward[2] Smithwick was determined by Mattie Erma Edwards Parker, from an undated deposition taken about 1682 in which Edward[2] said he was thirty-three years old, according to *North Carolina Colonial Records*, 2nd ser., vol. 2, p. 423, note 5. There is no concrete proof for the marriage of Elizabeth[2] Smithwick to Robert Warburton although the couple did, however, name a son Smithwick[3] Warburton. Mary[2] Smithwick's existence is proved by an undated deed from her brother Edward[2] to his [then married] sister Mary[2] Gregory, wife of Thomas Gregory, according to Chowan Co., NC, Deed Book W#1, p. 68. All "Smithwick" descendants bearing that last name are the progeny of Edward[2]—John[2] had only daughters.

Edward[2] Smithwick was married first to **Lydia** [__] by 5 Feb 1678, at which time he received a patent of 200 acres on the south side of Matacommack Creek, which he registered on 29 Mar 1680 for imporation rights, listing himself and wife Lydia, and John and Lydia Shearing, in Haun, *Old Albemarle County North Carolina Book of Land Warrants and Surveys, 1681-1706*, f. 182 (p. 111). He was married second to **Elizabeth** [__] by 29 Mar 1680, when he registered his rights for 4 headrights: himself, wife Elizabeth, and John and *Elizabeth* Shearin, in Haun (*op. cit.*), f. 30 (p. 25). Edward[2] Smithwick and his third wife

Africa [__] sold land to John Jones, Sr., of Chowan on 1 Dec 1702, according to Chowan Co., NC, Deed Boook W#1, p. 33. It has also been assumed that Africa [__] Smithwick was the widow of David Jones, but since the importation rights of David Jones of Shaftesbury precinct were reigstered on 5 Feb 1679, it seems somewhat unlikely that she would still be of child-bearing age in 1694. See Caroline B. Whitley, *North Carolina Headrights, A Lits of Names, 1663-1744*, p. 123 and p. 144, wherein on 1 Apr 1694, Jonathan Jones, son of David, registered his rights. Moreover, there is no proof of blood connection between the Joneses and Smithwicks. By *ca.* 1707, Edward[2] and his fourth wife **Sarah** made a deed of gift to his sister Mary[2] (Smithwick) Gregory, as noted above. There is an excellent biography of Edward Smithwick in Powell, *Dictionary of North Carolina Biography*, vol. 5, *P-S*, pp. 392-93. It should supercede the information in Bennett.

Evidence of Herman Joyner's plea to the authorities down in the Albemarle (where the offending couple had settled) for a divorce, and Sarah's subsequent liaison with Capt. Woolard can be found in Isle of Wight Will & Deed Book 1, p. 294, dated 6 Dec 1673. William Woolard died testate in Albemarle Co., between 12 Nov $168^{4}/_{5}$ and 2 Feb $169^{1}/_{2}$, his will filed among NC Secretary of State loose wills. He named a granddaughter Margaret Holbrook, obviously the result of an earlier marriage. Woolard's wife Sarah was listed in his will as "Sarah Woolard *alias* Joyner," suggesting that the couple had not seriously considered repairing the error of their ways, or at least of Sarah's. The will of Sarah's third husband Thomas Gillyam was dated 10 Oct 1702, and was witnessed by step-granddaughter Margaret Holbrook, NC Secretary of State loose wills. No children were mentioned. The much-courted Sarah was still alive in $171^{5}/_{6}$ when Edward[2] Smithwick signed his will and addressed her fondly but namelessly as "his beloved wife." There is no reason to believe that Edward had married for a fifth time or that this final *tendresse* referred to yet another wife other than his fourth.

A braver soul than this can assigne Edward's children to his various wives. We may be fairly certain that there were none by his last. Childbearing does not seem to have been her *métier*.

The Children of Hugh Smithwick and Elizabeth [__]:

[1]+ a. **Edward[2] Smithwick**, born *ca.* 1649, died testate between 21 Jan $171^{5}/_{6}$ and Oct 1716, Chowan Co., NC, NC Secretary of State loose wills; married first, before Feb 1678, **Lydia** [__]; second, by Mar 1680, **Elizabeth** [__]; third by Dec 1702, **Africa** [__]; fourth, *ca.* 1703, **Sarah** [__] **Joyner-Woolard-Gillyam**, the *shameless* and adulterous wife of Herman Joyner of Isle of Wight Co., VA, and then bigamous widow of Capt. William Woolard and Thomas Gillyam, respectively.

[2] b. **Hugh[2] Smithwick**, *died young*.

[3] c. **Ralph[2] Smithwick**, *died young*.

[4] d. **Elizabeth[2] Smithwick**, married, as his second wife, **Robert Warburton**, who died testate between 25 Mar and 31 July 1733, Bertie Co., NC, Secretary of State loose wills.

[5]+ e. **John[2] Smithwick**, born *ca.* 1670, died testate between 28 Aug 1696 and 6 Jan 1696/7, NC Secretary of State loose wills, also recorded in NC Secretary of State vol. 874.2, p. 93; married, as her first husband, **Hannah[2] Kent**; she married second, **Farnefold[1] Green I**, who died testate 26 Oct 1711, Bath Co., NC, recorded in Secretary of State vol. 875, p. 10; she married third, Thomas Graves, who died testate between 11 Apr and 16 Sept 1730, NC Secretary of State loose wills.

[6] f. **Mary[2] Smithwick**, born *ca.* 1672, married **Thomas Gregory**, who died intestate *ca.* 1713, according to NC Secretary of State vol. 875, 1712-1722, p. 73: division of his estate among his children, Mary, Sarah, Samuel, Benjamin, and the children of Thomas Heath. Hathaway, in the *North Carolina Historical and Genealogical Register*, vol. 1, p. 46, gives a date of $171^{2}/_{3}$, and lists the distributees as Mary, Sarah, Luke, and Samuel. These are the Gregorys of Chowan.

168. Col. **John Snoad** appeared in the records of Bath on 26 Sept 1717 as a witness to the will of Emanuel Cleeves, recorded in Beaufort Co., NC, Deed Book 1, p. 285. He received a patent for 570 acres on the west side of the Pamticough River on the west side of Broad Creek, dated 4 Apr 1720, recorded in NC Land Patent Book 2, p. 319. The will of John Snoad was dated 21 June and proved 1 Sept 1743, recorded in NC Land Grant Book 4, no. 145. Tombstone records reveal that he was born Jan 1692 and died 30 June 1744. He married first, **Ann[2] Martin**, the daughter of **Joell Martin** and **Elizabeth[2] Alderson**, although she died before the signing of his will. John "Snode" wedded second, after Oct 1738, Beaufort Co., NC, the much-married **Elizabeth (Porter) Fry-Maule**, who was still Elizabeth Maule at that point (Beaufort Co., NC, Deed Book 2, p. 283). Elizabeth Snoad was identified as a widow in a deed of 3 ½-acre lots in Bath Town to her son John Fry on 11 Sept 1745, according to Beaufort Co., NC, Deed Book 2, p. 443.

Elizabeth's first husband Capt. Thomas Fry was baptized 26 May 1700, Milton, Hampshire, the son of Thomas Fry [FHL Fiche #6,358,139, 1/1], and died testate between 18 Mar $172^{4}/_{5}$ and Jan 1726, Bath Co., NC, Secretary of State loose wills, naming wife Elizabeth, no children by name, and his mother Elizabeth, the latter still a resident of the parish of Milton. Elizabeth (Porter) Fry was later the widow of Patrick Maule, according to Beaufort Co., NC, Deed

Book 2, p. 236, dated 3 June 1736, in which she mentioned the estate of her first husband, Thomas Fry, originally of London, who died testate between 18 Mar 172$^{4}/_{5}$ and Jan 1726, Bath Co., NC Secretary of State loose wills, also recorded in Secretary of State vol. 876, p. 101. Thomas Fry left everything to his wife Elizabeth and mentioned only his mother Elizabeth in Milton, Hampshire. Patrick Maule witnessed the will.

Elizabeth Porter's children by her first husband were named in the will of her brother Joshua Porter, who died testate between 17 Jan 1733 and 14 Sept 1734, Bath Co., NC, Secretary of State Will Book 876, p. 349, in which he named his cousins John and Elizabeth Fry. Elizabeth and Joshua were the children of John Porter, Jr., whose will was dated 8 Jan and proved 7 Aug 1713, Albemarle Co., NC, Secretary of State Will Book 875, p. 5 and p. 45; and his wife Mary (Sidney) Porter, will dated 12 Nov and proved 21 July [*sic*] 1717, of Chowan Co., NC, Secretary of State Will Book 875, p. 139. Elizabeth was not married as of the signing of her mother's will in 1717.

The Colonel named brothers-in-law William Martin and Walley Chancy as executors, along with son Henry^{2} Snoad. It was thought that perhaps Elizabeth, the colonel's second wife, was a sister of "brother-in-law" Walley Chancy, but records in Beaufort revealed a deed of gift—a slave purchased in Boston—to Walley Chauncey who had married Snoad's sister Mary^{1} Snoad, according to Beaufort Co., NC, Deed Book 2, p. 288, dated 10 Nov 1738.

Shortly before his death, John Snoad executed a deed of gift of slaves to his children: Henry^{2}, William^{2}, Mary^{2}, Ann^{2}, and Elizabeth^{2}. This occurred in Beaufort Co., NC, Deed Book 2, p. 282, and was dated 4 Nov 1738. One must assume that children Sarah^{2} and John^{2} were born after this date, since none of the above mentioned were even married at that time. Of course such instruments are usually executed to insure the inheritance of children of a first marriage soon before a second.

A suit of ejectment filed in Pitt Co., NC, July 1790, in the Court of Pleas and Quarter Sessions, enumerated the children of John Snoad [by his first wife] with their married names: Henry^{2} Snoad; Mary^{2}, wife John Lane; Ann^{2}, mother of James^{3} Bonner; Elizabeth^{2}, wife of Henry Bonner and mother of Henry Snoad^{3} Bonner. Depositions concerning the descent of the Snoad children were taken in 1792.

The Children of Col. John Snoad and Ann Martin:

[1] a. **Henry^{2} Snoad**, died testate after 14 Aug 1752, Beaufort Co., NC, Will Book F, p. 75b; married **Mary^{3} Peyton**.

[2] b. **William^{2} Snoad**, died testate between 15 Mar 1746 and 8 Apr 1747, Beaufort Co., NC, NC Secretary of State loose wills; married **Patience** [__].

[3] c. **Mary^{2} Snoad**, married **John Lane**.

[4] d. **Ann[2] Snoad**, married, as his first wife, **James[2] Bonner**, born *ca.* 1719, Bath Co., NC, who married second, **Mary Maule**.
[5]+ e. **Elizabeth[2] Snoad**, married **Henry[2] Bonner**, whose will was dated 16 Mar 1779, Beaufort Co., NC, Old Will Book, p. 145.

The Children of Capt. Thomas Fry and Elizabeth Porter:
[6] f. **John Fry**, born *ca.* 1721.
[7] g. **Elizabeth Fry**, born *ca.* 1723.

The Children of Col. John Snoad and Elizabeth (Porter) Fry-Maule:
[8] f. **Sarah[2] Snoad**, born *ca.* 1739.
[9] g. **John[2] Snoad**, born *ca.* 1741.

169. Capt. **John Spann** was born *ca.* 1695, and died intestate after 4 Sept 1754, Northampton Co., NC, his last appearance in the Northampton records, on which date he made a deed of gift to his son Richard[2] Spann for 250 acres on Elk Island, according to Northampton Co., NC, Deed Book 2, p. 181. He married, almost certainly, **Mary [__] Smith**, the widow of testator **Robert[1] Smith**, who died testate between 26 Jan and May 1726, Bertie Co., NC, his will filed among NC Secretary of State loose wills. Spann presented to court the inventory of Robert Smith's estate, according to Bertie Co., NC, Inventories of Estates, 1728-1744, p. 42, dated 24 Jan 172$^{7}/_{8}$.

Mary appeared with Spann 8 Aug 1741 on a deed of sale of 160 acres in the Upper Parrish of Bertie to Silvester Estes, Bertie Co., NC, Deed Book F, p. 275. Capt. Spann purchased land in Bertie Co., NC, on 12 May 1724, according to Bertie Co., NC , Deed Book A, p. 397. It is not inconceivable that John Spann migrated to Bertie from St. Stephen's Parish, Northumberland Co., VA, in whose seventeenth century records the names John and Richard Spann are found. This can be investigated in Beverley Fleet's *Virginia Colonial Abstracts*, vol. 1, *Northumbria Collectanea, 1645-1720*. Various internet sources trace him to Scotland, but without any proof.

The Children of Capt. John Spann and Mary [__] Smith:
[1]+ a. **Richard[2] Spann**, born *ca.* 1727, Bertie Co., NC, died testate by 24 Sept 1782, Northampton Co., NC, but the will was lost; married **Sarah [__]**, who died intestate by Dec 1788, according to Northampton Co., NC, Accounts, Sales, and Divisions, 1789-1801, p. 187.
[2] b. **John[2] Spann**, married **Sarah [__]**, as per the will of James[2] Smith of Halifax (John's half-brother), dated 3 Jan 1762, Will Book 1, p. 70. Two years later he and his wife were residents of Dobbs Co., NC,

according to Halifax Co., NC, Deed Book 9, p. 119, dated 18 Oct 1764. This was a sale of 250 acres on the south side of Great Creek, adjoining Reves and Crenshaw, to Robert Green of Halifax Co. Capt. Spann had purchased this land from John Baldwin on 28 Sept 1742 in Edgecombe Co., NC, Deed Book 5, p. 93.

170. John[1] Speir was a native of Nansemond Co., VA, where a much older Dr. John Speir had been a resident —of an age to be his grandfather—but with whom no connection can be proved other than a fondness for the practice of medicine, as seen in brother James[1] Speir. John Speir was born 25 Sept 1693, Nansemond Co., VA, and died testate 20 Apr 1764, Greenville, Pitt Co., NC, according to an article in the *Washington Progress*, dated 20 Dec 1892, p. 3, column 2, reported by the late John H. Oden III, in the *North Carolina Genealogical Society Journal*, vol. 22, nol. 2 [May 1996], p. 201. Speir's will was said to have been proved in Craven, although it was filed among the loose wills of the NC Secretary of State collection. Speir married first, **Patience[2] Cotton**, the daughter of **John[1] Cotton**, Sr., and Martha Godwin, born say 1695, Isle of Wight Co., VA, and who died as a result of injuries sustained in childbirth, attributed to her uncle Dr. James[1] Speir, 30 Nov 1725. This generated a lengthy (but nonetheless sensational!) lawsuit in which Patience (Cotton) Speir's parents sued Dr. James Speir and his wife Anne for murder, accusing him and his wife that they "on or about the twelfth day of November One thousand seven hundred and twenty five by force and Armes feloniously and voluntarily with her hand did tear out and destroy the body and womb of Patience Speir wife of John." John Speir married second **Martha** [__], the mother of his two other daughters. He married third, **Elizabeth Warren**, who died testate between 9 Oct 1773 and 23 Mar 1774, Pitt Co., NC, Secretary of State loose wills, naming, among others, her brother Joseph Warren. There were no children by the last marriage. A sketch of this family can be found in *Order of First Families of North Carolina, Ancestor Registry*, no. 1. John Speir had no male progeny, and all subsequent bearers of the Speir name must be descended from his brothers Dr. James[1] and William[1].

The information about the [second] marriage of John Spier to Martha [__] was discovered on the Beaufort Co., NC, Web-Site, under Robert A. Moore's *Transcriptions from the 1763 Kennedy Family Bible*. This information does not occur in this writer's OFFNC *Ancestor Registry*, vol. 1. The fact that Patience Spier would have to have been the last offspring of her mother and father has always made perfect sense—given that her mother obviously died from injuries in childbirth—but that her sisters therefore had to be older (so that she could be the youngest and last) posed problems which I found insolvable. Both sisters continued to bear children as if they had been born after Patience, and there was no record of Martha [__] Spier in *any* of the extant records. I am grateful for this information. It has been alleged that second wife Martha was actually Martha (Cotton) Benton, Patience's widowed sister, but I have found no proof for this, especially since her husband Francis Benton was probably alive into the 1740s.

The Children of John Speir and Patience Cotton:

[1]+ a. **Patience**^{2} **Speir**, born 12 Nov 1725, married *ca.* 1742, Edgecombe Co., NC, **Osborne**^{2} **Jeffreys**, son of **Simon**^{1} **Jeffreys** and Elizabeth [__] Hilliard.

The Children of John Speir and Martha [__]:

[2] b. **Cleare**^{2} **Speir**, born *ca.* 1727, married first, **John Hardee**; second *ca.* 1750, Pitt Co., NC, **Robert**^{3} **Salter** (Edward$^{2-1}$).

[3] c. **Apsley**^{2} **Speir**, born 27 Jan 1728, died 13 Nov 1800; married first, **John Holland**; second, 23 Sept 1762, Pitt Co., NC, **John Kennedy**.

171. Dr. **Godfrey Spruill**, possibly a native of the Glasgow, Scotland, area where the surname is extremely common, was born about 1650, according to a deposition taken 1 Aug 1689 in which he was 39 years old, Henrico Co., VA, Wills, Deeds, Etc., 1688-1697, p. 75, and died testate between 5 Aug 1718 and 29 July 1719, Chowan Co., NC. Godfrey Spruill, who spent his first years in the colonies in the Richmond, VA, area, was a surgeon, or *chirurgeon* (χειρ ἔργον). He married before 10 Mar $169^{3}/_{4}$, Henrico Co., VA, Will & Deed Book, 1688-1697, p. 566, **Johanna** [__], with whom he appeared on a deed of sale in Henrico to John Lowry, Henrico Co., VA. Joanna Spruill most likely predeceased her husband as she was not mentioned in his will. Spruill migrated to Chowan before 2 July 1694, according to the importation rights which he registered in Albemarle Co., NC, Book of Land Warrants and Surveys, 1681-1706, p. 32. Godfrey Spruill's will was recorded in NC Secretary of State vol. 875, p. 271. A sketch of this family can be found in *Order of First Families of North Carolina, Ancestor Registry*, no. 1.

The Children of Godfrey Spruill and Johanna [__], born Henrico Co., VA:

[1] a. **Susanah**^{2} **Spruill**, born *ca.* 1680, married **Cuthbert Phelps**, who died intestate *ca.* 1740, Tyrrell Co., NC, Estates Records.

[2] b. **Anna Margeritta**^{2} **Spruill**, born *ca.* 1682, married first, by 26 May 1701/2, Chowan Co., NC, **John Stuart** died testate, 1702-1706, Chowan Co., NC; second, by 1709, Chowan Co., NC, as his first wife, **Samuel Boutwell**.

[3]+ c. **Samuel**^{2} **Spruill**, died testate bafter 19 Aug 1760, Tyrrell Co., NC, Will Book 1, p. 8; married first, **Elizabeth**^{2} **Swaine**; second, **Mary**

[__].

[4] d. **Godfrey² Spruill**, Jr., born *ca.* 1690, died intestate by 7 Apr 1736, Tyrrell Co., NC, Deed Book 1 p. 22; married first, by 1720, **Ann** [__]; second, **Rebecca** [__].

[5]+ e. **Joseph² Spruill**, died testate between 2 Aug 1760 and Mar 1764, Tyrrell Co., NC, Will Book1, p. 30; married **Mary** [__]; their son Hezekiah³ married **Bridgett³ Baum**.

[6] f. **Mary² Spruill**, *no further record.*

172. William Strickland of Bertie, born *ca.* 1673, the son of progenitor Matthew^A Strickland and wife Elizabeth^A [__] of Isle of Wight Co., VA, died testate before May 1728, his undated will filed in the NC Secretary of State loose wills and also recorded in NC Secretary of State vol. 876, p. 145. Although William's father Mathew^A died intestate, William's connection to him was shown in a deed wherein William and his wife **Olive** [__] sold 200 acres of father Mathew's 1680 patent to Ratcliff Boon on 8 Mar 1715, according to Isle of Wight Co., VA, Will & Deed Book 2, p. 123. On 16 Mar 1723, William Strickland, Sr., was identified as a resident of North Carolina, according to Isle of Wight Co., VA, Will & Deed Book 2, p. 744. Forrest King compiled an excellent examination of the Stricklands entitled the "Descendants of Mathew Strickland (1648-1696) through Four Generations," published in the *North Carolina Genealogical Society Journal*, vol. 34, no. 2 [May 2008], pp. 111-42; continued in vol. 34, no. 3 [Aug 2008], pp. 219-52; and concluded in vol. 34, no. 4 [Nov 2008], pp. 293-326.

The Children of William Strickland and Olive [__], born Isle of Wight Co., VA:

[1]+ a. **Joseph² Strickland**, born *ca.* 1698, died testate after 25 Sept 1755, Northampton Co., NC, Secretary of State loose wills; married, as her first husband, **Elizabeth** [__], who married second, Roger Allen.

[2] b. **William² Strickland**, born *ca.* 1704, died after 1756, Edgecombe or Halifax counties, NC; married **Martha Brown**, daughter of William and Martha [__] Brown.

[3] c. **Matthew² Strickland**, born *ca.* 1706, died after July 1775, possibly Anson Co., NC; married [__].

[4] d. **John² Strickland**, born *ca.* 1708, died after 1744, probably Johnston Co., NC.

[5] e. **Samuel² Strickland**, born *ca.* 1710, died after Feb 1784, Johnston Co., NC; married **Mary** [__].

173. **George Sutton**, Quaker, was born *ca.* 1613 [his origins are as of yet officially unknown in spite of wildly imaginative information on the internet], and died 12 Apr 1669, Perquimans Co., NC. First a resident of New England, he married 13 Mar 1636/7, Scituate, Plymouth Co., MA, **Sarah Tilden**, the daughter of Nathaniel^A Tilden and Lydia^A Huckstep, baptized 13 Jan 1613, Tenterden, Kent, England, who died 20 Mar 1677, Perquimans Co., NC. The marriage record of George and Sarah can be found in Jeremy Dupertuis Bangs, *The Seventeenth-Century Town Records of Scituate, Massachusetts*, vol. 1, p. 24.

The Children of George Sutton and Sarah Tilden, born Scituate, MA:

[1]+ a. **Joseph^2 Sutton**, born *ca.* 1637, died testate between 20 Jan $169^4/_5$ and 8 Apr 1696, Perquimans, NC Secretary of State loose wills; married *ca.* 1680, Perquimans Co., NC, **Deliverance^2 Nicholson**, daughter of **Christopher^1 Nicholson** and Hannah (Redknap).

[2] b. **Daniel^2 Sutton**, baptized 20day.11mo.$16^{39}/_{40}$, First Church of Charlestown, married 15 Apr 1667, Charlestown, Middlesex Co., MA [Vital Records], **Mary Cole**. Daniel Sutton is almost certainly the testator of Burlington, NJ, with will dated 20 Feb $171^0/_1$, proved 23 July 1711, Liber 1, p. 322, *Calendar of New Jersey Wills*, vol. 1, *1670-1730*, p. 449. A tailor by profession, he named children Daniel^3, Robert^3, Mary^3, and Susan^3, and wife Mary.

[3] c. **William^2 Sutton**, born *ca.* 1641, married first, 11 July 1666, Eastham, Cape Cod, MA, **Damaris Bishop**; he married second, 3 Jan 1683/4, **Jane Barnes**. A Quaker, he removed to Piscataway, Middlesex Co., NJ.

[4]+ d. **Nathaniel^2 Sutton**, born *ca.* 1643, died testate between 20 Dec and 12 Mar 1683, Perquimans Co., NC, Secretary of State loose wills; married 12 Aug 1668, as her first husband, Nansemond Co., VA, **Deborah "Astin"** or **Austen** [see below].

[5] e. **Lydia^2 Sutton**, baptized 13 Sept 1646, Scituate, MA, *no further record.*

[6] f. **Sarah^2 Sutton**, baptized 3 Dec 1648, Scituate, MA, *died young.*

[7]+ g. **Sarah^2 Sutton**, baptized 15 Sept 1650, Scituate, MA, married 1 Feb 1668, Perquimans Co., NC, **John Barrow**, Sr., who died tesate 10 June 1718, Perquimans, NC Secretary of State loose wills, also recorded in NC Secretary of State vol. 875, p. 74.

[8]+ h. **Elizabeth^2 Sutton**, baptized 28 Aug 1653, Scituate, MA, died 21 Jan $^{1699}/_{1700}$, Perquimans; married 11 Mar 167[4], Perquimans Co., NC, **Ralph Fletcher**. J. R. B. Hathaway, in "Miscellaneous Items," *The North Carolina Genealogical and Historical Register*, vol. 2, no. 2 [April 1901], p. 298, makes a reference to a deposition made by Fletcher giving his year of birth as 1632. I have not yet located this

in the colonial records.

174. Nathaniel Sutton, the son of **George[1] Sutton** and Sarah Tilden, was born *ca.* 1643, Scituate, Plymouth Co., MA, and died testate 29 Dec 1682, Perquimans, NC Secretary of State loose wills. He married 12 Aug 1668, Perquimans, **Deborah Astin/Austen**, the daughter of Robert[A] Austen and his wife Sarah [__]. Deborah Sutton married second, 10 May 1685, Perquimans, John Whedbee, son of Richared Whidbey and [--] his wife, "late of Virginia." On 23 Mar $169^{6}/_{7}$, John Whidby executed a deed of gift to his two chidren Richard and Deborah with the proviso that should they die without issue, the property should devolve onto the grantor's brother George Whidby. This document had the feel of a last will and testament. John Whidby died 5 Apr 1700, Perquimans.

Deborah married third, by 2 July 1702, Daniel Maclendon, according to Perquimans Co., NC, Court Minutes, 1688-1738, p. 49, at which time Joseph Sutton, Sr., guardian for Deborah Whidby, sued Dennis "Mecklenden and Debro" his wife for property belonging to estate of Debro Whitbey given to her by her father John Whidbey.

The Children of Nathaniel Sutton and Deborah Austen, born Perquimans Co., NC:

[1] a. **George[2] Sutton**, born 2 Mar $16^{69}/_{70}$, married **Rebecca** [__].

[2]+ b. **Joseph[2] Sutton**, born 6 Aug 1673, died testate between 11 Jan and 10 Mar $172^{3}/_{4}$, Perquimans, NC Secretary of State loose wills, also recorded in Secretary of State vol. 876, p. 19; married first, 18 June 1695, Perquimans, **Perthenia[2] Durant**; she married second, 17 Mar 1726, Perquimans, **John Stevens**.

[3] c. **Rebecka[2] Sutton**, born 8 Aug 1676, married first, 30 Sept 1695, Perquimans Co., NC, **Jacob Peterson**; married second, 24 Aug 1697, Perquimans Co., NC, **John Bird**.

[4] d. **Nathaniel[2] Sutton**, died testate between 23 Feb and 30 mar 1725, Perquimans, NC Secretary of State vol. 876, p. 35.

The Children of John Whedbee and Deborah (Austen) Sutton, born Perquimans Co., NC:

[5] e. **William Whedbee**, born 28 Jan $168^{5}/_{6}$.

[6] f. **Richard Whedbee**, born 2 Feb 1687, married 4 Feb 1709, Perquimans, **Sarah[3] Durant** (John[2], George[1]).

[7] g. **Folk Whedbee**, died 12 Oct 1688.

[8] h. **Deborah Whedbee**, born 28 Jan 1689.

175. Stephen Swaine, the son of John^{A} Swaine and Mary^{A} Weare, was born 21 Nov 1666, Nantucket, Nantucket Co., MA, and died testate after 24 Jan $171^{2}/_{3}$, Chowan Co., NC. His will was filed among the NC Secretary of State loose wills and recorded in NC Secretary of State vol. 875, p.57. Stephen's birth can be found in William C. Folger, "A Record of Births, Deaths, and Marriages on Nantucket, beginning in 1662," in *The New England Historical and Genealogical Register*, vol. 7, no. 2 [Apr 1853], pp. 181-82. Stephen Swaine predeceased his father John^{A} Swaine, whose will, dated 9 Feb $171^{4}/_{5}$ and proved 27 Jan $171^{7}/_{8}$, was recorded in Nantucket Co., MA, Probate Book A, no. 1, 1706-1730, p. 32 (FHL# 906,832). John^{A} Swaine made a made a bequest of 5 shillings to "son Stephen['s] heirs," which demonstrates that he and his father had been in some type of communication. Stephen married first, by 5 Apr $169^{2}/_{3}$ [*sic*], **Elizabeth White** of Knotts Island, Princess Anne Co., VA [later Currituck Co., NC], the daughter of Patrick White^{A} and wife Elizabeth [__], according to a deed registered in May 1693, Princess Anne Co., VA, Deed Book 1, p. 34. This first marriage has heretofore escaped detection. He married second, as her first husband, **Patience** [__], who died testate Feb $173^{8}/_{9}$, Bertie Co., NC.

Although this writer has for years clung desperately to the notion that Swaine's second wife was Patience *Gardner* of Nantucket (born there 29 June 1675, to Richard Gardner and Mary Austin) with an origin similar to that of Stephen's, he reluctantly admits that Patience [__] Swaine *might* have been a daughter of the Richard Stiball who died testate after 18 Sept 1695, Albemarle [Chowan] Co., NC, Secretary of State loose wills, recorded also in NC Secretary of State vol. 874.1, p. 17. Richard$^{(1)}$ Stiball left two daughters and a wife: [1] Mary$^{(2)}$ Stiball, who according to Chowan Co., NC, Deed Book W#1, p. 18, dated 2[--] Mar 1701, married Robert Murry, the latter of whom sold his and his wife's interest in her father Richard Stiball's plantation to James Ward; [2] Patience$^{(2)}$ Stiball, who would have divided her father's land with sister Mary. Did her portion descend to Stephen Swaine *in uxoris jure*? Although it did eventually come into the Swaine family's possession, the surviving (recorded) chain of land transfers is not only incomplete but confusing, as is the provenance of the land: a tract of 400 acres, sold by son John^{2} Swaine and his wife Mary on 3 Dec 1718 to John Porter, according to Chowan Co., NC, Deed Book B#1, p. 646, the lands formerly belonging to Richard Stiball, but with intermediate possession by William Wilkinson, David Perkins, and Charles Haughton, not necessarily in that order—no originals of these transfers being extant; [3] Widow Hannah [__] Stiball, who according to *North Carolina Higher-Court Records, 1670-1696*, p. 138, dated Feb/Mar $169^{4}/_{5}$, married second, James Ward, who later purchased his stepdaughter Mary (Stiball) Murry's interest in her father's land.

To quash further this writer's own "Patience Gardner" theory, we have the will of Patience Gardner's father, Richard Gardner "of Sherborne on the

Island of Nantucket." Richard did not mention in his will a daughter named Patience, nor any Swaine grandchildren, suggesting that his daughter Patience must have died young and unmarried. Richard's will was recorded 17 July 1728, Nantucket Co., MA, Probate Book A, no. 1, 1706-1730, p. 135 (FHL# 906,832). On the off chance that Patience Gardner *did* actually marry Stephen Swaine, she could have been omitted from her father's will in view of the fact that she had been well provided for and in possession of a second husband—a *femme couverte*. This writer, quite frankly, does not know which view to take. He awaits further information, which, unfortunately, may never be forthcoming.

Patience [__] Swaine married second, Henry Speller, who died testate between 5 Apr 1727 and the date that letters of administration were granted on his estate—9 Jan 172⁷/₈, his will filed among NC Secretary of State loose wills, and also recorded in NC Secretary of State vol. 876, p. 124. He named his wife Patience and his two children Thomas and Ann Speller. The will of Patience Speller was dated 3 Feb 1738 and proved that same month, NC Secretary of State loose wills and also recorded in NC Land Grant Book 4, no. 79. She named the following children: son James[2] Swain, daughter Anne (Speller) Ward, son Thomas Speller, son Richard[2] Swain, daughter Patience[2] (Swaine) Ray, and her Smithwick[3] grandchildren. This indicates that the following children were by Stephen Swaine's first wife Elizabeth White: John Swain, daughter Elizabeth (Swaine) Spruill, and Mary Swaine.

An inventory of the estate of Thomas Speller, the son of Henry and Patience, reveals even more intermingling of the various families. A division of Thomas Seller's estate was ordered 24 Jan 1759 with 1/3 paid to Samuel "Sprewel" in right of his wife Elizabeth, and 2/3 to be divided among the minor children of the deceased. A division of the Negroes was had 12 Mar 1759 as follows: [1] to *Samuel Spruel* for his wife Elizabeth, Chloe and Moll; [ii] to *Joseph Knott*, Jr., in right of his wife [__], Mingo; [iii] to *Henry Speller*, Isaac; [iv] to *Thomas Speller*, [*Jr*.], [--].

The only Swain genealogies consulted were [1] Robert H. Swain's *Swains of Nantucket, Tales and Trails*, pp. 9-10, pp. 34-36, and p. 81. It was helpful in sorting out the spouses of the Swain children; and [2] Orlando and Orlando Swain, *The Swain Family in America, The families of the First Ten Generations*, traced other descendants of John Swaine and Mary Weare who migrated to Quaker settlements in Guilford Co., NC.

The Children of Stephen Swaine and Elizabeth White:

[1] a. **John[2] Swaine**, died testate between 6 Apr and 5 Dec 1749, Tyrrell Co., NC, Secretary of State loose wills; married **Mary** [__], who died testate between Aug 1773 and May 1774, Tyrrell Co., NC, loose wills.

[2]+ b. **Elizabeth[2] Swaine**, born *ca*. 1695, married, as his first wife, **Samuel[2]**

Spruill, who died testate after 19 Aug 1760, his will filed among Tyrrell Co., NC, loose wills, also recorded in Tyrrell Co., NC, Will Book 1, p. 8; he married second, Mary [__].

[3] c. **Mary[2] Swaine**, married **John[3] Smithwick**, who died testate between 13 June 1761 and Apr 1762, Bertie Co., NC, Will Book A, p. 4; married second, **Sarah[2] Swaine** [see below]

The Children of Stephen Swaine and Patience [__]:

[4] d. **James[2] Swaine**, died testate between 11 Apr and June 1763, Tyrrell Co., NC, loose wills; married **Elizabeth Smithwick**, who died testate between 5 May and July 1777, Martin Co., NC, Will Book 1, p. 138.

[5] e. **Richard[2] Swaine**, died by 27 Feb 1761, Bertie Co., NC, according to Bertie Estates Records, the presentation of his inventory to court by his widow **Ann[2] Charlton**.

[6]+ f. **Patience[2] Swaine**, married **Alexander Ray**, born *ca.* 1697, died testate after 4 Nov 1769, Bertie Co., NC, Will Book A, p. 113.

[7] g. **Sarah[2] Swaine**, born *ca.* 1715, married, as his second wife, **John[3] Smithwick**, son of Edward[2], who died testate between 13 June 1761 and Apr 1762, Bertie Co., NC, Will Book A, p. 4. Children Sarah[3], John[3], and Elizabeth[3] Smithwick were named in the will of their grandmother Patience Speller.

The Children of Henry Speller and Patience [__] Swaine:

[8] h. **Thomas Speller** married **Elizabeth** (**Lawrence**) **Sutton**, the widow of **Thomas[3] Sutton**; she married third, as his second wife, **Samuel[3] Spruill**, son of **Samuel[2]** and **Elizabeth[2]** (**Swaine**) **Spruill**, the former of whom (Samuel) died testate between 25 May 1765 and Mar 1766, Tyrell Co., NC, loose wills (he bequeathed Elizabeth a slave named Chloe, and she in turn gave Chloe her freedom) and died testate between 7 Apr 1787 and Feb 1788, Bertie Co., NC, Will Book D, p. 85, leaving all her property to Lawrence relatives.

[9] i. **Ann Speller**, married **William Ward**, according to Tyrrell Co., NC, Deed Book 4, part 1, dated 28 Sept 1762, in which William Soane of Tyrrell sells to John "Lenier" acreage which had belonged to Henry "Spelor," and which descended to his heirs, Thomas Spellor and Ann Spellor, and William Ward, "husband of [--]," and which had been transferred to John Lanier.

176. Thomas Symons, the elder (surviving) son of William[A] Symons of East Hampton, Long Island, Suffolk Co., NY, was born *ca.* 1648, and died testate 2.18.1706, aged 57 or 58 years, Pasquotank Monthly Meeting, having signed his will 11.20.$170^{2}/_{3}$. His will was proved 16 July 1706, Pasquotank Co., NC, Secretary of State loose Wills. Thomas and his wife **Rebecca** were in North Carolina as early as 1679, as Rebecca witnessed the marriage of Solomon Poole to Margaret White at the house of Henry White, Jr., 4.24.1679. Rebecca Symons died 2.25.1718, Pasquotank Montly Meeting, aged about 64 years, (born, therefore, 1654). William[A] Symons was in East Hampton, Long Island, as early as 17 Nov 1651, at which time he, in addition to William Edwards, William FFithian, Richard Brookes, and Samuel Parsons, was allotted six loads of thatch, according to *Records of the Town of East-Hampton, Long Island, Suffolk Co., N. Y.*, vol. 1, p. 19, in the original records, Book 2, p. 16. William[A] Symons and his wife, known to us only as "Goodwife Symons," who was involved in the only witchcraft trial of record in East Hampton, were both deceased by 7.28.1685, at which time Thomas Symons of Pasquotank Co., NC, wrote two letters to East Hampton requesting that David Gardiner, as his attorney, sell his deceased father's remaining land on Long Island. This can be found in *Records of the Town of East-Hampton, Long Island, Suffolk Co., N. Y.*, vol. 2, pp. 172-73, in the originals, Book A, p. 78. See below.

It has been assumed that Thomas Symons' wife **Rebecca** was the daughter of Henry[1] White, Sr., and of wife Rebecca (Arnold) of the Albemarle, due to the fact that Henry's son Arnold[2] White in his Perquimans will, dated 22 Apr 1690, and proved 5 Aug 1690, NC Secretary of State loose Wills, made the following statement: "I leve to my trusty and well beloved Brothers Henry[2] White [*torn*] / Simons..." At that date [1690], Arnold's neice Damaris[3] had not yet married John[2] Symons, so the "brother" relationship, almost certainly meaning "brother-in-law" would have to revolve on another connection. In fact, Henry[1] White, Sr., [as Henry *Wight*] died testate between 14 Nov $16^{69}/_{70}$ [*sic*] and 6 May 1670, NC Secretary of State loose wills, naming wife Eleanor, sons Arnuill and John, his unnamed "eldest daughter," and his youngest daughter Elizabeth. Ten years later in 1680, Henry's estate was administered by the "nearest concerned," Anthony Waters, according to NC Secretary of State vol. 842.2 (1677-1701), p. 26. Supposed first or second wife "Rebecca Arnold" does not appear in any connection with Henry the testator of 1669 and has proved to be a complete fiction, receiving nevertheless quite a bit of press in the literature, including a short article in the *Dictionary of North Carolina Biography*, vol. 5, *T-Z*, p. 178. If it could be proved that Henry[1] White, Sr., married a "Rebecca Arnold" between the signing of his will and its probate, then it might have been possible for his new widow to have married second, Thomas[1] Symons. If, on the other hand, Rebecca [__] Symons was *née* White and a sister of Arnold[2], then the chronology might be more reasonable; and "Rebecca Arnold" might have been Henry's unrecorded first wife. There was a Henry White in Isle of Wight Co., VA, connected with the Moores and the Pylands, but there is **NO** reason to believe that the two were the same. Moreover, a possibility which seems never to have occurred to anyone is that the Symons reference might pertain to *Jeremiah* Symons, or possibly to someone completely unconnected with this family.

However, **Robert West**, who died testate between 28 Mar 1689 and 4 Jan 16$^{89}/_{90}$, Chowan precinct, Albemarle Co., NC, his extremely mutilated will filed among NC Secretary of State loose wills, very clearly named his "brother in law Thomas: Simonds" as a trusteee to his last will and testament. According to *Old Albemarle County North Carolina Book of Land Warrants and Surveys, 1681-1706*, f. 17: "This may certify all whom it may concerne that Mr. Tho. Pollok has proved thirteen Rights whose names are upon Record & hereund^{r}. written, Robt. West, Jr., Sarah West, Mary West, Ffrancis West, *Rebecca West*, Jno. West, Benj^{a}: West, Deb. West, and five Indians. Certifyed y^{e}. 17th of March 1693." Therefore, in spite of the fact that the Whites and Symons were thrown together quite a bit as Quakers of the same monthly meeting, Thomas Symons married by 1677, **Rebecca West**, the daughter of Robert West, Sr., and the sister of testator **Robert West**. It is curious that William Perry Johnson did not know of the Symons-West connection. It is entirely possible that, the original not having yet surfaced, Johnson had access only to the shorter version of West's will filed in NC Secretary of State C.C.R.187 This shorter version did not mention bequests to Robert West's siblings or to his brother-in-law, and did not appear in Grimes' *Abstracts of North Carolina Wills*.

Thomas Symons' brother Jeremiah[1] migrated with Thomas to Pasquotank, where records of his family can be found in Pasquotank Monthly Meeting. Jeremiah[1] died testate in Pasquotank between 30 Mar 1713 and 12 Dec 1715, NC Secretary of State loose Wills, leaving a large family. His death was recorded in Pasquotank Monthly Meeting as 6.21.1714, "aged about 60 years."

In the letter (referred to above) which Thomas Symons wrote to David[3] Gardiner, he added: "Remember my love to thy son in Law James & his wife, and to thy brother Jeremiah & his wife & mickell [*uncle*?] and aunt, & all my Cosins." In an earlier letter dated Oct 1684 from Little River, Albemarle Co., NC, Thomas Symons mentioned his uncle Ffithian, who would probably be William Ffithian, the immigrant. This can be found in East Hampton record vol. 2, p. 151, listed therein as Book A, p. 78. "Jeremiah and his wife" are obviously Jeremiah Concklin and wife Mary[3] Gardiner, the sister of David[3] Gardiner (1636-1689), both Gardiners being the children of Lyon[2] Gardiner and Mary Willemsen Duercant. David Gardiner's "son-in-law James" was James Parshall who married David's daughter Elizabeth[4]. Elizabeth[3] Gardiner married Arthur Howell.

An excellent, detailed, but unfinished genealogy of the Symons family was begun by William Perry Johnson in *North Carolina Genealogy*, vol. 14, no. 1 [Spring 1968], pp. 2064-72. The venerable Mattie Erma Parker wrote a short entry for Thomas Symons in the *Dictionary of North Carolina Biography*, vol. 4,

P-S, p. 494, but, astonishingly, was unaware of William Perry Johnson's work—unless, possibly, she had written her article for publication before Perry had submitted his. Mr. Johnson's "supplement," as it is called, should be the standard reference work for this family.

The Children of Thomas Symons and Rebecca West, born Pasquotank Monthly Meeting:

[1] a. **John^2 Symons**, born 3.22.1678, died testate between 13 Oct 1741 and Jan 174$^1/_2$, Pasquotank, NC Secretary of State loose wills; married 6.8.1700, Little River, Pasquotank Monthly Meeting, at the house of Henry White, **Damaris White**.

[2] b. **Francis^2 Symons** [daughter], born 4.2.1680, died 2.[--].1687.

[3] c. **Thomas^2 Symons**, born 7.15.1682.

[4] d. **Peter^2 Symons**, born 10.8.1684, died 6.22.1715, Pasquotank Monthly Meeting; married 12.7.1705, Pasquotank Monthly Meeting, **Martha^2 Pritchard**.

[5]+ e. **Mary^2 Symons**, born 12.4.1687, married 9.4.1703, Pasquotank Monthly Meeting, **John^1 Morris**, born 3.31.1680, Pasquotank Monthly Meeting; he died testate 9.20.1739, Pasquotank Monthly Meeting, his will filed among NC Secretary of State loose wills.

[6] f. **Elizabeth^2 Symons**, born 2.22.1691, married 1.11.170$^7/_8$, Pasquotank Monthly Meeting, **Zachariah Nicholson**.

177. Phillip Torksey was born *ca.* 1656, according to a deposition taken in Middlesex Co., VA, on 4 Nov 1678, in which he stated his age to be about 22 years, Middlesex Co., VA, Court Orders, 1677-1680, p. 150. Two years after the birth of their first child, he married 31 July 1683, Christ Church Parish, Middlesex Co., VA, [the child's mother] **Mary$^{[3]}$ (Scarborough) Frence**, the daughter of John Scarborough and his wife [__]$^{[2]}$ Moore, and the widow of [__] Frence. Phillip died testate between 16 Jan 172$^0/_1$ and 18 July 1727, Pasquotank Co., NC, NC Secretary of State loose wills. This family is treated in *Adventurers of Purse and Person*, 4th ed., vol. 2, *Families G-P*, pp. 685-90, and pp. 693-95. John Scarborough's wife was the daughter of Augustine$^{[1]}$ Moore.

An additional descent from Elizabeth^2 (Torksey) Morgan has been found in the will of her daughter Judith^3 Morgan who married William Gregory; and in her will, dated 21 Oct 1753 and proved Jan 1754, Pasquotank Co., NC, NC Secretary of State loose wills, she named her brother Joseph Morgan. Her husband William Gregory predeceased her, dying testate between 24 Nov 1751 and Apr 1752, Pasquotank Co., NC, NC Secretary of State loose wills. I am grateful to OFFNC member **#250** for opening this new line. The vital records for

Mary[2] Torksey's husband Henry Hayman can be found in F. Edward Wright, ed., *Maryland Eastern Shore Vital Records, 1648-1725*, 2nd ed., p. 121.

The Children of Phillip Torksey and Mary (Scarborough) Frence, first two baptized Christ Church Parish, Middlesex Co., VA:

[1]+ a. **Elizabeth[2] Torksey**, bapt. 10 Apr 1681, married **Robert Morgan**, who died testate between 22 Oct 1727 and 27 Nov 1730, Pasquotank Co., NC, Secretary of State loose wills.

[2] b. **Phillip[2] Torksey**, bapt. 8 June 1684; married **Margaret Raymond**.

[3] c. **John[2] Torksey**, died testate between 10 Nov 1746 and Apr 1747, NC Secretary of State loose wills; he married [__].

[4] d. **Mary[2] Torksey**, married **Henry Hayman**, born 26 Nov 1688, Somerset Co., MD, the son of Henry Hayman and Martha Standridge, and died testate between 23 May and 18 July 1727, Pasquotank Co., NC, Secretary of State loose wills.

[5] e. **Sarah[2] Torksey**, married **Edward Faircloth**, died intestate before 19 July 1726, Pasquotank Co., NC.

[6] f. **Robert[2] Torksey**, *no further record.*

178. Susannah [__] **Travis**, the widow of **Daniel Travis** of Pasquotank, married second, as his first wife, by 10 Oct 1694, **Francis[1] Delamare** at which time he and the recently widowed Susannah applied to administer the estate of her first husband. This is to be found in Wills, Administrations, Inventories, Deeds, 1677-1790, NC Secretary of State vol. 874.2 (1677-1701), p. 51. Susannah was deceased by 1701, at which time Francis had married second, as her second husband, Ann (Mayo) Pope. Francis Delamare died by 20 Oct 1713, Pasquotank Co., NC, at which time his second wife Anne was named as his widow and relict, according to Pasquotank Co., NC, Deed Book A, p. 63. Very little is known about Daniel Travis. He does not yet appear to be related to the Travis/Travers families of Virginia or of New England.

The Child of Francis Delamare and Susannah [__] Travis:

[1]+ a. **Francis[2] Delamare**, will proved Mar 1741, Craven Co., NC, Secretary of State loose wills, and also recorded in NC Land Grant Book 4, no.161; married **Susannah** [__].

The Children of Francis Delamare and Ann (Mayo) Pope-Scarborough:

[2] b. **Stephen[2] Delamare**, died testate Oct 1732, Pasquotank, NC Secretary of State loose wills; he did not marry, but named his sister Ann, then married to Stockley, and her children.

[3] c. **Isaac[2] Delamare**.

[4]+ d. **Anne[2] Delamare**, died testate between 23 Oct 1767 and 9 Mar 1773, Craven Co., NC, Secretary of State loose wills; married, first, **Joseph Stoakley**, died testate between 12 Dec 1729 and Jan $17^{29}/_{30}$, Pasquotank, NC Secretary of State loose wills; second, 10 Jan $173^{3}/_{4}$, Pasquotank Co., NC, **William[2] Bryan (Edward[1])**, died testate between 12 Dec 1746 and June 1747, Craven Co., NC, Secretary of State loose wills.

179. Henry Turner died testate between 20 Jan and Feb $174^{8}/_{9}$, Edgecombe Co., NC, his will filed among NC Secretary of State loose wills. He was born apparently by 1690, almost certainly in Isle of Wight Co., VA (given his associations), and was a resident of Chowan Co., NC, by 1 Mar 1719, at which time he received a grant for 476 acres, according to NC Land Patent Book 8, p. 186. Henry Turner, on 13 June 1723, sold 376 acres of this patent to Thomas Hart, according to Bertie Co., NC, Deed Book A, p. 176; then, on 6 Aug 1736, already of Edgecombe precinct, he "made over" the remaining 100 acres to the same Thomas Hart, Bertie Co., NC, Deed Book E, p. 147. Henry married **Mary** [__], whom he named in his will.

Since there is basically no difficulty in determining the identity of the other children of Henry[1] Turner, the problem focus of this sketch will be the identity of son Thomas[2] Turner and his possible wife and progeny. Throughout his "career" in land transfer, Henry[1] Turner in his land sales and purchases was continually associated with a constellation of the following families: James and Ann Turner of Isle of Wight, Thomas Turner of Isle of Wight, and the Harts, Walls, and Boykins of Bertie, Northampton, Edgecombe, and later Halifax (as the county borders evolved). It is not completely clear that Thomas Turner of Isle of Wight and Thomas of North Carolina were two distinct persons, given that the two areas were not that far apart. Besides those two Thomases, we have also a Thomas Turner connected with a John Turner of New Hanover Co., a Thomas Turner of Granville, a Thomas Turner of New England, and a Thomas who married Mary, the daughter of David Hix.

Thomas[2] Turner has long been said to have died intestate by May 1749, his estate in Edgecombe administered by James Smith, according to Edgecombe Co., NC, Estates Records. The fact that Joseph[2] Turner's land devolved *in toto* onto eldest son Solomon[2] Turner in 1761 poses a slight problem of intestate descent based upon the laws of primogeniture. Either there were no intermediate brothers to share such property left by the death of Joseph[2], or, more likely, Solomon[2] as eldest son would naturally inherit. Therefore, whether Thomas[2] Turner was alive in 1761 is a moot point. Who, therefore, was the Thomas Turner of Edgecombe who on 12 May 1758 sold 90 acres on the Cattail Marsh, adjoining Marmaduke Norfleet, to James Smith, according to Edgecombe Co.,

NC, Deed Book 6, p. 303? How, moreover, did the land come into the possession of that Thomas Turner? Another myth circulated about Thomas[2] Turner has been that his sole surviving heir was his daughter Millea[3] who married James Smith. We shall see. See my discussion on the Smiths and Turners in the sketch on **Nicholas[1] Smith**.

If we may posit two scenarios, let us begin with the hypothesis that Thomas[2] Turner died intestate in Edgecombe in May 1749, at which time his inventory was taken by **James[2] Smith**, according to Joseph W. Watson, *Estate Records of Edgecombe County, North Carolina, 1730-1820*, p. 270. Once again, there is no formal information about his children, but we might assume that his son-in-law James Smith was the administrator of his estate. There is, moreover, no indication from the North Carolina records concerning whom Thomas Turner married.

Two years later an inventory was taken for the estate of [possibly] another Thomas Turner in Isle of Wight Co., VA, just over the state line, appraisal by Daniel Herring, Henry Johnson, and Robert Johnson, and signed by wife Martha (Joyner) on 5 Sept 1751, recorded 6 Feb 1752, Isle of Wight Co., VA, Will Book 5, p. 393. Were these two Thomases the same, with property in different counties and in different states? This writer does not know.

Alternatively, Thomas Turner, the grantor of 1758, seems to have acquired his tract on the Cattail Marsh from the bequest of his father Henry Turner, unless he was somehow Henry's grandson. There is a discrepancy of 10 acres, but that is almost negligible. Did our Thomas really die in 1749? Once again, this writer does not know. Much more research needs to be done on the land records of James Smith of Halifax to see if any language in the deeds themselves will identify the provenance of James' land on Cattail Swamp.

The Children of Henry Turner and Mary [__]:

[1]+ b. **Solomon[2] Turner**, born *ca.* 1726, died testate before May 1807, Halifax Co., NC, Will Book 3, p. 465; married **Polly[3] Merritt**, daughter of **William[2] Merritt**, whose will was proved 1784, Halifax Co., NC, Will Book 3, p. 54.

[2] b. **Thomas[2] Turner**, bequeathed 150 acres bought of Robert Council, Edgecombe Co., NC, Deed Book 5, p. 407, 5 Jan 1745, 100 acres on the Cattail Marsh, adjoining Thomas Whitmell and John Nairn.

[3] c. **Olive[2] Turner**.

These last two children were under age at the writing of Henry's will, 20 Jan 174$^{8}/_{9}$:

[4] d. **Joseph[2] Turner**, was bequeathed 150 acres bought of Daniel McDaniel, on 7 Aug 1727, Bertie Co., NC, Deed Book B, p. 309; as Solomon[2] Turner possessed this tract on 17 Feb 1761, which he

had received from Joseph[2] Turner; it seems that, Joseph having died intestate and childless, the tract devolved onto Solomon[2], Halifax Co., NC, Deed Book 7, p. 240; this was confirmed by Halifax Co., NC, Deed Book 9, p. 21, dated 20 Feb 1764.

[5] e. **Mary[2] Turner**. Did she marry Thomas Gray?

180. Matthias(2) Tyson/Tisson, or "Mathias Tice," the son of John(1) Tyson and Sussaninka [__] of Northampton Co., VA, was born *ca.* 1660, Accomack Co., VA, and died testate after 5 Apr 1710, Bath Co., NC, his will filed in NC Secretary of State loose wills. Matthias' father signed his will, dated 1 Mar 1681 and recorded 28 Aug 1683 in Northampton Co., VA, Orders, Wills, XV, No. 12, 1683-1689, p. 15, as "John Mattison," using his last name typically as a Dutch patronymic to indicate "John, son of Matthias." After John(1) Tyson's death, Susanika married second, Robert Thompson, according to Northampton Co., VA, Deeds, Wills, Etc., XIV, No. 11, 1680-1692, in which Robert Tompson and Susannika his wife, late wife of John Tyson decd., and son her Mathias Tyson, all of Accomack, deeded land to Charles Parkes. Robert Tompson was deceased by 1 Mar 1702, Northampton, and Susanna was the administratrix of his estate, according to Northampton Co., VA, Orders, Wills, Etc., XVIII, no. 14, 1698-1710, p. 127. Susannika is said to have married, third, Robert Hamilton.

Matthias Tyson married *ca.* 1695, **Mary** [__], who was born *ca.* 1661, and who died after 7 Feb 173$^7/_8$, Beaufort Co., NC. She married second, George Hill, who named her in his will and who died testate between 17 Apr 1722 and 30 Mar 1723, Beaufort Co., NC, his will filed among NC Secretary of State loose wills. George Hill's will was also recorded in NC Secretary of State vol. 876, p. 26. The Tyson and May Genealogy Committee's *The Tyson and May Genealogy of Pitt County*, is helpful, but virtually bereft of documentation.

Matthias named the following children in his will: John[2], Edward[2], Cornelius[2], Edmond[2], Thomas[2], Samuel[2], Susannah[2], Matthias[2], and grandson Aron[3].

The Children of Matthias Tyson and Mary [__]:

[1] a. **John[2] Tyson**.

[2] b. **Edward[2] Tyson**, died after Mar 1751, Hyde Co., NC, his last appearance in the deeds, Hyde Co., NC, Deed Book A, p. 381 (282); married before 1719, **Ann** [__], who appeared with him on a deed of land to their son Daniel[3] Tyson, who purchased land from his uncle Mathyas[2] Tyson, Hyde Co., NC, Deed Book A, p. 212 (170).

[3] c. **Cornelius[2] Tyson**, died after 1749, Beaufort Co., NC; married [__] **Mills**, daughter of John Mills of Beaufort, who died testate in Beaufort after 2 Jan 1739, Old Wills, pp. 28-29; he made bequests to

his Tyson grandchildren: Courtney[3], Moses[3], and made "[--][3] Tyson" his executor. Unfortunately Mill's will was mutilated.

[4]+ d. **Edmond[2] Tyson**, died after 1765, Beaufort Co., NC; married **Mary** [__].

[5]+ e. **Thomas[2] Tyson**, died before 1755, Beaufort Co., NC, married **Sabra[2] Mason**, who appeared on the 1755 Tax List for Beaufort Co., NC.

[6] f. **Susannah[2] Tyson**, born 16 June 1701, died 8 Aug 1785; married *ca.* 1728, Col. **John Hardee**, born 13 Apr 1707, died 12 Dec 1784; both, according to David L. Hardee's *The Eastern North Carolian Hardy-Hardee Framily in the south and Southwest*, pp. 277-278, are buried in the old Hardee-Smith Cemetery, Greenville, Pitt Co., NC.

[7] g. **Jonas[2] Tyson**, *no further record.*

[8] h. **Samuel[2] Tyson**, died testate between 1 May and 1 Sept 1736, Bath Co., NC, will filed among NC Secretary of State loose wills, and recorded in NC Secretary of State vol. 877, p. 209; married **Margera** [__].

[8] i. **Mathyas[2] Tyson**, died after 31 Aug 1756, Hyde Co., NC, his last appearance as a grantor of Beaufort, Hyde Co., NC, Deed Book A, p. 618 (117), *no further record.*

181. Thomas[(3)] Tyson, the son of **Matthias[(2)] Tyson** and Mary [__], was born *ca.* 1699, Accomack Co., VA, and died before 1755, Beaufort Co., NC, a date chosen for the fact that his wife's name, and not his, appeared in the 1755 Beaufort Tax list. He married, as her first husband, **Sabra[2] Mason**, the daughter of **John[1] Mason** of Hyde Precinct, She died *ca.* 1798, Fayetteville, Cumberland Co., NC. She married second, by 1771, Thomas Wilson. Since Matthias[1] Tyson died testate in Beaufort Co., NC, after Apr 1710, having named Thomas[2] among his children, we may assume that Thomas was in the colony at that time as well. The Tyson and May Genealogy Committee's *The Tyson and May Genealogy of Pitt County*, is helpful, but not very well documented.

Son Mason[2] Tyson was named in the will of his grandfather John[1] Mason.

The Children of Thomas Tyson and Sabra Mason:

[1] a. **Mason[2] Tyson**, married **Rachel** [__], who married second, John Bonner; she married third, Charles Tyndal.

[2] b. **John[2] Tyson**, Esq., born *ca.* 1720, married **Bethany** [__].

[3]+ c. **Cornelius[2] Tyson**, born 22 Jan 1722, died 10 Mar 1795, Moore Co., NC; married **Jane Cheek**.

[4] d. **Thomas[2] Tyson**, married **Jane** [__].

182. Jeremiah Vail was born *ca*. 1675, possibly Southhold, Long Island, Suffolk Co., NY, and died intestate 10 Sept 1741, Chowan Co., NC. He married **Mary**[2] **(Lillington) Swann**, the daughter of **Alexander**[1] **Lillington** and Elizabeth Cooke, and the widow of Samuel Swann, born 22 Apr 1683, Perquimans Co., NC, died 1757, Chowan Co., NC. Jeremiah Vail was a resident of Chowan Co., NC, by 1697, at which point he purchased 560 acres on Albemarle Sound. There are excellent biographies of Jeremiah and of his son Edward in William S. Powell's *Dictionary of North Carolina Biography*, vol. 6, *T-Z*, p. 82. According to this last source, the Vail family Bible still exists and was, at last report, in the possession of a Lillian Smith Hough of Eden, NC. A thorough search of Henry H. Vail's *Genealogy of Some of the Vail Family Descended from Jeremiah Vail at Salem, Mass., 1639*, failed to identify our ancestor, even though the name "Jeremiah," which persisted in the NC branch, would seem to indicate a relationship with the Long Islanders.

J. R. B. Hathaway's "The Edenton Tea Party," in *The North Carolina Historical and Genelogical Register*, vol. 3, no. 1 [Jan 1903], p. 116, footnote, touches on some of the connections of the Vails with other Chowan families.

In Chowan Co., NC, Deed Book G-1, p. 217, dated 3 June 1754, Mary Vail of Chowan for love and affection gave 5 Negro slaves to daughter Sarah[2] Blount, formerly in the possession, by grantor's permission, of John Blount.

The Children of Jeremiah Vail and Mary (Lillington) Swann:

[1] a. **Moseley**[2] **Vail**, one time Clerk of Court, Chowan Co., NC, according to Chowan Co., NC, Deed Book W-1, p. 227, dated 10 Apr 1734.

[2] b. **Mary**[2] **Vail**, died testate between May 1764 and Jan 1765, Craven Co., NC, Wills, Deeds, Etc., 1756-1765, p. 80; in her will she named nephews John[3] and Miles[3] Gale, and nieces Mary[3] and Margaret[3] Vail, and called herself the widow of **Roger Moore**.

[3] c. **Jeremiah**[2] **Vail**, Jr., was of New Hanover Co., NC, on 23 Dec 1748, when for 5 shillings he gave 560 acres to his brother Edward[2]—land which his father had purchased of Edmond and Sarah Smithwick, Chowan Co., NC, Deed Book E-1, p. 289; married **Margaret Merrick**; she was named as sister in the will of John Merrick, merchant, dated 11 Feb 1756, proved May 1756, New Hanover Co., NC, Deed Book D, p. 190.

[4]+ d. **Edward**[2] **Vail**, born 6 Aug 1716, died testate after 29 Nov 1775, Chowan Co., NC, Will Book A, p. 319; married **Susannah**[2] **Salter**, according to Beaufort Co., NC, Deed Book 3, p. 278, dated 14 Apr 1756, in which Edward Vail and wife Susannah, both of Chowan, sold to Simon Jones 510 acres on the Pamptico, bequeathed her by the last will and testament of her father **Edward**[1] **Salter**.

[5] e. **Martha**[2] **Vail**, married 6 Aug 1745, Chowan Co., NC (marriage bond), **Miles Gale**, Jr.
[6] f. **John**[2] **Vail**, died testate after 13 Nov 1765, Chowan Co., NC, Will Book 1, p. 21; married first, 20 Sept 1748, Chowan Co., NC (marriage bond), **Elizabeth Swann**; married second, **Mary** [__].
[7] g. **Sarah Elizabeth**[2] **Vail**, married **John**[3] **Blount**, son of **John**[2] **Blount** and Elizabeth Davis.

183. Thomas Vinson, the son of Thomas[A] Vinson and Sarah [__], was born say 1690, either Surry or Charles City counties, VA, and died testate between 15 Jan 1762 and Feb 1764, Northampton Co., NC, Will Book 1, p. 86. He married **Isobel** [__], named in his will, and listed as his wife on Bertie deeds from 1723 onwards (Bertie Co., NC, Deed Book A, p. 67). From John Molton on 19 July 1716, Vinson purchased 200 acres of land upon Meherrin Creek, adjoining John Cropley, according to Chowan Co., NC, Deed Book B#1, p. 341. A sketch of this family can be found in *Order of First Families of North Carolina, Ancestor Registry*, no. 1.

The Children of Thomas Vinson and Isobel [__]:
[1] a. **John**[2] **Vinson**.
[2] b. **Thomas**[2] **Vinson**, married **Hannah** [__].
[3]+ c. **William**[2] **Vinson**, born 1715-20, died testate before 1797, Mecklenburg Co., NC, Will Book F, p. 204; married [__], the widow of [__] **Pinnian**.
[4] d. **Jesse**[2] **Vinson**.
[5]+ e. **James**[2] **Vinson**, died testate between 26 Oct and Dec 1797, Northampton Co., NC, Will Book 2, p. 164; he married **Unity** [__].
[6] f. **Peter**[2] **Vinson**.
[7] g. **David**[2] **Vinson**.
[8] h. **Charity**[2] **Vinson**, married [__] **Carter**.
[9] i. **Sarah**[2] **Vinson**, married [__] **Fuller**.
[10]+ j. **Susanna**[2] **Vinson**, born by 1728, married *ca.* 1750, **Robert Morgan**, will proved 3 Mar 1801, Franklin Co., NC; his [loose] will is not listed in Mitchell.
[11] k. **Isabel**[2] **Vinson**, married **Robert Duke**; he died testate between 12 Oct 1766 and Feb 1767, Northampton Co., NC, Will Book 1, p. 150.

184. Thomas Waller, who died testate 2 July 1687, Perquimans Co., NC, married, say 1680, Perquimans Co., NC, as her first husband, **Elizabeth**[2] **Durant**, the daughter of **George**[1] **Durant** and Ann Marwood, born 13 Feb

1661/0, Perquimans Precinct, NC. She married second, shortly after her husband's death, *ca.* 1688 [--], Perquimans, John Harris, one of the witnesses to Thomas Waller's will. Thomas Waller's first entry in the court records of colonial North Carolina was as a plaintiff who was awarded 1500 pounds of tobacco from the estate of William Therrill in Mar 1680.

The Children of Thomas Waller and Elizabeth Durant, born Perquimans Precinct, NC:

[1]+ a. **Anne[3] Waller**, born say 1681, married, first, say 1695, **Benjamin Massagny**; she married second, say 1698, Perquimans Co., NC, **Thomas Boswell**, Sr.

[2] b. **George[3] Waller**, born 20 Aug 1683, died 23 [--] 1687.

[3] c. **Elizabeth[3] Waller**, born 7 Nov 1685.

185. Robert West, Jr., the son of a "hypothetical" Robert West, Sr., was born *ca.* 1640, and died testate between 28 Mar 1689 and 4 Jan $16^{89}/_{90}$, Chowan precinct, Albemarle Co., NC, his extremely mutilated will filed among the NC Secretary of State loose wills. According to *Old Albemarle County North Carolina Book of Land Warrants and Surveys, 1681-1706*, f. 17: "This may certify all whom it may concerne that Mr. Tho. Pollok has proved thirteen Rights whose names are upon Record & hereund[r]. written, Rob[t]. West, Jr., Sarah West, Mary West, Ffrancis West, Rebecca West, Jn[o]. West, Benj[a]: West, Deb. West, and five Indians [*i.e.*, native Americans]. Certifyed y[e]. 17th of March 1693." Robert West, Jr., married, after 1 May 1681, Albemarle Co., NC, **Martha[2] Cullen**, the daughter of **Thomas[1]** and Sarah (Alderstone) **Cullen**, baptized 1 May 1663, St. Mary the Virgin, Dover, Kent, and died 17 Feb $170^{1}/_{2}$, Chowan precinct, Albemarle Co., NC. Martha married second, as his first wife, 19 June 1690, Chowan precinct, Albemarle Co., NC, North Carolina Governor Thomas Pollock, born 6 May 1654, Glasgow, Scotland, and died 30 Aug 1722, Chowan Co., NC, the son of Thomas Pollock of Bal-gra, Glasgow, Scotland. Among other children who lived to adulthood, Thomas Pollock and Martha (Cullen) West had two sets of twin girls, neither of which pair survived. In his will, Robert West named his brothers John and Benjamin West, and his brother-in-law **Thomas[1] Symons**, who married Rebecca[1] West. The list of children from Martha Cullen's second marriage is taken from the *Thomas Pollock Papers, 1708-1859*, in the North Carolina State Archives, and a copy of the Bible record itself was graciously supplied to this writer by genealogist Forrest King.

The will of Thomas Pollock was dated 8 Aug 1721 and not proved until Aug 1753, Chowan Co., NC. According to records listed in the sketch on **Ann (Bigg) Batchelor-Fewox**, after the death of Martha (Cullen) West, Pollock married Esther (Jenkins) Sweatman-Wilkinson, who died testate between 30 May

1712 and Mar 1723, Chowan Co., NC, Secretary of State loose wills. He apprarently married third, Mary [__] Lawson-Fewox, the widow of Nathaniel Lawson and James Fewox, respectively. Regardless of her huband of the moment, she always referred to herself as "Mary Lawson." For a discussion of Esther's marriages, see John Anderson Brayton, "Madame Esther Pollock of Kent Co., MD, and Chowan Co., NC, and the Lutens," in *The North Carolina Genealogical Society Journal*, vol. 24, no. 4 [November 2000], pp. 376-92.

As for the marriages of the three West children, the following records apply: [1] Thomas Harvey, whose will was dated 10 Apr 1729, proved 10 Nov 1729, Perquimans Co., NC, Secretary of State loose Wills, called Col. Robert West "brother-in-law" and named nieces Martha^3, Sarey^3, and Mary^3 West. [2] Martha Blount was the daughter of John Blount who, according to J. R. B. Hathaway, *The North Carolina Genealogical Register*, vol. 1, no. 3 [July 1900], p. 445, came into court, 7 Apr 1722, on behalf of his daughter Martha West, administratrix of Thomas^2 West, deceased. In John Blount's will, dated 27 Jan $172^5/_6$, proved 18 May 1726, NC Secretary of State loose Wills, she was called Martha Worsley, indicating a second marriage. [3] According to Chowan Co., NC, Deed Book W-1, p. 124, dated *ca.* 1713, Elizabeth West gave power of attorney to her father Richard Rose. She is said to have married second, Thomas Boyd, according to Hathaway, vol. 3, no. 2 [Apr 1903], p. 249, but she did not. In the the will of John^2 West, dated 10 July 1719 and recorded in NC Secretary of State vol. 875, p. 77, the testator named wife Elizabeth, and did not mention children. However, the record of the second marriage in Hathaway took place in in the first decade of the 1700's, and refers to John^1 West, Sr., uncle of the aforesaid John^2, whose widow was Winifred [__], not Elizabeth. As Winifred Boyd, she died testate in 1720, naming West children.

The Children of Robert West and Martha Cullen:

[1] a. **Robert^2 West**, married **Mary Harvey**.
[2]+ b. **Thomas^2 West**, married **Martha Blount**; she married second, between 1722 and 1725, Chowan Co., NC, [__] Worley/Worsley.
[3] c. **John^2 West**, died testate after 10 July 1719, Chowan Co., NC, Secretary of State vol. 875, p. 77; married **Elizabeth Rose**.
[4] d. **Richard^2 West**, *no further record.*

The Children of Thomas Pollock and Martha (Cullen) West:

[5] e. **Martha Pollock**, born 26 Mar 1691, died 29 Oct 1691.
[6] f. **Elizabeth Pollock**, born 26 Mar 1691, died 7 Sept 1691.
[7] g. **Elizabeth Pollock**, born and died, 22 Jan $169^2/_3$.
[8] h. **Martha Pollock**, born and died, 22 Jan $169^2/_3$.
[9] i. **Martha Pollock**, born 4 Mar $169^3/_4$, called "Mary" in her father's will; she married 10 Feb $171^3/_4$, **James Bray** of New Kent Co., VA.

[10] j. **Thomas Pollock**, born 9 Nov 1695, died testate in Bertie Co., NC, between 16 Apr 1732 and 20 Jan 173$^{2}/_{3}$, NC Secretary of State loose wills; he married 12 Feb 17$^{29}/_{30}$, **Elizabeth (Sanderson) Crisp**, who married third, Samuel Scolley of Bertie Co., NC.

[11] k. **Cullen Pollock**, born 27 Sept 1697, died testate between 18 Aug 1749 and June 1751, Tyrrell Co., NC, Secretary of State vol. 879, p. 23, the original filed among Tyrrell Co., NC, loose wills; he married **Frances West**.

[12] l. **George Pollock**, born 25 Oct 1699, died testate between 18 Oct 1736 and 29 July 1738, Chowan Co., NC, NC Land Grant Book 4, no. 82; he married first, 25 July 1725, **Sarah Swann**; he married second, 18 Apr 1734, **Elizabeth^{2} Whitmell**, born 1717, who married second, 2 Feb 173$^{6}/_{7}$, Thomas Blount; she married third, 2 Oct 1746, William^{3} Williams (**William^{2}**, John^{1}).

186. William Weston was almost certainly born by 1685 in Isle of Wight Co., VA, where a Weston family with numerous Williams had resided for a couple of generations. He married no later than 1716, Chowan Co., NC, **Catherine^{2} Blanchard**, the daughter of **Benjamin^{1} Blanchard** and Catherine [__]. Blanchard named two of Weston's sons in his 5 June 1719 will, indicating that Weston and Catherine had already been married at least three years. William Weston died testate after 12 Nov 1747, Bertie Precinct, NC, his will filed among NC Secretary of State loose wills. Catherine was still alive on 11 Feb 1754, according to Bertie Co., NC, Deed Book H, p. 84, occupying her deceased husband's plantation.

An interesting deed in Chowan for the docking of an entail, dated 13 Oct 1744 and recorded in Chowan Co., NC, Deed Book A#1, p. 306, recites that John Weston/Wesson of Bertie, then of full age, had sold land to Ephraim Blanchard of Chowan, with the full advice of William Weston of Bertie and Catherine his wife, John's lawful father and mother. The tract contained 100 acres and was known as Meherin Neck near Catherine Creek in Chowan, being part of a patent to Benjamin Blanchard of the Upper parish of Nansemond Co., VA, dated 4 Sept 1714, which by the last will and testament of the said Benjamin descended to "Catterene Wesson and her son John," the value of which entail not being of sufficient value to disturb the land values of other neighboring land-holders.

The Children of William Weston and Catherine Blanchard:

[1] a. **John^{2} Weston**, born *ca.* 1716.

[2]+ b. **William^{2} Weston**, born *ca.* 1718, was of Craven Co., SC, when he died testate between 17 Oct 1770 and Feb 1772, Johnston Co., NC, loose wills [this will is not listed in Mitchell]; married 7 May 1744,

Chowan Co., NC (marriage bond), **Sarah^{3} Luten**.

[3] c. **Ephraim^{2} Weston**.

[4] d. **Thomas^{2} Weston**.

[5] e. **Malichi^{2} Weston**, married **Sarah** [__], according to Chowan Co., NC, Court Minutes, 1749-1754, p. 263, dated Oct 1752, wherein Malachi "Wesson" and wife Sarah, William Harloe and wife Deborough sold land to John Hoskins. On p. 272 of that same volume, dated Jan 1753, appeared the notice that William Lewis made a deed of gift to the same Sarah Weston, now the wife of Malachi.

[6] f. **Rachel^{2} Weston**.

187. Thomas White, the son of John^{A} White, the testator of 4 Mar 1718, Isle of Wight Co., VA, Will & Deed book 2, p. 649, was born *ca.* 1696, Isle of Wight Co., VA, and died testate 10.30.1761, Perquimans Monthly Meeting, his will recorded in Perquimans Co., NC, Will Book C, p. 1. He married 7.13.1719, Chuckatuck Monthly Meeting, Nansemond Co., VA, **Rachel[4] Jordan**, the daughter of Joshua[3] Jordan (Thomas[2-1]) and Elizabeth (Sanborne), born *ca.* 1700, Nansemond Co., VA, and died testate 6.16.1768, Perquimans Monthly Meeting, although her will was never signed or probated. Thomas White was a resident of Perquimans Co., NC, by 10 Jan $172^{4}/_{5}$, according to Perquimans Co., NC, Deed Book B, #183. This family has been traced in the chapter on "Thomas Jordan," in *Adventurers of Purse and Person*, 4th ed., vol. 2, *Families G-P*, pp. 363-416, especially pp. 378-79, and pp. 412-16.

The Children[5] of Thomas White and Rachel Jordan, born Perquimans:

[1] a. **Lydia^{2} White**, born 12 Nov 1720, married 6 Apr 1737, **John Robinson**.

[2] b. **Elizabeth^{2} White**, born 19 Dec 1722, married *ca.* 1740/1, **Joseph Pritchard**, who married second Elizabeth Newby; third, Sarah Barrow.

[3] c. **Joshua^{2} White**, born 26 Jan $172^{6}/_{7}$, married **Mary** [__].

[4]+ d. **Joseph^{2} White**, born 6 Mar 1728, married **Gulielma Newby**.

[5] e. **Jordan^{2} White**, born 20 May 1729, died 175[ ].

[6] f. **Thomas^{2} White**, born 25 Feb $173^{0}/_{1}$, married **Ann Barrow**.

[7] g. **Rachel^{2} White**, born 25 Feb $173^{0}/_{1}$, married 10 Mar 1752, **John Winslow**.

[8] h. **John^{2} White**, born 7 May 1733, married 15 May 1757, **Lydia Winslow**, who married second, John Cornwell.

[9] i. **Mary^{2} White**, born 29 Apr 1735, married before 1753, **Joseph Winslow**.

[10] j. **Matthew² White**, born 10 May 1738, married *ca*. 1762, **Mary Robinson**.

[11] k. **Caleb² White**, born 8 May 1740, married 14 Jan 1761, **Rebecca Toms**.

[12] l. **Sarah² White**, born 5 Dec 1744, married 17 Nov 1762, **Nicholas Nicholson**.

[13] m. **Benjamin² White**, born 7 Dec 1742, married 25 Mar 1767, his cousin **Millicent Henley**.

188. Joseph Whitehead, the son of Col. **William Whitehead** and Rachel [__], married **Faith Lane**, the sister of Joseph Lane of Edgecombe Co., NC, whose will was dated 6 Dec 1757, proved Nov 1758, in the NC Secretary of State Loose Wills collection. Faith (Lane) Whitehead married second, by 6 Dec 1757, the date of her brother's will (which named her as Faith Bynum), William Bynum. She was alive as late as 14 Feb 1772, in a deed with her second husband in which she relinquished her dower rights in a sale of land to Joseph Whitehead, according to Halifax Co., NC, Deed Book 12, p. 145.

In cases concerning the qualification of younger ancestors such as Joseph Whitehead, it has been necessary to prove that each was born before or during the time his father lived in colonial North Carolina, and 12 July 1729, especially since William had a narrow window of opportunity to qualify as an OFFNC ancestor. William Whitehead was in North Carolina by 5 Apr 1720, at which time he received a land grant for 490 acres in Chowan Co., NC, on the north side of the Morratuck River, adjoining Thomas Bryan. This can be found in NC Land Patent Book 3, p. 13. A sketch of this family can be found in *Order of First Families of North Carolina, Ancestor Registry*, no. 1.

With Joseph Whitehead, eligibility as an OFFNC ancestor is not a problem if we can assume that he was at least 21 years old (and therefore born before 1722) when he first purchased 200 acres of land on Deep Creek from John Briggs on 17 Aug 1743, Edgecombe Co., NC, Deed Book 5, p. 196. Joseph would have been a child when his father moved from Isle of Wight to Chowan Co., NC. At any rate, even if Joseph had been born after 1729, entertaining the notion of his purchase of land at the age of 14 would be ludicrous.

Joseph Whitehead died intestate by May 1752, at which time the account of sales of his estate which his widow and administratrix, Faith, presented to the court was recorded, Edgecombe Co., NC, Estates Records.

Proof that Joseph² Whitehead was the son of Joseph¹ lies in Halifax Co., NC, Deed Book 12, p. 115, dated 26 Aug 1771, in which Joseph², with wife Pheraby's consent, sells the same tract which his father had acquired from James Bandy in Edgecombe Co., NC, Deed Book 4, p. 393. Using the same logic, we may include Benjamin Whitehead among Joseph's orphans. According to

Halifax Co., NC, Deed Book 9, p. 420, dated 9 Oct 1765, recorded Jan 1767, Benjamin^2 Whitehead sold to William Bynum the 200A which his putative father had acquired from John Briggs in Edgecombe Co., NC, Deed Book 5, p. 196, dated 17 Aug 1743.

The Children of Joseph Whitehead and Faith Lane, born Edgecombe Co., NC, possibly others:

[1]+ a. **Joseph^2 Whitehead**, died testate between 17 Feb and Nov 1781, Halifax Co., NC, Will Book 3, p. 1; he married, as her first husband, **Pheraby Applewhite**, the daughter of Martha [__] Applewhite who died testate between 5 Apr and Nov 1788, Halifax Co., NC, Will Book 3, p. 158. Martha named, among others, her daughter Phereby Wilkins (she had remarried) and her Whitehead grandchildren: Martha^3, John^3, Tobias^3, Betsey^3, and Joseph^3.

[2] b. **Benjamin^2 Whitehead**.

189. Col. **William Whitehead**, the son of Arthur^A Whitehead and Mary^A Godwin (William^B), was born say 1675, Isle of Wight Co., VA, and died intestate by 1750, according to Edgecombe Co., NC, Estates records. He married before 12 Feb 1722, when she appeared on a deed of sale with her husband, Bertie Co., NC, Deed Book A, p. 124, **Rachel** [__], who survived him and died intestate after Dec 1764 in Halifax Co., NC, according to Halifax Co., NC, Deed Book 9, p. 128, in which she distributed part of her estate to her children and grandchildren. William Whitehead was in North Carolina by 5 Apr 1720, at which time he received a land grant for 490 acres in Chowan Co., NC, on the north side of the Morratuck River, adjoining Thomas Bryan. This can be found in NC Land Patent Book 3, p. 13. A sketch of this family can be found in *Order of First Families of North Carolina, Ancestor Registry*, no. 1.

Just after their father's death, the Whitehead brothers engaged in a flurry of land sales to each other: Edgecombe Co., NC, Deed Book 3, p. 513, dated 6 June 1750, William, son of William, deceased, top brother Jacob; p. 514, dated same, William to brother Tobias; p. 516, same date, William for filial love to brother Abraham; p. 517, Joseph for love to his brother Lazarus, dated 16 Aug 1750.

The Children of William Whitehead and Rachel [__]:

[1] a. **William^2 Whitehead**, Jr., died testate between 24 Jan and Apr 1765, Halifax Co., NC, Will Book 1, p. 162; he married (possibly as his second wife) 5 July 1758, Southampton Co., VA (bond, Marriage Register, p. 4, dau. of William Bynum), **Abby Bynum**.

[2] b. **Jacob^2 Whitehead**, married **Mary** [__], with whom he sold land to

Samuel Saxon in Edgecombe Co., NC, Deed Book 4, p. 451, dated 20 Dec 1753.

[3] c. **Abraham^{2} Whitehead**, died testate between 28 May and July 1766, Halifax Co., NC, Will Book 1, p. 187; he named his four surviving brothers (Jacob^{2}, Arthur^{2}, Lazarus^{2}, and Tobias^{2}), and mentioned (without naming) the orphans of his two deceased brothers, William^{2} and Joseph^{2}.

[4] d. **Lazarus^{2} Whitehead**, married [__]; he, styled as Lazarus, Sr., witnessed a deed with Lazarus, Jr., presumably his son, dated 24 Feb 1767, Halifax Co., NC, Deed Book 9, p. 416.

[5]+ e. **Tobias^{2} Whitehead**, died testate between 17 June 1773 and May 1774, Halifax Co., NC, Will Book 1, p. 334; married **Susannah** [__].

[6]+ f. **Joseph^{2} Whitehead**, born *ca.* 1720, died intestate before May 1752, Edgecombe Co., NC, according to Edgecombe Co., NC, Estates Records; he married, as her first husband, **Faith Lane**.

[7] g. **Arthur^{2} Whitehead**.

190. William Whitfield, probably the son of Matthew Whitfield and his unknown first wife (before Matthew's second marriage to Priscilla Lawrence), was born by 1689, possibly in Nansemond Co., VA, and died sometime after his last appearance in the Bertie deeds, 13 Nov 1740, at which time his wife Elizabeth released her dower in a deed which had originally been dated 24 Oct 1729, Bertie Co., NC, Deed Book F, p. 173. What was almost certainly his last appearance was on 18 Mar $174^{1}/_{2}$, Bertie Co., NC, Deed Book F, p. 342, in which he sold 300 acres of land at Pottecasie Branch, adjoining Thomas Jones at Thomas's Path (the plantation whereon John Graddy formerly lived, and where Wm., Jr., now lives) to Thomas Walker. Witnesses were Edward and Patience Outlaw, Daniel Sellevent, and William^{2} Whitfield, Jr. This 300 acres was a tract which William, Sr., purchased of John and Margaret [__] Beverley on 14 Oct 1721, according to Chowan Co., NC, Deed Book F#1, p. 200. William married **Elizabeth** (said to be **Goodman**), whose last appearance in the records was on the deed above. William Whitfield and his wife Elizabeth sold 300 acres of land in Bertie called the "Red Ridge," to Thomas Johnson on 29 Jan 1723, according to Bertie Co., NC, Deed Book A, p. 205.

The list of William's children has been taken, with certain reservations, from Emma Morehead Whitfield, *Whitfield, Bryan, Smith, and Related Families*, Book One, *Whitfield*, pp. 54-63, and adjusted with information from *Herring Highlights III*, and primary source documents. While the list below is entirely plausible, it would be helpful to have had more concrete records of filiation, besides the proved relationship between William^{1} and his son William^{2}, Jr.

The putative Children of William Whitfield and Elizabeth [Goodman], born Chowan and Bertie counties, NC:

[1]+ a. **William^2 Whitfield**, born 20 May 1715, died testate 31 Mar 1795, Wayne Co., NC, Will Book A, p. 558; married first, 6 Nov 1741, **Rachel^2 Bryan**, born 10 June 1723, died Nov 1780; married second, **Frauzan** [__], named in his will. He and his first wife were buried at Seven Springs on the south bank of the Neuse River, Wayne Co., according to Susan Fergusson and Eleanor Powell, David Williams Chapter, DAR, Goldsboro, *Miscellaneous Records of Wayne County, North Carolina, Families and Some of the Their Ancestors*, p. 2 of 6.

[2] b. **Matthew^2 Whitfield**, born *ca.* 1717, said to have migrated to Marion Co., SC, and to have married [__] **Warren**.

[3] c. **Luke^2 Whitfield**, born 1722, said to have died after 1773, Florence Co., SC; said to have married married **Rachel Powell**.

[4] d. **Mary^2 Whitfield**, died 20 Dec 1791; married *ca.* 1733, **John Graddy**, born 1710, died 12 Mar 1787, his will dated 9 Feb 1773 and proved Apr 1787, Duplin Co., NC, Will Book A, p. 152, the son of William Graddy and [Anne] Barfield; the Barfield connection appeared in a deed from Richard Barfield and wife Mary to grandson John Graddy, dated 11 May 1725, Bertie Co., NC, Deed Book A, p. 440.

[5] e. **Patience^2 Whitfield**, married by Feb 1739, Bertie Co., NC, **Edward Outlaw III**, according to Bertie Co., NC, Deed Boo F, p. 31, in which he described himself as son of Edward Outlaw, Sr., dec., and mentioned his brother George Outlaw; Patience relinquished her dower; Edward died testate after 22 Mar 1758, Duplin Co., NC, Will Book A, p. 369.

[6] f. **Margaret^2 Whitfield**, married first, **Solomon Barfield**; second, [__] **Winkfield**.

[7] g. **Elizabeth^2 Whitfield**, married first, **Jonathan Taylor**; second, **John Beck**, who died testate between 2 Sept and Oct 1790, Duplin Co., NC, Will Book A, p. 20.

[8] h. **Sarah^2 Whitfield**.

[9] i. **Charity^2 Whitfield**, married first, **Frederick O'Daniel**, who died between 1761 and 1773; second, 2 May 1782, **Daniel Herring**; there were no children by the second marriage.

[10] j. **Constantine^2 Whitfield**, born 6 Mar 1728, died testate between 28 Oct 1797 and June 1798, Craven Co., NC, Will Book B, p. 46; married **Barbara^4 Williams** (James^3, John$^{2-1}$).

191. Thomas Whitmel II was the son of Mary[A] [__] and Thomas[A] Whitmell I, the latter of whose will was proved 4 Dec 1693, Charles City Co., VA, Court Orders 1687-1695, p. 473. His executrix Mary [__] married second, Arthur Cavanaugh, according to the same volume, 5 Aug 1695, p. 579. The Whitmel Family Bible provides the information that Thomas Whitmel II was born 16 Sept 1688, Charles City Co., VA, and died testate 24 Nov 1735, Bertie Co., NC. He married *ca.* 1712, as her first husband, **Elizabeth[2] Bryan**, the daughter of **Lewis[1] Bryan**(t), and Elizabeth [__]. Thomas Whitmel's will was dated 23 Nov and proved Dec 1735, his will recorded in NC Land Grant Book 4, no. 22. The birth and death dates for Thomas Whitmel were taken from a family Bible said to be still in the family's possession, according to John Bennett Boddie, "Whitmel of Bertie," in *Southside Virginia Families*, vol. 1, p. 394. Elizabeth (Bryan) Whitmel married second, **Robert[2] Hunter**, the son of **William[1] Hunter** and Ann [__], and died before he signed his will. Hunter's will was dated 3 June, proved Aug 1753, Bertie Co., NC, and filed among NC Secretary of State loose wills. Although there were no children by Elizabeth's second marriage, Robert Hunter did mention his stepdaughter Elizabeth[2] (Whitmel) Williams, then the wife of William[4] Williams of Martin Co., NC.

Thomas Whitmell made his "brother" John Gray, who had married Ann Bryan [Elizabeth (Bryan) Whitmel's sister], an executor of his will. Only daughter Elizabeth Pollock was married at the time his will was signed. Mary[2] (Whitmel) Pugh-Thompson lived to great age and left her remaining estate to her son Thomas[3] Thompson, born after his father's death.

An entire assemblage of the surviving children of Thomas Whitmel II and Elizabeth Bryan deeded in common 3 Negro slaves to Winefred Whitmel and Mary Whitmel in an undated instrument, recorded Nov Court 1743, Bertie Co., NC, Deed Book F, p. 545. For love and affection, Robert Hunter, Elizabeth Hunter, Thomas Whitmel, Thomas Blount, Elizabeth Blount, John Hill, Martha Hill, Henry Hunter, and Sarah Hunter gave the two Whitmel girls slaves Phillis, Penny, and Nancy, to be equally divided between them at marriage.

The Children of Thomas Whitmel II and Elizabeth Bryan:

[1]+ a. **Thomas[2] Whitmel III**, born 9 Dec 1713, died testate 1778, Martin Co., NC, Will Book 1, p. 133; married **Elizabeth[3] West**.

[2] b. **Mary[2] Whitmel**, born 1715, *died 1728.*

[3] c. **Elizabeth[2] Whitmel**, born 1717, married first, by 1735, **George Pollock**; second, 27 Oct 1736, Capt. **Thomas Blount**; third, by 1748, Col. **William[4] Williams** (Samuel[3], **William[2]**, John[1])

[4] d. **Sarah[2] Whitmel**, born 1719, married her stepbrother **Henry[3] Hunter** (Robert[2], William[1]).

[5]+ e. **Martha[2] Whitmel**, born 20 Feb 1721, married John Hill, who died testate after 12 June 1762, Bertie Co., NC, Will Book A, p. 85, the

son of Isaac Hill of Chowan.

[6] f. **Ann[2] Whitmel**, born 1724, *died 1727.*

[7] g. **Janet[2] Whitmel**, born 1724, *died 1730.*

[8] h. **Winifred[2] Whitmel**, married after 1743, **Philip[2] Alston**.

[9] i. **Lewis[2] Whitmel**, born 1732, *died young.*

[10] j. **Mary[2] Whitmel**, died testate between 10 June and Aug 1807, Bertie Co., NC, Will Book F, p. 38; married first, after 1743, **Francis[2] Pugh**, who died intestate before Oct 1762, Bertie Co., NC, Court Minutes 1758-1762, p. 305; second, **Hezekiah Thompson**, who died testate between 25 Jan and Mar 1771, Bertie Co., NC, Will Book A, p. 132.

[11] k. **William[2] Whitmel**, born 1735, *died young.*

192. John Williams, Jr., weaver, son of progenitor John[A] Williams and Anne [__], was born *ca.* 1669, Isle of Wight Co., VA, and died testate well into his eighties between 26 Feb 1757 and Jan 1758, Bertie Co., NC. He married by 1691, Isle of Wight Co., VA, **Anne** [__], who died after 13 Mar 1745, the signing of her husband's will, Bertie Co., NC. On the Tax List of Chowan Co., NC, for 1717, John Williams was shown to own 1050 acres of land. A sketch of this family can be found in *Order of First Families of North Carolina, Ancestor Registry*, no. 2.

The Children of John Williams and Anne [__], born Isle of Wight Co., VA:

[1] a. **John[2] Williams**, born *ca.* 1692, died testate in what was then Albemarle Co., NC, between 26 Jan 1721 and 18 May 1722, Secretary of State loose wills; did not marry.

[2] b. **Theophilus[2] Williams**, born *ca.* 1694, died after 1760, most likely Onslow Co., NC; married by 1720, Chowan Precinct, NC, **Christian** [__]. A Catherine Busbey, in her will dated 22 Jan 173$^{8}/_{9}$, proved Feb 173^{8}[$/_{9}$], Bertie Co., NC, Secretary of State loose wills, made a bequest to Hester[3] Williams, daughter of Theophilus, and after a few other bequests, left the remainder of her estate to Theophilus[2] to be divided among his children. No connection between the Busbeys (possibly of Surry Co., VA), and the family of Theophilus has been discovered.

[3]+ c. **Anne[2] Williams**, born *ca.* 1696, married by 1716, as his second wife, **Samuel[1] Herring**,who died testate between 22 Oct 1750 and 20 Mar 175$^{0}/_{1}$, Johnston Co., NC, Secretary of State loose wills.

[4] d. **Isaac[2] Williams**, born *ca.* 1698, died intestate before 1760, Johnston Co., NC; married **Martha[2] Hodges**, who died testate between 31 Aug 1760 and [--] 1761, Johnston Co., NC, Secretary of State loose

wills.

[5] e. **Sarah**[2] **Williams**, born *ca.* 1700, died after June 1749, Bertie Co., NC; married **James Castellaw**, who died intestate after 1738, Bertie Co., NC.

[6]+ f. **Mary**[2] **Williams**, born *ca.* 1702, married [**Abraham**?] **Herring**.

[7] g. **James**[2] **Williams**, born *ca.* 1704, died testate between 21 Aug 1736 and Feb 1737, Bertie Co., NC, Secretary of State loose wills; married by 1727, Chowan Precinct, NC, as her first husband, **Elizabeth**[2] **Bryan**.

[8] h. **Arthur**[2] **Williams**, born *ca.* 1706, died testate between 28 Jan and May 1775, Society Parish, Bertie Co., NC, loose wills; had children by **Elizabeth Butler**.

193. Lewis Williams was born by 1650 and died testate between 1 Oct 1716 and 16 Apr 1717, Chowan Precinct, NC, his will filed among the NC Secretary of State loose wills. He married first by 1675, [__], the mother of most of his children, and second, by 1700, **Mary** [__], who survived him and was alive as late as July 1723, Chowan Precinct, NC—as demonstrated by her inclusion in a lawsuit as the executrix of Lewis Williams, deceased, against Joshua Porter and Catherine [__] Glover-Porter, in *North Carolina Higher-Court Records*, vol. 5, *1709-1723*, p. 376, 403. Mary was almost certainly the mother of daughter Priscilla[2], not mentioned in 1694, but married by 1717.

A Lewis Williams occurred twice as a headright in Virginia: [1] once for Arthur Allen of Surry Co., Edwd. Thelwell and Robt. Horneing of Nansemond, dated 29 Nov 1679, in VA Land Patent Book 7, p. 16; [2] and again for Giles Limscott of Isle of Wight Co., dated 20 Apr 1680, VA Land Patent Book 7, p. 20. In earlier references, a Lewis Williams appeared as a headright for persons patenting land in New Kent or in Old Rappahannock counties.

Researchers have concluded from the above records that Lewis Williams first owned land in Nansemond Co., VA, and that he subsequently removed to Chowan Precinct, NC, sometime in the last decade of the seventeenth century. Of course, due to the destruction of records in Nansemond, we have no idea if the Lewis Williams who patented land in Nansemond sold his land and migrated to Chowan, or remained in Virginia. Our Lewis Williams first received a patent for land in Chowan in 1697—apparently two or three years after his date of entry into North Carolina. But thus far, there is no reason to give him a Nansemond Co., VA, origin.

On 25 May 1694, Lewis Williams proved his rights for 9 importees: Lewis Williams, Sr., Lewis Williams, Jr., Elizabeth Williams twice, An Williams, Anthony Williams, Johana Williams, Katherine Williams, Edw. Redman, according to Caroline B. Whitley, *North Carolina Headrights, A List of*

Names, 1663-1744, p. 104. In July 1694, Lewis Williams once again registered his rights for four more importees: Thomas Stanbridge and his wife Mary, his daughter Mary and David Blake, according to Whitley, same volume, p. 123. A quick glance at this writer's article "The Hayman Family of Somerset Co., MD, and Pasquotank Co., NC," in *The North Carolina Genealogical Society Journal*, vol. 31, no. 3 [August 2005], pp. 248-54, will reveal that there is no ostensible connection between the Standridges, Mary (Standridge) Blake and Lewis Williams. At least, not so far. The above record suggests that daughter Priscilla Williams was born after the 1694 registration. Over the decades, genealogists have developed a rule of thumb pertaining to the Virginia headright system which suggests a three-year lapse between the submission of a petition for land and the actual recording of the patent. But no such time frame has yet been theorized for colonial North Carolina, to this writer's knowledge.

The information revealed by Lewis Williams' importation record has thrown a colossal wrench into traditional Williams genealogy, especially that compiled by this genealogist. And it necessitates a completely different interpretation of the curious will of Lewis Williams, Sr. The oddest piece of data is that of the two Elizabeths designated as "transported twice," which this writer can only interpret as the presence of an older and a younger Elizabeth. Another problem arises with the two Elizabeths, of course. Without the mention of Lewis' wife Mary in the importation documernt—she does not appear in the Chowan land records until 1700—we have the following question: was the first Elizabeth Williams mentioned Lewis' ["then"] wife, or is this a case of two daughters both named Elizabeth?

In his will, Lewis Williams named several of his grandchildren without revealing exactly who their parents were. As a result of this, it has been necessary to dig rather deeply into the records to make sure that each grandchild has been properly placed. The identities and families of Anthony^2 Williams, Ann^2 Jones, and Priscilla^2 West have been established without much difficulty. But one wonders whether LewisWilliams was consistent in the disposition of his property among his living children and the heirs of his deceased ones.

The problem with assigning a Williams daughter to the proper Sowell husband has been greatly relieved by the luxury of an extra Elizabeth^2 to dispose of. In fact Charles Sowell of Chowan and Bertie counties appeared with wife Elizabeth in the land records as early as 10 Apr 1721, according to Chowan Co., NC, Deed Book F#1, p. 121, in which they sold land to John Jordan—400 acres on Old Town Creek Swamp, adjoining Jordan, John Pusell, and Ballard. Elizabeth was still his wife when their land had been cut off into Bertie, according to Bertie Co., NC, Deed Book C, p. 208, dated 10 Feb 1729, in which they sold 100 acres on the west side of the Chowan River to John Graves. However, by the time Charles signed his will on 25 Nov 1738, Elizabeth Williams had died, and Charles had remarried Martha [__]. Several things in

Charles' will struck this writer as evidence of his intimate connection with the Lewis Williams family: [1] Charles' son Charles[3], Jr., had received 100 acres from his grandfather Lewis[1] Williams; [2] Charles named a son *Lewis*[3] Sowell, to whom he bequeathed 100 acres adjoining "*Patchett*," also a devisee of Lewis Williams; [3] Charles elected to name two daughters Elizabeth[3], an oddity which seems more than a mere coincidence given this writer's argument for the two Elizabeths just a generation before. This writer is also aware that he goes against every other piece of written genealogical literature [including some of his own] by denying the existence of a Margaret (Williams) Sowell, but he stands by his argument. Elizabeth Williams existed in the importation document, and there was no mention of a Margaret.

The existence of Elizabeth[2] Rutland was discovered in the land records; and although the deed of gift from Lewis[1] Williams to her and her husband was badly worded, it seemed reasonable to include her as a daughter of Lewis Williams—and most likely recently married. However, the odd wording of the deed of gift makes one wonder if possibly James Rutland was actually a son-in-law of Lewis Williams—bringing up the possibility that wife Mary [__] Williams was a widow Rutland with a son Thomas—and that his wife Elizabeth was completely unrelated to the Williams family. Elizabeth[2] was not mentioned at all in the will. A thorough study of the land records of Thomas Rutland revealed no language indicating any blood relationship with the Williams family. On 6 Apr 1708, Chowan Co., NC, Deed Book W#1, p. 81, Lewis Williams, for affection to James and Elizabeth Rutland, his son and daughter-in-law [*sic*], gave them 100 acres for their lives and then to their first begotten child. Was this a scribal error? Probably not, as we do have the importation record of one Elizabeth as a guarantee of her presence in Lewis' family. The "disconnect" appeared later in the land records when Elizabeth[2] and James Rutland described how they had obtained their land, and Mary Williams was mentioned merely as a casual by-stander, emphasizing her role as step-mother. It also determines that there were two daughters named Elizabeth.

Under the terms of his grandfather Lewis Williams' will, grandson John[3] Patchett received 100A of land adjoining the land of Lewis[3] Jones, on the north side of the western fork of the Poplar Run. It is likely that our John[3] Patchett is the John[3] Padgett who died intestate in Craven Co., NC, leaving wife Mary [__] as his administratrix. By 1738, according to Bertie Co., NC, Deed Book E, p. 451, dated 2 Feb 1738, John[3] Patchett had sold his inheritance from his grandfather and had removed to Craven Co., NC. His parents have not been identified, and he is, unfortunately, untraceable.

This writer has not been to place Johanna and Katherine Williams in the Williams family. Either they died between 1695 and 1716, they were related to Lewis in some other way, or they have been buried in the records so successfully that research has not yet been able to unearth them.

The Children of Lewis Williams and [__], born Chowan Precinct, Albemarle Co., NC:

[1]+ a. **Anthony² Williams**, born *ca.* 1675, died testate between 3 Dec 1717, Apr 1718, Chowan Co., NC, Secretary of State loose wills; married by 1700, as her first husband, **Martha Bush**; she married second, William Corlee.

[2] b. **William² Williams**, died before1695, married [__].

[3]+ c. **Elizabeth² Williams**, born *ca.* 1678, married by 1695, as his first wife, Chowan Precinct, NC, **Charles Sowell**, Sr., who died testate between 25 Nov 1738 and Feb 173⁸/₉, Bertie Co., NC, Secretary of State loose wills. He married second, Martha [__].

[3] c. **Ann² Williams**, born *ca.* 1680, married by 1700, Chowan Precinct, NC, as his first wife, **John Jones**, Jr., who died testate between 6 Aug 1739 and 18 Oct 1744, Chowan Co., NC, Secretary of State loose wills; he married second, Florence [__].

[4] d. **[Daughter]² Williams**, married [__] **Patchett**.

[5] e. **Elizabeth² Williams**, born *ca.* 1690, married *ca.* 1708, Chowan Precinct, NC, **James Rutland**, who died intestate in Bertie Co., NC, after 1742.

The Child of Lewis Williams and Mary [__], born Chowan Precinct, Albemarle Co., NC:

[6] f. **Priscilla² Williams**, born 1696-1700, married by 1717, Chowan Precinct, NC, Col. **Peter West**, who died testate between 31 July 1749 and May 1751, Bertie Co., NC, Secretary of State loose wills.

194. William Williams, the son of progenitor John^A Williams and Anne [__], was born *ca.* 1671, Isle of Wight Co., VA, and died testate between 9 Dec 1711 and 15 Apr 1712 in Chowan Precinct of Albemarle Co., NC. William Williams married *ca.* 1689, Isle of Wight Co., VA, **Mary** [__]. A sketch of this family can be found in *Order of First Families of North Carolina, Ancestor Registry*, no. 2. William Williams had at least two daughters, his "garls," whom he mentioned in his will, but did not name.

There is one lingering question about the fate of Mary [__] Williams raised by the following deed abstract:

Isle of Wight Co., VA, Deed Book 4, p. 100, dated 19 Mar 1730, rec. 22 Mar 1730/31; Henry Cobb and Mary his wife to JOHN WILLIAMS, for a valuable consideration, 75A on the s.s. Main Blackwater, the sd. dividend of land being part of a patent for 600A granted to WILLIAM WILLIAMS by the sd. Hon. Francis Nicholson 28

Oct 1702, and bounded by Boons Branch, a small Branch which divided Joseph Godwin's land and Edward Cobbs, a line dividing Francis Braces land, Joseph Godwin's, and Edward Cobbs land; except for a parcel of ground eight feet square being the burying place of Edward Cobb the said Henry Cobb's father; wit: Richard Williams, John Johnson, Jo^{n}: Daughtrey; signed: Henry C Cobb, Mary M Cobb; Mary relinquishes dower 22 Mar 173$^{0}/_{1}$.

The land which William bequeathed to his wife Mary had absolutely no restrictions put upon it, neither upon her re-marriage, nor the coming of age of their children. Did she marry, second, Henry Cobb and live for at least another eighteen years? If William had been born in 1671, then Mary would only be about 60 years old in 1730. Or was the grantee one of the unnamed Williams daughters who married Henry Cobb?

The Children of William Williams and Mary [__], born Isle of Wight Co., VA,

[1] a. **John**[2] **Williams**, born *ca.* 1690, married (possibly) **Mary** [__].

[2] b. **Steven**[2] **Williams**, born *ca.* 1691, removed to Onslow Co., NC; married **Elizabeth** [__].

[3] c. [**Daughter**][2] **Williams**, *no further record.*

[4] d. [**Daughter**][2] **Williams**, *no further record.*

[5]+ e. **Samuel**[2] **Williams**, born *ca.* 1701, died testate between 24 Oct 1753 and Feb 175$^{3}/_{4}$, Edgecombe Co., NC, Secretary of State loose wills; married, as her first husband, **Elizabeth**[2] **Alston**,daughter of **John**[1] **Alston**.

195. Robert Willson, Quaker, was born by 1630 and died testate 21 Dec 1696, Perquimans Co., NC. His will was dated 2.28.1693 and proved 7.11.1696, filed among the NC Secretary of State loose wills and recorded in NC Secretary of State vol. 874.2, p. 76. He married **Ann** [__], named as wife in his will, born *ca.* 1643, and died 21 May 1702, Perquimans Co., NC. Ann died testate 21.5mo.1702, the date her will was signed, Surry Co., VA, Deeds, Wills, Etc., No. 5, p. 248, the date of her will being also her death date, assuring her identity as Robert's widow. [*Why* was she in Surry?] Robert Willson did not marry Ann[3] Blount, the daughter Ann Willson named in the will of **Thomas**[2] **Blount** (**James**[1])—it is unlikely that Robert would have predeceased this father-in-law by ten years, and it would be more reasonable to search within Chowan for Ann Blount's Willson husband. Another reason for this opinion is that Robert Willson named grandchidlren in his will, suggesting that he was a generation older than Thomas Blount. Moreover, it is difficult to see how Thomas Blount, as a son of the leader of Culpeper's Rebellion would have let a daughter marry a pacifist. According to Caroline B. Whitley, *North Carolina Headrights, A List of*

Names, 1663-1744, p. 124, Robert Willson registered importation rights for 8 persons on 2nd Monday Apr 1694: Robert Wilson and wife Anne, Isaack Wilson, Sarah Wilson, Isaack Wilson and his wife An, David Sherwood and his wife. The last three rights were then assigned to John Pricklow, 14 July 1694. Another fact against the Blount connection is the fact that Robert's wife Ann Willson was imported into the colony. She would not have appeared as an importee had she already been born in the Albemarle.

Robert Willson wrote his will as a resident of Chuckatuck Monthly Meeting, Nansemond Co., VA, and a note was recorded in the minutes of that meeting concerning a gift of £18 left to his daughter Sarah Belman, the wife of John Belman. Another glimpse into Robert's life explains, possibly, the reason he made bequests to his Willson grandchildren rather than directly to his son Isaac. In Perquimans Monthly Meeting, Isaac[2] Willson had "by evil advice... left his plantation & gone to another that might be like to be his ruin" and was "advised to return to his former being."

The Children of Robert Willson and Ann [__]:

[1] a. **Isaac[2] Willson**, born *ca.* 1665, died testate between 13 June and 13 July 1714, Perquimans, NC Secretary of State loose wills; married first, by 1688, Perquimans Monthly Meeting, **Ann** [__]; he married second, 31 Mar 1701, Perquimans, **Ann Barker**, bapt. Apr 1672, Ashchurch, Gloucestershire, the daughter of Robert and Hannah [__] Barker. Isaac had the following children by his first wife, registered at Perquimans Monthly Meeting: [*i*] Robert[3] Wilson, born 8.10.1690; [*ii*] Ann[3] Wilson, born 7.16.1692; [*iii*] Benjamin[3] Wilson, born 10.1.1694; and the one son by Ann Barker, registered in Perquimans vital records: [*iv*] Isaack[3] Wilson, born 18 Nov 1702, the childless, unmarried testator of 3 Oct 1724, will proved 29 Dec 1724, NC Secretary of State loose wills; Isaac[2] Willson married third, by 1714, **Ann[1] (Walker) Hancock-Norman**, who married fourth, John Pettiver, mentioned in the will of her stepson Isaac, Jr.

[2]+ b. **Sarah[2] Willson**, born *ca.* 1668, married 19 Aug 1687, Perquimans Co., NC, also recorded in Perquimans Monthly Meeting, **John Belman**, who died testate between 5 Nov 1706 and 12 Jan $170^6/_7$, Perquimans, NC Secretary of State loose wills.

196. William Willson was born by 1695 and died testate after the signing of his will on 1 Jan 1745, Northampton Co., NC, filed among the NC Secretary of State loose wills. William Willson married first, between 1 Mar $17^{19}/_{20}$ and 10 Nov 1724, Bertie Co., NC, **Rebecca[3] Braswell**, born *ca.* 1697, who was the mother of all his children except for Elisha Moore[2] Willson. On the latter date, William

Wilson and wife Rebecca sold 265 acres on Meherrin Creek to Thomas Clerk, land formerly granted to Rebecca Brassell for 530 acres, 1 Mar 1719, Bertie Co., NC, Deed Book A, p. 341. The patent in question was land granted directly to Rebecca Braswell, dated 1 Mar $17^{19}/_{20}$, for 530 acres in Chowan on the south side of Maherrin River, adjoining Braswell's branch and the country line, NC Land Patent Book 8, p. 184. Rebecca was almost certainly the daughter of Richard and **Eleanor**[2] **(Bryant)** Braswell.

William married second, **Judith Moore**, daughter of Elizabeth [__] and Epaphroditus Moore of Bertie Co., NC, the testator of 11 June 1757, whose will was proved Oct 1757, NC Secretary of State loose wills, and who named therein his grandson Elisha[2] Wilson. Epaphroditus was still of Nansemond as of 11 Nov 1729, as a grantee in Bertie Co., NC, Deed Book C, p. 166. Judith (Moore) Wilson married second, according to the will of her father, John Hurst, and had children by him. John Hurst died testate after 11 Feb 1769, Bertie Co., NC, Will Book A, p. 103.

James[2] Wilson was omitted from his father's will, but received from William[1]Willson a gift of 180 acres of land in Ursara Meadow, his father's dwelling plantation, on 10 Apr 1741, Bertie Co., NC, Deed Book F, p. 240. Judith signed with William[1] on the deed. Son John[2] Wilson further identified his father's holdings after William[1]'s death in a deed recorded in Northampton Co., NC, Deed Book 1, p. 303, dated 1 Feb 1746. John[2] sold 150 acres of land in Ursara Meadow, whereon his father had lived, to John Dawson of Northampton. This land adjoined Robert Ruffin, William Cotton, and Thomas Cotton, and was "all the land deeded to William by *Richard Braswell.*"

The Children of William Wilson and Rebecca Braswell:

[1] a. **James**[2] **Wilson**.
[2] b. **Isaac**[2] **Wilson**.
[2] b. **Katherine**[2] **Willson**.
[3] c. **Elinor**[2] **Willson**.
[4] d. **Mary**[2] **Willson**.
[5] e. **Charity**[2] **Willson**.
[6] f. **Anne**[2] **Willson**.
[7] g. **John** [2]**Willson**.

The Child of William Wilson and Judith Moore:

[8]+ h. **Elisha Moore**[2] **Wilson**, died testate *ca.* 1811, Sampson Co., NC, Sampson loose wills; married **Sarah** [__]

The Children of John Hurst and Judith (Moore) Wilson:

[9] i. **Mary Hurst**, married [__] **Green**.
[10] j. **William Hurst**.

197. Lidia^{2} Windley, named as daughter in the will of of **Robert^{1} Windley** and Jane [__], married by 1694, **Nicholas Daw**, who died testate between 9 Jan 1716 and 2 July 1717, Hyde precinct, Bath Co., NC. Nicholas' will was recorded in Beaufort Co., NC, Deed Book 1, p. 282. Lydia was mentioned but not named in the will of her husband, and died after 22 Mar 1718, probably in Beaufort Co., NC.

The Children of Nicholas Daw and Lidia Windley:

[1]+ a. **William^{2} Daw**, born *ca.* 1695, died testate between 23 Jan and Mar 174$^{5}/_{6}$, Beaufort Co., NC, NC Secretary of State vol. 877, p. 35; married **Dinah** [__].

[2] b. **Ann^{2} Daw**, married first, *ca.* 1718, **William Stone**, who died testate between 29 Mar and 20 July 1720, Bath [Craven] Co., NC, his will recorded in NC Secretary of State vol. 875, p. 277; she married second, **Richard Harvey**, according to Carteret Co., NC, Deed Book B, pp. 83-85, dated 3 Mar 172$^{3}/_{4}$, in which both she and her husband acknowledged inheritance of land from William Stone, deceased. On 4 Apr 1730, Beaufort Co., NC, Deed Book 2, p. 39, Richard Harvey made a deed of gift to his son Peter Harvey. No spouse signed, and there was no indication in the deed concerening Peter's age, although on 15 Feb 173$^{3}/_{4}$, Peter Harvey witnessed a deed, Beaufort Co., NC, Deed Book2 , p. 109. He was possibly older than 13. By June 1731, Richard Harvey was married to Mary [__], who signed with him in a deed in Beaufort Co., NC, Deed Book 2, p. 233. Therefore, the maternity of Peter Harvey will remain unresolved until further information comes to light concerning his age.

[3] c. **Priscilla^{2} Daw**.

198. Robert^{1} Windley was born by 1630 and died testate between 31 July 1688 and 7 Apr 1690, Albemarle Co., NC, but the name of his wife, a widow with at least two unidentified daughters—one who married George Pearcy leaving a son John and another who married John Tailor, also leaving a son John—did not appear in the probate records. Robert's original will was filed among the NC Secretary of State loose wills. Although Windley wished to be buried in the manner of the Friends, he did begin his will with that oath which was anathema to Quakers: "In the name of God amen." Almost twenty years after his death, on 30 Mar 1709, Chowan Co., NC, Deed Book B#1, p. 214, **Jane [__] Windley-Gaskill**, late wife of Robert Windley of Chowan, and Hannah the wife of William Powers, for £16 sterling sold to Nicholas Crisp 280 acres of land formerly patented by Robert Winley on 29 Mar 1680, according to NC Land Patent Book 1, p. 146. The name is spelled "Gaskin," however, in NC Secretary of State vol. 847.2, p. 32. The implication is that either Jane and Hannah Powers were closely related or that they had both come into the possession of his one patent. The will of William Gaskill of Pasquotank, planter, was dated 4 May and proved 20 July 1703, NC Secretary of State loose wills. He named [second] wife **Jane**, and the following children: William Gaskill, Thomas Gaskill, Jean Gaskill, and Elizabeth (Gaskill) Durant. After only thirteen years of marriage at most, Jane [__] Windley-Gaskill could not be the mother of married daughter Elizabeth Durant. As a result, the maternity of the Gaskill children is uncertain.

The Windley name is rare enough in Virginia to warrant the assertion that our Robert was the headright of 1652 in Mr. John Browne's patent for 1000 acres in Northampton Co., VA, dated 27 Nov 1652, according to VA Land Patent Book No. 3, p. 138. Nine years later, Robert Windley received a patent for 500 acres in Northampton Co., VA, at the "seabord side," near Matchepungo, called "Allens Quarter," adjoining Thomas Hannans, dated 12 Apr 1661, according to VA Land Patent Book No. 4, p. 407. There were Windleys in Accomack-Northampton as early as 1632, but there is no evidence of Robert's relationship to or interaction with any of them. What became of his patent is a mystery both to this writer and to Mr. Ralph Whitelaw.

Several deeds in Chowan document the transfer of lands between Messrs. Pearcy and Tailor. On 1 Apr 1700, Chowan Co., NC, Deed Book W#1, p. 8, John Tailer of Chowan precinct sold 100 acres of land to George Pearcy, being a tract on the east side of the easternmost branch of Matoromot Comet Creek, adjoining Will Waters and formerly belonging to Robert Winley. On 8 Mar 1700, George Pearssy and wife Magdalon sold 100 acres, just acquired from Tailer, adjoining Edward Smithwick, "formerly Robert Winley's," as surveyed by Will James, according to Chowan Co., NC, Deed Book W#1, p. 10. According to Caroline B. Whitley, *North Carolina Headrights, A List of Names, 1663-1744*, p. 151, George Peircy received 187 acres in Chowan on 1 Jan 1694 for the following importees: John Crew, Elizabeth Crew, and Eliz. Crew, Jr.

The Children of [__] and Jane [__]:

[1] a. **Magdalon** [__], married **George Pearsy**.

[2] b. [**Daughter**] [__], married **John Taylor**.

The Children of Robert Windley and Jane [__] [__]:

[3] c. **William**[2] **Windley**, removed to Bath Co., according to Chowan Co., NC, Deed Book W#1, p. 150, dated 1 July 1707; he married **Ann**[2] **(Hoskins) Cox**.

[4]+ d. **Lidia**[2] **Windley**, married **Nicholas**[1] **Daw**, born by 1673, died testate between 9 Jan and 2 July 1717, Hyde precinct, Bath Co., NC,

Beaufort Co., NC, Deed Book 1, p. 282

✠ **199. Henry[1] Woodward**, the son of testator Francis[A] Woodward of Norfolk Co., VA, who named him in his will dated 21 Apr and proved 15 Aug 1679, Norfolk Co., VA, Will Book 4, p. 55, was born say 1665, Norfolk Co., VA. According to Annie Laurie Wright Smith's *The Quit Rents of Virginia, 1704*, p. 100, in that year Henry Woodward still owned 280 acres in Norfolk Co., VA. He received a deed of gift from his father-in-law Joell Martin for 300 acres in Bath Co., NC, adjoining Thomas Worsley on the west side of Town Creek, dated 20 Sept 1709, Beaufort Co., NC, Deed Book 1, p. 146. Henry Woodard married **Mary[2] Martin**, the daughter of **Joell[1] Martin**, both of whom Joell named in his 1715 will. After this 1715 mention, Henry Woodward disappeared from the records, although his son John[2] in his own will mentioned that Henry[1] had made a verbal will—which we would call nuncupative—but there is no record of such a document.

Descent through this ancestor has been temporarily closed. The actual son of John[2] Woodard [listed below], was not the testator of Edgecombe Co., NC, in 1761, with wife Margaret. John[3] Woodard was the testator of 1785 of Beaufort who named his uncle William Martin (brother of his grandmother), his deceased brother Henry, and mentioned the bequest of land from his grandfather to his father. Until future correct descents are found, this also eliminates **Edward Cannon**.

The Child of Henry Woodward and Mary Martin:

[1] a. **John[2] Woodward**, died testate between 21 Nov and 10 Dec 1734, St. Thomas Parish, Bath Co., recorded in NC Secretary of State vol. 876, p. 343; married **Sarah[2] Cannon**.

[2] b. **Joel[2] Woodward**, named in will of brother John.

200. Thomas Wynne was born *ca.* 1685 and died testate between 25 July 1755 and 8 Sept 1757, Tyrrell Co., NC. His will was filed among the loose wills of Tyrell Co., NC. He married **Anna** [__], named in his will. Thomas Wynne's name occurs on a 1706 road crew in the lists of Robert Fewox and Joseph Spruill. This list appeared in a publication called *Swamproots, Tyrrell County 1729-1979*, Fall 1979, p. 14, and was itself taken from a publication said therein to be entitled *North Carolina Historical and Genealogical Review*. While this writer does not especially doubt the veracity of the claim, he cannot locate the latter periodical.

Thomas Wynne worked with a road crew that operated from Spruill's Back Landing in Scuppernong to a Mrs. Long's in South Lancaster.

The Children of Thomas Wynne and Anna [__]:

[1] a. **John**[2] **Wynne**.

[2] b. **Lydia**[2] **Wynne**, married [__] **Davenport**.

[3]+ c. **Jeremiah**[2] **Wynne**, died *ca.* 1763, Tyrrell Co., NC; married **Mary**[3] **Hassell**, who married second, 18 Feb 1765, Tyrrell Co., NC (marriage bond), Adkins Massey.

[4] d. **Peter**[2] **Wynne**.

Appendix

[201] The will of Abraham Baum, Currituck, 1729:

Abraham Baum: Currituck, will dated 18 Sept 1729, proved 7 Apr 1730, Hayes Collection, Microfilm Reel 2, 1694-1770, folder 1729, Southern Historical Collection, Wilson Library, UNC, Chapel Hill.

In the name of God amen I ABRAHAM BAUM of the precinct of Corrotuck in / The province of North Carolina Being Sick & weak of Body but of perfect and / Sound mind and memory Thanks be to God for it Calling to mind the mortal / =aty of my Body & Knowing it is apointed for all men once to Dye Do make / Ordain Constitute and appoint this to be my last will and testament in / Manner & form following principally and first of all I Recomend my Soul / into the hands of almighty God who gave it me & my Body to the Earth to be / Decently Buried at the Discretion of my Executrix hereafter named and as / for my worldly Goods I Give and Dispose of in Manner and form follow / =ing, Imprimis I Give and Bequeath the plantation & Land Belonging / to it which I now Live on and the Land I Bought of JONATHAN JARVIS, To / be Equally to my two Sons PETER and MAURICE BAUMS, the Plantation to / Remain in my son PETERs possession and my Son MAURICE to have his / priviledge to Build & Settle my part of the S^{d} Land Except where the / Plantation now is and the said Land to be Equally Betweene my two Sons / afs^{d}, and the heirs of the Bodys Lawfully Begotten forever; and if Either / of my S^{d} Sons PETER or MAURICE should die without Lawfull Issue as / afors^{d} the part of the land Belonging to Him that Shall So Decease to / fall and be to the next of my Sons in age and their heirs as afores^{d}

Item I Give and Bequeath to my two Sons JOHN & ADAM BAUMS The / Plantation and land Belonging to it on the Sandy Banks to them and the / heirs of their Bodyes Lawfully Begotten forever in the same Manner & form / as the other Land Given to my other two Sons PETER and MAURICE

Item I Give and Bequeath to my four Sons PETER MURICE JOHN & ADAM / BAUMS Each of them one heifer and her Increase to them & their heirs forever

Item I Give to my Daughter MARY BAUM one two year old heifer & her Incr / =rease to her and her heirs forever

Item I Give and Bequeath to my Daugh / =ter SARAH BAUM one Cow Calf to be paid out of my Stock the first that Shall fall after the Date hereof & her increase to her & her heirs forever

Item I Give & Bequeath to my Daughter ELIZABETH BAUM one Cow Called Good / = luck and her future Increase to her and her heirs forever

Item I Give & Bequeath to my Loving APPOLONIA BAUM all the Remaining / part of my Estate Both real & personal after my just Debts are paid & / Satisfyede to her & her heirs forever I also appoint my Loving wife / APPOLONIA my whole and Sole

Executrix of this my Last will & Testament / Revoking all other wills or Testaments by me heretofore made and this to

Carried Over

f. 2

be my last will and testament ass witness my hand & Seal this 18th day / of September in the year of our Lord Christ 1729 his

Signed Sealed & Delivered ABRAHAM B BAUM Seal

In presence of mark

PETER LUTS

JOHN MARTYN

The foregoing will was by APPOLONIA BAUM Executrix Herein named Exhibited to / Court this Seventh day of April anno Dom 1730 and was proved in Lawful / Manner and at the Request of S^{d}. Executrix was Ordered to be Recorded / and was accordingly Recorded in the Records of Currituck

by JOHN MARTYN

This instrument of writing is a True Copy from off the Records of Currituck / County Examoned the 17th day of February Anno Dom 1785 / [*faded*]

[202] Bryan & Co., Information

Craven Co., NC, loose wills, the will of Joseph Bryan, 1770 [mutilated on both edges]

In the Name of God Amen I / JOSEPH BRYAN of North Carolina in Craven Cou[nty being] / in Sound and perfect Mind and memory Doe Ma[ke this] / my Last Will and Testament in Manner and f[orm] [--] / of My will is That my Debts & financial Charges be [paid] / [I] Give To my beloved Wife SARAH 100 Acres of [land on] / [the] Side Nuce River & North Side of Swift Creek [--] / [--] [N]ame of The miry branch I also Give as afore[said] [--] / [h]ousehold Goods and furniture The afore s^{d}. Land [--] / [--] [I] Give to her and her Heirs for Ever

[I] Give and Unto [*sic*] my Son GEORGE my Lands and [--] / [wh]ich I bought of George Moringar 160 Acres the [--] / [I] Give to him and his heires for Ever

[I] Give To my Son JOSEPH all my Lands on Nuce [River on] / [B]oth Sides known by the Name of holing with fery [--] / [--] Land I Give to him and his heires for [ever]

[I] Give To my Son JOHN all my Lands at Swif[t] [--] / [Ri]dge on both Sides ye Creek The Lands that I [bought of] / [J]arret Johnson and that on ye Other Side That I [--] / [--] afore s^{d} Lands I Give to him and his heirs fo[rever]

[I] Give To my Son WILLIAM The plantation Where [--] / [--] [d]well with all the Land Joyning there To also [--] / [--]ill on Maules Run and Land There unto be[longing] / [--] afore S[d] Lands and Mill I Give to Him & his he[eirs for] / [ever]

[I] Give and bequave To my Beloved Wife The foll[owing] / [Negros] Andrew Nan Defay & Sillah to her and her h[eirs forever] / [--] The Use of the plantation During her Widowhoo[d] [--]

f. 2

[I] Give the Remander of my Slave To b[e equally] / [Divi]ded a between my Seven Children Viz [GEORGE] / [JO]SEPH JOHN MARY SARAH WILLIAM ANN [& ELIZABETH] [--] / [arr]iv To the Age of Twenty One yeares or the Day [of] / [their] Marriage The afore S[d]. Negroes to be put in / a Lott and the first at age to Draw & at his Lo[t] / [--] On Lott the youngest Come to the afores / [S[d]] Day of Mareage and after So Drawn They / [- -] entitled to any of the Remaining Slaves or / [--]ase and My Will is That my Stock of Cattle / [--] Mare Sheep & hogs be Devided is afores[d] / [--] my Will is That my Excutors Devide them afore s[d] / [--] Stock Between my afore S[d] Children

And my Will further is that The Slaves be keept at [--] / [--] the plantations Till my Sons Come to his or their [Age] / by the Decrestions of my Escutors [ ] She Be[--] / [t]ender and Loving Mother Till The afore S[d] [--] / [--] Them for Ever

[And] I further Will That my Vesells be Sold at [--] / [--] Newbern To pay Debts of the Tarkil whe[--] / [--]and Debts Due To me will Not answer the [--]e Estate

And if any Moneys be Left after Debts is p[aid] / [--] Estate Setled more then Supports the f[--] / [--] it be Devided as afore S[d] and my wife [--] / [--] her Equal part of S[d] Money with Share [--] / [--] at the Last Devision and [--] Equal pa[rt] [--] / Turn Over

f. 3

[I] Constitute and Opoint my Loving Brother [--] / [--] BRYAN Reading Blount John Maule and [my Son] / JOSEPH BRYAN Executors of this my Last [Will and] / Testament and Do hereby Revoke Disannul and [--] / all former Wils and Testaments by me here to [fore made / In Witness whereof I the S[d] JOSEPH BRYAN [--] / [--] Last will and Testament have Set my hand [and] / Seal in The year of Our Lord 1763 This 7th [--]

JOSEPH BRYAN

Sealed published & and Delivered
[The] Last Will and Testament in [--]cute
[--] Worsley
[--]ry Worsley
his
[--] E Clark
mark

f. 4

[N[o]] Carolina March Craven Inferior [Court]

Present his Majestys Justices [--]

[--] then last Will and Testament of JOSEPH BRYAN [--] / [--]ly proved in open Court by the Oath of James Cl[ark] / [one of] the subscribing Witnesses thereto At the same [time] / [--] BRYAN and JOSEPH BRYAN two of the Execut[ors] / [--] Quallified as such agreeable to Law

Ordereth that M^r^. Secretary have [--] / [--] that letters Testamentory issue there[--] / [accor]dingly

Test Chris [--]

JOSEPH BRYAN
Will
March Court 1770

Craven Co., NC, Estates Records, Joseph Bryan, 1798

State of North Carolina }
WILLIAM BRYAN & other } Petition for
vs. } Legacy
GEORGE BRYAN Exec^r^. of }
JOSEPH BRYAN }

Hear before Levi Dawson John Dawson / & Thomas A. Guin Esqr. and others their [ ] / Justices of the peace of the County Court of Pleas and / quarter Sessions held for the County of Craven at / the Court House in Newbern on the Second Monday / in September XXIII of Independence A Domini 1798

Be it remembered that heretofore, to wit, on the second Monday in June 1797 / GEORGE BRYAN Executor of the last Will and Testament of JOSEPH BRYAN dec^d^. / were Summoned to answer to the Petition of W^M^. BRYAN & W^m^. Grimes and / ANN his wife, which Petition is as follows.

State of N^o^. Carolina } To the Worshipfull the Justices of the Court
County of Craven } of Pleas and quarter Sessions for the County afores^d^.

The Petition of WILLIAM BRYAN, and William Grimes and ANN / his Wife humbly Shewith, that the said WILLIAM BRYAN is the Son and the / said ANN the daughter of JOSEPH BRYAN formerly of said Craven County / deceased, who was in his life time, and untill his death, possessed among other / things of a large and Valuable Stock of Cattle, Horses, hogs and Sheep / of the Value of not less than Three Hundred pounds, which were his own / proper Goods and Chattles. Your Petitioners alledge that the said JOSEPH / died sometime in the year of our Lord One thousand, Seven hundred & Seventy / having previously made his last Will and Testament, and therein and thereby / bequeathed his Stock aforesaid to be equally Divided between his Wife and his / Seven

Children to wit The Petitioners, the said WILLIAM BRYAN and ANN / GRIMES & GEORGE, JOSEPH, JOSEPH [*sic*], JOHN, MARY and SARAH, his Sons and daugh / =ters, and soon after making his said Will, the said Testator died, having / Named and appointed amongst other Persons his Sons JOSEPH, & GEORGE BRYAN / Executors of his said Will, who along caused the same to be proved, and took / upon themselves the burthen of the Execution thereof, and afterwards the said / JOSEPH one of the said executors died, and the said GEORGE became the sole / surviving acting executor, and as such possessed himself of all the Goods / & chattles of the said Testator, and of the Stock aforesaid And your / petition[rs]

f. 2

Petitioners say: that tho' the other legatees have received satisfaction for their / Share of the Stock and legacy aforesaid, yet no part thereof or any Satisfaction / therefor has ever been delivered to your Petitioners or either of them, though often / Demanded Wherefore your Petitioners pray that the said GEORGE executor as afores[d]. / may be summoned to appear before your Worships, at the next Court to be held / for the County of Craven aforesaid, at the Court House in Newborn on the second / Monday in June next then and there to answer this Petition and to Shew / Cause if he can why he should not be compelled to deliver to your Petitioners / their Shares of said Stock of pay thim the Value thereof or in Some other Way / do justice to your Petitioners

And your Petitioners will ever pray / Thomas Badger / for Petitioners

Where upon the Defendant by Edward Graham Esquire / his Attorney appeared & filed the following Answer

The Answer of GEORGE BRYAN, Surviving Executor of the last / Will & testament of JOSEPH BRYAN, Surviving Executor of the last / Will & testament of JOSEPH BRYAN deceased defendant, to / the petition of WILLIAM BRYAN & William Grimes and ANN / his Wife. Petitioners

The Defendant saving to himself all benefit of exception / to the imputations in the said petitions in his Answer thereto / Sayth that he admits that JOSEPH BRYAN in the petition / named the father of the petitioner William & ANN died in the / Year of our Lord 1770 having previously & duly made his last / Will and testament, And this Defendant further further admits that / the said testator JOSEPH BRYAN did by such Will appoint / his Sons JOSEPH & GEORGE this defendant Executors thereof who / Caused the Same to be proved and took upon themselves the / burthen of the Execution thereof & the said GEORGE now has the / Probate of this Will ready to produce to this Court that after / wards the said JOSEPH One of the said Executors died, to wit in / the Month of December in the year of our Lord 1780 Whereby the said

f. 3

GEORGE became the sole Surviving Executor this defendant, further / Admits that the said testator at the time of his death was / possessed of a Stock of Cattle, hogs, and Sheep the parties [ ] / Of Which may appear by the inventory returned and filed in / the Clerks Office of Craven County Court

But this defendant does diny that he ever was possessed by / Virtue of his Office as executor to his fathers Will or in any other way / Of the whole or any part of the Stock of which his testator left it / his death. he does not know of nor can he recollect at this distance / of time of what this Stock consisted, neither of the Number, nor of the / Kind, but he is well assured & convinced that the Stock of the testator / at his death was far more inconsiderable & inferior in Value than / what the petitioners States – with regard to the petitioners allegations / that the testator bequeathed his Stock aforesaid to be equally divided / between his Wife and his Seven Children to wit the petitioner the said / WILLIAM BRYAN and ANN GRIMES & GEORGE JOSEPH JOHN MARY & / SARAH his Son & daughters And that though the other legatees have / Received Satisfaction for their Share of the Stock of [ ] yet no / Part thereof or any Satisfaction therefor has ever been delivered to / the petitioners or either of them though often demanded; this defendant / Cites the following clauses of said Will as relative to & connected with / the said bequest

Item I also give & bequeath to my beloved Wife / the use of the plantation during her Widowhood

Item I also / Give the remainder of my Slaves to be equally divided between my Seven / Children Viz. GEORGE, JOSEPH, JOHN, MARY, SARAH, WILLIAM, and ANN as / they come to the Age of twenty one Years or the day of Marriage / the aforesaid Negroes to be put in equal lots and the first at / Age to draw out his lot, and doe on till the youngest comes to

f. 4

the aforesaid Age or day of Marriage and after So do come they shall / not be intitled to any of the remaining Slaves or their increase And / my Will is that my Stock of Cattle, Horses, mares, Sheep, & Hogs, / be divided as aforesaid & my Will is that my executors divide the / aforesaid Slaves and Stocks between my aforesaid Children, And my / Will further is that the Slaves be kept at Work on the plantation / till my Sons come to heir them and that my Wife have the Care of / bringing up the Children by the discretion of my executors, while she / Behave as a tender & loving Mother till the aforesaid Children receive / their fortune, And I further will that my Vessells be sold, also, / two lots in Newbern to pay debts of the tarkilns when burnt of and / Debts due to me will not answer the debts of the estate, And if any / monies be left after debts paid and the estate settled more than / Supports the family it be divided as aforesaid & my Wife to take / her equal part of said money with the Children at the last / Division and also the equal part of the Stock this defendant / States that when in consequence of the death of his testator he in / conjunction with his Brother JOSEPH took upon himself the execution / of their Father's Will they found the estate indebted in the amount / of at least Seven hundred pounds that the provision made in / the Will for payment of debts was by no means adequate to / the Object, knowing that the discharge of these debts was their / first & necessary duty and receiving these debts as a common charge / on the legatees they concluded that instead of making an / immediate division of the Slaves &c and drawing out their / Shares, as contemplated by the Will, as they might well have / done being then of age they would suffer all the property

f. 5
To remain in common and be employed to the best advantage first / for the Support of the Widow, these Executors and the other Children / then making all one Family and Secondly that the Surplus should / be applied towards the payment of the aforesaid Debts, the Defend / =ant further States that all the slaves belonging to the estate were / in pursuance of this plan employed for five years in making t[ ] / that whatever Stock the testator left was suffered to remain with the / Widow on the plantation for the plantation use and for the use / And subsistance of the Slaves who were employed in raising money to / pay the debts and of the family as well the petitioner as others that / in the year 1775 the Slaves were divided and that the Children then of / Age drew their Shares, the Shares of the Children under age Still / remaining with the Widow But this defendant does deny that any / division then or at any other time was made of any Stock on the / Contrary he States that whatever Stock then remained (if any) was / left on the plantation with the Widow for her Use And the bringing / up of the younger Children this defendant States that when the debts were / paid and the Slaves divided & the shares of the Children under age / left with their Mother (who continued a Widow till her death) for / the Support & Use of the Children, as was by the will within the / Discretion of the Executors he supposed that he had fulfilled his / Executors Ship, this Defendant further States this his Coexecutor / JOSEPH died in the year 1780 that the petitioners are the two youngest /children of the testator and lived with their mother the Widow / that ANN the petitioner the youngest of the Children was of age / in February 1783 And that the Widow died in the year 1796 / that this defendant never heard of any claim set up or demand / made by these Petitioners on Account of any Stock till October / 1796....

f. 6
Pirsuant to the annexed Order of Court We the / Subscribers made a Division of the Estate of JOSEPH / BRYAN deceased in the following Manner Namely / to the Widow, A Negro Fellow called Harry, ten head / of Cattle, Six old, Sheep and three lambs, One Bed and / Furniture, One Bed Stead, One frying Pan, One Pewter / Bason, One Dish, four Plates & one Spoon, three Chairs / 1 Trunk, two Hoes, One Ax, One plough, One Gun, One / Saddle, One Canoe, One Table, One bar plough, 1 Iron pot

To the Heirs (they paying the Widow by agreement / of Parties on Six Months Thirty Seven pounds twelve Shil / lings Specie,) A Negro Wench called Ace and her Child / A Negroe Fellow called Gambo, Eleven Head of cattle, Seven / old Sheep & 3 lambs, two Beds & furniture, two Bed Steads, One Pewter Bason, One Dish, two plates, two Spoons, three / Chains, One Table, three Hoes, One Ax, One plough, One / Gun, One Hand mill, a Ferry Flatt, 2 Iron Pots / The Devision made Saturday March 16th 1782

Jacob Blount
Joseph Campbell
Wm. Blount

Craven Co., NC, loose wills, the will of Sarah (Maule) Bryan, 1796 [mutilated]

I SARAH BRYAN of Craven county in the / State of North Carolina being at present weak / and Inform [in Body but of Sound] memory / and [Mind] / death and for the [better settling of my worldly] / Estate which it hath [pleased God to bless] / me with [I will] and [bequeath in the following manner and form]

First I Give and Bequeath my Soul to Almi / ghty God that gave it my Body I to the / Earth to be decently Enterred at the Discre / tion of my Executors [--] / Thus My desire is that all My Lawful / Debts and funeral Charges be paid

Item I Give and Bequeath to my Daughter / MARY BRYAN my Negro Man Dozey [Moses] / and [Clear the aforesaid Negroes are] Given [to] / her and her heirs for[ever]

Item I Give to my daughter SARAH BRYAN / My Negro [man named Will] / [my Negro man Elleck] / My negro Woman [Cillar my Negro woman Esther my] Negro Girl / Named [Ary] My Negro Boy named / Will to her and her heirs for Ever

Item I Give and bequeath to my Daughter / ELIZABETH GRIST One feather bed and / Turn Over

f. 2

Furniture and one Square Mahogney Table / to her and her heires for Ever

Item I Give and bequeath to my Grand Son / CHRISTOPHER DAWSON My Negro Woman Named / Peggy [and my] Will is that her first / child be Given to My Grand Son EDWD. DAWSON / [to him and his heirs forever and her Second child to be given to my Grand Son JOHN BRYAN DAWSON] / and her third Child be given to my / Grand Son LEWIS DAWSON the Sd. three Negroes / Given to my Abovemed [*sic*] Grand Sons to them / and their heirs for Ever Then the sd. Negroe / Peggy I geve and bequeath to my first / Mentioned Grand Son CHRISTOPHER DAWSON / to him and his heirs for Ever

Item I Give and bequeath unto my Grand / Daughter SARAH GRIMES my Negro Girl / Named [Moll] to her and her heirs for ever

Item I Give and Bequeath Unto my Sons GEORGE / BRYAN and WILLIAM BRYAN EDWARD BRYAN and / LEWIS BRYAN and My Daughter [ANN] / GRIMES and GARRETT DAWSON Each of them / [one Shilling Sterling] to them and their / heirs for ever

Item And my Will is that the Rest of my / Estate which is Not [above] mentioned / in my will be Equally Divided

f. 3
Between my Two Daughters MARY BRYAN / and SARAH BRYAN to them and their heirs / for ever

Item And my Will is that [--] Daughters / MARY and SARAH BRYAN shall Di[scharge] / [my debt and Funeral charges out] / of their Legaceys [before mentioned And I do constitute and appoint my son] / LEWIS BRYAN [Executor] and my Daughter / MARY BRYAN Executrix of this my Last / Will and Testament and Do hereby Revoke / Disannul and make Void all former / Wills and Testaments by me heretofore / made In Witnes I the sd SARAH BRYAN / to this my Last Will and Testament have / Set my hand and affixed my Seal / in the Year of Our Lord one Thousand / Seven Hundred and Ninety Six and on / the 30th of July
Signed Sealed Publisht
and Declared to be the
Last Will and Testament
In Presence of
James Fillingim
Isaac W[illis]

f. 4
letters issued Sept / 1796

[203] The will of William Maunsel Crisp, Martin Co., NC, 1783:

Martin Co., NC, Will Book 1, p. 107:

North Carolina}
Martin County}

In the name of God amen I WILLIAM CHRISP of the / S^{d}. province and County being under the / Afflicting of God but of A perfect and Sound mind and Memory / thanks be to god for the same and Calling to mind the Mortallity / of my Body and that it is Appointed for all men once to die Do make / Ordain Constitute and Appoint this to be my Last Will & Testament / in the following Form and Manner First I Recommend my Soul / into the hands of god who gave it and my Body to the earth to be / Buried in A Christian Manner at the Discretion of my Executors / and as touching those Worldly Good that god has blest me with I give / and Dispose of in the following form and Manner

First I Lend unto my beloved Wife FRANCIS CHRISP the use of all my / Estate of What kind soever During of hir Widowhood and at the end / of her Widowhood I give unto my Son JESSE CHRIST the Manner plantation / Where I now live that is all the S^{d}. plantation and Land Lying between / the Creek and the Little Branch that Runs through the s^{d}. plantation / all the s^{d}. Land to SUSANNA PRESCOAT's Line and SAMUELL

CHRISPs / line to him and his heirs forever

Item I give unto my Son SAMUELL CHRISP the Land and plantation / Where he Now lives and is bounded as is expressly Set forth

p. 108

Beginning at the Creek at FRANCES CHRISPs [*faint*] / the Creek to the County Line thence Along the County line and the Marked / line of the sd. SAMUEL CHRISP to Widow PRESCOATs line Down the s^{d} po[ ] / line to the s^{d} FRANCIS CHRISP line Along that line to the first Station to her / and his heirs forever

Item I Give unto my BENJAMIN CHRISP one hundred and fifty Acres of Land / Lying between the Great Branch and the horsepen Branch Beginning at the / Mouth of the further Little branch then Running Across Northwardly to the / horsepen branch thence Down the said branch to A White Oak Corner tree / thence N°. 55th 60 pole thence Wst. 120 pole to A pine thence S^{o}. to the Creek / thence Across the Creek the Mouth of the Great Branch thence up s^{d}. Branch to / the first Station to him and to his heirs forever.

Item I give unto my Son EZEKIEL CHRISP all my Land lying on the South Side / of the Great Branch Runing Along the Little Branch that goes through the / ~~Great~~ Plantation to the County line and to the head line to him and to his / heirs forever

I Likewise Give unto my Sons SAMUEL CHRISP and JESSE CHRISP my New Entry / Land Lying between the Great branch and the horsepen Branch Joining the / Land that I gave unto BENJAMIN CHRISP to them and their heirs for Ever

Item I give unto my Daughter MARY WILKERSON Ten Pounds Current Money of / this State to her and to her heirs for ever

Item I Give unto my Daughter ANN ROSS ten pounds Current Money of this / State to her and to her heirs for Ever

Item I give unto my Daughter SARAH EDMUNSON Decd. Ten Pounds Current / Money of the sd. State to her and to her heirs for Ever

Item I give unto my Son JOHN CHRISP twenty Shillings Current Money of the / s^{d}. Estate [*sic*] to him and to his heirs for Ever

Item I give unto my Son WILLIAM CHRISP ten pounds Current Money of the / State to him and to his heirs forever

Item I give unto my Daughter SUSANNAH PRESCOAT Ten Pounds Current Money / of the S^{d}. State to her and to her heirs forever

Item i give unto my Daughter MARTHA FLAKE Ten pounds Current Money of the / s^{d}. State to her and to her heirs forever

Item I give unto my Son BRAY CHRISP Ten pounds Current Money of the S^{d}. State / to him and to his heirs for Ever

Item I give to my Daughter ELIZABETH LITTLE Dec^{d}. Ten pounds Current / Money of the S^{d}. State to her and to her heirs for Ever

Item I give unto my Son FRANCIS CHRISP Dec^{d}. Ten [pounds Current Money / of the S^{d}. State to him and to his heirs for Ever.

Item I give and Bequeath all my Negroes and their Increase Except old / [ ]ob and him to be Maintain'd and hir [*sic*] Children and all the Rest of my / [ ] have not been Mentioned and Legacees to be Equally Divided [ ]

p. 109
Amongst my Last wife's Children that is to Say WINIFRED GIBBS LEDE / WHITFIELD ISBALL WHITLEY, SAMUEL CHRISP, BENJAMIN CHRISP, SEALEY BULLOKE / JESSE CHRISP EZEKIEL CHRISP and A Childs part to be Divided Equally / Amongst my Daughter ELISABETH LITTLEs Children and A Childs part / to be Divided Equally Amongst my Son FRANCIS CHRISPs Children to / them and their heirs forever

I Likewise Nominate and Appoint SAMUELL CHRISP BENJAMIN CHRISP and JESSE CHRISP Executors to this my Last Will and Testament / Revoaking and Disannulling all Other Wills heretofore by me made / Ratifying and Confirming this and no Other to be my last Will & Testament / In Witness Whereof I the s[d]. WILLIAM CHRISP hath hereunto put my hand / & Seal this fourteenth Day of February in the year one thousand / Seven hundred and Eighty three
Signed Sealed Published Pronounced and Declared
this to be my Last will & Testament in presence of

Test — his
Edmon Andrews Jurat — WILLIAM **C** CHRISP (seal)
David Taylor — Mark
Joseph Taylor

[204] Depositions concerning the marriage of Christopher[2] deGraffenreid

Lunenburg Co., VA, Deed Book 16, p. 124:

South Carolina / Seal / Zach[a]. Bullock / acting Magistrate &c / Obediah Trimmier acting Magistrate

Before us personally appeared Edward Slocker / who being duly Sworn, on the Holy evangelists of almi / ghty God. Deposeth and Saith, That in the year of / our Lord one Thousand Seven Hundred and Fourteen he / was in the City of Charleston in the State of South Carolina / aforesaid, and then and there did See CHRISTOPHER / DEGRAFFENREIDT and BARBARA TEMPEST Joinid Together / in matrimony according to the Laws and Customs of / the County at that time Prevailing by a regular Clergy / man named Jones

Sworn and Subscribed this — Edward Stocker
27th Day of July in the year
Of our Lord one Thousand
Seven hundred & Ninety
Before us.

South Carolina / We hereby Certify that according to our Judgment & / Belief Edward Stocker is of Sound memory & Recollection / and would be Deemed a Competent witness in any of our / Courts of our State. Given under our Hands & Seale this / 27th Day of July in the year of our Lord one Thousand / Seven Hundred and Ninety

Zacha. Bullock (Seal)
Obediah Trimmier (Seal)

p. 125
South Carolina / (Seal) / Zach[a]. Bullock acting Magistrate (Seal) Obadiah Trimmier / acting magistrate

Before us also appeared Penewell Lambkin / who being duly Sworn on the holy Evangelists of almighty / God, deposeth and Saith that he this Deponent is aged / about Eighty Eight years as he verily Believes, and that / he Knows the deponent Edward Slocher, Named in the / Deposition above Written and Subscribed; and that he well / Recollects, the Said Edward Sloker to have been a man grown / when he this deponent was a Boy

his
Penewell x Lambkin
mark

Sworn and Subscribed this
2d Day of august in the year of our
Lord one Thousand Seven Hundred and
Ninety Before us

State of South Carolina

By his Excellency Charles Pinckney Governour / and Commander in Chief in and over the State aforesaid, / To all to whome these Presents Shall Come Greeting / Know ye That Zachariah Bullock and Obadiah Trimmier / Esquires Before whome the affadavits hereunto annexed were / Made are two of the Justices assigned to Keep the Peace / in the County of Union, in the Said State, Therefore all due / Faith Credit and authority are and ought to be had & / given to their Proceedings and Certificates as Such.

In Testimony whereof I Have hereunto Set my hand and / Caused to be affixed the Great Seal of the State in the City / of Charleston this Twenty Third day of August in the year / of our Lord, One Thousand Seven Hundred & Ninety and of the / Soveraignty and independence of the United States of / America the Fifteenth.

By his Excellencys Command
Peter Freneau
Secretary

CHARLES (SEAL) PINCKNEY

[205] The will of Patrick Henley, 1696

Patrick Henley: Albemarle Co., North Carolina, will dated 24 July 1696, will proved 28 Apr 1699; Philadelphia Co., PA, Patrick Henley 1698, File 54, Administration Book A, p. 258

The Last Will & / testamt of PATRICK HENLY

Albemarle Countie in the province of Carolina, / In the Name of God Amen I PATRICK HENLEY being in / perfect health & of Sound Memorie & withal being / Sensible of the Uncertaintie of Life & not knowing how / Soon the Lord May Remove me by death from this / troublesome world I make this my Last Will & testamt / revocking what ere to fore at the time or times hath been made by me of this nature. I give and bequeath my soul to God the Creator and Preserver thereof hoping that in and through the / meditations of our Lord and Savir jaesus Christ he will receive the same. And my bodie decentilie buried at ye discretion / of my Exsecrs hereafter menconed. But in Case my executrix should dye before her return then I Doe nominate and appoint DANIEL AKEHURST and THOMAS SYMONS to be my exec[rs] to perform my will.

Item I give & Bequeath / unto my loving Wife SARAH HENLY my Whole estate / real personal except one Negro girl which I give unto / my Daughter MARY HENLY, but in Case my Wife dye / befor her return this Voyage I give & bequeath my / estate in Mannr & fforme following

Item I give / & Bequeath unto my Daughter in law SARAH CULPEPPER / fiftie pounds to be paid her when she come of age / in this County Comodities beside what is due to her by / her father's Will.

I give unto my Daughter / MARIE HENLY One Negro girle to be Delivered her / when shee Comes of age

Item I give unto my Daughtr / ELIZABETH HENLY two Negroes when she comes of age / of Day or Marriage

Item I give unto the child that / My Wife Now goes withal, if it be a boy, two negroes / If it be a girle one Negro either boy or girl

Item I / also give & bequeath the rest of my whole estate both real & / psonal either in Europe or America to my Loving Son / JOHN HENLY, when I Nominate & appoint to be heir

Item I also [--] my brother in Law STEPHEN SCOTT / what hee owes mee, In witness wrof I have hereunto sett my / hands & affixed my Seal this 24th day of Julie 1696

I also / give unto my said executors, DANIEL AKEHURST & THOMAS SYMONS five pounds per piece for ye trouble, care, and pains in the performance of this my will. In witness hereunto set my hand and affixed my seal this 24th day of Julie, 1696. So subscribed

PATRICK HENLEY

Signed, sealed, and delivered in presence of us;
STEPHEN RICHARDSON
ELIZABETH SCOTT

ELLINER SCOTT

[206] The will of Isabel (Newby) Henley-Pritchard-Pierce, 1755:

Isabel Pierce: Chowan, will dated 3.4.1755, Hayes Collection, Microfilm Reel 2, 1694-1770, folder 1755, Southern Historical Collection, Wilson Library, UNC, Chapel Hill.

North Carolina } ISABEL PEIRCE wife of / THOMAS PEIRCE
Chowan County}

Being in a Very / Low State of Helth But of perfect Sences / and Sound Memmory Calling to Mind the Uncertainty / of my Time in this world do make and Ordain / This my Last Will and Testament In Manner and form / following Viz

Item I Give and bequeath unto My Son JOHN HENLEYs / Four Children Twenty Shillings a peace / to them there Heirs and assigse for ever

Item, I Give and bequeath unto my Son BENONJ PRITCHARD / Twenty pounds Thirten, Shillings and four pence / One Bed and firniture to him his Heirs assign for Ever

Item, I give and bequeath unto my Daughter MARY RIC / KS My Curtins Vallens Teaster & Heade Cloths / Which She Hath Received Allready to her / Her Heirs and assigns for Ever

Item, I Give and bequeath unto my Daughter HANNAH / PRITCHARD My Mallatto Boy Nam'd James / my Best Bed and firniture to her her Heirs / and assigns for Ever

Item I Give and bequeath unto my Son MATTHEW / PRITCHARD Three pounds Eightin Shillings / (One Bed and firniture) which he hath allready / Received to him & his Heirs and assigns fro Ever

Item I Give and bequeath unto My Daughter PENINNAH / WILLSON three pounds a Forth of my Estate, / More then Her Eaqual Divided of the Rem / ainding part that is Not Given out in Legases, / to Her and her Heirs for Ever

Item I Give and bequeath unto my Loving Husband

f. 2

THOMAS PEIRCE My Young mare to him his / Heirs and assigns for Ever

Item after my Just Debts and Legases are paid / I Give and bequeath unto My Five Youngest / Children all the Remaining Part of my / Estate to them there Heirs and assigns for / Ever Viz JESSE HENLEY PENINNAH WILSON / MATTHEW PRITCHARD HANNAH PRITCHARD / BENONI PRITCHARD

Lastly I Do Nominate and appoint My Sons JESSE HENLEY / MATTHEW PRITCHARD Executors to this my Last / Will and Testament: Hereby Revoke / all Former Wills Here to fore made / or Leguases Given Ratifieing and Confirm / ing This and No other to be My Last Will and / Testament In Witness where of I have hereunto / Set my hand and Fixed my Seal this third day / of the Fourth Month Anno Dom. one thous / and Seven Hundred & fifty Five

Signed Sealed in the ISABELL PEARCE
Presents of
THOMAS PEIRCE the younger
KERENHAPPUCK PEIRCE affirmat

Name Index

[1] Numbers below refer to items, not page numbers in the text
[2] Names may appear may more than once in each biography
[3] Names of deities and royalty have not been indexed
[4] Generational numbers have not been appended to persons sharing the same given name, nor have persons of the same name been distinguished by their parents
[5] "x" indicates that there was no marriage involved in the union

Location Index

I have not distinguished between precincts and counties.
The numbers refer to item numbers in [brackets], and not page numbers.

CITIES & TOWNS, Etc.

MONTHLY MEETINGS

PARISHES

Previous Publications

"The Maternal Ancestry of Gov. Augustus Hill Garland," in *The Arkansas Family Historian*, vol. 17, no. 1 [Jan-Mar 1979], pp. 25-27.[1]

"Wilkinsons of Virginia and Yazoo County, Mississippi," in *The Virginia Genealogist*, vol. 24, no. 4 [Oct-Dec 1980], pp. 178-80.

"Almost *Mayflower* Descendants in the Carolinas," in *Nexus*, vol. 8, no. 1 [Feb-Mar 1991], pp. 24-25.

"Following the Clues: The Family of Dr. Joel Walker," in *Tennessee Ancestors*, vol. 7, no. 1 [Apr 1991], pp. 55-59.

"The Ancestry of Tennessee Williams," in *Nexus*, vol. 8, nos. 3 & 4 [June-Aug 1991], pp. 108-112.

"The Maternal Ancestry of Henry Soane," in *The Virginia Genealogist*, vol. 35, no. 3 [July-Sept 1991], pp. 163-72.

"The Ancestry of Tennessee Williams," in *Tennessee Ancestors*, vol. 7, no. 2 [Aug 1991], pp. 159-204.

"The Descendants of Moses White of Rowan Co., NC," in *Tennessee Ancestors*, vol. 7, no. 3 [Dec 1991], pp. 303-66.

"Carter, Helms, and Presley--A Foray into the Piedmont *Non-Plantation South*," in *Nexus*, vol. 8, no. 6 [Dec 1991], pp. 204-06.

"Using Middle Names To Establish a *Burned County* Pedigree," in *The Virginia Genealogist*, vol. 36, no. 3 [July-Sept 1992], pp. 163-72.

A series of articles (concerning the English ancestry of the following families: Castlyn, Fisher, Knapp, Lake, Lucas, Oldham, Sowter, Whitman), in John Brooks Threlfall, *Twenty-Six Great Migration Colonists to New England and Their Origins*. Madison, Wis., 1993.

"Hollywood Gothic and the Alabama Three," in *Nexus*, vol. 10, no. 4 [Aug-Sept 1993], pp. 110-15.

---

[1] A work of extreme youth which should be treated with extreme caution.

The Complete Ancestry of Tennessee Williams. Jackson, Miss., 1993.

"An Illegitimate and a 'Legitimate' Royal Descent for John Fisher of Virginia," in *The Virginia Genealogist*, vol. 38, no. 4 [Oct-Dec 1994], pp. 283-89.

An Addendum to The Complete Ancestry of Tennessee Williams: *The Ancestry of Gen. James Robertson, "Father of Tennessee."* Jackson, Miss., 1995.

The Five Thomas Harrises of Isle of Wight County, Virginia. Jackson, Miss., 1995.[2]

"A Royal Descent for Christopher Calthorpe of York Co., VA," in *The Virginia Genealogist*, vol. 40, no. 1 [Jan-Mar 1996], pp. 64-67.

The Descendants of Cheney Boyce, "Ancient Planter," and of Richard Craven, for Seven Generations. Jackson, Miss., 1996.

"Joseph Bridger of Dursley, Gloucestershire," in *The Virginia Genealogist*, vol. 41, no. 3 [July-Sept, 1997], pp. 183-84.

"Subtle Recognition in Seventeenth-Century Virginia," in *The American Genealogist*, vol. 73, no. 1 [Jan 1998], p. 10.

"The Batte Family of Birstall, Yorkshire, and Bristol Parish, Virginia," in *The Virginia Genealogist*, vol. 42, no. 3 [July-Sept, 1998], pp. 214-30.

"William[3] Tooke's Children: A Reinvestigation," in *The Virginia Genealogist*, vol. 42, no. 4 [Oct-Dec, 1998], pp. 291-99.

Colonial Families of Surry and Isle of Wight Counties, Virginia. Vol. 2. *The Descendants of Robert Harris.* Jackson, Miss., 1999.

"The Will of Arthur Jones of Bermuda," in *The Virginia Genealogist*, vol. 43, no. 3 [July-Sept, 1999], pp. 227-31.

---

[2] This is actually the first volume of *Colonial Families of Surry and of Isle of Wight Counties, Virginia.*

"Of Things Clerical," in *Friends of the Virginia State Archives, Archives News*, vol. 9, no. 2 [Fall 1999], pp. 1 and 12.

Colonial Families of Surry and Isle of Wight Counties, Virginia. Vol. 3. *Isle of Wight Co., VA, Court Orders, Oct 1693-May 1695.* Jackson, Miss., 1999.

In collaboration with Kenneth W. Kirkpatrick, "Cottoniana, or 'That Cotton-Pickin' Somerby!' ", in *The New Hampshire Genealogical Record*, vol. 16, no. 4 [Oct 1999], pp. 145-70.

"By a Line of Marked Trees," Abstracts of Currituck Co., NC, Deed Books [1], 1-2, and 3, pp. 1-122. Jackson, Miss., 2000.

"The Ancestry of Robert Batte," in *The Virginia Genealogist*, vol. 44, no. 3 [July-Sept, 2000], pp. 163-71.

"America's Best Southern Genealogical Libraries," in *Friends of the Virginia State Archives, Archives News*, vol. 10, no. 2 [Fall 2000], pp. 1, 4-7.

"The Ancestry of Robert Batte [concluded]" in *The Virginia Genealogist*, vol. 44, no. 4 [Oct-Dec 2000], pp. 301-08.

"Madam Ester Pollock and the Cullens," in *The North Carolina Genealogical Journal*, vol. 26, no. 4 [Nov 2000], pp. 363-75.

"The Ancestry of Thomas Cullen," in *The North Carolina Genealogical Journal*, vol. 26, no. 4 [Nov 2000], pp. 376-92.

"The Ancestry of Edward Jones of Isle of Wight County, Virginia," in *The Virginia Genealogist*, vol. 45, no. 1 [Jan-Mar, 2001], pp. 66-70.

Colonial Families of Surry and Isle of Wight Counties, Virginia. Vol. 4. *The Descendants of Capt. John Jennings of Isle of Wight County, Virginia.* Jackson, Miss., 2001.

Colonial Families of Surry and Isle of Wight Counties, Virginia. Vol. 5. *Isle of Wight County, Virginia, Book A, Deeds, Wills, Conveyances.* Jackson, Miss., 2001.

Colonial Families of Surry and Isle of Wight Counties, Virginia. Vol. 6. *Isle of Wight County, Virginia, Will & Deed Book 1, 1662-1688. Deed Abstracts, 1715.* Jackson, Miss., 2001.

"The English Ancestry of Benjamin Laker of Perquimans Co., NC," in *The North Carolina Genealogical Society Journal*, vol. 27, no. 3 [Aug 2001], pp. 291-94.

"The Weepings and Wailings of a Disappointed Genealogist: A Partisan Revue of Volume 1 of *The Dictionary of Virginia Biography*," in *Friends of the Virginia State Archives, Archives News*, vol. 11, no. 2 [Fall 2001], pp. 6-8.

"The Ancestry of Henry Applewight of Isle of Wight Co., VA," in *The Virginia Genealogist*, vol. 45, no. 4 [Oct-Dec, 2001], pp. 243-253.

The Annotated Abstracts of Southampton County, Virginia, Deed Book One. Jackson, Miss., 2001.

"The English Ancestry of Christopher Gale, Attorney General of North Carolina, for Four Generations," in *The North Carolina Genealogical Society Journal*, vol. 28, no. 1 [Feb 2002], pp. 44-69.

"The Ancestry of the Rev. Francis Doughty of Massachusetts, Long Island, New Amsterdam, Maryland, and Virginia," in *The American Genealogist*, vol. 77, no. 1 [Jan 2002], pp. 1-16.

"Notes on the Roper Family of Somerset and Isle of Wight Co., Va.," in *The Virginia Genealogist*, vol. 46, no. 1 [Jan-Mar 2002], pp. 66-67.

"Historical Records as Literature," in *Friends of the Virginia State Archives, Archives News*, vol. 12, no. 1 [Spring 2002], pp. 3-6.

"Check the Original! Two Lessons Learned the Hard Way: Hardy of South Carolina—A 'Discreet Omission to Hide an Indiscretion,' " in *The National Genealogical Society Quarterly*, vol. 90, no 1 [Mar 2002], pp. 69-71.

"The Ancestry of the Rev. Francis Doughty of Massachusetts, Long Island, New Amsterdam, Maryland, and Virginia [concluded]," in *The American Genealogist*, vol. 77, no. 2 [Apr 2002], pp. 127-36.

Colonial Families of Surry and Isle of Wight Counties, Virginia. Vol. 7. *The Ancestry of the Pitt Family of Bristol, Gloucester, Charlestown, Massachusetts, and Isle of Wight County, Virginia*. Jackson, Miss., 2002.

"Thomas Mallory (1566-1644), Rector of Davenham and Dean of Chester," in *The Virginia Genealogist*, vol. 46, no. 2 [Apr-June, 2002], pp. 83-90.

"Just What are They Doing Over There, Anyway? Differences in American and English Genealogical Research Methodology," in *Friends of the Virginia State Archives, Archives News*, vol. 12, no. 2 [Summer 2002], pp. 3, 6-7.

"A Tentative Royal Descent for Daniel Dobyns of Essex Co., Va.," in *The Virginia Genealogist*, vol. 46, no.3 [July-Sept 2002], pp. 163-66.

"A Tentative Reconstruction of the Crowder Family of Bristol Parish, Charles City, and Prince George, Counties, 1680," in *Tidewater Virginia Families*, vol. 11, no. 2 [Aug-Sept, 2002], pp. 74-78.

"Notes on the Ancestry of Valentia (Sparke) Branch, Mother of Christopher Branch," in *The Virginia Genealogist*, vol. 46, no. 4 [Oct-Dec 2002], pp. 282-92.

"Notes on the Ancestry of Mary (Addy) Branch, Wife of Christopher Branch," in *The Virginia Genealogist*, vol. 46, no. 4 [Oct-Dec 2002], pp. 293-98.

"Rolfe/Relfe-Jennings: The Unclosed Case of an Unclosed Case," in *The North Carolina Genealogical Society Journal*, vol. 29, no. 1 [Feb 2003], pp. 3-43.

"Genealogical Notes from Virginia Colonial Decisions by William Ronald Cocke, III—A Correction and Another 'Burned County Pedigree,' " in *The Virginia Genealogist*, vol. 47, no. 1 [Jan-Mar, 2002], pp. 38-50.

"Early Riveses of the Tidewater," in *The Virginia Genealogist*, vol. 47, no. 2 [Apr-June, 2003], pp. 83-92.

"Robert, William, and Thomas Hicks of Flushing, Long Island, NY, and Granville Co., NC," in *The North Carolina Genealogical Society Journal*, vol. 29, no. 3 [August 2003], pp. 238-309.

"The Warwick Family of Middlesex Co., VA" in *The Virginia Genealogist*, vol. 47, no. 3 [July-September, 2003], pp. 198-214.

Transcriptions of Provincial North Carolina Wills, 1663-1729/30. Vol. 1, *Testators A-K*. Jackson, Miss., 2003.

"Notes on the Taborer Family of Derby, Derbyshire, England, and Isle of Wight County, Virginia," in *Magazine of Virginia Genealogy*, vol. 41, no. 3 [August 2003], pp. 177-92.

"Good News and Bad News in Applewight Research," in *The Virginia Genealogist*, vol. 47, no. 4 [Oct-Dec, 2003], pp. 267-71.

"The Other Philacrista," in *The North Carolina Genealogical Society Journal*, vol. 30, no. 1 [February 2004], pp. 47-64.

"Did the Rev. John Farnefold Have Descendants?" in *The Virginia Genealogist*, vol. 48, no. 1 [January-March, 2004], pp. 28-37.

"Some English Descendants of a North Carolina Colonist," in *Friends of the Virginia State Archives, Archives News*, vol. 14, no. 1 [Winter 2004], pp. 1 and 7.

"Nicholson and Redknap Families of Massachusetts and North Carolina," in *The North Carolina Genealogical Society Journal*, vol. 30, no. 2 [May 2004], pp. 173-97.

"From One Boston to Another: Notes on the Ancestry of Mary (Jackson) Woodward," in *The New England Historical and Genealogical Register*, vol. 158, no. 631 [July 2004], pp. 213-27.

"The Ancestry of Frances (Baldwin) Townshend-Jones-Williams," in *The Virginia Genealogist*, vol. 48, no. 3 [July-September, 2004], pp. 170-84.

"The Early Whitakers of Middlesex County, Massachusetts," in *The Genealogist*, vol. 18, no. 2 [Fall 2004], pp. 232-54.

Colonial Families of Surry and Isle of Wight Counties, Virginia. Vol. 8. *Isle of Wight Co., VA, Will & Deed Book 2, 1666-1719*. Jackson, Miss., 2004.

"The Ancestry of Mrs. Anne (Thoroughgood) Chandler-Fowke," in *The Virginia Genealogist*, vol. 48, no. 4 [October-December, 2004], pp. 243-56.

Transcriptions of Provincial North Carolina Wills, 1663-1729/30. Vol. 2, *Testators L-Z*. Jackson, Miss., 2005.

Order of First Families of North Carolina. *Ancestor Registry*. Vol. 1. Jackson, Miss., 2005.

"The Pasquotank Descendants of John Scarborough of Middlesex Co., VA, for Four Generations," in *The North Carolina Genealogical Society Journal*, vol. 31, no. 3 [August 2005], pp. 234-47.

"The Hayman Family of Somerset Co., MD, and Pasquotank Co., NC," in *The North Carolina Genealogical Society Journal*, vol. 31, no. 3 [August 2005], pp. 248-54.

"The Ancestry of Frances (Baldwin) Townshend-Jones-Williams, Part II," in *The Virginia Genealogist*, vol. 49, no. 3 [July-September, 2005], pp. 210-14.

Transcriptions of Provincial North Carolina Wills, 1663-1729/30. Vol. 2, *Testators L-Z*. Jackson, Miss., 2005.

"The Wrong James and Alice (__) Ashton, Alas!" in *The New England Historical and Genealogical Register*, vol. 160 [2006], p, 60.

Transcription of Norfolk Co., VA, Record Book D, 1655-1665. Jackson, Miss., 2007.

"Additions to the Ancestry of Sarah (Hawkredd) (Story) (Cotton) Mather of Boston, Lincolnshire," in *The Genealogist*, vol. 20, no. 1 [Spring 2007] and vol. 21, no. 2 [Fall 2007], pp. 191-217 (conclusion).

By a Line of Marked Trees. Vol. 2. *Abstracts of Currituck County, North Carolina, Deed Books 3-4*. Baltimore, Md., 2007.

"Brayton Family Record, Herkimer County," in *The New York Genealogical and Biographical Record*, vol. 138 [2007], pp. 300-01.

Order of First Families of North Carolina, Ancestor Registry, vol. 2. *The Descendants of John and Thomas Williams of Isle of Wight Co., VA*. Baltimore, Md., 2008.

Transcriptions of Provincial North Carolina Wills, 1663-1729/30. Vol. 2, *Testators L-Z*. 2nd Edition. Baltimore, Md., 2008.

"An Annotated Pedigree of a Medlock Family from the Louisa County, Virginia Chancery Suits," in *Magazine of Virginia Genealogy*, vol. 46, no. 3 [August 2008], pp. 188-202.

Colonial Families of Surry and Isle of Wight Counties, Virginia. Vol. 9. *The Family of George Williams, died 1672, Isle of Wight Co., VA. With Corrections and Additions to* Adventurers of Purse and Person, *4th Ed. Including the Families of Reynolds, Hunt, and Parker.* Baltimore, Md., 2008.

Abstracts of Pasquotank Co., NC, Deeds, 1750-1770. Baltimore, Md., 2008.

"The Pumphrey Family of Gloucestershire, Maryland, and North Carolina," in *The North Carolina Genealogical Society Journal*, vol. 35, no. 3 [August 2009], pp. 217-54.

"Corrections and Additions to *Adventurers of Purse and Person*, 4th ed., Rookings-Watson," in *Magazine of Virginia Genealogy*, vol. 47, no. 3 [August 2009], pp. 249-52.

"Daniel Tanner of Norfolk, Virginia, and Canterbury, Kent," in *Magazine of Virginia Genealogy*, vol. 47, no. 4 [November 2009], pp 257-61.

Colonial Families of Surry and Isle of Wight Counties, Virginia. Vol. 10. *Bridger of Godalming, Surrey; Slimbridge, Gloucestershire; and Virginia.* Baltimore, Md., 2010.

Transcription of Norfolk Co., VA, Record Book C, 1651-1655. Baltimore, Md., 2010.

Abstracts of Carteret County, NC, Deed Books A-F, 1713-1759. Baltimore, Md., 2010.

Abstracts of Beaufort County, NC, Deed Book 2, 1729-1748. Baltimore, Md., 2011.

Colonial Families of Surry and Isle of Wight Counties, Virginia. Vol. 11. *Transcription of Isle of Wight County, Virginia, Deed Book 1, 1688-1705.* Baltimore, Md., 2011.

Annotated Transcriptions of Currituck County, North Carolina, Wills. Baltimore, Md., 2011.